Making the Team: A Guide for Managers

Leigh L. Thompson

Kellogg Graduate School of Management
Northwestern University

Prentice Hall, Upper Saddle River, NJ 07458

VP/Editorial Director: Jim Boyd
Editor-in-Chief: Natalie Anderson
Acquisitions Editor: Jennifer Glennon
Managing Editor: Melissa Steffens
Executive Marketing Manager: Michael Campbell
Director of Production: Michael Weinstein
Production Manager: Gail Steier de Acevedo
Production Coordinator: Kelly Warsak
Permissions Coordinator: Monica Stipanov
Manufacturing Buyer: Natacha St. Hill Moore
Senior Manufacturing Manager: Vincent Scelta
Cover Design: Robert Weeks
Cover Illustration: Robert Weeks
Composition: Carlisle Communications, Ltd.

Library of Congress Cataloging-in-Publication Data
Thompson, Leigh L.
    Making the team : a guide for managers / Leigh L. Thompson.
      p.   cm. — (Executive education)
    Includes bibliographical references and index.
    ISBN 0–13–014363–4
    1. Teams in the workplace. 2. Performance. 3. Leadership.
  4. Organizational effectiveness. I. Title. II. Series: Executive
  education (Upper Saddle River, N.J.)
    HD66.T478   1999   99-35844
    658.4'02—dc21   CIP

Prentice-Hall International (UK) Limited, London
Prentice-Hall of Australia Pty. Limited, Sydney
Prentice-Hall Canada, Inc., Toronto
Prentice-Hall Hispanoamericana, S.A., Mexico
Prentice-Hall of India Private Limited, New Delhi
Prentice-Hall of Japan, Inc., Tokyo
Editora Prentice-Hall do Brasil, Ltda., Rio de Janeiro

Printed in the United States of America

10 9 8 7 6 5 4 3 2 1

For my home team:
Bob, Sam, Ray, and Anna

Contents

PREFACE   **xiii**

PART I   THE BASICS OF TEAMWORK   1

CHAPTER 1   Teams in Organizations: Facts and Myths   1

What Is a Team?   2

Types of Teams in Organizations   3

Why Should Organizations Have Teams?   5

Some Observations about Teams and Teamwork   7

Companies that use teams are not more effective than those that do not   7
Managers fault the wrong causes for team failure   8
Managers fail to recognize their team-building responsibilities   8
Experimenting with failures leads to better teams   8
Conflict among team members is not always a bad thing   10
Strong leadership is not always necessary for strong teams   10
Good teams can still fail under the wrong circumstances   10
Retreats will not fix all the conflicts between team members   11

What Managers Tell Us about Their Teams   11

Most common type of team   11
Team size   11
Team autonomy versus manager control   12
Team longevity   12
The most frustrating aspect of teamwork   12
Skill assessment   13
Skill development   13

A Warning   15

Conclusions   16

**CHAPTER 2   Performance and Productivity: Team Performance Criteria
and Threats to Productivity   17**

An Integrated Model of Successful Team Performance   18

Team Context   18

Organizational context   19
Team design   19
Team culture   19

Essential Conditions for Successful Team Performance   20

Knowledge and skill   20
Effort and motivation   23
Coordination strategies   27

Performance Criteria   29

The Team Performance Equation   33

Conclusions   33

CHAPTER 3   Rewarding Teamwork: Compensation and Performance Appraisals   35

Types of Team Pay   36

Incentive pay   38
Recognition   39
Profit sharing   42
Gainsharing   42

Team Performance Appraisal   43

What is measured?   44
Who does the measuring?   45
Developing a 360-degree program   47

Sources of Rater Bias   50

Homogeneity bias   51
Halo bias   51
Fundamental attribution error   51
Communication medium   52
Experience effect   52
Reciprocity bias   52
Bandwagon bias   52
Primacy and recency bias   52

Sources of Ratee Bias   52

Egocentric bias   52
Intrinsic interest   53
Social comparison   53
Fairness   53

Guiding Principles   54

Principle 1: Goals should cover areas that team members can directly affect   54
Principle 2: Balance the mix of individual and team-based pay   54
Principle 3: Consult with the team members who will be affected   55
Principle 4: Avoid organizational myopia   55
Principle 5: Determine eligibility (who qualifies for the plan)   55
Principle 6: Determine equity method   55
Principle 7: Quantify the criteria used to determine payout   55
Principle 8: Determine how target levels of performance are established and updated   57
Principle 9: Develop a budget for the plan   57

Principle 10: Determine timing of measurements and payments 57
Principle 11: Communicate with those involved 57
Principle 12: Plan for the future 57

Conclusions 58

PART II INTERNAL DYNAMICS 59

CHAPTER 4 Building the Team: Tasks, People, and Relationships 59

Building the Team 59

The Task: What Work Needs to Be Done? 61

How much authority does the team have to manage its own work? 62
What is the focus of the work the team will do? 62
What is the degree of task interdependence among team members? 63
Is there a correct solution that can be readily demonstrated and communicated to members? 65
Are team members' interests perfectly aligned (cooperative), opposing (competitive), or mixed in nature? 65
How big should the team be? 65

The People: Who Is Ideally Suited to Do the Work? 67

Diversity: SWOT analysis 69
Creating diversity 72

Relationships: How Do Team Members Socialize Each Other? 73

Group socialization 74
Role negotiation 75
Team norms: Development and enforcement 77
Cohesion: Team bonding 79
Trust 80

Conclusions 84

CHAPTER 5 Sharpening the Team Mind: Communication and Collective Intelligence 85

Team Communication 86

Message tuning 86
Message distortion 86
Biased interpretation 87
Perspective-taking failures 87
Transparency illusion 87
Indirect speech acts 87

The Information Dependence Problem 88

Common knowledge effect 88
Hidden profile 91
Practices to put in place 93
Things that don't work 93
Effective interventions 94

Collective Intelligence   96

Team mental models   96
The team mind: Transactive memory systems   99

Team Longevity: Routinization versus Innovation Trade-Offs   105

Conclusions   108

CHAPTER 6   Team Decision Making: Conformity, Pitfalls, and Solutions   109

Decision Making in Teams   109

Conformity: Why It Occurs and How It Works in Teams   110

The need to be right   110
The need to be liked   111

Decision-Making Pitfall 1: Groupthink   112

Learning from history   114
How to avoid groupthink   116

Decision-Making Pitfall 2: Escalation of Commitment   118

Project determinants   120
Psychological determinants   120
Social determinants   122
Structural determinants   123
Avoiding the escalation of commitment problem   123

Decision-Making Pitfall 3: The Abilene Paradox   124

How to avoid the Abilene paradox   126

Decision-Making Pitfall 4: Group Polarization   128

Conclusions   129

CHAPTER 7   Conflict in Teams: Leveraging Differences to Create Opportunity   131

Types of Conflict   132

Transforming A-type into C-type conflict   134

Team Dilemma: Group versus Individual Interests   135

Strategies to enhance cooperation and minimize competition   136

Perils and Pitfalls of Democracy   137

Voting rules   137
Drawbacks to voting   138

Group Negotiation   139

The BATNA principle   140
Avoid the fixed-pie fallacy   140
Build trust and share information   140

Ask questions   *141*

Provide information   *141*

Make multiple offers simultaneously   *141*

Avoid sequential discussion of issues   *142*

Construct contingency contracts and leverage differences   *142*

Be wary of intuition   *143*

Search for postsettlement settlements   *143*

Use team-on-team negotiation   *144*

Avoid majority rule   *144*

Beware of coalitions   *144*

Appeal to norms of justice   *145*

What to Do When Conflict Escalates?   146

Conclusions   148

**CHAPTER 8   Creativity: Mastering Strategies for High
Performance   150**

What Exactly Is Creativity?   151

Measuring creativity   *151*

Creativity through categorization of ideas and team diversity   *151*

Creativity through cognitive flexibility   *152*

Creativity and context dependence   *152*

Creative People or Creative Teams?   152

Team creativity   *153*

Analogical Reasoning   154

Expertise   *156*

Comparison and abstraction   *156*

Divergent versus Convergent Thinking   157

Group Brainstorming   158

Brainstorming on trial   *158*

What goes on during a typical group brainstorming session?   *160*

Trained facilitators   *161*

High benchmarks   *161*

Two-step approach: Solitary and group ideation   *162*

Nominal group technique   *162*

Stepladder technique   *162*

Delphi technique   *163*

Electronic Brainstorming   164

Advantages of electronic brainstorming   *164*

Disadvantages of electronic brainstorming   *166*

Capstone on brainstorming   *167*

Conclusions   168

PART III   EXTERNAL DYNAMICS   169

CHAPTER 9   Managing the External Environment   169

Team Boundaries   170

Insulating teams   171
Broadcasting teams   171
Marketing teams   172
Surveying teams   172

Team Identity   173

External Roles of Team Members   173

Networking: A Key to Successful Teamwork   173

Perfect and imperfect markets   175
Human capital and social capital   175
Boundary spanning and structural holes   177
Types of networks   178
Advice for the manager   179
Structural positioning   180

Distance   184

Time   186

Conclusions   186

CHAPTER 10   Leadership: Managing the Paradox   188

The Team Paradox   188

Leaders and the Nature-Nurture Debate: Great Person versus Great Opportunity
189

Great Opportunity: Some Evidence   190

Obedience to authority   190
Blind faith   191
Good Samaritans   193
Self-fulfilling prophecy   193
The power of labels   195
Head of the table effect   195
Random selection of leaders   196

Leadership Behavior: Routes to Influence   197

Vivid information   197

Leadership and Teamwork: Addressing the Paradox   200

Decision Analysis Model: How Participative Do You Want to Be?   202

Decision styles   202
Problem identification   202
Decision tree model   204

Strategies for Encouraging Participative Management   204

Task delegation   204

Parallel suggestion involvement   206
Job involvement   206
Organizational involvement   206

Freeing the Caged Bird: Effects of Empowerment   207

Team Empowerment   208

Red Flags on the Way to Greater Involvement   210

Conclusions   211

CHAPTER 11   Interteam Relations: Competition and Stereotyping   213

Overview   213

Group Membership: The Locus of Human Identity   215

Need for categorization   216
How categorization affects behavior   216
"Us" versus "them": The psychology of in-groups and out-groups   217
"We're better than they are": In-group supremacy and entitlement   218
"They all look alike": The out-group homogeneity effect   219
Minority groups   220
Performance evaluation   222
Extremism   222
Overt and covert racism   223
Unconscious discrimination at work   224

Strategies for Reducing Prejudice   225

Blinding   225
Consciousness-raising ("don't be prejudiced")   226
Contact   227
GRIT and bear it   228
Stress and fatigue reduction   229
Affirmative action   229

Conclusions   230

**CHAPTER 12   Teamwork via Information Technology:
Challenges and Opportunities   231**

Place-Time Model of Social Interaction   233

Face-to-face communication   233
Same time, different place   235
Different time, same place   237
Different place, different time   238

Information Technology and Social Behavior   240

Status and power: The "weak get strong" effect   240
The impact of technology on social networks   241
Risk taking   243
Social norms   243
Task performance   243

Enhancing Local Teamwork: Redesigning the Workplace   244

Virtual or flexible space   244
Flexible furniture   245
Hoteling   246

Virtual Teams   247

Strategies for Enhancing the Virtual Team   248

Collaboratory   248
Initial face-to-face experience   249
Temporary engagement   249
One-day videoconference   249
Touching base   249
Schmoozing   250

Transnational Teams   250
Conclusions   253

APPENDIX 1   Managing Meetings: A Toolkit   255

APPENDIX 2   Special Tips for Consultants and Facilitators   263

APPENDIX 3   A Guide for Creating Effective Study Groups   267

APPENDIX 4   Example Items from Peer Evaluations and 360-Degree Performance Evaluations   271

REFERENCES   277

AUTHOR INDEX   307

SUBJECT INDEX   313

Preface

When I first came to the Kellogg Graduate School of Management in 1995, there were only a small number of course offerings on group dynamics and teamwork. Sheer demand for more teamwork led to the development of a 3-day team-building program for executives. In this program, leading scholars—Deborah Gruenfeld, Dave Messick, Keith Murnighan, Brian Uzzi, and I—provide the latest team-building and management principles to managers and executives from different industries all over the globe. The participants are always as surprised as we are to see the commonality of concerns and interests regarding their teams. Most of the participants were hungry for a book that would pull together the basic and cutting-edge concepts they learned from the seminar. I searched for a book that would capture and supplement the broad and deep scope that this program reflected. Often, the popular book choices were not theory-based and the scholarly books not very practical. I set out to write a book that would do three things:

1. Provide an extremely engaging approach to teamwork by connecting models and theories with actual teams and companies.
2. Maintain a rigorous, cutting-edge research focus—all of the material in the book is produced by leading scholars in the field and represents hard science, in the strict sense of the word.
3. Provide a big-picture view of teamwork by giving the manager and team leader practical advice and solutions to problems.

Making the Team separates fact from fiction and outlines in a clear, step-by-step fashion how young managers, as well as seasoned executives, can improve the functioning of their teams. Each chapter opens with a case analysis of a real team. The reader of this book will learn how to diagnose the causes of team failure, conduct a performance evaluation of teams, leverage the team within the organization, determine effective leadership behavior, create opportunity from conflict, deal with global teamwork issues, set the stage for creative, breakthrough thinking in teams, reduce prejudice, and manage meetings and study groups for effective learning and decision making. In short, this book transforms the art of teamwork into a science to be studied and mastered.

I took the perspective of the manager when writing this book; arguably, I should have taken the perspective of the team. However, this choice was for expositional purposes, as all of the messages for the manager of the team apply to the team itself.

The 12 chapters are arranged into a sequence of three major sections: Part I covers the basics (types of teams, facts, and myths); part II covers internal dynamics of teamwork (building the team, collective intelligence, decision making, conflict, and creativity); and part III focuses on the external dynamics of teams in organizations (networking, leadership, interteam relations, and information technology).

The first chapter ("Teams in Organizations") lays out the basic concepts of the book and attempts to dispel some common myths about teamwork. It introduces the basic building blocks for analyzing and perfecting teamwork. Chapter 2 ("Performance and Productivity") tackles the question of how we know whether a team is performing well, and if not, what to do about it. Chapter 3 ("Rewarding Teamwork") deals with the question of rewarding teamwork in organizations, the impact of rewards on motivation and behavior, and the choices that organizations have in this regard.

Part II of the book focuses on the internal dynamics—or what is going on inside the team itself. Chapter 4 ("Building the Team") focuses on structuring tasks, selecting people, and fostering team relationships. Chapter 5 ("Sharpening the Team Mind") explores how teams communicate (and the most common reasons for failures), how teams process information, and how they create a collective team intelligence. Chapter 6 ("Team Decision Making") examines the four most common team decision-making pitfalls. It discusses the causes and consequences of conformity and how to deal with it. Chapter 7 ("Conflict in Teams") focuses on how to turn negative conflict into positive conflict for teams. Chapter 8 ("Creativity") examines how to design teams to be maximally creative.

Part III of the book focuses on external dynamics—or how the team fits in the organization. Chapter 9 ("Managing the External Environment") takes up the topics of team boundaries, interteam relations, networking, and boundary spanning. Chapter 10 ("Leadership") focuses on the dual tasks of effective leadership: Dealing with internal dynamics as well as external dynamics. Chapter 11 ("Interteam Relations") focuses on the issues of conflict and competition between teams in the organization. Chapter 12 ("Teamwork via Information Technology") examines the impact of information technology on global, as well as local, teamwork and some of the choices the manager has for maintaining high productivity.

I also included four appendices that the managers, executives, and students I have worked with told me they wanted to see in this book. Appendix 1 focuses on how to run a meeting. Appendix 2 contains tips for consultants and facilitators of meetings. Appendix 3 focuses on how to build and maintain an effective study group. Appendix 4 contains examples of 360-degree evaluations.

The research and ideas in this book come from an invaluable set of scholars in the fields of social psychology, organizational behavior, sociology, and cognitive psychology. During the past 12 years, my life has been enriched in very important ways by the following people with whom I have collaborated: Linda Babcock, Max Bazerman, Terry Boles, Jeanne Brett, Susan Brodt, Gary Fine, Craig Fox, Dedre Gentner, Robert Gibbons, Kevin Gibson, Rich Gonzalez, Deborah Gruenfeld, Reid Hastie, Peter Kim, Shirli Kopelman, Rod Kramer, Laura Kray, Terri Kurtzburg, John Levine, Allan Lind, Jeff Loewenstein, Beta Mannix, Vicki Medvec, Dave Messick, Terry Mitchell, Don Moore, Michael Morris, Keith Murnighan, Janice Nadler, Robin Pinkley, Vanessa Ruda, Harris Sondak, Tom Tyler, Kathleen Valley, Leaf Van Boven, Kimberly Wade-Benzoni, and Laurie Weingart. In the book, I use the pronoun *we* because so much of my thinking has been influenced and shaped by this set of eminent scholars.

Fourteen students who were enrolled in an advanced "managing groups" course at the Kellogg School read the book, criticized it, and improved it immensely during the fall of 1998. These people are Diego Lezica Alvear, Pablo Gonzalez Beramendi,

Geoffrey Bolan, Elmer Choy, Francesco Dalla Rovere, Read T. DuPriest, Shawna Gwin, Alison Hyman, Jean Johnson, Thomas Lott, Rebecca M. Mayne, Ryan Reis, Pamela L. Skonicki, and Carrie Tower. These people improved the book tremendously and humbled me in the process of doing so.

A number of people read this book in an earlier form and provided very helpful comments: Joan F. Brett, Karen Cates, John A. Drexler, Jr., and Jeff Polzer, and our reviewers Donald Ashbaugh, University of Wisconsin–Madison; Sigal Barsade, Yale University; Theodore Forbes III, University of Virginia; Daniel Gigone, Duke University; Cristina Gibson, University of Southern California; and Judith Gordon, Boston College.

Two other people played an enormously important role in this book: Avi Steinlauf and Greg Grieff. Avi Steinlauf conducted all of the information searches on the examples covered in the book based on real companies. His work was intensive, thorough, and creative and it made the book really come alive. Greg Grieff was the first-round high-level copy editor for the book. He raised the important questions, reorganized the flow of thoughts, made the logic clear, and provided much of the focus and direction of each chapter.

This book would not have had a chance without the dedication, organization, and editorial skills of Rachel Claff, who created the layout, organized the hundreds of drafts, mastered the figures, and researched various aspects of the book.

I completed this book while I was at the Kellogg Graduate School of Management, a place whose spirit is motivating, energizing, and inspirational. I feel honored to live and work in the midst of so many great people and I am indebted to Dean Donald Jacobs and the Kellogg Teams and Groups Center (KTAG) for their generous support of this book, and to Ken Bardach for helping to provide the vision for our team executive program. Very important, grants from the National Science Foundation's Decision Risk and Management Science Program have made it possible for me to conduct several of the research studies that I discuss in this book.

This book is very much a team effort of the people I have mentioned here, whose talents are diverse, broad, and extraordinarily impressive. I am deeply indebted to my colleagues and students, and I feel very grateful that they have touched my life and this book.

CHAPTER 1

Teams in Organizations: Facts and Myths

Scenario 1: The Miller Brewing Company opened its Trenton, Ohio, brewery in 1990. It was intended to be the brewery of the future, one that would give the company the flexibility to expand capacity and embody the most advanced staffing features. A planning and design team was set up for the Trenton project with a mandate to start from scratch and develop a totally new workplace design, abandoning all the traditional constraints of brewery operations. The team met for 6 months and came up with a completely new way to run a brewery, employing self-directed, cross-functional teams, ranging from 6 to 19 people. These teams handled brewing, packaging, and distribution. The payoff in terms of business results was a 30 percent increase in productivity, in comparison to Miller's other plants (Parnell, 1996).

Scenario 2: In the late 1980s as corporate America was embracing the concept of teams, Texas Instruments, the multi-billion-dollar electronics manufacturer in Dallas, joined the frenzy and began adding teams throughout the organization. "Depending on each team's focus, salespeople were grouped together with various employees, including engineers and sales support people. Management spoke of empowerment and self-direction" (Marchetti, 1997, p. 91). Management's message to employees was, "You're empowered; go do what you want to do." The initial results of this project were utter failure.

These two companies are household names and represent major players in their respective industries. One of the companies succeeded using teams, whereas the other failed. Why?

Virtually everyone who has worked in an organization has been a member of a task-performing group at one time or another. Why are some team experiences successful and others unsuccessful? Good teams are not a matter of luck; they result from hard work, careful planning, and commitment from the sponsoring organization. Team design from the inside out is a skill. It requires a thorough understanding of teams to ensure that the team works as designed. Although there are no guarantees, we believe that understanding what makes teams work will naturally lead to better and more effective teams. In this book, we introduce a systematic approach that allows managers, executives, teachers, and professionals to develop and maintain excellent teams in their organizations.

Our systematic approach is based upon a principle of learning and change. Implementing change requires that managers audit their own behavior to see where mistakes are being made, consider and implement new techniques and practices, and then examine their effects. Unfortunately, accomplishing these tasks in a typical organizational setting is not easy. This chapter sets the stage for effective learning by first defining what a team is—it's not always clear! Next, we distinguish four types of teams in organizations in terms of their authority and examine why teams are even necessary in organizations. We expose some of the most common myths about teamwork and provide some useful observations. Finally, we provide the manager with the results of our recent survey on how teams are used in organizations and the problems with which managers are most concerned. The problems cited by these managers cut across industries, from doughnut companies to high-tech engineering firms. These problems and concerns are examined in the chapters that follow.

WHAT IS A TEAM?

Not everyone who works together or in close proximity belongs to a team. A **team** is a group of people who are interdependent with respect to information, resources, and skills and who seek to combine their efforts to achieve a common goal. As is summarized in Box 1-1, teams have five key defining characteristics. First, teams exist to achieve a shared goal. Simply put, teams have work to do. Teams produce outcomes for which members have collective responsibility and reap some form of collective reward. Second, team members are interdependent regarding some common goal. Interdependence is the hallmark of teamwork. *Interdependence* means that team members cannot achieve their goals single-handedly, but instead, must rely on each other to meet shared objectives. There are several kinds of interdependencies, as team members must rely on others for information, expertise, resources, and so on. Third, teams are bounded and remain relatively stable over time. *Boundedness* means the team has an identifiable membership; members, as well as nonmembers, know who is on the team. *Stability* refers to the tenure of membership. Most teams work together for a meaningful length of time—long enough to accomplish their goal. Fourth, team members have the authority to manage their own work and internal processes. We focus on teams in which individual members can, to some extent, determine how their work gets done. Thus, although a prison chain gang may be a team in some sense, the prisoners have little authority in terms of managing their own work. Finally, teams operate in a larger social system context. Teams are not islands unto themselves. They do their

---

BOX 1-1

Five Key Characteristics of Teams (Alderfer, 1977; Hackman, 1990)

- Teams exist to achieve a shared goal.
- Team members are interdependent regarding some common goal.
- Teams are bounded and stable over time.

- Team members have the authority to manage their own work and internal processes.
- Teams operate in a social system context.

work in a larger organization, often alongside other teams. Furthermore, teams often need to draw upon resources from outside the team and vice versa—something we discuss in part III of this book.

A *working group*, by contrast, consists of people who learn from one another and share ideas, but are not interdependent in an important fashion and are not working toward a shared goal. Working groups share information, perspectives, and insights, make decisions, and help people do their jobs better, but the focus is on individual goals and accountability. For example, consider the operators who staff the phone lines at 1-800-MATTRESS. They share, via their computer network, specifications on hundreds of mattresses and bed frames. They may also share information among themselves on sales techniques, consumer demographics, or tie-in items. Yet they are individually evaluated based on their sales performance. These phone operators share resources, but not results. A team is a type of group, but not all groups are teams.

TYPES OF TEAMS IN ORGANIZATIONS

Organizations have come to rely on team-based arrangements to improve quality, productivity, customer service, and the experience of work for their employees. Yet not all teams are alike. Teams differ greatly in their degree of autonomy and control vis-à-vis the organization. Specifically, how is authority distributed in the organization? Who has responsibility for the routine monitoring and management of group performance processes? Who has responsibility for creating and fine-tuning the design of the group (Hackman, 1987)? Consider the four levels of control depicted in Figure 1-1.

The most traditional type of team is the **manager-led team.** In the manager-led team, the manager acts as the team leader and is responsible for defining the goals, methods, and functioning of the team. The teams themselves have responsibility only for the actual execution of their assigned work. Management is responsible for monitoring and managing performance processes, overseeing design, selecting members, and interfacing with the organization. Manager-led teams provide the greatest amount of control over team members and the work they perform; they allow the leader to have control over the process and products of the team. In addition, they are efficient, in the sense that the manager does the work of setting the goals and outlining the work to be done. In manager-led teams, managers don't have to sit by and watch the team make the same mistakes they did. Manager-led teams also have relatively low start-up costs. The key disadvantages are diffusion of responsibility and conformity to the leader. In short, members have less autonomy and empowerment. Such teams may be ideally suited for simple tasks in which there is a clear overriding goal, such as task forces or fact-finding teams. Specific examples include military squads, flight crews, and stage crews.

In **self-managing or self-regulating teams,** a manager or leader determines the overall purpose or goal of the team, but the team is at liberty to manage the methods by which to achieve that goal. Self-managed teams are increasingly common in organizations. Examples include executive search committees, managerial task forces, and so on. For example, at Whole Foods Markets, the largest natural-foods grocer in the United States, the culture "is premised on decentralized teamwork. The team, not the hierarchy, is the defining unit of activity. Each of the 43 stores is an autonomous profit center composed of an average of 10 self-managed teams—produce, grocery, prepared foods, and so on—with designated leaders and clear performance targets" (Fishman, 1996).

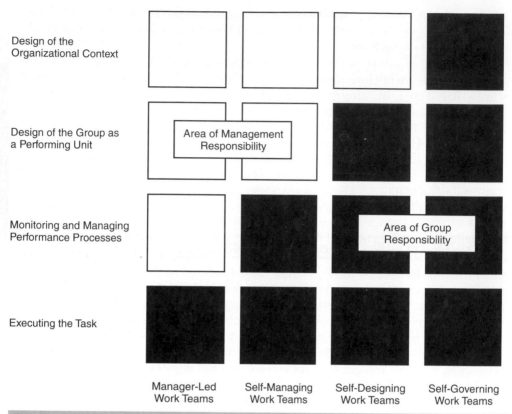

FIGURE 1-1 Authority of Four Illustrative Types of Work Groups

Source: Hackman, J. R. 1987. "The Design of Work Teams." In J. W. Lorsch (Ed.), *Handbook of Organizational Behavior.* Upper Saddle River, NJ: Prentice Hall.

Self-managing teams build commitment, offer increased autonomy, and often enhance morale. The disadvantage is that the manager has much less control over the process and products, making it difficult to assess progress. Self-managing teams can also be more time-consuming.

Self-directing or self-designing teams determine their own objectives and the methods by which to achieve them. Management has responsibility only for the team's organizational context. Self-directed teams offer the most potential for innovation, enhance goal commitment and motivation, and provide opportunity for organizational learning and change. However, self-directed or self-designing teams are extremely time-consuming, have the greatest potential for conflict, and can be very costly to start up. (For a step-by-step guide to setting up self-designing teams, see Orsburn, Moran, Musselwhite, & Zenger, 1990.) Furthermore, it can be extremely difficult (or impossible) to monitor their progress. Other disadvantages include marginalization of members and lack of team legitimacy. Self-designing teams may be ideally suited for complex, ill-defined, or ambiguous problems and next-generation planning. At the Harley-Davidson Motor Company, there is a "commitment to making the company a high-performance work organization, where the people closest to a job have the authority and responsibility to do it the best way they can. Part of the company's management approach is freedom and teamwork—it encourages each plant to solve its problems in its own way" (Imperato, 1997, p. 104). According to CEO Rich Teerlink, "The issues are always the same . . . quality, productivity, participation, flexibility, and cash flow. But each plant deals with them in a different way. We don't have cookbooks because there isn't a cookbook. We're on a journey that never ends. And the day we think we've got it made, that's the day we'd better start worrying about going out of business" (p. 104).

Self-governing teams and boards of directors are usually responsible for executing a task, managing their own performance processes, designing the group, and designing the organizational context. They are the extreme in terms of control and responsibility. In many companies, the president or chief operating officer has been replaced with an executive, self-governing team (Ancona & Nadler, 1989). Examples of this approach are John Reed's structuring of Citicorp's senior management when he succeeded Walter Wriston, and Walter Shipley's creation of the "three president" structure at Chemical Bank in the 1980s. When British Steel took the construction industry by storm by developing a unique, patented steel-skinned concrete panel system called the bi-steel system, it did so with the use of "a semi-autonomous team within a giant conglomerate not widely credited for encouraging innovative virtually self governing teams" (Greek, 1997, p. 19).

In certain cases, firms want to set up a self-governing (autonomous) team, similar to the independent counsel's office, to investigate serious problems, such as the sexual harassment case at Mitsubishi (e.g., the team headed up by Lynn Martin; Holland, 1996). The way the military has handled problems with sexual harassment stands in sharp contrast, not only in terms of the kinds of teams set up to examine the problems, but also in terms of the results they have achieved. In other cases, these kinds of teams could be disastrous, such as a committee composed of boards of directors—employees could be intimidated by the authority of these individuals and, therefore, unwilling or unable to provide a critical perspective on the status quo.

There are trade-offs involved with each of these four types of teams. Self-governing and self-directed teams provide the greatest potential in terms of commitment and participation, but are also at the greatest risk of misdirection. When decisions are pushed down in organizations, team goals and interests may be at odds with organizational interests. Unless everyone in the organization is aware of the company's interests and goals, poor decisions (often with the best of intentions) may be made. An organization that chooses a manager-led group is betting that a manager can run things more effectively than group members can. If it is believed that the group can do the job better, a self-governing or self-designing team may be appropriate. One implication of this is that the manager's traditional role as a collector of information is less and less important. If shared control over the performance situation and processes is preferred, a self-managing group is chosen.

WHY SHOULD ORGANIZATIONS HAVE TEAMS?

Teams and teamwork are not novel concepts. In fact, teams and team thinking have been around for years at companies such as Procter & Gamble and Boeing. In the 1980s, the manufacturing and auto industries strongly embraced a new, team-oriented approach when U.S. firms retooled to combat Japanese competitors who were quickly gaining market share (Nahavandi & Aranda, 1994). During collaboration on the B-2 stealth bomber between the U.S. Air Force, Northrop, and some 4,000 subcontractors and suppliers in the early 1980s, various teams were employed to handle different parts of the project. "As new developments occurred or new problems were encountered during the program, the Air Force/Northrop team formed ad hoc teams made up of [their] own experts and specialists from other companies and scientific institutions" (Kresa, 1991).

Managers discovered the large body of research indicating that teams can be more effective than the traditional corporate hierarchical structure for making decisions quickly and efficiently. Even simple changes like encouraging input and feedback from workers on the line can make a dramatic improvement. For instance, quality control (QC) circles and employee involvement groups are often vehicles for employee participation (Cole, 1982). It is a mark of these programs' success that this kind of thinking is considered conventional wisdom nowadays. But, although these QC teams were worthy efforts at fostering the use of teams in organizations, the teams needed for the restructuring and reengineering processes of the future may be quite different (Nahavandi & Aranda, 1994). This point is brought home even more clearly in light of A. T. Kearney's findings that nearly seven out of ten teams fail to produce the desired results ("*The Trouble with Teams,*" 1995).

At least three challenges of the future suggest that building and maintaining effective teams will be of paramount importance. The first has to do with *specialization.* As the economy expands and organizations grow accordingly, firms become ever more complex, both in their tasks and in the markets they serve. Thus, the activities of individuals in these firms are necessarily becoming more specialized. An increasingly global and fast-paced economy requires people with specialized expertise. Yet the specialists within a company need to know how to work together. Moreover, as acquisitions, restructurings, outsourcing, and other structural changes take place, the need for coordination becomes all the more salient. Changes in corporate structure and increases in specialization imply that there will be new boundaries between the members of an organization. Boundaries both separate and link teams within an organization (Alderfer, 1977; Friedlander, 1987), although the boundaries are not always obvious. These new relationships require team members to learn how to work with others to achieve their goals. Team members must integrate through coordination and synchronization with suppliers, managers, peers, and customers.

The second challenge has to do with *competition.* In today's economy, a few large firms are emerging as dominant players in the biggest markets. These industry leaders often enjoy vast economies of scale and earn tremendous profits. The losers are often left with little in the way of a market—let alone a marketable product (Frank & Cook, 1995). Think, for example, of Microsoft's Windows operating system and Office Products market share dominance. The division that develops the Office Products software—which includes Word, Excel, PowerPoint, Outlook, and Access—employs thousands of people. Those products share a lot of code with each other, and so teamwork is critical to coordinate the activities of the various component groups that make up the Office Products Division (Anonymous, 1996). With so much at stake, firms are aggressively competing in a winner-take-all battle for market share. Thus, bringing out the best in individuals within the firm has become ever more important. This means that people can be expected to specialize more and more in their areas of expertise, and these areas of expertise will get ever more narrow and interdependent. Both firms and individuals will have to increasingly rely on others to get access to their expertise. This is the core structure of a team-based approach to work.

A third factor is the *emergence of the information age.* Computer technology extends the firm's obligations and capacity to add value to its customers. For example, Toyota has a Monday-to-Friday design-to-delivery program, in which a customer "designs" a car on a computer terminal on Monday, and the factory automatically receives the specifications and has manufacturing completed by Friday of the same week (Cusumano, 1985). With ever-improving ability to communicate with others anywhere on the planet (and beyond!), people and resources that were once remote can now be reached quickly, easily, and inexpensively. This has facilitated the development of the virtual team—groups linked by technology so effectively that it is as if they were in the same building. Technology also gives managers options they never had before, in terms of which resources they choose to employ on any particular project. The role of management has shifted accordingly; they are no longer primarily responsible for gathering information from employees working below them in the organizational hierarchy and then making command decisions based on this information. Their new role is to identify the key resources that will best implement the company's objectives and then to facilitate the coordination of those resources for the company's purposes. The jobs of the team members have also changed significantly. This can be viewed as a threat or a challenge. Millions of jobs have been altered dramatically or have disappeared completely since the advent of computers. For example, George David, CEO of United Technologies Corp., believes that 18 million U.S. workers (almost one in six) are "at risk" because their jobs are "prone to automation" (Zachary, 1996). Decisions may now be made far from their traditional location; indeed, sometimes even by contractors who are not employees of the firm. This dramatic change in structure requires an equally dramatic reappraisal of how firms structure the work environment.

SOME OBSERVATIONS ABOUT TEAMS AND TEAMWORK

There is a lot of folklore and unfounded intuition when it comes to teams and teamwork. We want to set the record straight by exposing some of the observations that managers find most useful.

Companies That Use Teams Are Not More Effective Than Those That Do Not

When companies are in trouble, they often restructure into teams. However, putting people into teams does not solve problems; if not done thoughtfully, this may even cause more problems. For every case of team success, there is an equally compelling case of team failure, as indicated by this chapter's opening example. Teams can outperform the best member of the group, but there are no guarantees. Admitting the inefficiency of teams is hard, especially when most of us would like to believe in the Gestalt principle that the whole is greater than the sum of its parts! As we discuss in later chapters, teams can suffer from many drawbacks, such as too much emphasis on harmony or individualism, causing a feeling of powerlessness and creating discord (Griffith, 1997). Teams are not a panacea for organizations; they often fail and are frequently overused or poorly designed. In the best circumstances, teams provide insight, creativity, and cross-fertilization of knowledge in a way that a person working independently cannot. In the wrong circumstances, teamwork can lead to confusion, delay, and poor decision making.

Managers Fault the Wrong Causes for Team Failure

Imagine yourself in the following situation: The wonderful team that you put together last year has collapsed into lethargy. The new product line is not forthcoming, conflict has erupted, and there is high turnover. What has gone wrong? If you are like most managers, you place the blame on a clash of personalities: Someone is not behaving as a team player, or petty politics are usurping common team goals.

Misattribution error is a tendency for managers to attribute the causes of team failure to forces beyond their personal control. Leaders may blame individual team members, the lack of resources, or a competitive environment. By pointing to a problem team member, the team's problems can be neatly and clearly understood as emanating from one source. This saves the manager's ego (and in some cases the manager's job), but stifles learning and destroys morale. It is more likely that the team's poor performance is due to a structural, rather than personal, cause. Furthermore, it is likely that several things are at work, not just one.

Managers Fail to Recognize Their Team-Building Responsibilities

Many new managers conceive of their people-management role as building the most effective relationships they can with each individual subordinate; they erroneously equate managing the team with managing the individual (Hill, 1982). These managers rarely rely on group-based forums for problem solving and diagnosis. Instead, they spend their time in one-on-one meetings. Teamwork is expected to be a natural consequence. As a result, many decisions are based upon limited information, and decision outcomes can backfire in unexpected and negative ways (see Sidebar 1-1).

Experimenting with Failures Leads to Better Teams

It may seem ironic, but one of the most effective ways to learn is to experience failure. Evidence of this is provided by the fallout that accompanied the Los Angeles Police Department's (LAPD) handling of the riots that broke out following the Rodney King beating verdict in 1992. A *Los Angeles Times* editorial following the incident stated that "successful policing is a team effort; likewise, unsuccessful policing of the magnitude that occurred the night the riots broke out is a team failure" (*Los Angeles Times,* 1992, p. B4). The aftermath of the criticisms levied upon the LAPD and the people who run the department caused an overhaul within the management ranks of the department. A failed team effort should be viewed as a critical source of information from which to learn. The problem is that failure is hard to take: Our defense systems go into overdrive at the mere inkling that something we do is not above average. The true mark of a valued team member is a willingness to learn from mistakes. However, this learning can only come when people take personal responsibility for their actions.

Sidebar 1-1. Team-Building Responsibilities

Steve Miller, managing director of the Royal Dutch/Shell Group of Companies, develops exercises that allow teams to assess their performance as a group and the impact a leader has on the group. For example, one of his exercises involves giving each team a video camera. Each team has 90 minutes to come up with a 5 or 6 minute video that illustrates the old culture of the company and the new culture of the company. This exercise instigated a major change in the Austrian business offices of Royal Dutch/Shell.

In the first program involving the video camera exercise, the Austrian team was clearly lagging behind all the other teams in terms of motivation, participation and enjoyment. What's more, it was obvious to the Austrians as well as the other teams that they were not performing well. Needless to say, their morale was suffering, and Miller was uncertain how to help the struggling team turn things around.

At one point during the week, the team leader for the Austrian group was called away suddenly and was not present for the video exercise. At first, this seemed to be the worst thing that could happen to the Austrian team—they were leaderless and facing a real out-of-the-box problem.

The Austrian team surprised everyone by coming up with a powerful and humorous video. The video showed a man who needs to use the bathroom very urgently. The "old Shell" video depicts the man walking around in great discomfort, looking for a toilet. The doors are locked; there is all kinds of bureaucratic paperwork to complete and needless rubber-stamping. The clip ends with the man nearly collapsing in the men's room. That was the Austrian's idea of the "old Shell".

The next clip depicted the "new Shell" culture. The same man immediately finds the men's room, is greeted by a hospitable attendant and is offered personal toilet paper and amenities. The video concludes with the service attendant trying to zip up the man's fly.

Everyone watching the video was completely stunned by the creativity and humor of the video. Clearly, the Austrians had won this competition, which turned out to be the beginning of a dramatic shift in their motivation, performance, and participation in the entire event. When the Austrian leader returned, he began to realize how capable and motivated his team really was. This single event was a turning point in how the team and the leader worked together; the team went on to dramatically improve their business in Austria (Pascale, 1998).

The truth is, teams have a flatter learning curve than do most individuals; it takes teams longer to "get on their feet." However, teams have greater potential than do individuals. We discuss this further in chapter 2.

Conflict among Team Members Is Not Always a Bad Thing

Many managers boast that their teams are successful because they never have conflict. However, it is a fallacy to believe that conflict is detrimental to effective teamwork. In fact, conflict may be necessary for effective decision making in teams. Conflict among team members can foment accuracy, insight, understanding, and development of trust and innovation. We discuss conflict in teams in greater detail in chapter 7.

Strong Leadership Is Not Always Necessary for Strong Teams

A common myth is that to function effectively, teams need a strong, powerful, and charismatic leader. In general, leaders who control all the details, manage all the key relationships in the team, have all the good ideas, and use the team to execute their "vision" are usually overworked and underproductive. Teams with strong leaders may succumb to flawed and disastrous decision making.

As we discuss in chapter 10, a leader has two main functions: A *design* function, meaning that the leader structures the team environment (working conditions, access to information, incentives, training, and education); and a *coaching* function, meaning that the leader has direct interaction with the team (Hackman, 1996).

Good Teams Can Still Fail under the Wrong Circumstances

Teams are often depicted as mavericks: Bucking authority, striking out on their own, and asking for permission only after the fact. Such cases do occur, but they are rare and tend to be one-shot successes. Most managers want consistently successful teams. This is particularly important in industries where considerable tooling up is required for team members.

To be successful in the long run, teams need ongoing resources and support. By resources, we mean more than just money. Teams need information and education. In too many cases, teams tackle a problem that has already been solved by someone else in the company, but a lack of communication prevents this critical knowledge from reaching the current task force.

To lay the best groundwork for teams before the problems begin, it is important to consider such factors as the goals and resources of the team: Are the team's goals well defined? Does everyone know them? Are the goals consistent with the objectives of other members of the organization? If not, how will the inevitable conflict be managed? Does everyone on the team have access to the resources necessary to successfully achieve the goal? Is the organizational hierarchy set up to give team members access to these resources efficiently? If not, it might be necessary to reconsider the governance structure within which the team must operate. What are the rights of the team members in pursuing their duties, who can they contact, and what information can they command? It is also important to assess the incentive structure existing for team members and for those outside the team with whom team members must interact. Does everyone have the right incentives (to do the things they are supposed to do)? Are team members' incentives aligned with those of the group and the organization; for instance, to cooperate with one another and to fully share information and resources? There is no cookie-cutter solution to team structure. For instance, it may be appropriate for team members to compete with one another (in which case, cooperation may not be an achievable feature of the group dynamic). Choosing the structure of the group and the incentives that motivate the individuals inside it are essential factors contributing to the success of any team.

Retreats Will Not Fix All the Conflicts between Team Members

Teams often get into trouble. Members may fight, slack off, or simply be unable to keep up with their responsibilities, potentially resulting in angry or dissatisfied customers. When conflict arises, people search for a solution to the team problem. A common strategy is to have a "team-building retreat" or "corporate love-in," where team members try to address underlying concerns and build trust by engaging in activities—like rock climbing—that are not part of what they ordinarily do as a team.

A team retreat is a popular way for team members to build mutual trust and commitment. A retreat may involve team members spending a weekend camping and engaging in cooperative, shared, structured activities. This usually results in a good time had by all. However, retreats fail to address the structural and design problems that plague the team on a day-to-day basis in the work environment. Design problems are best addressed by examining the team in its own environment while team members are engaged in actual work. For this reason, it is important to take a more comprehensive approach to analyzing team problems. Retreats are insufficient because they allow managers to blame team interpersonal dynamics on the failures, rather than deeper, more systemic problems, which are harder to identify.

WHAT MANAGERS TELL US ABOUT THEIR TEAMS

To gain a more accurate picture of what managers face in their organizations in the way of teamwork, we conducted a minisurvey of 149 executives and managers from a variety of industries.[1] Here are some highlights of what they told us.

Most Common Type of Team

By far, the most common teams were cross-functional project groups, followed by service, marketing, and operations teams (see also Katzenbach & Smith, 1993). Cross-functional teams epitomize the new challenges outlined earlier in this chapter. They represent the greatest potential, in terms of integrating talent, skills, and ideas, but because of the diversity of training and responsibility, they provide fertile ground for conflict.

Team Size

Team size varied dramatically, from 3 to 25 members, with an average of 8.4. The modal team size was 5. These numbers can be compared to the optimum team size: As we discuss later in the book, teams should generally have fewer than 10 members—more like 5 or 6.

---

[1]Survey results are based on the responses from executives in attendance at the Kellogg Team-Building for Managers Program, 1996–1999.

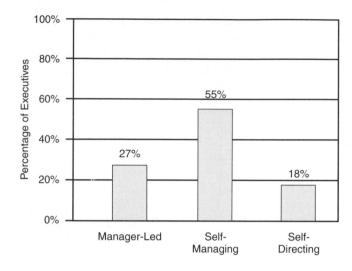

FIGURE 1-2 Team Autonomy versus Manager Control

Team Autonomy versus Manager Control

Most of the managers in our survey were in self-managing teams, followed by manager-led teams, with self-directing teams distinctly less common (see Figure 1-2). There is an inevitable tension between the degree of manager control in a team and the ability of team members to guide and manage their own actions. As a general principle, manager-led teams provide more control, but less innovation that stems from autonomy. We do not suggest that all teams should be self-directing. Rather, it is important to understand the trade-offs and what is required for each type of team to function effectively.

Team Longevity

The teams in our survey varied a great deal in terms of how long they had been working together. On average, teams had been in existence for 6 to 12 months (see Figure 1-3).

The Most Frustrating Aspect of Teamwork

Managers considered several possible sources of frustration in managing teams. The most frequently cited cause of frustration and challenge in teams was developing and sustaining high motivation, followed by minimizing confusion and coordination problems (see Figure 1-4). We discuss issues of motivation in chapter 2 as well as in a special chapter that focuses on team compensation and incentives (chapter 3). We look at conflict and ways to effectively manage it within a team in chapter 7.

Not surprisingly, the skills on the most-wanted list for managerial education were (1) developing and sustaining high motivation; (2) managing conflict productively; (3) providing leadership and direction; (4) fostering creativity and innovation; and (5) minimizing confusion and coordination problems. Consequently, we have designed this book to prepare managers and reeducate executives in how to effectively deal with each of these concerns.

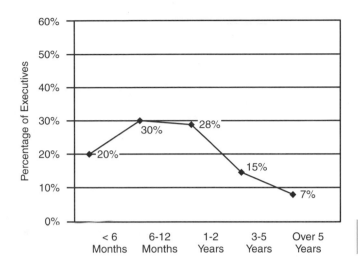

FIGURE I-3 Team Longevity

Skill Assessment

We asked managers to rate their own skills along a continuum from most to least proficient (see Figure 1-5). Managers felt most proficient in their decision-making, goal-setting, and leadership skills. They felt less proficient about fostering creativity and innovation, managing conflict, and compensation issues.

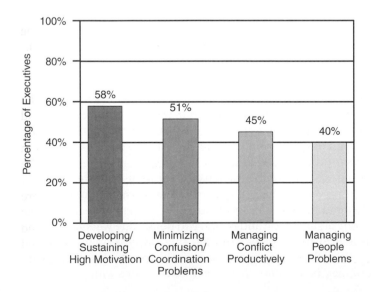

FIGURE I-4 The Most Frustrating Aspects of Teamwork

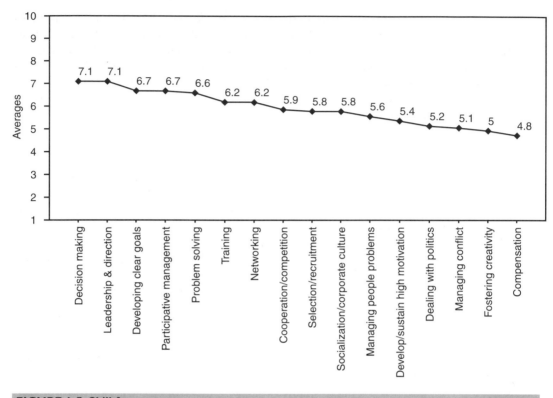

FIGURE 1-5 Skill Assessment

DEVELOPING YOUR TEAM-BUILDING SKILLS

This book focuses on two skills: Accurate diagnosis and theory-based intervention.

Skill 1: Accurate Diagnosis

One of the biggest shortcomings of managerial effectiveness is an inability to accurately diagnose situations; for instance, is a team performing well or poorly? It is very rare to identify a simple, obvious measure of team functioning because effectiveness is hard to define. For example, perhaps your firm beat the competition in winning a large contract, but the contract didn't turn out to be so profitable. Was this a victory or a failure? What will be the implications for future competition?

Many people make the mistake of looking for causes *after* they find effects. In the scientific literature, this is known as **sampling on the dependent variable.** For example, if your goal is to identify the determinants of a successful team, it may appear useful to look for effective teams in your organization and then try to determine what is common to all of them. This sounds logical, until you realize that there may be many common factors that have nothing to do with making a team successful, like the fact that everyone wears clothes! Or there may be common features that interfere with good teamwork, but are nonetheless difficult to detect—perhaps precisely because they are common to all the teams, successful or not. One important example of this is the institutional background of the firm; for example, taking certain established practices for granted, such as operating procedures, information sources, and even contractual relationships. In this case, the team may be effective, but not as effective as it might otherwise be. A more serious problem is that a manager who is also entrenched in the institutional framework of the firm may perceive a team as effective, while overlooking its shortcomings. Thus, it is essential to be as independent and critical as possible when analyzing team effectiveness.

How do you avoid the trap of sampling on the dependent variable? From a methodological point of view, you can do one of two things: (1) have a control group—that is, a comparison group (in this case, unsuccessful teams)—and look for differences between the two; or (2) do an experiment in which you provide different information, education, communication, and so on to one group (randomly assigned) but not the other. Then look for differences. Unfortunately, most executives do not have the time or resources to do either of these things. This book provides insights based upon research that has done these things before drawing conclusions. However, nothing can substitute for a thoughtful understanding of the environment in which the team operates, the incentives facing team members, and so on. We will discuss these factors throughout this book.

Another problem is called **hindsight bias** (Fischhoff, 1975), or the "I knew it all along" fallacy. This is the tendency to believe that something seems obvious, even inevitable, *after* you learn about it when you have not predicted (or cannot predict) what will happen in advance. This can result in an unfortunate form of overconfidence: Managers think they know everything, when in fact they know nothing useful when it is time to make the decision. We often see managers engage in post hoc justification rather than careful reasoning. The best way to avoid this trap is to read actively in order to learn about other possibilities, critically examine your own assumptions, and be open to a change of mind once you have the facts. As you read this book, some things will surprise you, but much will seem obvious. As a general principle, do not rely on your intuition; rather, test your assumptions.

Skill 2: Theory-Based Intervention

Once a problem or area of improvement has been identified, a manager still needs to deal effectively with it. This involves identifying reasons and remedies, such as finding ways to change the motivational structure of the task, the composition of the group, and so on. Mechanisms for transferring information from those who have it to those who need it must be developed as well as a means to manage power, politics , and conflict involving the group. All this is much easier said than done, of course. For every managerial problem, there are a dozen purported solutions and quick fixes. How can a manager knowledgeably choose among them?

The interventions presented in this book have a key quality going for them: They are all theory-based and empirically sound. This means that they are not based on naive, intuitive perceptions; rather, they have been scientifically examined. This book was written to provide managers with up-to-date, scientifically-based information about how best to manage their teams.

A WARNING

We believe that teamwork, like other interdependent social behaviors, is best perfected in an active, experimental, and dynamic environment. Thus, to fully benefit from this book, it is necessary for you to actively engage in teamwork and examine your own behavior. It may seem somewhat heretical to make the point in a textbook that team-building skills cannot be learned exclusively from a textbook, but we do so anyway.

We strongly urge you to work through the models and ideas presented here in the context of your own experience. We can think of no better way to do this than in a classroom setting that offers the opportunity for on-line, applied, experiential learning. It is easy to watch, analyze, and critique other teams, but much more challenging to engage in effective team behavior yourself. We hope that what you gain from this book, and the work you do on your own through team-building exercises, is the knowledge of how to be an effective team member, team leader, and team designer. In the long run, we hope this book will help you in developing your own experience, expertise, and models about how you can best function with teams.

CONCLUSIONS

There is no magic scientific formula for designing and maintaining an effective team. If there were, it would have been discovered by now. In some ways, a team is like the human body: No one really knows an exact regimen for staying healthy over time. However, we have some very good information about the benefits of a lean diet, exercise, stress reduction, wellness maintenance, and early detection of disease. The same goes for teamwork. Just as we rely on science to cure disease and to advance health, this book takes an unabashedly scientific approach to the study and improvement of teamwork in organizations. This is extraordinarily important because there is a lot of misperception about teams and teamwork. Intuition and luck can only take us so far; in fact, if misapplied, they may get us into trouble. In the next chapter, we undertake a performance analysis of teamwork, asking these questions: How do we know a healthy and productive team when we see it? What are the biggest "killers" and "diseases" of teams? And, more important: What do we need to do to keep a team functioning effectively over time? In chapter 3, we deal with the question of incentives and rewards for good teamwork. Part II focuses on internal team dynamics, and part III focuses on the bigger picture—the team in the organization.

CHAPTER 2

Performance and Productivity: Team Performance Criteria and Threats to Productivity

Team A is a top-management team in a rapidly growing pharmaceutical company. When team members are asked to reveal their "secret" for incredible growth, they have no idea how to respond. The team developed with no mission statement, goals, or strategic plan. The vice president of marketing put it this way: "We know we're doing something right, but we sure as hell don't know what it is." But when faced with new challenges, team members are afraid to change anything for fear of messing up a good thing.

Team B is also a top-management team in a farm and mining equipment company that is going through an extremely slow period. Profits are down. It is clear that something has to change. When team members retreat to make decisions, each has a different theory of what to do: Someone argues they should restructure around "values"; others want to get back to basics and empower workers; still others argue for greater centralization.

Team A and Team B have opposite fates, but the same problem: Neither one knows what drives their productivity or lack thereof.

> *A business person once stated "there is nothing as practical as a good theory."*
> —Lewin, 1943

The management teams in both of these organizations each need the same thing: A clear understanding of why and how to use teams in their companies. Ideally, they would like a model that would tell them what to do in each of the circumstances facing them. Such a model would serve two purposes: **Description,** or the interpretation of events so that managers can come up with an accurate analysis of the situation; and **prescription,** or a recommendation on what to do to fix the situation.

In this chapter, we introduce a model of team performance. The model tells us what factors and conditions have to be in place for teams to function effectively and how to address problems with performance. The remainder of the chapter focuses on different parts of the model and provides choices to enact change.

AN INTEGRATED MODEL OF SUCCESSFUL TEAM PERFORMANCE

We think that the best models of teamwork are ones that put the team in the context of the organization—that is, they deal with internal processes of teams as well as the team in the larger context of the organization (see Hackman, 1987, 1990; Hill, 1995). Figure 2-1 is a descriptive-prescriptive model of team performance: It tells us what to expect in terms of team performance and suggests ways to improve the functioning of teams. As promised in chapter 1, the model in Figure 2-1 is based upon empirical research. This chapter steps through each piece of the model.

The message of the model is actually quite simple. It asserts that the context of the team (referring to its internal processes and external constraints and opportunities) affects the team's ability to do three essential things: Perform effectively, build and sustain motivation, and coordinate people. These essential conditions are the causal determinants of the team's performance—that is, whether it succeeds or fails. The remainder of the chapter is divided into three key sections corresponding to the three pieces of the model: Team context, essential conditions, and team performance. We begin with the team context.

TEAM CONTEXT

The **team context** includes the larger organizational setting within which the team does its work, the design of the team in terms of its internal functioning, and the culture of the team. High performance teams cannot be created through simple instruction or exhortation. Instead, there are a number of organizational conditions that, when in place, increase the likelihood that a team's work will be successful (Hackman, 1990). In part, this means that the team relies on the organization to provide resources, funding, individuals for membership, and so on. In chapter 1, we stated that teams operate in a social context, which shapes and confines behavior. As we discuss in parts II and III, the

FIGURE 2-1 Integrated Model of Teamwork

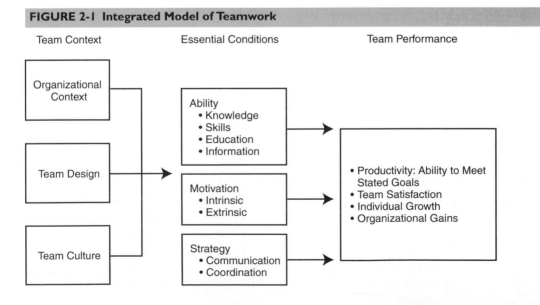

team leader must not only think about the internal functioning of the team (i.e., ability, motivation, and coordination), but also the external functioning of the team, including the organizational context, team design, and group norms.

Organizational Context

The organizational context includes the basic structure of the organization (e.g., lateral, hierarchical), the information system, the education system, and the reward system. It includes organizational policy and material and physical resources required to accomplish group tasks. Even if a team possesses spectacular skills, motivation, and coordination, lack of critical organizational infrastructure such as information, tools, equipment, space, raw materials, money, and human resources will hurt team performance. Teams ideally need a supportive organizational context—one that recognizes and welcomes their existence; responds to their requests for information, resources, and action; legitimizes the team's task and how they are achieving it; and expects the team to succeed (Bushe, 1986).

Team Design

Team design refers to the observable structure of the team (e.g., manager-led or self-managing). It refers to the leadership style within the team, functional roles, communication patterns, composition of the team, and training of members. We examine team design in part II of the book.

Team Culture

Culture is the set of shared meanings held by team members that make teamwork possible. In contrast to team design, which is often deliberate and explicit, team culture includes the unstated, implicit aspects of the team that are not discussed in a formal fashion, but nevertheless shape behavior. Member roles, norms, and patterns of behaving and thinking arise from team design and the structure and system of the organization in which the team operates. One way in which teams develop their culture is by imposing ways of thinking and acting that are considered acceptable. A **norm** is a generally agreed upon set of rules that guide behavior of team members. Norms differ from organizational policies in that they are informal and unwritten. Often, norms are so subtle that team members are not consciously aware of them. Team norms regulate key behaviors such as honesty, manner of dress, punctuality, and emotional expression. Norms can either be **prescriptive,** dictating what should be done, or **proscriptive,** dictating behaviors that should be avoided.

Norms that favor innovation (Cummings & Mohrman, 1987) or incorporate shared expectations of success (Shea & Guzzo, 1987a) may especially foster team effectiveness. Firms that report success in applying work teams have had similar cultures, often guided by philosophies of top managers (Galagan, 1986; Poza & Marcus, 1980; Walton, 1977). Often, culture is more a property of work units than the entire organization. This means that norms may exist in work groups, but not the larger organization. For example, an organization may not have any particular behaviors at lunchtime, but a work team might create a culture where it is expected that people will eat together and brainstorm over lunch.

Norms develop as a consequence of precedent. Whatever behaviors emerge at a team's first meeting will usually define how the team operates—just look at the consistency of seating arrangements. Norms also develop because of carryovers from other situations or in response to an explicit statement by a superior or coworker. They may also result from critical events in the team's history. We cover norms in greater detail in part II of the book.

ESSENTIAL CONDITIONS FOR SUCCESSFUL TEAM PERFORMANCE

Obviously, there are a number of factors that must be in place for a team to be successful (Hackman, 1987; Steiner, 1972). The team members must

1. bring adequate *knowledge and skill* to bear on the task;
2. exert sufficient *motivation and effort* to accomplish the task at an acceptable level of performance; and
3. *coordinate* their activities and communication.

Next, we discuss each of these essential conditions in greater detail.

Knowledge and Skill

For teams to perform effectively, members must have the requisite ability, knowledge, and skill to perform the task. This requires that the manager appropriately match people with the right skills to the tasks at hand and to the organizational human resource structure itself. An effective team needs people not only with technical skills, but also interpersonal skills, decision-making skills, and problem-solving skills. Interpersonal skills are crucial for effective management. Executives spend 78 percent of their working time interacting with others, and as much as 50 percent of that time in interactions with subordinates (Mintzberg, 1973). Subordinates reporting good relationships with superiors are better performers, assume more responsibility, and contribute more to their units than those reporting poor relationships (Liden & Graen, 1980).

How do you know whether you have an effective working relationship with someone? As a start, you can consider where your relationship stands on each of the dimensions listed in Table 2-1. If the majority of the dimensions of your relationship are listed on the right-hand side, this means that an effective relationship has developed.

Teamwork is often beneficial because individuals working independently lack the time, skills, and resources necessary to accomplish their goals. However, even talented people may lose confidence in their abilities in the presence of others. We focus on those patterns that interfere with individuals' ability to perform their best in certain social situations and, in particular, in the context of a team. Examples of this may include shyness (when someone is uncomfortable speaking up in a group meeting but may have valuable contributions to make on paper), a fear of acting in public (such as a fear of public speaking), aggressive or overbearing behavior (such as when an uncomfortable social situation causes someone to act loudly or aggressively), and so on. The paradoxical performance effect, or *choking under pressure,* occurs when a person's performance declines despite incentives for optimal performance (Baumeister, 1984).

For example, consider Lorraine. When she is questioned or challenged by other team members about something she is not an expert on, she becomes extremely

TABLE 2-1   Summary of Dyadic Dimensions Along Which Relationships Develop

From	*To*
Openness and Self Disclosure[a, b, c, d, f] Limited to "safe," socially acceptable topics	Disclosure goes beyond safe areas to include personally sensitive, private, and controversial topics and aspects of self
Knowledge of Each Other[b, d, e, f] Surface, "biographic" knowledge: Impressionistic in nature	Knowledge is multifaceted and extends to core aspects of personality, needs, and style
Predictability of Other's Reactions and Responses[b, d, e, f] Limited to socially expected or role-related responses, and those based on first impressions or repeated surface encounters	Predictability of the other's reactions extends beyond stereotypical exchange and includes a knowledge of the contingencies affecting the other's reactions
Uniqueness of Interaction[a, b, e] Exchanges are stereotypical, guided by prevailing social norms or role expectations	Exchanges are idiosyncratic to the two people, guided by norms that are unique to the relationship
Multimodality of Communication[a, b] Largely limited to verbal channels of communication and stereotypical or unintended nonverbal channels	Includes multiple modalities of communication, including nonverbal and verbal "shorthands" specific to the relationship or the individuals involved; less restrictiveness of nonverbal
Substitutability of Communication[a, b] Little substitution among alternative modes of communication	Possession of and ability to use alternative modes of communication to convey the same message
Capacity for Conflict and Evaluation[a, b, c, e] Limited capacity for conflict; use of conflict-avoidance techniques; reluctance to criticize	Readiness and ability to express conflict and make positive or negative evaluations
Spontaneity of Exchange[a, b, c] Interactions tend to be formal or "comfortably informal" as prescribed by prevailing social norms	Greater informality and ease of interaction; movement across topical areas occurs readily and without hesitation or formality; communication flows and changes direction easily
Synchronization and Pacing[a, b] Except for stereotyped modes of response, limited dyadic synchrony occurs	Speech and nonverbal responses become synchronized; flow of interaction is smooth; cues are quickly and accurately interpreted
Efficiency of Communication[a, b] Communication of intended meanings sometimes requires extensive discussion; misunderstandings occur unless statements are qualified or elaborated	Intended meanings are transmitted and understood rapidly, accurately, and with sensitivity to nuance
Mutual Investment[b, g] Little investment in the other except in areas of role-related or situation interdependencies	Extensive investment in other's well-being and efficacy

a. Altman & Taylor, 1973, pp. 129–136.
b. Levinger & Snoek, 1972; Levinger & Rausch, 1977, pp. 100–109.
c. Jourard, 1971.
d. Hinde, 1979, pp. 133–134.
e. Swensen, 1973, pp. 105–106, 230–237, 455.
f. Triandis, 1977, pp. 191–193.
g. Secord & Backman, 1964.

Source: Galegher, J., Kraut, R. E., & Egido, C. 1990. *Intellectual Teamwork: Social and Technological Foundations of Cooperative Work.* Mahwah, NJ: Lawrence Erlbaum & Associates.

defensive. She is aware that this behavior is not useful and is trying to respond to others in a nondefensive fashion. Last week, a colleague challenged Lorraine and she responded in a highly relaxed and receptive fashion. However, when Lorraine was meeting with her team yesterday, someone questioned her, and she became highly defensive. What is going on?

Lorraine is not alone in her seemingly strange behavior. Being around other people is stimulating. This arousal or stimulation enhances our performance on tasks that we are experts in, but hinders our performance on novel tasks. Consider, for example, what happens to pool players when they are observed by others in pool halls (Michaels, Brommel, Brocato, Linkous, & Rowe, 1982): Novice players perform worse when someone is watching. In contrast, expert players' games improve dramatically when they are observed. Similarly, joggers speed up on paths when someone is watching them and slow down when no one appears to be in sight (Worringham & Messick, 1983). People giving impromptu speeches perform worse in the presence of others than when alone. What determines whether someone's behavior improves or falters in the presence of a group?

Social facilitation is the predictable enhancement in performance that occurs when people are in the presence of others. **Social impairment** occurs when people are the center of attention and they are concerned with discrepancies between their performance and standards of excellence.

The key question for team players is how to ensure that their behavior is the optimal response. There are two routes. *Expertise* is one way: Experts are trained to focus on what matters most. *Practice* and *rehearsal* is another strategy: It modifies the behavioral response hierarchy, so that the desired response becomes second nature. However, being an expert does not completely protect people from choking. Just look at professional players on sports teams. In the championship series in professional baseball and basketball, the home team is significantly more likely to lose the decisive game than it is to lose earlier home games in the series (Baumeister & Steinhilber, 1984). Why? Remember that expertise is the result of overlearning. The pressure to perform well causes people to focus their attention on the process of performing—the focus of attention turns inward. The more pressure, the more inwardly focused people become. The problem is that when people focus on what are overlearned or automated responses, this actually interferes with performance (Lewis & Linder, 1997). As an example, consider shoelace tying. Most adults are experts at tying their own shoes. This comes from years of practice. Most people can carry on conversations without thinking about the process of shoelace tying when they are engaged in the act. Now, suppose that you had to tie your shoes onstage in front of an audience that was watching and timing you. You might become so preoccupied with the process that you would actually perform worse than if you were not under pressure. In short, hyper-self-awareness interferes with the ability to perform.

It is best to avoid trying to learn difficult material or perform complex tasks in groups, because peer pressure will obstruct performance. However, if team members are experts, they will likely flourish under this kind of pressure. Practice not only makes perfect, but it makes performance hold up under pressure. Not all teamwork needs to be done in a team setting; sometimes it is beneficial to allow team members to complete work on their own and bring it back to the group.

Effort and Motivation

It is not enough for members of a team to be skilled, they also must be *motivated* to use their knowledge and skills to achieve shared goals. Contrary to popular opinion, motivation is not strictly based on external factors, like reward and compensation. Motivation comes both from within a person and from external factors. People by nature are goal directed, but a poorly designed team or organizational environment can threaten team dedication and persistence. At certain times, members of a team can develop a defeatist attitude: They may feel that their actions do not matter, that something always goes wrong to mess things up (for example, a sports team on a losing streak), or that their input is not listened to. This can also happen if team members feel they are unable to affect their environment or cannot rely on others. As a case in point, consider Sidebar 2-1.

Sidebar 2-1. Game of Envelopes and Money

Consider the "envelopes and money" game (Murnighan, 1992). In this game, an envelope is passed around a room and team members can choose to donate money to the envelope. The instructor (or leader) states that if a certain amount of money is collected, all group members will be given a bonus of $10, but that their original donation will not be returned, as it is anonymous. Theoretically, it is possible for all group members to make a positive profit, but this requires trust on the part of members that all others will contribute. Inevitably, the group donations fall short of what is needed to gain bonuses.

Social Loafing

A German agricultural engineer named Max Ringelmann was interested in the relative efficiency of farm labor supplied by horses, oxen, machines, and men. In particular, he was curious about their relative abilities to pull a load horizontally, such as in a tug-of-war. In one of his experiments, he had groups of 14 men pull a load and measured the amount of force they generated; he also measured the force that each of the men could pull independently. There was nearly a linear decline in the average pull per member as the size of the rope-pulling team increased. One person pulling on a rope alone exerted an average of 63 kilograms of force. However, in groups of three, the per-person force dropped to 53 kilograms, and in groups of eight, it reduced to only 31 kilograms per person—less than half of the effort exerted by people working alone (Ringelmann, 1913; summarized by Kravitz & Martin, 1986). This detailed observation revealed a fundamental principle of teamwork: People in groups often do not work as hard as they do when alone. This is known as **social loafing.**

Team performance increases with team size, but the rate of increase is negatively accelerated; the addition of new members to the team has diminishing returns on productivity. Similar results are obtained when teams work on intellectual puzzles (Taylor & Faust, 1952), creativity tasks (Gibb, 1951), perceptual judgments, and complex reasoning (Ziller, 1957). Social loafing has been demonstrated in many different cultures, including India (Werner, Ember, & Ember, 1981), Japan (Williams & Williams, 1984), and Taiwan (Gabrenya, Latané, & Wang, 1983). The general form of the social loafing effect is portrayed in Figure 2-2.

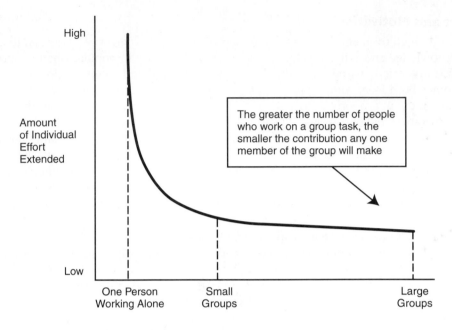

High

Amount
of Individual
Effort
Extended

The greater the number of people
who work on a group task, the
smaller the contribution any one
member of the group will make

Low

One Person
Working Alone

Small
Groups

Large
Groups

Number of People Working

FIGURE 2-2 The Social Loafing Effect

Source: Greenberg, J. 1996. *Managing Behavior in Organizations,* Upper Saddle River, NJ: Prentice Hall. (p. 189)

Free Riders

Many team leaders have asked: Is my team working as hard as it can? Their suspicions may be correct: People's motivations often diminish in a team. Also, the larger the team, the less likely it is that any given person will work hard. For many team tasks, there is a possibility that others can and will do most or all of the work necessary for the team to succeed. This means that free riders benefit from the efforts of others while contributing little or nothing themselves. Team members are sensitive to how important their efforts are perceived to be: When they think their contributions are not going to have much impact on the outcome, they are less likely to exert themselves on the team's behalf.

Suggestions for Avoiding Free-Rider Problems   How do teams react once a free rider has been detected? As a general principle, people don't like free riders one bit. Team members want equitable working arrangements. Indeed, a strong work ethic holds in most teams, with greater rewards coming to those who work harder. If someone is not working as hard, the other team members might attempt to reduce that person's reward (e.g., not allow Stan to put his name on the group report if he has not contributed) or reduce their own inputs (i.e., the other members of the group might stop working hard). Obviously, this kind of behavior by one person can undermine the effectiveness of the team on several dimensions. However, the company itself bears the greatest cost from this kind of behavior: When everyone stops working hard in retaliation against someone else's bad conduct, ultimately, the work does not get done or done well. In this case, the free rider may suffer no direct repercussions. Hence, this kind of behavior can be a serious threat to team productivity in the workplace.

Why do people loaf and free ride? Three reasons: Diffusion of responsibility, a reduced sense of self-efficacy, and the sucker effect.

Diffusion of Responsibility

In a team, a given person's effort and contributions are less identifiable than when that person works independently. This is because everyone's efforts are pooled into the team enterprise and the return is a function of everyone's contribution, considered jointly. Thus, it becomes difficult to separate one person's contribution from another. At an extreme, this can lead to **deindividuation**—a psychological state in which a person does not feel a sense of individual responsibility. As a result, the person is less likely to perform or contribute. Consider, for example, a dramatic, real-world illustration. A woman named Kitty Genovese was on her way home from work late one evening in New York (based upon Latané & Darley, 1968). She was attacked by a man and stabbed to death. Thirty-eight of her neighbors in the apartment building where she lived witnessed the attacker approach and slay her; however, not a single person so much as called the police.

Upon hearing this story, most people are horrified and attribute the neighbors' lack of assistance to social and moral decay. We might look at this, however, from another perspective: People are more likely to free ride as the number of others in the group increases. Observers in the apartment building who knew that others were also watching felt less responsible and so less inclined to intervene. In effect, they told themselves, "Someone else has probably already called for help." Why inconvenience yourself when it is likely the woman will receive help from someone else? Of course, if everyone thinks this way, the probability that the victim eventually gets help decreases dramatically.

Reduced Sense of Self-Efficacy

In some cases, it is not diffusion of responsibility that hinders people from contributing to a team effort, but rather the feeling that their contributions will not be as valuable, efficacious, or worthwhile as they might be in a smaller group. The individual may feel that any contribution will not be sufficient to justify the effort. Consider, for example, the problem of voting. Most everyone agrees that voting is a good practice. Why then did only 48 percent of the eligible U.S. population turn out to vote during the presidential election of 1996? Individuals may feel that their vote has such a small impact on the outcome that voting is not worthwhile. Similarly, team members may feel they lack the ability to positively influence a team's outcome.

Sucker Effects

A common concern held by team members is whether someone will be left doing all of the work and getting little or no credit (Kerr, 1983). Because everyone wants to avoid being taken advantage of, team members hedge their efforts, and wait to see what others will do. The problem is that when everyone does this, no one contributes. When people see others not contributing, it confirms their worst fears. The sucker effect becomes a self-fulfilling prophesy.

Suggestions for Enhancing Successful Team Performance

Suppose you are managing a team that processes insurance claims. Prior to the formation of teams, you measure average claim processing time and find it to be 3 days. After forming the teams, you find the average has increased to about 9 days. Has your team fallen victim to social loafing? Your upper-division manager advises you to immediately dismantle the teams. Someone else tells you that the company's incentive system needs to be overhauled. What do *you* think?

Before you dismantle the teams or completely restructure the company's entire pay structure, consider the following strategies:

Public Posting: Make Individual Team Members' Contributions Identifiable   When each member's contribution to a task is displayed where it can be seen by others (e.g., weekly sales figures posted on a bulletin board or e-mail), people are less likely to loaf, or slack off, than when only overall group (or companywide) performance is made available (Kerr & Bruun, 1981; Williams, Harkins, & Latané, 1981). Whole Foods subscribes to this line of thinking by collecting and distributing vast amounts of performance data throughout all levels of the organization. Sensitive figures on store sales, team sales, profit margins, and even salaries are available to every person in every location. It collects and distributes information to an extent that would be unimaginable almost anywhere else. In fact, the company shares so much information so widely that the Securities and Exchange Commission (SEC) has designated all 6,500 employees "insiders" for stock-trading purposes (Fishman, 1996). However, the key is not identifiability per se, but rather the evaluation that identifiability makes possible (Harkins & Szymanski, 1987; Harkins & Jackson, 1985).

Make the Task Involving, Interesting, and Challenging   Social loafing may be eliminated if the task is sufficiently involving (Brickner, Harkins, & Ostrom, 1986), attractive (Zaccaro, 1984), or intrinsically interesting (Petty, Cacioppo, & Kasmer, 1985). When the task is challenging and interesting, people feel more motivated to perform. Generally, when tasks are highly specialized and routinized, monotony sets in; in contrast, when team members are responsible for all pieces of a work product or service, they feel more responsibility for the work. This is perhaps why many companies, such as IBM Credit Corporation, restructured into teams that handle all aspects of a credit application. The walk-through time in IBM Credit Corporation for a single credit application decreased from 9 days to 2 days. This is largely because teams of individuals feel personally responsible for a particular client in a way that they did not feel before the restructuring.

Reward Team Members for Performance   This means that team members should recognize and reward contributions by individuals. This need not mean large financial incentives. Symbolic rewards are often more powerful than money. Sales managers may strategically use symbolic rewards, such as high-performer sales clubs or plaques and ceremonies honoring exemplary service, to deliver messages to the salesforce. These can be used to underscore the values of the sales organization and help shape salesperson behavior.

It is often more important for team members to feel appreciated and acknowledged by the members of their team than by outsiders. There can be serious consequences if people feel they are not valued and respected, so much so that people are more likely to cheat and steal from the organization when they feel they have been unfairly treated (Greenberg, 1988). For example, Blaine began his career motivated to do well; however, he put in a lot of work on a redesign team, and none of his suggestions were implemented. After that, he began to make personal long-distance calls and take office supplies, feeling that he was owed these things due to his unappreciated hard work.

Build Trust among Team Members   People worry a lot about being a sucker, especially when the norms of a team are created early on and people get labeled. Leaders can demonstrate trust by putting themselves in a vulnerable position. By showing vulnerability and requiring trust, leaders show they trust the team and set that expectation. Cohesive teams are less inclined to loaf (Williams, 1981).

Make People Feel Personally Responsible and Accountable for the Team's Actions
The buck stops with the team. When teams set their own performance goals, they are less likely to loaf (Brickner, Harkins, & Ostrom, 1986).

Team Contract   Ideally, at the outset of teamwork, members should develop a written statement of objectives and practices. This should be written up and posted. According to Katzenbach and Smith (1993), the best teams in their extensive study invest a tremendous amount of time and effort exploring, shaping, and agreeing on a purpose that belongs to them collectively and individually. This "purposing" activity continues through the life of the team. In contrast, failed teams rarely develop a common purpose. The best teams also translate their common purpose into specific performance goals.

Team Performance Review and Feedback   Team members should periodically review and evaluate others. This can be conducted on a formal or informal basis.

Decrease Team Size   As the team gets larger and larger, personal contributions to the team become less important to the team's chances of success (Olson, 1965; Kerr, 1989). In short, as team size increases, feelings of anonymity increase.

Suppose that you implement the preceding steps, and your team's performance is still less than what you think is possible. What should you do? Consider the third source of threats to productivity: Coordination problems.

Coordination Strategies

Ability and motivation are essential and desirable, but insufficient for effective team functioning. A team needs to *coordinate* the skills, efforts, and actions of its members so as to effectively enact team strategy. For example, distributed.net is a coordinated team of computer programmers and enthusiasts. Armed with tens of thousands of computers linked over the Internet, distributed.net solved the Data Encryption Standard (DES) Challenge II sponsored by RSA Data Security, Inc. The goal of the challenge was to break the 56-bit security code provided by the government's DES and recover the secret key used to encrypt messages. As the *PR Newswire* reported on February 26, 1998: "The distributed.net team met the challenge in 39 days, less than half the 90 days of computing time it took the original challenge to be solved by a university team. The distributed.net organization utilized the idle time of computers throughout the world to solve particularly arduous computing tasks. For the DES Challenge II, the team managed to coordinate the efforts of 22,000 participants throughout the world, linking together over 50,000 computers to power through 72 quadrillion possible keys. One by one, the computers crunched through all possible combinations until the winning key was found to decode the message encrypted with the DES algorithm." This feat was possible because the team was highly coordinated.

Coordination problems must be surmounted for a team to be effective. Team members may be individually good at what they do, but unless they coordinate their activities, like distributed.net, they will not meet their team objectives.

Coordination is the combined synchronization of the strategies of all members. Teams vary in terms of their coordination or synchrony. Consider a football team—the slightest misunderstanding about a play can lose the game. Another example is a rowing team or a dance troupe—unless everyone is synchronized, they cannot achieve their performance goals, no matter how skilled and motivated the individuals. This is why teams often sing or chant to synchronize their movements and actions. Sir Adrian Cadbury, former chairman of Cadbury Schweppes, rowed in the 1952 Olympics. "Sir Adrian took more than the lesson of timing from the world of rowing when he entered corporate life. 'What has always been important to me is the team—rowing taught me that. More importantly, trust.' Rowing is certainly a sport that places more emphasis on team harmony than others—there's less scope for those with individual flare to shine. 'The beauty of racing in a crew is that you learn that any victory is the combined effort of everyone. In the same way company results reflect the performance of the whole firm.'" (Phelps, 1996, p. 110).

Coordination problems increase with team size and do so in an accelerating manner. The number of ways in which a team can organize itself (e.g., divide responsibilities, combine contributions, coordinate efforts) increases rapidly as the team gets larger (Kelley, 1962).

Most of the threats to team productivity are attributable to coordination problems, but most managers, used to thinking in terms of ability and motivation, fail to realize this—an example of the misattribution problem discussed in chapter 1.

Most people take coordination and communication in teams for granted. In other words, they do not anticipate that their handwriting will be misread by a teammate or that a fax won't go through. People have a biased sense about the clarity of their own messages and intentions. They may not be as clear as they think they are. The problems in communication and coordination are compounded when the medium of communication is less rich, such as in e-mail, fax, and videoconferencing (a topic discussed in part III on global teamwork).

What are some practical steps to ensure better coordination of efforts within teams?

Use Single-Digit Teams

Most teams are too large. As the number of people on a team increases, it is that much harder to schedule meetings, move paperwork, and converge on ideas. The incidence of unanticipated failure increases. As a rule of thumb, teams should have fewer than 10 members and just enough to cover all needed skill areas.

Have an Agenda

Members need a clear sense of where they are going and how they will get there. If the team does not know where it is going, its efforts will be fragmented and members will waste time and energy.

Train Team Members Together

Team members who train together, as opposed to separately, work more effectively. This is because they have an opportunity to coordinate their strategies. A side benefit of training team members together is that training provides an opportunity for building trust.

Practice

Teams are low on the learning curve when the team members begin to work with one another. A team might be motivated and highly skilled, but naive in terms of communicating with one another in a highly synchronized and coordinated fashion. Teams require more practice than individuals.

Minimize Links in Communication

For most tasks, it is better for team members to be able to directly access one another rather than going through others (gatekeeping).

Set Clear Performance Standards

Every team needs clear performance standards. In the absence of performance standards, it is impossible to evaluate the effectiveness of a team. The most common means by which individuals are evaluated by organizations is through a performance appraisal, which we discuss in detail in the next chapter. Many performance appraisals are routine and occur on a regular basis. In the best of circumstances, they are objective, based upon hard facts and deliverables. People receive valuable and telling feedback about what they are doing well and what they need to work on. Should performance appraisals be used when evaluating team performance?

If so, how do we know whether a team is performing effectively? If this question is hard to answer, then it will be difficult to pull together a high-performance team and diagnose problems before they threaten team performance. Furthermore, even if you happen to be in the fortunate position of working on a successful team, unless you understand what makes your team effective, you may make the wrong choices or be indecisive at inopportune times.

Team performance evaluation is more difficult than individual performance evaluation. Teams are harder to track, and higher turnover can blur the relationship between the actions that people take and the results achieved by the team. Nevertheless, it is still possible to do a rigorous performance evaluation on teams, just as it is with individual employees. In this chapter, we consider *what* factors are important to consider in assessing team performance. In the next chapter, we deal with the thornier issue of *how* to do the actual measuring and structure the incentive system.

PERFORMANCE CRITERIA

What are the criteria by which we should evaluate team effectiveness? By performance criteria, we mean those factors used to evaluate the success or failure of a team effort. Hackman (1987) identified three key criteria in his model of group effectiveness: Productivity, satisfaction, and individual well-being. To this, we add a fourth criterion, organizational gains, suggested by Gruenfeld (1998).

Productivity is probably the most important measure of team success. Did the team achieve its goals? Team productivity requires that the team have a clear goal and be able to adapt accordingly as new information arrives, goals change, and organizational priorities shift. This also holds true for changes in the marketplace—for example, the entrance or exit of a competitor or a stock market plunge. There are many different dimensions to productivity. For instance: What was the team's output? How does the output correspond to the team's original goals? How quickly or timely were results achieved? How effective was the outcome? What is the correspondence between the team output and a measurable accomplishment (such as improved market share, new product development, etc.) by the firm? Efficiency is also important: If the team's goals were accomplished, at what cost did this happen? Was it worth it? The productivity of a team is highly correlated with its goals, as well as the ability of the team to adapt, change, and accommodate the goals in the face of new information, changing organizational priorities, and the changing marketplace.

The productivity criterion asks whether the team's output meets the standards of those who have to use it—that is, the end user. It is not enough that the team is satisfied with the output or even that it meets some objective performance measure. If the team's output is unacceptable to those who have to use it, the team is not effective.

For these reasons, it is important to identify the legitimate clients of the team. The various end users who depend upon the team's output may focus on different performance standards (e.g., quantity, quality, cutting costs, innovation, and timeliness).

For many people, the buck stops here; anything else is inconsequential. We disagree. A second major criterion on team performance is *team satisfaction and well-being.* Did the team learn something from working together and are its members better able to work together in the future? Sometimes, teams meet their goals, but relationships suffer and are not dealt with in a way that allows members to work productively together in the future. "Mutual antagonism could become so high that members would choose to accept collective failure rather than to share knowledge and information with one another" (Hackman, 1990, p. 6). In an effectively functioning team, the capability of members to work together on future projects is maintained and strengthened.

It is worthwhile to ask why team satisfaction is important, as opposed to being just a nice side benefit. For example, if a team successfully puts a person on the moon, is this not a success regardless of whether the team experienced satisfaction? The main reason has to do with the future of the team or project. If the team effort really and truly is a one-time effort, then maximizing team satisfaction may not be necessary. However, most of us want to build teams that will last for some meaningful length of time. If team members do not enjoy working on a team, performance will suffer. A manager in Societé Generale, a French investment bank and corporate finance institution, summed it up by saying, "I ask myself whether I want to work with these people again. If the answer is yes, then the team was successful. If the answer is no, the team was not successful."

Successful teamwork means that the team accommodates to changes in membership due to additions, growth, and turnover. A prime example of this kind of teamwork is evident at Whole Foods Market Inc. Everyone who joins Whole Foods quickly grasps the primacy of teamwork. That's because teams—and only teams—have the power to approve of new hires for full-time jobs. Store leaders screen candidates and recommend them for a job on a specific team. But it takes a two-thirds vote of the team, after what is usually a 30-day trial period, for the candidate to become a full time employee. Successful teamwork means that team members may need to routinely reject candidates. According to CEO John Mackey, teams do not become effective until they have rejected someone: "They're saying, 'This person isn't good enough to be on our team.' They're standing up to the leader, taking ownership of their team, saying, 'Go back and try again'" (Fishman, 1996, p. 103).

In addition to the functioning of the team as a whole, the development and satisfaction of the individual members is also important. Thus, a third major criterion of successful teamwork is *individual growth.* Simply stated, teams should represent growth and development opportunities for the individual needs of the members. Human beings have a need for growth, development, and fulfillment. Some teams operate in ways that block the development of individual members and satisfaction of personal needs. In short, members' needs should be more satisfied than frustrated by the team experience. Teams should be sensitive to members and provide opportunities for members to develop new skills. This does not mean that teams, or for that matter, organizations, exist to serve individual needs; rather, successful organizations create opportunities that challenge individual members. Whole Foods addresses this potential problem by putting the fate of the team in the hands of the team members. "The company's gain-sharing program ties bonuses directly to team performance—specifically, sales per labor hour, the most important productivity measure at Whole Foods. Democracy reinforces discipline: Vote for someone who doesn't perform, and your bonus may go down within months" (Fishman, 1996, p. 103).

Another perspective is that of the larger organization. Thus, a fourth criterion of team performance is *organizational gains.* Does the organization benefit from the team? In many instances, the team becomes so self-serving and egocentrically focused that it loses sight of the organization's larger goals. (This is most likely the case with teams that have greater autonomy.) This can occur when the team's goals are incompatible with those of other departments or areas. If, for instance, a company's salesforce dramatically improves sales over a short period of time, this does no good for the company. In fact, it could even hurt the company, if the manufacturing group cannot fulfill the promises made by the salesforce or if the technical support group cannot handle the new customer calls. This is an example where the sales strategy backfired at the organizational level.

In other cases, different teams in the organization may reinvent things already developed by the organization because they are not able to learn from outside their group.

At the heart of this issue is **integration:** It is important for teams to understand the organization's goals in order to work effectively toward them. Teams need to integrate with other units in the organization. Practically, this means that teams must disseminate information, results, status reports, failures, expertise, and ideas in a timely and efficient manner.

Achieving organizational gains requires solid planning and coordination with the rest of the firm. According to Jeff McHenry, Director of Executive Development at Microsoft, "the single most important factor is that effective teams have a clear goal. They work toward something. And everybody understands what the goal is. We tend to hire people who are achievement-oriented and results-driven. When they don't have a

---

BOX 2-1

Team Performance Analysis

Conduct a performance analysis of your team using the following four criteria as a baseline. Remember, you don't have to wait until the team is finished with its task to begin an evaluation. It is actually best to continually assess performance as the team is working toward its goal.

TEAM PRODUCTIVITY

- Does the team have a clear goal?
- What objective performance measures have been established at the outset of teamwork?
- Who are the legitimate clients of the team?
- Does the team's output (e.g., decisions, products, services) meet the standards of those who have to use it?
- Under what conditions should the goal change?
- What sources of information should the team consider to assess whether the initial goal might need to be changed?

TEAM SATISFACTION

- Do the team members enjoy working together?
- What conditions could lead to feelings of resentment?

- What conditions could prevent team members from working together in the future?
- How can team members best learn from one another?
- How are team members expected to accommodate to changes, such as additions to the team, growth, and turnover?

INDIVIDUAL GROWTH

- Do the individual team members grow and develop as a result of the team experience?
- Do team members have a chance to improve their skills or affirm themselves?
- What factors and conditions could block personal growth?
- Are individuals' growth needs understood and shared by group members?

ORGANIZATIONAL GAINS

- How does the team benefit the larger organization?
- Are the team's goals consistent with those of the larger organization?
- What other groups, departments, and units are affected by the team?
- What steps has the team taken to integrate its activities with those of others?

---

goal, they tend to flounder because they have nothing to work toward. When they do have a goal, their achievement orientation takes over—and great things happen" (Anonymous, 1996).

Box 2-1 is an executive summary of our team performance analysis, which can be performed by team members or team leaders. The relative importance of each of the four criteria vary across circumstances, and there is no single best set of conditions for optimizing performance. There are many ways a team can perform work well and, unfortunately, more ways for it to be ineffective. Teams are governed by the principle of

equifinality (Katz & Kahn, 1978)—a team can reach the same outcome from various initial conditions and by a variety of means.

THE TEAM PERFORMANCE EQUATION

Now that we have discussed the four critical measures of team performance and the three key ingredients for team success, we can put all these factors together in a single equation for the manager to use when assessing team performance (Steiner, 1972):

$$AP = PP + S - T$$

Where AP = Actual Productivity;
PP = Potential Productivity;
S = Synergy;
T = Performance Threats.

The actual productivity of a team is a function of three key factors: The potential productivity of the team, synergy, and threats. The first factor, the **potential productivity** of a team, depends on three subfactors: Task demands, the resources available to the team, and the team process.

Task demands are the requirements imposed on the team by the task itself and the rules governing task performance. Task demands determine the resources needed for optimal performance and how to combine resources. **Resources** are the relevant abilities, skills, and tools possessed by people attempting to perform the task. **Process** concerns the way teams use resources to meet task demands. *Team process* describes the steps taken by the team when attempting the task and includes nonproductive as well as productive actions. The task demands reveal the kinds of resources needed; the resources determine the team's potential productivity; and the process determines the degree of potential realized.

Synergy refers to everything that can and does go better in a team compared to individuals working independently (Collins & Guetzkow, 1964). **Performance threats** refer to everything that can go wrong in a team. Unfortunately, teams often fall below their potential; there is considerable **process loss,** or underperformance, due to coordination problems and motivational problems (Davis, 1969; Laughlin, 1980; Steiner, 1972). As a general principle, managers can more easily control threats than synergies. Synergies can emerge, but they usually take more time than anyone expects. Therefore, the manager's job is to set the stage for synergies by attempting to minimize all possible threats.

CONCLUSIONS

Unless a team has a clear goal, it will be impossible to achieve success. However, having a clear goal in no sense guarantees successful team performance. Successful team performance is a multidimensional concept. To be sure, managers want their teams to satisfy the end user or client, but they also need to make sure that teamwork is satisfying and rewarding for the members. If the team does not enjoy working together, sustaining long-term productivity will be impossible. Moreover, managing a team successfully must include managing and investing in the individual team members. Thus, teamwork ultimately needs to be a growthful and rewarding experience for team members. Finally, as organizations move toward flatter structures and greater team empowerment, the possibility arises that team goals may become superordinate to those of the larger organization. A successful team is integrated with the larger organization. Putting teams on a course to achieve these four markers of success requires a combination of managing the internal dynamics of teams (ability, motivation, and coordination) as well as the external relations of teams within the larger organization. One of the most effective things a manager can do to ensure team success is to adopt a preventative approach and undertake an analysis of the essential conditions affecting team performance. One of the biggest managerial shortcomings in terms of teamwork is a failure to account for threats to team performance. This is unfortunate because managers can more easily control threats than synergies.

CHAPTER 3

Rewarding Teamwork: Compensation and Performance Appraisals

At Johnsonville Foods Company, a midsize sausage maker, slipping behind in produc-tion can cost workers money. The company's 725 employees operate in self-managed teams and divide up profit-sharing bonuses each month. Teams split the cash based on how well members have satisfied customers and achieved previously negotiated goals. Here, actions speak louder than words. For example, when several headquarters staffers failed to deliver a financial analysis to the food-service division on time, teammates re-turned 20 percent of some members' expected bonuses to the corporation. What do team members think of the system? "Alternately, we are all very happy with this system and un-happy with it," says Michael Garvey, the financial-service team's coach and company con-troller (Lublin, 1995, p. R4).

The move to self-managing teams begs the question of reward and compensation in teams because hierarchical pay plans centered on individuals may not make sense in the context of teams and may, in fact, be detrimental. If pay plans reward the individual but the corporate message is teams, then teamwork may be undermined. Perhaps it is for this reason that 76 percent of businesses with self-directed teams tie team members' compensation partly to team performance (Lawler, Mohrman, & Led-ford, 1995). This does not mean, however, that team members should all be paid equally. People in teams know that there is variable performance among members.

Team compensation is not as simple as it might seem. For example, rewarding team performance could set up a system where teams compete viciously with other teams in their same company (see, for example, Sidebar 3-1). Even though teams may be per-fectly capable of allocating pay or rewards to individuals in the team, this may some-times mean that superstars are not rewarded unless other teammates forgo part of their own profit sharing.

Even if a compensation system can be set up that appropriately rewards team effort, some team members may be unwilling to determine their coworkers' pay. For example, teams in the Dallas office of New York Life Insurance Company conducted "peer re-views" to assess members' contributions to a team's performance, but team members were not comfortable deciding the size and recipients of the resulting incentive awards. So, management decided for them (Lawler, Mohrman, & Ledford, 1995). Other compa-nies, such as Johnsonville Foods, address the problem by creating more objective stan-dards to evaluate team members' performance. For example, three Southwest-region Johnsonville teams prepare a detailed weekly scoreboard to set and track specific activ-ity, such as the number of sales calls. As we discuss in this chapter, team members feel more comfortable when performance criteria are based on objective standards.

> ### Sidebar 3-1. When Team Pay Backfires
>
> The Levi Strauss Corporation moved from a piecemeal system to a team system, in which workers were no longer paid by how much they produced personally, but rather by the performance of the team (King, 1998). Levi Strauss did this for seemingly good reasons—to give employees more variety in their work, making it more interesting and less likely that employees would be injured due to repetitive stress disorders, and so on. But the results were disastrous. Workers with more skills resented those with fewer skills because they ended up with less pay than before, even though the average pay increased across the board. The conflict among team members was fierce. Yet given the structure that was set up, conflict almost seemed inevitable and there was little that employees could do to change the situation. In fact, highly skilled workers promoted the antagonism of less capable workers, including those with injuries, to get them to quit (and thus increase the average productivity of the group).
>
> Consider also what happened at Solar Press in Naperville, Illinois (Garfield, 1992). Employees were assigned to specific machines and divided into work teams with four or five members. The more a team produced during a given month, the bigger the bonus for each of its members. Teams competed for additional dollars. The bonus plan, put in place in the spring of 1984, had an immediate effect: Packaging machines ran faster than ever and production rates doubled. But there were also problems. Because of the pressure to produce, teams put off routine maintenance, so machines broke down more often. Employees who found more efficient ways of working hoarded the information to prevent others from winning their bonuses. Moreover, the plan did not take into account unfair distributions of work assignments, or the fact that some jobs demanded more work than others. According to Sue Smith, the Solar Press Scheduling Manager, the "system totally dismantled any feeling of team work or company-wide spirit" (Garfield, 1992, p. 252).

This chapter examines the types of team pay and the choices companies have for rewarding their teams. We discuss the advantages and disadvantages of each method. In the second section of the chapter, we take up the question of performance appraisals: What are they? What should be measured? Who should do the measuring? We examine 360-degree evaluations in detail. In the third section of the chapter, we examine the types of biases that can play havoc on performance appraisals and discuss what to do about these biases. We conclude the chapter by providing a step-by-step guide for implementing a variable team-based pay structure.

TYPES OF TEAM PAY

There is no all-purpose team compensation plan. In this section, we consider four types of team pay or reward: Incentive pay, recognition, profit sharing, and gainsharing (see Table 3-1). Pay, in a large measure, is a communication device. According to Gross (1995), pay is one of the loudest and clearest ways a company can send a message to an employee. People tend to behave according to the way they are evaluated and paid. Therefore, if the organization values teamwork, team members must be ultimately rec-

TABLE 3-1   Team-Based Pay

Type	Description/Types	Advantages/ Applications	Disadvantages
Team incentives	A team of employees receives money based on increased performance against predetermined targets	• Can combine a focus on individual and team performance • Team can be given opportunity to allocate	• Employees averse to thinking of selves as team members • Risky if base pay is reduced • Guided by upper management and corporate initiative
Recognition: Spot awards	One-time award for a limited number of employees or groups for performing well beyond expectations or for completing a project, program, or product	• Easy to implement • Distributed at the local (team level) • Introduced easily, quickly, and inexpensively without layers of approval • Comparatively simple	• Employees concerned they won't be recognized for own contributions • Risky if base pay is reduced • Carry less front-end motivation
Profit sharing	A share of corporate profits is distributed in cash on a current basis to all employees, (driven by financial factors)	• Serves communication purpose by signaling that rewards are in balance across the organization • Informs and educates employees about financial well-being of organization	• Too far removed from workers' control to affect performance
Gainsharing	A percentage of the value of increased productivity is given to workers under prearranged formula (driven by operational factors (e.g., quality, productivity, customer satisfaction))	• Geared toward production-oriented workers • Add-on to compensation, so easily accepted by employees	• Too far removed from workers' control to affect performance

ognized and compensated for teaming. First and foremost, employees must understand how the incentive system works in their company. Generally, the simpler, the better. For example, burying incentives and recognition for team membership in the company's basic compensation package can dampen the intended motivating effect on individuals. Second, an incentive system should be comprehensive enough that people feel fairly treated. Employees compare their pay with that received by others. An incentive system that appears unfair can result in trouble (see Sidebar 3-2, for example).

Sidebar 3-2. Women Are Still Paid Less Than Men for the Same Work

It is well known that women earn significantly less money for doing the same work as men: Women presently comprise almost 46 percent of the paid labor force, and 62 percent of married mothers with children younger than the age of 6 are now employed (U.S. Bureau of Census, 1995). Yet despite a number of gains, women's annual earnings remain at 71 percent of men's (U.S. Bureau of Labor Statistics, 1993).

In the traditional model of compensation, base pay was designed to attract and retain employees. Incentives and bonuses were reserved for managers, salespeople, and higher executives. Now, many companies are moving to align pay systems with business strategies (Gross, 1995). Individual incentives, commissions, profit sharing, and gainsharing are different methods of variable pay that are offered to motivate and reward performance. However, they are not designed to motivate and reward teams. Rather, the two most common practices for rewarding and motivating team performance are team incentives and recognition.

Incentive Pay

In terms of salary and pay, **base pay** is how companies determine an individual's base salary. This is an integration of internal equity (based on job evaluation) and external equity (based on market data). The second issue in pay is **variable pay.** One type of variable pay is incentive pay. In general, variable pay should not be more than 15 to 20 percent for individuals in the lowest levels of the company. As employees move up the organizational chart, the proportion of variable pay should increase—along with their amount of control over the situation.

Many organizations have incentive-based pay plans based on individual performance. Because the focus of this book is on teams, we deal with team-based pay. When teams are an organization's choice approach to job design, it often makes little sense for the organization to use systems that reward individual performance. Particularly destructive are performance appraisal systems for individuals that require a fixed number of positive and negative rations or provide fixed pots of budget money that need to be divided up differentially among individuals in a group; these practices put team members in competition for rewards (Lawler, 1992).

Incentive strategies can combine a focus on individual performance and team performance to reflect the degree to which a job calls for individual work and teamwork. For example, a bonus pool may be created based on the performance of the overall team. The bonus pool can be divided among the individuals who are members of the team based on how well the individuals performed. (For an example of the implementation of bonus pay, see Sidebar 3-3.) To ensure that team members do not compete in a destructive fashion, a 360-degree feedback method can be used (which we discuss in detail in the next section). Another alternative is to have two separate reward systems operating in tandem. One system provides bonuses to teams based on their performance; the second rewards individuals, based on how well they have performed. These systems can be based on separate budgets so that they do not compete.

A critical question is whether to reward behavior or to reward results. Traditional thinking may lead managers to link team performance to their results. For goals such as cost reduction, this is easy to quantify, but for other areas, this is much more difficult. For example, Motorola's David Goodall, corporate director of compensation, argues that "It's unfair to reward cross-functional teams solely on the basis of results, because they are often put into positions to move organizations forward by taking risks. Sometimes the risks they take might not be successful. The worst thing to do would be to rap their knuckles" (Pascarella, 1997, p. 16). One solution is to redefine or broaden the meaning of success—much as the previous chapter reviewed the four measures of team productivity (goal achievement, team satisfaction, individual growth, and organizational gains). Thus, many managers reward *competencies* rather than *results*—for ex-

Sidebar 3-3. Team Bonus Pay

One large national retail corporation with more than 800 outlets was exploring ways to increase sales (see Shea & Guzzo, 1987a). Management believed that increasing group incentives to sell would increase sales and service by increasing salespeople's customer orientation and cooperativeness. Consequently, the salesforce went from being paid an hourly wage to being paid an hourly wage plus a group bonus. The bonus depended on sales gains in the current calendar month over sales for that month in the preceding year. The bonuses were distributed noncompetitively; each person could earn an hourly bonus that ranged from a few cents to over a dollar for each hour worked in a month, depending on the size of the team's sales. No financial penalties existed for sales losses. Posting the weekly sales figures meant that groups received continual feedback regarding their opportunity to earn bonus money. During the 7-month period of this study, sales gains corporationwide averaged approximately 28 percent. At the work group level, outcome interdependence increased significantly, and marked changes occurred in the patterns for work interaction among group members. Rewarding entire groups for focusing on sales was associated with an increase in mutual assistance and a decrease in members' blocking or hindering each other's work.

ample, does the person display participative behavior? Does the person empower others? Does the person listen in a team environment?

Companies are more likely to add incentives to support team activity when a person is assigned full time to a project. At TRW Inc.'s Cleveland-based automotive group, Project ELITE (Earnings Leadership In Tomorrow's Environment), a number of people are temporarily assigned to a team effort and it is expected that they will return to their units or to a full-time permanent position sometime in the future. A significant portion of their pay is tied to the accomplishment of their goals and the organization's goals, which are clearly articulated.

Although team incentives offer significant advantages, there are some potential drawbacks (see DeMatteo, Eby, & Sundstrom, 1998). Most important, the use of team-based rewards may create the potential for motivational loss (that is, social loafing and free riding). This may result from perceptions of inequity when other team members are perceived as free riders, but rewards are nevertheless allocated based on equality. Moreover, team rewards may not foster cooperation in teams (Wageman, 1995). In fact, team rewards may foster competition between teams, leading to suboptimization of the organizational goals (Mohrman, Lawler, & Mohrman, 1992).

Recognition

The power of positive recognition often is severely underestimated. Furthermore, it can cost virtually nothing—just a little time, energy, and forethought. According to Gross (1995, p. 129), "One of the smartest things companies can do is to develop a systematic program of recognition of team results." Recognition, rewards, spot cash awards, or "celebrations of success" reward contributions after the fact, when performance is known.

The idea behind team recognition is that money is not everything. There are infinite sources of nonmonetary recognition—plaques, trophies, small gifts, vacations, and

TABLE 3-2 Implementing Recognition Awards: A Guide	
To have maximum possible impact, recognition awards should have the following features	
Purpose/objective	The program should clearly recognize what has been accomplished by the team and how that effort is linked to the company's values.
Eligibility	Companies must clearly determine whether teams or individuals will be recognized; lower, middle, and upper management; and how frequently employees are eligible for awards.
Program award levels	Use a few levels to recognize different accomplishments and different degrees of contributions: (a) application noncash awards (up to $250); (b) awards for significant financial contribution ($250–$2,500) for team members whose efforts significantly exceed expectations, support the unit's efforts, and produce measurable results; (c) awards for "extraordinary financial results" ($2,500–$10,000) for team members whose efforts have exceptional bottom-line impact.
Benefit implications	Recognition awards are not considered benefit bearing.
Funding	Recognition programs are typically funded out of the expense budget of the business unit and department, and are often stated as a percentage of the payroll.
Types of awards	(noncash versus cash)
Nomination procedures	For appreciation award level, nomination procedure should be as simple as possible; for companywide rewards, nomination procedures may be much more elaborate with peers, customers, and supervisors all having opportunity for input.
Timing	All awards should be given as close to the event as possible to reinforce the actions that led to the event.
Award presentation	This should be a positive experience, that makes the winner(s) feel proud; comments should be personalized and refer to details of the achievement; the connection between the accomplishment and the company's business strategy should be made clear; never present the award in passing; publicize the award (e.g., via memo, e-mail, bulletin board, or newsletter).
Program evaluation	Annually, a rewards and recognition committee should be chartered to evaluate the program in terms of its effectiveness.

Source: Adapted from Gross, S. E. 1995. *Compensation for Teams: How to Design and Implement Team-Based Reward Programs.* New York: AMACOM.

dinners with company officers. The most important feature of any of these is to give the gift respectfully, personally, and sincerely. First and foremost, this means that people and teams are singled out—if everyone gets the same recognition, it doesn't work. The reward should be chosen with the people in mind. Not everyone likes sporting events or ballet, for example. It is important to clearly tie the recognition to team performance; it will lose its effect if the organization waits 2 months to reward the team. Bernie Nagle, principal consultant at Price-Waterhouse-Coopers, advises management to recognize and celebrate the team. Also, team members should be encouraged to speak to management and explain how they achieved their objectives. (For some general guidelines for implementing recognition awards, consult Table 3-2.)

Cash and Noncash

Spot awards (also known as lightning bolts) can either be cash or noncash. Noncash awards, which are the most common, are given out for a job well done and are usually of nominal value. Cash awards can be far more substantial, although usually they are small bonuses. There is a lesson to be learned about cash and noncash recognition awards: "To recognize efforts and activities above expectations, give non-cash awards. To get results, pay cash" (Gross, 1995, p. 130).

Recognition awards are regarded to be effective, according to the 1994 Hay survey of 86 large U.S. corporations represented in the Business Roundtable, an association of 200 chief executives of the largest U.S. companies. The size of recognition awards varies significantly, from $100 to $15,000, with the average much closer to the low end. Cash awards need to be significant enough to merit being awarded. This usually means over $250. Steven Gross (1995) uses the VCR test as a rule of thumb: If someone can't buy a VCR with the award, it is probably not enough.

There are an infinite variety of noncash rewards that companies can give to teams to recognize contributions, ranging from thank-you notes to time off to lavish, all-expenses-paid trips for two to exotic places. Such rewards often reinforce the company image and strengthen the connection between the employer and the employee. To be effective, recognition needs to be clearly focused on the team whose achievements are being celebrated, rather than on a general self-congratulatory party for the entire unit or organization.

An especially thorny issue is whether recognition awards to teams should equally recognize all team members. (For an example of how recognition could backfire, see Sidebar 3-4.)

Sidebar 3-4. When Recognition Backfires

Recognition can invite complaints. Motorola's Goodall cites the case of an international team made up of six people representing different businesses from different regions. When they successfully completed their project, the organization decided it would give each individual a $1,000 after-tax bonus. Three of the six members felt the money was unnecessary: "We've already had the satisfaction of being on the team, having the recognition of being able to report back to the senior staff." These team members were further disturbed by the fact that, irrespective of the level they were in the organization, each received the same dollar amount: "We want to be rewarded for the effort we put in as individuals" (Pascarella, 1997). Team members may say to themselves, "We saved the company millions and they only give me a thousand."

James A. Tompkins, president of Tompkins Associates Inc., a Raleigh, N.C. consultancy, warns that management needs to be careful about anything that may be viewed as "buying" the team. He gives the following example: "If I'm stuck on the side of the road and you stop and help me change a flat tire, and I give you $10, you are insulted. But if I send your wife a bouquet of flowers, you are complimented" (Pascarella, 1997, p. 16). The gesture must be meaningful to the group. For example, giving team members tickets to an evening ball game in reward for putting in long hours on a project may be deflating to team members with families.

Many consultants believe that teams should be given a role in distributing recognition awards—letting the team decide which members get how much. This practice is consistent with the whole idea of self-managing teams: Autonomy and self-management (see Box 3-1).

According to the 1994 Hay Compensation Conference Survey, recognition awards are more widely used by companies (38 percent) than are special pay programs for

---

BOX 3-1

Seven Ways to Praise Teams

Bob Nelson, author of *1001 Ways to Reward Employees* (1994), suggests these seven methods of recognizing the accomplishments of a team as well as the achievements of individual team members:

1. Have managers pop in at the first meeting of a special project team and express their appreciation for the members' involvement.

2. When a group presents an idea or suggestion, managers should thank members for their initiative.

3. Encourage a lunch meeting with project teams once they've made interim findings. Have managers express their appreciation. Encourage continued energy. Provide the lunch.

4. Promote writing letters to every team member at the conclusion of a project thanking them for their contribution.

5. Encourage creative symbols of a team's work, such as T-shirts or coffee cups with a motto or logo.

6. Have managers ask the boss to attend a meeting with the employees during which individuals and groups are thanked for their specific contributions.

7. Suggest catered lunches or breakfasts for high-performing groups.

---

teams (12 percent). Two types of incentive pay systems that are not designed specifically for teams but are popular in participative management companies and are consistent with many team-based approaches are profit sharing and gainsharing. They can be tailored for teams.

Profit Sharing

Many companies use profit sharing schemes, wherein a portion of the bottom-line economic profits is given to employees. These internally distributed profits may be apportioned according to equality or equity. In the typical profit sharing plan, profit sharing bonuses are put into retirement plans. This makes it more difficult to clearly relate rewards to controllable performance. Thus, most profit sharing plans have little impact on the motivation and behavior of employees (Lawler, 1992).

Profit sharing plans serve an important communication purpose by signaling to everyone that rewards are in balance across the organization. Second, they inform and educate employees about the financial health of the organization. Finally, profit sharing makes the labor costs of an organization variable, thus adjusting them to the organization's ability to pay (Weitzman, 1984).

Gainsharing

Gainsharing involves a measurement of productivity combined with the calculation of a bonus, designed to offer employees a mutual share of any increases in total organizational productivity. In gainsharing plans, an organization uses a formula to share financial gains with all employees in a single plant or location. The organization establishes a historical base period of performance and uses this to determine whether or not gains in performance have occurred. Typically, only controllable costs are measured for the purpose of computing gain. Unless a major change takes place in the company's products or technology, the historical base stays the same during the entire history of the plan. Thus, the organization's performance is always compared to the time period before it started the gainsharing plan. When the organization's performance is better than it was in the base period, the plan funds a bonus pool. When its performance falls short, no bonus pool is created; when performance is met or exceeded, the typical plan pays about half of the bonus pool to employees and the rest is kept by the company. Payments are usually made on a monthly basis, with all employees receiving the same percentage of their regular base pay. A trend of large corporations that have their own gainsharing plans has led more companies to adopt gainsharing.

Gainsharing plans appear to work. Gainsharing enhances coordination and information sharing among teams, instigates attitude change, raises performance standards, and enhances idea generation and flexibility (Lawler, 1990b). (For an in-depth discussion of gainsharing, see Lawler, 1992, chapter 11.) Gainsharing plans are more than just pay incentive plans; they are a way of managing and a technology for organizational development. For gainsharing to work successfully, it should be developed in collaboration with the people it will affect. It is important that employees understand and know how to influence the formula, that the standards seem credible, that bonuses be timely, and that some mechanism exists for change. A company needs a participative management system for the plan to work because it requires employees to take ownership of the success of the company (Blinder, 1990; Lawler, 1990b).

Profit-sharing plans are typically less effective than gainsharing plans in influencing employee motivation and changing culture than are gainsharing plans (Blinder, 1990; Lawler, 1990b). This lack of effectiveness is largely attributable to the disconnection between individual performance and corporate profits—even with high-level involvement. This depends on how salient profit-sharing benefits are made to the workers. Consider the firm that boldly posts its stock value for all employees to see in public areas—people see the value literally.

These four systems for rewarding employees—incentive pay, recognition, profit sharing, and gainsharing—should not be looked at as competing approaches, but rather as compatible systems that accomplish different, important objectives. For example, the combination of gainsharing and profit sharing deals directly with an organization's need to have variable labor costs and helps to educate the workforce about financial information. There is no surefire plan or formula that works for most teams. It depends on the organization. We offer these differing plans to increase the possibilities. Next, we turn to the issue of how to evaluate performance.

TEAM PERFORMANCE APPRAISAL

Individual performance appraisal is an evaluation of a person's behaviors and accomplishments in terms of the person's work in an organization. Performance appraisals are a source of feedback, a basis for personal development, and a determination of pay. The rise of teams presents special challenges for performance appraisal. It is difficult for a supervisor to conduct a traditional performance appraisal of an individual who is serving at least part time on a team. When the individual is part of a self-managed, self-directing, or self-governing team, it is virtually impossible, because supervisors are rarely close enough to the teams to evaluate them. The catch-22 is that if they were, they might hinder the performance of the team. We saw in chapter 2 that it is useful for teams and managers to focus on four measures of team productivity. Here, we deal with the question of exactly how performance should be measured and by whom.

What Is Measured?

A change in traditional performance appraisals, precipitated by the rise of teams, concerns what is measured in performance reviews. In many traditional control-oriented organizations, the major determinant of employees' pay is the type of work they do or their seniority. The major alternative is competency-based pay. Companies are increasingly recognizing that dynamic factors, such as competencies and skills, may be a better way to measure success than static measures, such as experience and education. In the following paragraphs, we review job-based pay, skill-based pay, and competency-based pay.

Job-Based Pay

Job-based pay is determined by a job evaluation system, which frequently takes a point factor approach to evaluating jobs (Lawler, 1990b). The point factor approach begins with a written job description that is scored in terms of duties. The point scores are then translated into salary levels. A key advantage of job-based pay systems is that organizations can determine what other companies are paying and can assess whether they are paying more or less than their competitors. Another advantage of job evaluation systems is that they allow for centralized control of an organization's pay system.

Skill-Based Pay

To design a skill-based pay system, a company must identify those tasks that need to be performed in the organization. Next, the organization identifies skills that are needed to perform the tasks and develops tests or measures to determine whether a person has learned these skills. For this reason, it is important to specify the skills that an individual can learn in a company. Employees need to be told what they can learn given their position in the organization and how learning skills will affect their pay. People are typically paid only for those skills that they currently can and are willing to perform. Many skill-based plans give people pay increases when they learn a new skill. One system of skill-based pay is a technical ladder, in which individuals are paid for the depth of skill they have in a particular technical specialty. Procter & Gamble started using skill-based pay in the late 1960s to support the development of work teams. In the P&G system, production employees are paid for horizontal skills and, in some cases, upwardly vertical skills. In a few cases, they are also paid for learning downwardly vertical skills, such as cleaning and routine production tasks. (For an example of how one skill-based pay plan failed to work, see Sidebar 3-5.)

Competency-Based Pay

Competency-based pay differs from skill-based pay in that employees prove they can *use* their skills. After all, it is possible for people to attain skills (e.g., training and mentoring programs) but never use them—or be ineffective when using them. For example, Volvo gives every employee in a work area a pay increase when the employees in that area prove they can operate without a supervisor (Lawler, 1992). It is important

> ### Sidebar 3-5. When Skill-Based Pay Doesn't Work
> John Powenski, the HR manager at Frito Lay in Kirkwood, New York, helped to orchestrate a performance and productivity improvement at the 800-employee facility, with initially strong results. A Leadership Team, composed of manufacturing, distribution, planning, technical, and HR managers, challenged the plant to become more customer-focused, team-based, and owner-driven. Teams trained together, met to discuss production plans, and give each other 360-degree feedback. However, "'All hell broke loose when we linked pay to performance,' Powenski says. It was a radical departure, and employees had not been included in development of the new compensation structure. 'They didn't like a peer affecting their pay and had concerns about the integrity of the whole system,' Powenski notes. 'We had not included the technicians in the pay restructuring, and that was a big mistake.' Recognizing that the change had not been accepted, the Leadership Team returned to the previous system" (Novak, 1997).

for organizations to focus on demonstrated competencies, rather than accumulated accreditations.

Competency-based pay is regarded as a much more sensible and ultimately profitable approach to use in a team-based organization. First, competency-based pay systems promote flexibility in employees: When employees can perform multiple tasks, organizations gain tremendous flexibility in using their workforce. This, of course, is the concept of cross-training. In addition to the benefits of cross-training, individuals who have several skills have an advantage in terms of developing an accurate perspective on organizational problems and challenges. When employees have an overview of the entire company, they are more committed. When they are broadly knowledgeable about the operations of an organization, they can increase their self-managing, coordinate with others, utilize organizational resources, and communicate more effectively.

However, competency-based pay systems are not perfect. An organization using a competency-based pay system typically commits to giving everyone the opportunity to learn multiple skills and then to demonstrate them; thus, the organization has to make a large investment in training and evaluation. There is a trade-off between getting the work done and skill acquisition and demonstration.

Who Does the Measuring?

The standard is the employee's supervisor, or some set of top-level persons. With the increasing use of teams, peer review is becoming more common and more necessary in organizations. Popularly known as **360-degree** or **multirater feedback** methods, the peer review procedure involves getting feedback about an employee from all sides: Top (supervisors), bottom (subordinates), coworkers, suppliers, and end-user customers or clients (see Figure 3-1). Typically, several people (ideally 5 to 10) participate in the evaluation, compared with a traditional review where only one person, usually a supervisor, provides feedback. Anonymity is the key to building a nonbiased feedback system, especially for peers and subordinates. Otherwise, the entire system is compromised. General Electric's CEO, Jack Welch, explains how his company does it: "Every employee is graded on a 1–5 scale by his manager, his peers, and all his subordinates in areas such as team-building, quality focus and vision. Some people think it's bureaucratic. But it

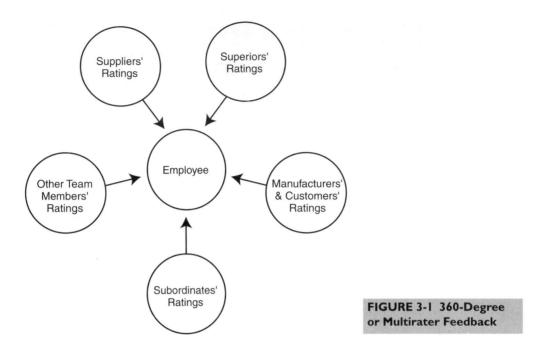

FIGURE 3-1 360-Degree or Multirater Feedback

embodies our values (which come out of years of discussions with employees). And the subordinates clearly provide the best input. Peers are a little more careful, and the boss is always a little more cautious" (Hillkirk, 1993, p. 5B).

A big disadvantage of the top-down performance review is evaluation bias. The multiple data points and aggregate responses provided by 360-degree feedback make the bias of a single person less of a problem.

A second major disadvantage of single-source evaluation is that it is easy to dismiss the information. "If my boss tells me something, I can easily ignore it," says Mark Edwards of Teams, Inc. With multiple sources, the information becomes more credible and is more difficult to discount. As Jarman (1998) puts it, "If in the course of a day you meet a disagreeable person, chances are you've met a disagreeable person. But if in the course of a day you meet five disagreeable people, chances are you're the disagreeable person" (p. D1).

As an example of how companies put 360-degree feedback in place, consider the Long Term Credit Bank of Japan, or LTCB, which bases its annual bonuses for managers in part on evaluations by their subordinates. LTCB, which previously adopted a skill-based pay system, is trying to increase the transparency of its performance evaluation methods by inviting the rank and file to grade bosses. In the system, managers select a group of up to 20 subordinates, colleagues, and supervisors to grade their job performance. Of the group, as many as nine employees, including two or three who work directly under the manager, evaluate their boss. Managerial employees receive a monthly base pay plus two bonuses; over 30 percent of their bonus is based on the evaluations (Dow Jones News Service, April 14, 1998).

At Phelps Dodge, 360-degree evaluations were first administered to the company's top 180 executives worldwide, including Chairperson Douglas Yearley. The company developed a set of core competencies, such as demonstrating sound business judgment, driving for results, fostering teamwork, and creating an ownership philosophy among employees, and evaluated executives on these dimensions. Because the core competencies used to evaluate employees are part of the company's or department's mission statement, the 360-degree process helps bring performance of individual employees in line with company goals and values. In fact, companies beginning to develop 360-degree evaluations are encouraged to start with their mission statement.

In theory, the 360-degree process provides a multifaceted view of the team member. However, putting it into practice can be difficult: If the number of feedback sources is limited, raters are not guaranteed anonymity and may fear retaliation. The system is subject to abuse if members make side deals to rate one another favorably. Many people going into it are against the idea, and it takes time to make several evaluations!

However, despite its difficulties, 360-degree or multirater feedback is usually regarded to be a more fair assessment of performance than is top-down review (for an argument of how information systems [IS] can benefit from 360-degree feedback, see Sidebar 3-6). Although team members are often best qualified to rate each other, there are some weaknesses to this approach. Team members unpopular for reasons other than performance can suffer. Team members do not always grasp the big picture in terms of organizational goals. As raters, peers can suffer from evaluation biases.

Sidebar 3-6. Why Information Systems (IS) Need 360s

Michael Schrage jokes that "whenever managers talk about 360-degree job reviews, I think of that joke about the nattering egomaniac at the cocktail party: 'But enough about me; let's talk about you. What do you think about me?' " (Schrage, 1998, p. 33).

Schrage quite seriously goes on to argue that the key reason why IS should passionately embrace 360s is that these reviews represent the best way to promote better communication of expectations. Basically, 360s force technical people and businesspeople to communicate about something other than the tasks, specs, and deadlines at hand. Properly managed, 360s hold the promise of creating new networks of interactions around the challenge of creating productive relationships.

Developing a 360-Degree Program

It is impossible to develop a 360-degree evaluation program overnight. Most teams are not ready to base all of their pay on multisource performance management, especially when teams are relatively new. Most teams are hesitant to have all of their pay tied to team member evaluations; at the same time, they scoff at individual pay performance systems. The key is to set up a system of feedback that is anonymous and private and slowly build into an open feedback, public knowledge system. Often, team members will let companies know when they are ready to have pay based on their individual performance as evaluated by relevant others.

There is no standard method for 360-degree implementation. Some companies administer and develop the whole system. Some allow outside consultants to prepare and analyze feedback to ensure anonymity. For example, Groupe Schneider, an international firm, invites its managers to participate in 360-degree evaluations by choosing nine

---

BOX 3-2

Things to Think About Before Developing a 360-Degree Program in Your Company

Companies should ask themselves the following questions before undertaking 360-degree evaluation programs (Hoffman, 1995; Milliman, Zawacki, Powell, & Kirksey, 1994):

- Should only the 360-degree feedback be used or should the process be combined with other appraisal systems?
- Should an outside consultant be used?
- Can a program be purchased off the shelf or should the process be customized for the organization?
- Is a computer-based or paper and pencil form best for the organization?

- How many raters should be used? (The ideal is 5 to 10; fewer than 5 limits perspectives; more than 10 makes the system too complex and time-consuming.)
- Who should do the rating?
- Who selects the raters?
- How does the organization define *peer, internal customer, supervisor, subordinate,* and so on?
- How many questions/items should be included on the form?
- Should the feedback be anonymous?
- How should employees be trained on giving and receiving constructive feedback and the nature of 360-degree feedback?

---

people to provide confidential evaluations. The entire evaluation is carried out by an outside consulting firm that collects and prepares all of the results, which are completely confidential. Often, the survey used to evaluate employees is developed by a cross-sectional team of company employees. In addition to specifying evaluation criteria, the group also determines the makeup of the evaluation teams and how they will be selected. This team also makes decisions on who will get to see the results of the evaluations and devises a follow-up program to ensure that employees take action on the feedback they receive.

As a start for developing 360-degree evaluation systems, consider the steps outlined in Box 3-2 (see Milliman et al., 1994; Hoffman, 1995).

The answers to the questions in Box 3-2 will be different for every organization. Duplicating systems used by world-class companies is not necessarily the best approach. Each organization should develop the 360-degree system that will optimize effectiveness within its organizational design. Companies should first use a test 360-degree program that is not tied to compensation and is not public. In the beginning stages, only the employee sees all of the feedback; gradually, the supervisor is brought into the loop. Eventually, it is important to tie employee compensation to the 360-degree evaluation. Yet there is considerable variation on this. For example, at Phelps Dodge, 360-degree feedback is used as a development and training tool and not the basis for performance evaluation and pay. In contrast, Farm Credit uses 360-degree reviews to evaluate the performances of its 68 employees and determine their compensation levels.

At Johnson & Johnson Advanced Behavioral Technology, which has many teams but still retains traditional hierarchical reporting relationships, ratees develop a list of

---

BOX 3-3

Prescriptions for Legally Defensible Appraisal Systems
(Adapted from Bernardin & Cascio, 1988)

1. Job analysis to identify important duties and tasks should precede development of a performance appraisal system.

2. The performance appraisal system should be standardized and formal.

3. Specific performance standards should be communicated to employees in advance of the appraisal period.

4. Objectives and uncontaminated data should be used whenever possible.

5. Ratings on traits such as dependability, drive, or attitude should be avoided.

6. Employees should be evaluated on specific work dimensions rather than on a single, global, or overall measure.

7. If work behaviors rather than outcomes are to be evaluated, evaluators should

have ample opportunity to observe ratee performance.

8. To increase the reliability of ratings, more than one independent evaluator should be used whenever possible.

9. Behavioral documentation should be prepared for ratings.

10. Employees should be given an opportunity to review their appraisals.

11. A formal system of appeal should be available for appraisal disagreements.

12. Raters should be trained to prevent discrimination and to evaluate performance consistently.

13. Appraisals should be frequent, offered at least annually.

---

key internal and external customers with whom they interact and then recommend 5 to 10 people to serve as raters. The supervisor has the ultimate responsibility for the appraisal. In contrast, at Digital Equipment, the ratee has the primary responsibility for selecting the raters. The Digital ratee works with the team leader to select a panel consisting of a coach and three other employees to be objective advocates. Raters are then selected at random from the ratee's team by a computer-generated system and notified by e-mail to participate in the appraisal. The random system ensures that a fair distribution of raters is created.

As companies begin to challenge old assumptions about performance appraisals, they need to be careful not to cross the line of legal liability (see Box 3-3). If people other than management are involved in the appraisal process, then they must be trained on the legal issues involved with discrimination law, the Americans with Disabilities Act, and other relevant legislation. Stated more eloquently:

> The use of multiple raters is becoming more popular as many firms move toward team-based management systems. Use of multiple raters reduces the influence of idiosyncratic rating policies on personnel decisions. However, sharing ratings to arrive at a consensus is not an acceptable way of offsetting the bias of a single rater (*Loiseau v. Department of Human Resources*, 1983). An important caution in the use of multiple raters as illustrated in the Hopkins

case, is that illegal bias on the part of one or two raters can taint the entire process with legal discrimination. (Austin, Villanova, & Hindman, 1996, p. 283; reference to *Price Waterhouse v. Hopkins,* 1989, which involved gender bias in a consensus promotion decision made by PW partners)

For a detailed look at actual items used in 360-degree evaluations, consult appendix 4.

SOURCES OF RATER BIAS

Peers are often best qualified to evaluate a team member's performance. Lots of empirical research indicates that peer assessment is a valid and reliable evaluation procedure (Huber, Neale, & Northcraft, 1987). In addition, the team's supervisor and the team's customers or clients (either internal or external, if available) are also valuable sources of input. These information sources are valuable, but can also be biased. Raters are not perfect; below we discuss several serious sources of bias that can threaten the quality of peer evaluation.

Extrinsic Incentives Bias

Most managers believe that employees are primarily motivated by extrinsic incentives (e.g., job security and pay) and less motivated by intrinsic incentives (e.g., learning new things). For example, Douglas McGregor (1960) explicitly acknowledged this tendency when he described a social fault line between managers who inferred motivations incorrectly and those who inferred them correctly. He bemoaned the commonness of Theory X managers (who believe that employees dislike work, wish to avoid responsibility, and desire security above all) and the scarcity of Theory Y managers (who believe that employees like work, wish to develop their skills, and desire to participate in tasks that advance worthy organizational goals). Consider a survey of 486 prospective lawyers, who were questioned by Kaplan Educational Centers during a preparation course for the Law School Admissions Test (Lawler, Mohrman, & Ledford, 1995). The prospective lawyers were asked to describe their own motivations for pursuing a legal career and then those of their peers. Although 64 percent said that they were pursuing a legal career because it was intellectually appealing or because they had always been interested in the law, only 12 percent thought this about their peers. Instead, 62 percent thought that their peers were pursuing a legal career because of the financial rewards. Indeed, most of us have claimed that "they're only in it for the money" many more times than we have claimed "I'm only in it for the money" (Heath, 1998).

According to Frederick Taylor, "What workers want most from their employers beyond anything else is high wages" (Taylor, 1911). In contrast, McGregor (1960) and other members of the human relations school of management argued that intrinsic features motivated employees.

The extrinsic incentives bias states that people believe that others are more motivated than themselves by motivations that are situational or extrinsic, and less motivated than themselves by motivations that are dispositional or intrinsic (Heath, 1998). For example, in one survey, 74 M.B.A. students ranked the importance of eight different motivations (benefits, pay, job security, learning new skills, praise from manager, developing skills, accomplishing something worthwhile, and feeling good about oneself) for themselves and predicted the rank order that would be provided by their classmates and by actual managers and employees (customer service representatives at Citibank; Heath, 1998). The M.B.A. students overestimated how highly the Citibank managers would rank extrinsic incentives: They predicted that the top four incentives would be primarily extrinsic (pay, security, benefits, and praise); however, the actual Citibank employees listed only one extrinsic incentive in their top four (benefits).

If managers falsely assume that others' motives are less noble than their own, then they may fail to communicate the importance and relevance of the organization's goals (Bennis & Nanus, 1985). Corporate managers may spend too little time highlighting the satisfaction of solving customer problems; nonprofit managers may spend more time describing the joys of charity balls than the pleasures of community service. When managers fall prey to the extrinsic incentives bias, they may overlook the importance of feedback, neglect opportunities to make jobs more interesting, and underestimate the employee's desire to participate in team and organizational decisions. Managers could substantially improve their ability to understand the motivations of others if they would assume that others are motivated exactly as they are (Heath, 1998).

People work hard for a lot of different reasons. It is a mistake to think that the only thing that drives performance is monetary incentives and that people hoard effort until incentives justify greater contributions. Many managers incorrectly believe that people are primarily motivated by monetary reward. However, they view themselves as having loftier reasons. For example, most people overestimate the impact that financial reward exerts on their peers' willingness to donate blood (Miller & Ratner, 1998).

In sum, evolutionary biology, neoclassical economics, behaviorism, and psychoanalytic theory all assume that people actively and single-mindedly pursue their self-interest (Schwartz, 1986). However, organizational science research tells a different story: People often care more about the fairness of procedures they are subjected to than the material outcomes these procedures yield (Tyler, 1990); they often care more about a group's collective outcomes than about their personal outcomes (Dawes, Orbell, & van de Kragt, 1988); and their attitudes toward public policies are often shaped more by values and ideologies than the impact they have on material well-being (Sears & Funk, 1990, 1991).

Homogeneity Bias

Generally, appraisers rate appraisees who are similar to themselves more favorably than those who are different from them. This means that in general, white male superiors tend to favor white male subordinates over females and minority supervisees (cf. Kraiger & Ford, 1985).

Halo Bias

Once we know one positive (or negative) fact about someone, we tend to perceive all other information we learn about them in line with our initial perceptions. This has several serious implications, the most obvious of which is the fact that physically attractive people are evaluated more positively than are less attractive people—even when holding constant their skills and competencies.

Fundamental Attribution Error

We tend to perceive people's behaviors as reflecting their personality rather than temporary, situational factors. This can obviously be a good thing for someone who seems to be doing well, but very problematic for a person who seems to be performing under par.

Communication Medium

Performance appraisers give poor performers substantially higher ratings when they have to give face-to-face feedback as opposed to anonymous written feedback.

Experience Effect

Experienced appraisers tend to render higher quality appraisals. Thus, training and practice can reduce error in ratings (Klimoski & Inks, 1990).

Reciprocity Bias

People feel a strong social obligation to return favors. Thus, a potential flaw of 360-degree programs is that they are subject to collusion: "I'll give you a good rating if you give me one." Providing for anonymous rating may reduce both biases. However, this is difficult to achieve when team size is relatively small.

Bandwagon Bias

People want to "jump on the bandwagon," meaning that they will want to hold the same opinion of someone as does the rest of the group.

Primacy and Recency Bias

People tend to be overly affected by their first impression of someone (primacy) or their most recent interaction with this person (recency).

There is no simple solution to overcoming these biases. Awareness is an important first step. We suggest that everyone in the business of providing performance evaluations be made aware of these biases. Employees in companies probably do receive some form of training on conducting performance appraisals, but hardly anyone receives training on the biases that afflict ratings. As a second step, we suggest that only objective behavior and productivity measures be used—they are less susceptible to biases than are judgment traits and attitudes. As a rule of thumb—if you can't observe it directly, then don't measure it.

SOURCES OF RATEE BIAS

In addition to the rater biases discussed earlier, the quality of a 360-degree process can be compromised by the ratees themselves. Although countless articles and books have dealt with sources of rater bias, virtually no attention has been paid to bias on the part of ratees—as if feedback, once delivered, is perfectly received by the recipient. In fact, that is not the case. The more managers know about ratee bias, the better able they will be to anticipate the impact of a performance review on the employee.

Egocentric Bias

Most people feel underrecognized for the work they do and the value they bring to their company. This feeling is largely attributable to the human cognitive system, which is primarily egocentric in nature. In short, people give themselves greater credit than do others. This means that in a typical 360-degree evaluation, no matter how positive it may be, people will feel that they are underappreciated by others. There is no perfect solution to dealing with this. Our suggestion is that the supervisor (or person providing the feedback) should present as many facts as possible to justify the ratings and feedback.

It is important to focus on behaviors rather than attitudes when assessing others, because it is more difficult to misinterpret objective information (e.g., "you've been late 18 out of the last 20 days").

Intrinsic Interest

As we noted earlier, people are strongly motivated by intrinsic interest, rather than extrinsic rewards. However, this is not to say that people don't care about extrinsic rewards. Furthermore, this does not mean that intrinsic interest will always flourish. In fact, even positive feedback, if not carefully administered, may undermine intrinsic interest (Freedman, Cunningham, & Krismer, 1992). That is, employees may do something for purely intrinsic reasons, such as the joy of learning new things or expressing themselves; however, if a supervisor or a person of obvious importance praises the work and administers large extrinsic rewards for the work, this may lead the employees to believe that they are doing the work for the money (or other extrinsic rewards). In some cases, external reward may undermine intrinsic interest. For example, Kohn (1993) argues that incentive or pay-for-performance systems tend to make people less enthusiastic about their work.

We are not suggesting that companies should never offer extrinsic (e.g., pay-based) rewards to their employees. Rather, the manager should emphasize, when providing the reward, what is valued about the work and how the company views the employee. The research evidence supports this: When high effort is rewarded, people are more industrious. Just as people can be reinforced for working hard, they can be reinforced for creativity (Eisenberger & Selbst, 1994). Thus, for fabulous work effort, a supervisor or company may give the team a special cash reward or noncash recognition and clearly communicate to the team that the company values their inspiring motivation, creativity, and attention to detail. It is important to clearly indicate what is being rewarded.

Social Comparison

People have a basic drive to compare themselves with others. This is why, students feel less value in receiving an A if they find out that everyone has received an A. Thus, supervisors must anticipate that team members will talk and compare notes, one way or another, about the feedback they receive. It is often these comparisons that drive how employees interpret feedback.

Supervisors should anticipate that social comparison will occur, and be frank about feedback to employees and team members. For example, it would be wrong to imply that an employee was the only stellar performer if, in fact, over 60 percent performed at the same level. (For this reason, it may be useful to provide information about averages and standard deviations to employees.)

Fairness

People evaluate the quality of their organizational experiences by how fair they regard them to be. Whether the ultimate outcome is positive or negative, people are more likely to accept the outcome if they think the procedure has been fair. The fairness of procedures is determined by the extent to which the employee has a voice in the system, among other things (Lind & Tyler, 1988). Supervisors should actively involve the employee in the performance review, because people who are invited to participate regard procedures and systems to be fairer than those who are not invited. For example, superiors may ask employees to anticipate the feedback they will receive and to suggest how to best act upon it.

Although there is no surefire way to eliminate the biases on the part of the ratee, awareness of the bias is key. A second step is to recognize that many ratee biases are driven by a need to maintain or enhance self-esteem. Thus, it is important to put evaluations in a positive light and to help employees view them as opportunities to grow, rather than marks of failure. A third step is to involve employees actively in the evaluation procedure before they receive their results. For this reason, an early planning meeting, months ahead of the evaluation, can be an ideal opportunity for teams and leaders to work together to identify and clarify goals. Finally, it is important to recognize that performance appraisals, in any form, tend to be stressful for all involved. However, they provide an opportunity for everyone to gain feedback about what otherwise might be an "undiscussable problem." Tools such as 360-degree evaluations have the power to break down the barriers of fear in the organization. However, this can only be effective if managers are trained and skilled at using the information to break down barriers instead of building new ones.

GUIDING PRINCIPLES

An organization that wants to institute some kind of variable team-based pay structure needs to follow a step-by-step approach. However, even before that, the organization needs to adhere to some basic guiding principles (Gross, 1995).

Principle 1: Goals Should Cover Areas That Team Members Can Directly Affect

"Otherwise, the team is disempowered. Compensation won't motivate employees unless there is a direct line of sight between performance and results. For example, when incentives are tied only to the final profit of a company or group, which can be affected by all sorts of market forces, the connection between performance and reward is weakened. At the same time, pay should bear some kind of relationship to the company's bottom line. If the company is in the red, team rewards appear nonsensical—unless management is confident that ultimately the team's superior productivity and quality will help turn the company around" (Gross, 1995, p. 20).

In effective programs, rewards are contingent upon performance. This is in perfect contrast to a Las Vegas slot machine, in which payouts are contingent upon luck. Furthermore, a system that always pays out is ineffective. The key is to devise a system that equitably spreads the risk between the team and the company, offers a potential gain that makes the risk worth taking, and gives employees a fair shot at making more by working harder, more intelligently, and in a more coordinated fashion.

Principle 2: Balance the Mix of Individual and Team-Based Pay

For many teams, a thoughtful balance of individual and group incentives may be most appropriate. A good rule of thumb is to balance this proportion in line with the amount of individual and team-based work an employee is expected to do or the percentage of control and responsibility the individual and the team have.

Principle 3: Consult with the Team Members Who Will Be Affected

The process by which an organization introduces a program is more important than the program itself. The programs with the greatest likelihood of success are those that have input from all levels of the organization, including members of the team, teams that support or interface with the team, those who will administer the plan, management, and customers. The feasibility of the team pay program is determined through a full understanding of the business, the wants and needs of the management and employees, the impact of the current compensation program, and the company's ambitions for the new plan.

If people remain ignorant or uninformed about a process, they are more likely to reject it out of hand when they see it—even if it is perfectly compatible with their interests. In short, people want to be involved. The team members who are affected will have greater buy-in to the program if they had a hand in shaping it, and they can be valuable sources of information. In addition, employees need to feel that nothing is set in stone—if something does not work, employees will feel better knowing it can be changed. (For an example of how this can be effectively done, see Box 3-4.)

Principle 4: Avoid Organizational Myopia

Many programs fail not because they are inherently flawed, but rather because they create problems with other teams, groups, and units within the organization. Managers often are myopic about their own team issues; good leaders are able to ask the question of how the particular team compensation system fits into the larger organization. This is the heart of what we referred to in the last chapter as "organizational gains."

Principle 5: Determine Eligibility (Who Qualifies for the Plan)

Every member of the team should be eligible for the plan, and the plan should indicate when someone becomes eligible or loses eligibility. (Another complication concerns full- and part-time membership.)

Principle 6: Determine Equity Method

There are two basic variations: Same *dollar* amount (wherein each team or each member is given the same amount of pay) and same *percentage* amount (wherein each team or each member is given the same percentage of pay).

Principle 7: Quantify the Criteria Used to Determine Payout

There are two main ways to measure team results: Financial and operational. *Financial* measures tend to be "bigger," encompassing profit and loss (measured either companywide or in terms of the teams' contribution) or revenues. *Operational* measures are typically productivity-based (e.g., cycle time). There are several drawbacks to financial measures that primarily stem from the inability of team members to control the corporate-level decisions that will affect their microfinances. Operational measures are more firmly within the team's grasp.

BOX 3-4

Honeywell's Participative Pay Team

Honeywell's Commerican Avionics Division charged a group of employees to align compensation with business goals (Caudron, 1996). The team's decision to link workers' pay to division profitability got better buy-in because it was employee driven. In their plan, a percentage of each employee's yearly pay is based on the achievement of annual company objectives. In many cases, employees are resistant to this kind of risk-sharing plan because if results fall short of expectations, then paychecks are cut. But, Honeywell's incentive program met with little resistance because it was the employees themselves, through a group of 25 volunteers called the Participative Pay Team, who decided how the plan would work.

The first step in this plan was for human resources (HR) to teach the members of the team, which included secretaries, machine shop workers, engineers, and department managers, the principles of compensation in a 2.5-day training workshop. Armed with this basic knowledge, the team members then were assigned to do additional research on their own. The HR department provided no guidelines as to how the plan should work; it was up to team members to make recommendations to the company's executive leadership.

The end result of the team effort was a self-funded gainsharing program in which a percentage of each employee's pay is at risk, pending the achievement of business goals linked to Honeywell's profitability. Second, employees also have the opportunity to earn more than their annual salary when the company has an exceptionally good year.

The biggest challenge was explaining the program to employees. Honeywell realized it had to educate its workforce on business fundamentals, so it developed a course called Business Basics to provide information on how to calculate the three measures used to determine company performance: profit, working capital, and economic value added. Conducted by the participative pay team members, the course participants get a big picture of their work in the company. The communication effort to support the plan was supported by HR, which produced two publications about the plan: a comic book depicting two employees having a dialogue about the new pay system, and a typical HR document distributed in an orientation course. The plan embodies key principles:

- Emphasizing the direct stake all employees have in the continued success of the business
- Emphasizing the importance of executives and employees working toward similar business goals
- Recognizing and rewarding employees' impact on major improvement opportunities
- Improving employee understanding of the division's financial performance
- Supporting the culture of teamwork, employee involvement, and participation

Now that the plan is in place, the focus of the participative pay teams has shifted: It works with the finance department to monitor the books. The crux of their role is to provide a "trust" message to the workforce—to validate what is being reported by management.

Principle 8: Determine How Target Levels of Performance Are Established and Updated

Goals can either be based on past performance or projected performance. There are advantages and disadvantages to each. The most immediate advantage of the historical approach is that people can readily accept it. However, many managers like to set stretch goals. One popular compromise is **raising the bar,** in which the baseline is increased and employees are given a one-time payment to compensate them for lost incentive opportunity. However, there is likely to be conflict over the amount of the payout. The **rolling average** method sets the baseline against which performance is measured as an average of some relevant period of time. (For a detailed discussion of payment options, see Gross, 1995.)

Principle 9: Develop a Budget for the Plan

All plans should pay for themselves, with the exception of safety plans. This means that the improvements must be quantifiable.

Principle 10: Determine Timing of Measurements and Payments

Shorter measurement periods and faster payouts motivate employees more and—particularly when pay is at risk—are fairer. However, there are a number of disadvantages with a short turnaround system that include administrative overhead and manipulation of results.

Principle 11: Communicate with Those Involved

As stated earlier in the chapter, it is important for companies to be completely straightforward about what counts and how things are going. For example, Richard Semler states:

> Nothing matters more than those vital statistics—short, frank, frequent reports on how the company is doing. Complete transparency. No hocus-pocus, no hanky-panky, no simplifications. On the contrary, all Semco employees attend classes to learn how to read and understand the numbers, and it is one of their unions that teaches the course. Every month, each employee gets a balance sheet, a profit and loss analysis, and a cash flow statement for his or her division. Everybody knows the price of the product. Everybody knows the cost. Everybody has the monthly balance sheet that says exactly what each of them makes, how much bronze is costing us, how much overtime we paid, all of it. And the employees know that 23% of the after-tax profit is theirs. (Garfield, 1992, p. 253)

Principle 12: Plan for the Future

As teaming becomes more developed and the organization experiences shifts in culture or focus, a new mix of rewards needs to be defined to keep the organization in alignment.

CONCLUSIONS

Many organizations promote and value teamwork, yet pay people based upon individual accomplishments. Individuals operating under this system feel the tension. Just as college basketball players who feed their teammates instead of shooting will not compile impressive scoring statistics and are less likely to be drafted by the pros, managers who devote energy to organizational goals will often not forward their own career. Viewed in this sense, it is rational for team members to think of themselves first and the team second. The organization that wants otherwise had better "walk the walk"—and the walk involves serious thought about performance evaluation and compensation. This chapter does not provide easy answers to team compensation problems because there are none. However, there are some fundamental questions to think about and there exist choices for managers and organizations.

CHAPTER 4

Building the Team: Tasks, People, and Relationships

The first rule of teamwork at SEI, the money management firm headquartered in Oaks, Pennsylvania, is that there are remarkably few rules. Teams have anywhere from 2 to 30 members and every team is structured differently. Most employees belong to one "base team" as well as three or four ad hoc teams. These ad hoc teams give SEI a sense of perpetual motion. Work is distributed among roughly 140 self-managing teams. Some are permanent, designed to serve big customers or important markets. But many are temporary: People come together to solve a problem and disband when their work is done. The result is a workplace that is always on the move. "We call it fluid leadership," says SEI's Chairman and CEO Al West. "People figure out what they're good at, and that shapes what their roles are. There's not just one leader. Different people lead during different parts of the process" (Kirsner, 1998, p. 130).

Seasoned managers recognize that their success in large part depends on how effectively they can build and maintain a well-functioning team. Managing an effective team involves two sets of responsibilities: (1) Managing the internal dynamics of the team itself—that is, specifying the task, selecting the members, and facilitating the team process; and (2) managing the external dynamics of the team—scanning the organizational environment and managing relationships with those on whom the team is interdependent (Ancona, 1990). We refer to these dual processes as "internal team management" and "external team management." Beginning with this chapter in part II, we focus on internal team dynamics. The starting point for this chapter presumes that the manager has determined that teams are necessary to do the work required. For expositional purposes, we take the point of view of the manager when we discuss building the team. However, we do not presume a manager-led team; all of our messages can be extended to the team as its own manager (i.e., as in the case of self-managing and self-designing teams). This chapter takes you through the steps involved in building a team and keeping it running smoothly. The goal of this chapter is to create a toolkit for the busy manager to use in developing and maintaining teams. In part III, we focus on external team dynamics.

BUILDING THE TEAM

Any team, whether it is suffering from declining sales, brainstorming about a new product, attempting to solve a difficult problem, or hiring a new recruit, can be better understood by examining its internal dynamics. It is particularly disturbing, then, that in a 1995 survey distributed to 134 separate project teams in 88 companies in the United States, respondents indicated that "despite positive indications on some of the key team building elements, overall results show companies are generally doing a poor job of team building. Lack of effective rewards, inadequate individual and team performance feedback mechanisms, lack of project management skills, and inadequate individual and team goal-setting are all weak areas" (Tippett & Peters, 1995, p. 29). (For an example of poor team design that was eventually turned around, see Sidebar 4-1.)

Sidebar 4-1. Turning Poor Team Design Around

When Rexam Custom in Matthews, North Carolina, a division of Rexam PLC, first employed teams, the outcome was a failure. Why? The team was too large, which made meetings impossible for anything other than information sharing and updating; there was a lack of goals or objectives, which led to members attending meetings with the sense that anything was fair game. Thus, they addressed everything from capital improvements to pay and benefits. The resulting frustrations often led to extended gripe sessions. Teams were poorly structured and, as a result, members often had different and competing interests. Members did not share information, and meetings became a competition between conflicting priorities. Consequently, meetings rarely resulted in any action steps or outcomes. After identifying and correcting these key problems, Rexam was able to successfully implement their team-based approach (Pope, 1996).

Contrary to popular thought, it is more important to have a well-designed team than a team with a good leader. For example, in an intensive study of customer service teams at Xerox with team sizes ranging from 3 to 12 persons, well-designed teams were more successful on a number of key organizational effectiveness criteria—assuming collective responsibility, monitoring their own performance, managing their own task strategies, and customer approval—than were poorly designed teams (Wageman, 1997). Poorly designed teams, even under good leadership, were significantly less effective. In the case of Xerox, team effectiveness was judged by supervisors as well as customers, thus providing a comprehensive view of team effectiveness.

Once it is determined that a team is desirable for the work and viable within the organization, then the manager must focus intently on three key aspects of building a team: The *task*, the *people*, and the *relationships* among team members. These three critical internal dynamics are illustrated in Figure 4-1: Phase 1 concerns the **task** facing the team. Does it call for creativity or problem solving? Is it cooperative or do members compete with one another? Phase 2 concerns the **people** on the team. How should team members be selected? What level of diversity is best? Phase 3 involves the **relationships** among the group members in terms of how they do their work together. Is there a norm of challenging one another? Do members feel cohesive? Do team members trust one another?

These three factors—tasks, people, and relationships—form the basic, internal system of teamwork. Just like Rome, the building and maintenance of a team is not something that is accomplished in a day. We begin by discussing the task, then we move to the people, and we conclude by discussing the relationships.

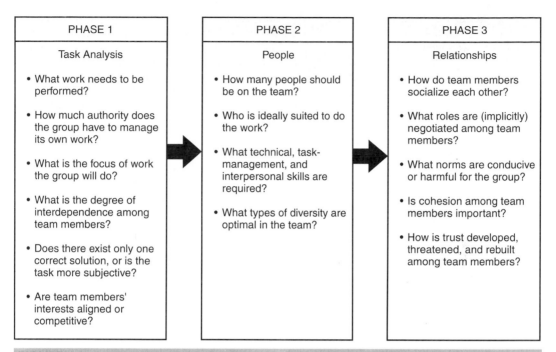

FIGURE 4-1   Internal Dynamics: Key Questions to Ask When Building the Team

THE TASK: WHAT WORK NEEDS TO BE DONE?

What practices and structures need to be put into place to achieve highly functioning teams? To a great extent, this is determined by the nature of the work that groups are doing. For example, some teams make products, some teams provide services, other teams make decisions, and still others provide advice and consultation. The nature of the work sets constraints on design. However, there is much variation in team design, even among companies doing very similar types of work—and sometimes even large variation among teams within the same company!

Obviously, there is no single recipe for optimal team design—it depends upon the type of work the team is doing, the structure of the organization, and so on. However, managers often do not think carefully about team design, leaving it up to the team to work out on their own or falling back on traditional, functional practices. If left to their own devices, teams rarely explicitly plan or develop performance strategies (Hackman, Brousseau, & Weiss, 1976; Weingart, 1992). Those that do, however, usually perform better, especially when the appropriate performance strategy is not obvious (Hackman et al., 1976). It is useful to distinguish **preplanning** (before actually performing the task) and **on-line planning** (during the task itself; Weingart, 1992). Teams permitted to plan between periods of task completion perform better than those that plan only during periods of task completion or do not have opportunities to discuss and develop plans (Shure, Rogers, Larsen, & Tasson, 1962).

TABLE 4-1 Types of Work That Teams Do

Broad Objective	Dominant Feature	Process Emphasis	Threats
Tactical	Clarity	• Directive, highly focused tasks • Role clarity • Well-defined operational standards • Accuracy	• Role ambiguity • Lack of training • Communication barriers
Problem solving	Trust	• Focus on issues • Separate people from problem • Consider facts, not opinions • Conduct thorough investigation • Suspend judgment	• Failure to stick to facts • Fixate on solutions • Succumb to political pressures • Confirmatory information search
Creative	Autonomy	• Explore possibilities and alternatives	• Production blocking • "Lumpy" participation

Source: Adapted from Larson, C. E., & LaFasto, F. M. 1989. *Teamwork: What Must Go Right/What Can Go Wrong.* Newbury Park, CA: Sage.

In keeping with our goal of providing choices for managers, we raise some critical team design issues in the following sections. We suggest that managers and team designers work through each of these issues when thinking about team design and redesign.

How Much Authority Does the Team Have to Manage Its Own Work?

In short, what is the ratio of team governance to managerial governance? This issue was raised in chapter 1, where we presented four types of teams: Manager-led, self-managing, self-directing, and self-governing. There is an inherent trade-off here: The more authority team members have to manage their own work, the more likely they are to be motivated and highly involved in the work. However, this comes at a loss of control for the manager. Furthermore, when teams set and carry out their own objectives, they may not be aligned with those of the larger organization.

What Is the Focus of the Work the Team Will Do?

Obviously, the possibilities are endless. However, it is helpful to characterize team tasks into one of three basic kinds: Tactical, problem-solving, and creative, following Larson and LaFasto (1989). Table 4-1 describes tactical, problem-solving, and creative teams and the disadvantages and advantages of each.

Tactical teams are those in which the key objective is to execute a well-defined plan. For tactical teams to be successful, there must be a high degree of task clarity and unambiguous role definition. Some examples of tactical teams include cardiac surgery teams, military teams, many sports teams, and other teams that are tightly organized (see Larson & LaFasto, 1989).

Problem-solving teams are those that attempt to resolve problems, usually on an ongoing basis. To be effective, each member of the team must expect and believe that interactions among members will be truthful and of high integrity. Thus, a key feature of problem-solving teams involves trust and respect. Some examples of problem-solving

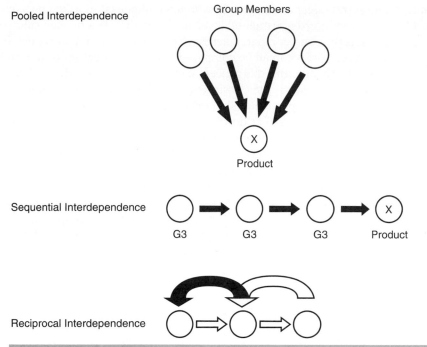

FIGURE 4-2   Levels of Interdependence

teams include the American Leadership Forum, the Centers for Disease Control, and other teams that are focused on solving a problem (see Larson & LaFasto, 1989).

Creative teams are those in which the key objective is to create something, think out-of-the-box, and question assumptions. The process focus of creative teams is that of exploring possibilities and alternatives. We will discuss creative teams in much more depth in the last chapter of part II. Some examples of creative teams include the IBM PC team, the Chicken McNugget project team, many research and development (R&D) teams, and other teams that are focused on coming up with new ideas, products, and services (see Larson & LaFasto, 1989).

Sometimes, teams are mischaracterized—for example, a team that is supposed to be creative uses a problem-solving perspective, or a team that really requires problem solving is organized as a tactical team. This may happen when the goals of the team are not clear. This can also happen when teams are not apprised of the organization's objectives. Managers must take a hard look at the type of team they need and guide members' understanding of the relationship between the goal and the design of the team.

What Is the Degree of Task Interdependence among Team Members?

By definition, team members are interdependent. However, there are many types of task interdependence that affect the way teams get their work done (Thompson, 1967, see Figure 4-2). Consider three types of task interdependence:

- **Pooled interdependence** means that group members work independently and then pool their work. For example, a furniture department within a department store is comprised of several salespeople, each of whom is compensated based on sales performance. On an interdepartmental level, however, the sales of each salesperson are added together and compared across departments, so that cosmetics, furniture, and men's accessories can all be compared and added together to determine overall store profit. Throughout this process, each salesperson is independent.

- **Sequential interdependence** is the classic assembly line or division of labor; each member of the team has a particular skill or task to perform. Members are more interdependent, with those further down the line more dependent on others. For example, as a new car proceeds through the factory at the Ford Taurus manufacturing plant in South Chicago, pieces are added to it at certain stages of the process which could not have been added prior to that stage.

- **Reciprocal interdependence** is the highest form of interdependence. Every member is dependent upon others at all levels—not just in a simple linear fashion, as in sequential interdependence. For example, when software developers are writing code, each person must have a high degree of familiarity with the other pieces of the program, otherwise the likelihood of bugs increases significantly. Charles Parnell of the Miller Brewing Company epitomizes the complexities of reciprocal interdependence. During a speech delivered at Marquette University, Parnell gave an example of teamwork at Miller: "If Marketing wants to launch a group of new products, they will set up a task force and call in someone from Finance, Human Resources and Operations. The Operations people will explain to the Marketing Group the realities of brewing, packaging and shipping more than 40 brands of beer in more than twenty eight hundred different can, bottle, keg, package and label configurations. This means that if Marketing had been thinking about introducing 10 new brands next year, they will understand that's a virtual impossibility for the Operations people and they will know why" (Parnell, 1998).

Recent studies of team performance reveal that high levels of task interdependence, which require interactions among group members to obtain crucial resources (such as in the Miller Brewing Company) consistently enhance performance (Fan & Gruenfeld, 1998). Highly dependent members come up with solutions faster, complete more tasks, and perform better than teams whose members are not highly dependent upon one another.

The degree of interdependence has design implications for teamwork. To the extent that tasks are easily divisible and threats to performance (chapter 2) have been adequately ironed out, pooled interdependence may be very effective for groups. For example, in a customer service call center, members do roughly the same type of work. However, pooled interdependence often cannot work for teams because completing the tasks requires specialization and division of labor. Thus, sequential or reciprocal interdependence is necessary. For example, in a Saturn assembly line, members' tasks are highly differentiated and specialized. To a large degree, greater specialization means greater interdependence, because team members must rely on others to complete their portion of the work. The start-up times for reciprocal interdependence may seem daunting, but it may be especially important for highly complex tasks that require high levels of customer satisfaction. Another advantage of reciprocal interdependence is that all team members know the overall objectives of the team and may feel more accountable (thus reducing the motivational problems discussed in chapter 2).

Is There a Correct Solution That Can Be Readily Demonstrated and Communicated to Members?

Some tasks have one correct solution; other tasks are more subjective. Contrast, for example, a team assembling a house, in which each component (the framework, the windows, the insulation, and so on) has to conform to a specified blueprint, versus a consulting team outlining a strategy proposal for a company. In the case of the construction team, the blueprint is the criterion by which the team will be judged. This kind of team task is known as a **demonstrable** task (Steiner, 1972).

In contrast, no single best answer exists for the consulting team. This kind of team task is known as a **nondemonstrable** task. In nondemonstrable tasks, it is important for team members to discuss the indices they will use to assess their performance as a team. Otherwise, there could be considerable disagreement after the work is completed—not only among team members, but between the team and the client!

Are Team Members' Interests Perfectly Aligned (Cooperative), Opposing (Competitive), or Mixed in Nature?

In many team-based organizations, reward structures are constructed so that some portion of team members' pay is contingent on the performance of the team as a whole, to promote cooperation and reduce the incentive for competition among team members.

It is important to determine the extent to which members have an incentive to work with one another or compete with other group members for monetary gain (such as might exist within some sales teams), promotion, and so on. For example, IBM's manufacturing and marketing/sales departments have very closely aligned interests. In contrast, Andersen Consulting and Arthur Andersen have highly opposing interests. Teams that are rewarded for a mix of both individual and team performance outperform teams whose rewards are purely individual or purely group-based (Fan & Gruenfeld, 1998).

How Big Should the Team Be?

One final issue about task design concerns how many people to put on the team. Obviously, this depends on the nature of the work to be done and the level and overlap of skills among team members. Generally, teams should be fewer than 10 in number. In fact, it is wise to compose teams using the smallest number of people who can do the task (Hackman, 1987). Unfortunately, there is a pervasive tendency for managers to err on the side of making teams too large. There are many reasons for this—it is easier to include others than to exclude them to the fact. Unfortunately, managers seriously underestimate how coordination problems can geometrically increase as team members are added. This is an example of how managers inadvertently focus on individuals, rather than the team.

Teams that are overgrown can have a number of negative effects on performance (Nieva, Myers, & Glickman, 1979). Further, larger teams are less cohesive (McGrath, 1984) and members of large teams can be less satisfied with team membership, participate less often in team activities, and are less likely to cooperate with one another (Kerr, 1989; Markham, Dansereau, & Alutto, 1982). People are more likely to behave in negative and socially unacceptable ways in larger teams, perhaps because team members feel more anonymous or are less self-aware (Latané, 1981; Prentice-Dunn & Rogers, 1989).

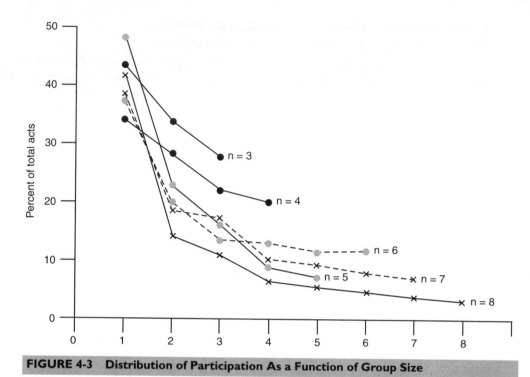

FIGURE 4-3 Distribution of Participation As a Function of Group Size

Source: Shaw, M. E. 1981. *Group Dynamics: The Psychology of Small Group Behavior* (3rd ed., p. 170). New York: McGraw-Hill. Reprinted with permission.

As team size increases, the frivolity of conversation increases and people tend to avoid serious subjects. One reason is that people tend to become aroused in the presence of others and, therefore, are more self-conscious and concerned about projecting the right image. It is safer for people to avoid serious topics.

A big problem of large teams has to do with the equality of member participation. For example, in a team of two to three, one person may do more of the talking, but all may participate. As the size of the team grows, more and more people do less talking relative to others. Sometimes, a few members say and do nothing. As can be seen in Figure 4-3, the equality of individual members' contributions decreases dramatically as group size increases.

In contrast, there are advantages to smaller, even understaffed teams. Members of understaffed teams work harder, engage in a wider variety of tasks, assume more responsibility for the team's performance, and feel more involved in the team (Arnold & Greenberg, 1980; Perkins, 1982; Petty & Wicker, 1974; Wicker, Kermeyer, Hanson, & Alexander, 1976; Wicker & Mehler, 1971).

If smaller teams are more advantageous, why are they relatively rare? The problem is that managers of teams appear to have an overstaffing bias: When team leaders are asked whether their teams could ever become too small or too large, 87 percent believe that understaffing is possible, but only 62 percent agree overstaffing is possible (Cini, Moreland, & Levine, 1993).

Once managers have some idea of the task design issues facing them, they are ready to turn to the people part of team building—how to best select members for their team. Obviously, the freedom to select team members is constrained in many ways: Managers may be limited to selecting members from a particular department, of a particular status, and so on. In other cases, managers may go outside the organization to recruit. At the opposite extreme, some managers do not have a choice about who is on their team; existing departmental structures determine team membership. Many teams are built by accretion and swapping members, not just created from scratch. Whatever their position is in terms of selection opportunity, managers need to know some basic facts about team composition.

THE PEOPLE: WHO IS IDEALLY SUITED TO DO THE WORK?

What manager has not wrestled with the question of who to put on the team? As illogical as it may sound, many managers form their team without too much thought and subsequently, attempt to figure out how to capitalize upon and match up people's skills. A much better approach is to carefully think about the task in terms of the work to be done, and then choose people on the basis of their skills relevant to that work. For example, think back to the three basic purposes of teamwork described earlier: Tactical, problem-solving, and creative. Obviously, creative types are not as well suited for tactical teams as are highly organized, results-driven people, and vice versa.

As a manager faced with the opportunity to build a team, how do you begin? The more you know about the task, the better able you are to suit people to the task. The following skills are important to think about when forming any team:

- **Technical or functional expertise:** If the task calls for open-heart surgery, a chemist or a lawyer will not suffice, no matter how great they are at what they do. Team members must have demonstrated competence to perform what they need to do for the team to accomplish its goals. In most team tasks, it is necessary to recruit members with diverse skills. In an age of increasing specialization, it is rare for one person to be knowledgeable in all aspects of a complex task.
- **Task-management skills:** It is not enough for team members to simply perform their functional area of expertise. They need to coordinate the efforts of the team, set goals, carry out plans, and so on. Task-management skills involve planning the work, monitoring performance, dealing with disappointments and unknowns, and dealing with coordination problems. The list of key task-management skills is potentially endless, but for starters, see Table 4-2. The left-hand side focuses on task-management skills; the right-hand side focuses on interpersonal skills.
- **Interpersonal skills:** People on teams are not just automatons who simply carry out their tasks according to some predetermined plan. Because members of teams are people first—with their own issues, problems, and agendas—and team members second, the people side of teams is always present and a powerful influence on productivity. Interpersonal skills include attributes such as the ability to give constructive criticism, objectivity, ability to give recognition, ability to learn from

TABLE 4-2 Task-Management and Interpersonal Skills

Task-Management Skills	*Interpersonal Skills*
• **Initiating:** Suggesting new goals or ideas	• **Encouraging:** Fostering team solidarity by reinforcing others
• **Information seeking:** Clarifying key issues	• **Harmonizing:** Mediating conflicts
• **Opinion seeking:** Clarifying attitudes, values, and feelings	• **Compromising:** Shifting one's own position on an issue to reduce conflict in the team
• **Elaborating:** Giving additional information—examples, rephrasing, implications—about points made by others	• **Gatekeeping:** Encouraging all team members to participate
• **Energizing:** Stimulating the team to continue working when progress wanes	• **Commenting:** Pointing out the positive and negative aspects of the team's dynamics and calling for change if necessary
• **Coordinating:** Pulling together ideas and suggestions	• **Following:** Accepting the ideas offered by others and serving as an audience for the team
• **Orienting:** Keeping team headed toward its stated goal	• **Standard setting:** Expressing, or calling for discussion of, standards for evaluating the quality of the team process
• **Detailing:** Caring for operational details	
• **Recording:** Performing a "team memory" function by documenting discussion and outcomes	
• **Challenging:** Questioning the quality of the team's methods, logic, and results	

Source: Adapted from Benne, K. D., & Sheats, P. 1948. "Functional Roles of Group Members." *Journal of Social Issues, 4,* 41–49.

others, and so on. Consult the right-hand side of Table 4-2 for examples of interpersonal skills in groups.

The type and blend of skills needed on a team depend largely on the task the team does. For example, problem-solving tasks often require more interpersonal skills; tactical teams require more organizational skills. Unfortunately, there is no simple paper and pencil test that neatly measures and classifies people. However, by drawing upon the following sources of information, the manager can go a long way toward making thoughtful and accurate assessments of skills:

- **Self-report:** What do employees regard to be their key strengths (and weaknesses)?
- **Past accomplishments:** What projects have employees been involved with that called for these skills?
- **360-degree reports:** What do employees' peers, supervisors, and subordinates regard to be their key strengths and weaknesses vis-à-vis these tasks?

The well-rounded team member, who possesses exquisite technical, task-management, and interpersonal skills, is a statistical rarity. More often, team members excel in one area. Thus, a key task of the manager is not to search for Jacks and Jills of all team skills, but rather to focus on the task of *diversifying* the team so as to meet and exceed performance objectives. This is a harder goal, because it requires the manager to think in terms of multiple dimensions and blends of team members, rather than evaluating team members solely on their individual merits.

At the heart of this issue is *diversity* in team membership. This being said, how do managers best optimize the diversity of their teams?

Diversity: SWOT Analysis

The purpose of a SWOT (Strengths, Weaknesses, Opportunities, and Threats) analysis of diversity is fourfold: To examine strengths inside, weaknesses inside, opportunities outside, and threats outside.

Strengths of Diversity

Diversity is currently a hot topic in organizations for a lot of reasons. First, it is the correct thing to do. It is illegal to discriminate on the basis of gender, race, sexual orientation, or disability status. However, diversity goes beyond gender and race issues. Diversity is also valuable in terms of functional skills. Diversity in and of itself is an extremely important tool for the team, the manager, and the organization as a whole.

- **Expanded talent pool:** First and foremost, the company that does not tolerate or promote diversity has access to a smaller amount of corporate talent; the less diversity, the less likelihood of recruiting and maintaining talented individuals. Thus, diversity is consistent with the firm's bottom line.
- **Multiple viewpoints:** Diverse (or heterogeneous) teams are more likely to come up with creative solutions and solve problems more accurately than are homogeneous teams—a topic we take up in chapter 8 (creativity). Heterogeneous groups are more effective than are homogeneous groups at solving complex problems (for a review, see Shaw, 1981).
- **Competitive advantage:** The key reason why diversity is so advantageous is that by sampling from a larger pool of potential team members, teams increase their competitive advantage. That is, nondiverse teams have a smaller talent pool to recruit from, which can only hurt their performance.

Weaknesses

Diversity is not without its challenges, however. The following are some key challenges in creating and managing diversity within a team:

- **Diversify on what?** Just exactly what dimensions should be diversified? The number of possibilities, such as demographics (age, race, sex, nationality, ethnicity, socioeconomic status), task-related knowledge, values, beliefs and attitudes, personality and cognitive style, or status in the organization, is infinite.
- **How much diversity?** The question of how much diversity to strive for is not always clear. A team that is so diverse that it has little or no overlap in terms of interpersonal style or disciplinary or strategic background and training will have a difficult time getting anything done. As a general principle, however, managers tend to err in the direction of not diversifying enough. We suggest that managers should specify those skills they see as necessary to perform the job and then sample from *all* persons who meet those requirements.
- **Managing cultural diversity:** If improperly managed, culturally diverse groups may not perform up to their potential. In a study of culturally diverse work

groups over a 15-week period (Watson, Keimar, & Michaelsen, 1993), homogeneous groups reported more process effectiveness than did heterogeneous groups during the early period (first few weeks). The diverse groups (composed of one white American, one black American, one Hispanic American, and one foreign national) reported more difficulty in agreeing on what was important and in working together, and they frequently had members who tried to be too controlling. The result was lower total task performance for the culturally diverse groups over the first 9 weeks. However, at 9 weeks, the diverse and homogeneous groups performed about the same. Diverse groups improved at generating ideas, but homogeneous groups remained superior in overall task performance. "It would seem unwise to expect newly formed groups with a substantial degree of cultural diversity to be able to solve problems very effectively" (p. 598).

- **Conflict:** Diverse teams will often (but not always) experience more conflict than will homogeneous groups, as individuals attempt to reconcile one another's views or simply decide upon a single course of action. (This might explain why some "lazy" managers opt for less diversity.) For example, in a study of top-management teams in bank holding companies, heterogeneity with respect to age and experience outside the industry was positively related to turnover rates (Jackson et al., 1991).

Opportunities

Fortunately, there are several opportunities—almost more than ever—to capitalize on diversity. Changing workforce demographics mean that work teams can be diversified in terms of gender, race, ethnicity, national origin, area of expertise, and organizational affiliation on an increasing level. As the 1980s drew to a close, the U.S. Department of Labor projected a rapid increase in the cultural diversity of the labor supply (Johnston & Packer, 1987). Only 58 percent of new entrants into the labor force were expected to come from the "majority" population of white native-born Americans. The remaining 42 percent were expected to be mostly immigrants (22 percent), followed by an approximately equal number of African Americans and Hispanic Americans. In some states, racial diversity is growing even more rapidly; in California, racial diversity is fast approaching the point at which no single group will represent a majority. Although the proportion of African Americans has remained relatively stable, their employment patterns have shifted considerably, resulting in higher degrees of racial integration in clerical, technical, and skilled craft jobs (Tuch & Martin, 1991).

Women are entering the labor force in growing numbers. By the year 2000, the workforce is expected to be almost completely gender-balanced. Furthermore, gender-based segregation in the workforce is declining. Although they are still seldom seen in corporate boardrooms, women currently represent more than 35 percent of the administrative and managerial workforce (Selbert, 1987).

In terms of age and diversity, the shrinking rate of growth in the labor pool is pushing employers to hire at both extremes of the age distributions, with the result that both student interns and former retirees are being hired to fill vacant positions (Hopkins, Nestleroth, & Bolick, 1991). Variability in age may create conflict, because team members with different training and experience are more likely to have different perspectives about their jobs (Pfeffer, 1983). Also, teams whose members vary more widely in age have greater turnover (Wagner, Pfeffer, & O'Reilly, 1984).

Threats Outside

The popular trend is toward diversity, but diversity has become a mantra rather than a practical prescription. Unfortunately, there are several psychological and social forces that work against diversity. We describe these in detail in part III on interteam relations, but we highlight the key threats here:

Homogeneity Bias   The homogeneity bias is the basic tendency for people to be attracted to those who are similar to themselves. The homogeneity bias, or *similarity-attraction effect,* characterizes everything from mate selection—with people choosing mates that are similar to them in background, race, attractiveness, and so on—to corporate recruitment. Not surprisingly, then, teams form among similar people (Feld, 1982; Fontana, 1985). People are attracted to teams whose members are similar to themselves (Royal & Golden, 1981) and teams prefer people who are similar to existing members. In fact, people who belong to the same groups even resemble one another (Magaro & Ashbrook, 1985; McPherson & Smith-Lovin, 1986). A variety of factors perpetuate the homogeneity bias. For example, teams often recruit new members through social networks of friends and relatives (Stark & Bainbridge, 1980). (Of course, this is not necessarily evidence of a preference for similarity. It could simply indicate that people are lazy in terms of how they search for new members.)

The question is: Why does the homogeneity bias exist? People find it easier to communicate and build a sense of rapport with others who are similar. As an exercise, think about the last time you met someone whose first language was not your own and with whom you had difficulty communicating. You probably found yourself not wanting to prolong the conversation, but instead, wanting to join in a conversation with people who spoke the same language as you.

Another reason for the homogeneity bias is that being around people who are similar to us validates who we are. However, the downside is that in teams, it is not ideal to have people who always agree and come up with similar ideas. This can lead to excessive like-mindedness—a problem we discuss in chapter 6 (decision making). People seem to have a preference for supporting others who are similar to them—in other words, they find it difficult to criticize people they like and identify with. Supporting ideas in a team can become part of the team identification process, in which a critique may violate an "us against them" norm.

Heterogeneity Aversion   Complementing the human tendency toward homogeneity is a bias that repels people away from those who seem different. Heterogeneity aversion is not the same thing as homogeneity bias. Homogeneity bias simply says that people are attracted to those who are similar. Heterogeneity aversion is more sinister: It says that people are repelled by what seems different. People are often repelled by groups whose members seem different from themselves (Bouma, 1980) and groups are often repelled by people who seem different from their own members (Brinkerhoff & Burke, 1980).

Consider a "token" group member. Many teams, especially those in traditional organizations, contain teams with a single token member. Because they are different, token and minority members (e.g., women in predominantly male groups) attract more attention from others (Lord & Saenz, 1985; Taylor, Fiske, Etcoff, & Ruderman, 1978) and are more aware of the characteristics that distinguish them from others (Cota & Dion, 1986; Frable, Blackstone, & Scherbaum, 1990; McGuire & Padawer-Singer, 1976). This visibility can distract token members from their task and interfere with their performance (Lord & Saenz, 1985). Token females may experience a variety of problems in work teams, ranging from social isolation to role entrapment to powerlessness (Izraeli, 1983; Kanter, 1977; Lord & Saenz, 1985; South, Bonjean, Markham, & Corder, 1982). Token males do not experience the same problems as token females (Craig & Sherif, 1986; Crocker & McGraw, 1984). Token females who have higher status in the team (Fairhurst & Snavely, 1983) or who adopt certain behavioral styles toward males (e.g., Ridgeway, 1982) are less likely to experience problems.

Self-Fulfilling Prophesy   The self-fulfilling prophesy is the tendency for our beliefs about someone to become true. As an example, consider what happens to men and women in mixed-sex teams. Membership in a mixed-sex group reminds people of their conventional sex roles, which may in turn lead them to adopt those roles in the team, either through personal choices or through the self-fulfilling prophesy process. That is, if someone expects a team to have certain beliefs and preferences (e.g., women are afraid of numbers and prefer homemaking), then they begin to act toward them in a way that may elicit that very behavior (e.g., "Don't bother to do the math, Loretta"; "Wouldn't you like to take some time off to be with your kids, Jeanne?"). Out of context, these statements sound harmless, perhaps even helpful, but if all employees are not treated the same way, this behavior is discriminatory.

It may be that behavioral confirmation is responsible for the differences observed in mixed-sex teams; that is, males are (1) more active and influential than females; (2) more likely to engage in **agentic activities** (e.g., decision making, problem solving), but less likely to engage in **communal activities;** and (3) more concerned than women about resolving issues of status, power, and wealth (for reviews, see Smith-Lovin & Robinson, 1992). Furthermore, the more uneven the proportion of males and females in a team, the more likely that these sex roles will become even more salient (Mullen, 1983).

Creating Diversity

Diversity may raise challenges for the managers, but these are not insurmountable problems. In contrast, the problems associated with a *lack* of diversity may be insurmountable. A properly managed workplace meets these challenges, and it is worth the effort that it will take to iron out these problems because a diverse workforce greatly benefits the firm and the team. However, it would be inaccurate to imply that once diverse teams are created, everything is fine. Managing diversity is an ongoing process. We outline here a four-pronged plan:

Publicly Commit to Valuing Diversity
An important first step is for firms to publicly commit themselves to valuing diversity. For example, the diversity (or lack thereof) in recruiting teams sent out to business schools is a public statement about diversity. Ideally, this statement should not be forced upon the firm (although it may have to be); rather, it should be something that the firm regards to be part of its own mission. (For examples of companies that use their Web sites to promote diversity, refer to Sidebar 4-2.)

Sidebar 4-2. Commitment to Diversity

Evidence of commitment to diversity is sometimes provided by visiting the corporate recruiting Web sites of many global companies.

- **Intel's** Workplace Web site contains information on "a multicultural workplace," "People of color at Intel," "women at Intel," and a "diversity of viewpoints" (http://www.intel.com/intel/ community/workplace/index.htm)
- **British Telecom's** Web site contains an area dedicated to valuing diversity (http://search.bt.com/search/edit?www.bt.com&80&/World/community/diversity/&bt.doc&/World/community/diversity/)
- **Exxon Corp.** has a supplemental area of its Web site which details its "Workplace Diversity—Strategies and Objectives" as well as its "Minority and Women-Oriented Community Activities" (for Exxon's 1997 on-line supplement, visit http://www.exxon.com/exxoncorp/main_frame_2.html)
- **S.C. Johnson Wax** promotes diversity by mentioning that they were nominated as one of the best companies for working mothers (http://www.scjohnsonwax.com/htdocs/we_are/ whoerwkm.html)

Solicit Ideas and Best Practices from Employees on How to Diversify

Managers should pay attention to what team members say, and implement at least some of these ideas. Part of this plan also includes asking team members to suggest ways to deal with conflict before it erupts. It is less useful to ask members how to deal with conflict after it erupts because once embroiled in conflict, people are less objective and more egocentric in their suggestions. Along these lines, asking members to identify the causes of conflict will inevitably lead to finger-pointing or blame-finding attributions.

Educate Members on the Advantages of Diversity

Rather than just stating the advantages of diversity, managers should explain in hard numbers the facts. Instead of preaching to the team (e.g., "you should diversify because it is the right thing to do"), managers should explain why diversity is in the members' best interests.

Diversify at All Levels

It is probably not enough for organizations to simply hire more diverse people and hope they intermix. Thus, in addition to diversity at the individual level, the organization must commit to and work toward diversity at the team level and the governing level.

Now that we have talked about diversity in detail and laid out an action plan for creating and maintaining diversity, we need to consider the other issues that face the manager when designing the internal dynamics of teams.

RELATIONSHIPS: HOW DO TEAM MEMBERS SOCIALIZE EACH OTHER?

Someone could get the idea from reading this chapter that teams are built from scratch and that, once built, the manager's work is largely done. This assertion, of course, is false.

Teams are not built from scratch; instead, a member or two is added to a team that is changing its direction; members leave teams for natural (and other) reasons. In short, members of teams are continuously entering and exiting; as a consequence, the team itself is constantly forming and reconfiguring itself. Group socialization is the process of how individuals enter into and then (at some point) leave teams. The process is disruptive, to be sure, yet it need not be traumatic or ill-advised.

When people begin to work together as a team, they immediately begin a process of socialization, such that members of the team mutually shape each other's behavior. More often, teams may undergo changes in membership, such that some members may leave and new ones may enter. The process of socialization is essential for the ability of team members to work together and coordinate their efforts. We begin by describing the basic processes involved in team socialization. Then, we discuss the process of role negotiation, norm development and maintenance, cohesion, and trust.

Group Socialization

Group socialization is the process by which a person becomes a member of a group. Most people think of socialization as a one-way process, wherein the team socializes the individual member—usually a newcomer—in the norms and roles of the team. However, this is an overly narrow and inaccurate view. As any parent can attest, the introduction of a newcomer to a family is a process of joint socialization.

Think about a time when you joined an existing team. Perhaps you joined a study group that had been previously formed, took a summer internship with a company that had ongoing teams already in place, or moved to a different unit within your organization. In all of these instances, you went through a process of group socialization (Moreland, 1985; Moreland & Levine, 1982, 1984, 1988). Three critical things go on during group socialization that can affect key productivity criteria of teams:

- **Evaluation:** Teams evaluate individual members, and individual members evaluate teams. In short, the individuals and the team "size each other up." Basically, people do a primitive sort of cost-benefit analysis when it comes to appraising teams. For example, if team members receive (or expect to receive) relatively high returns from team membership while enduring few costs, they probably like their team. Teams, too, evaluate a member positively who makes many contributions to the collective while exacting few costs (Kelley & Thibaut, 1978; Thibaut & Kelley, 1959). In addition to this direct cost-benefit analysis, some people are simply attracted to teams, whereas others are not. For example, people with either little prior experience or negative experiences in teams often avoid working in groups (Bohrnstedt & Fisher, 1986; Gold & Yanof, 1985; Hanks & Eckland, 1978; Ickes, 1983; Ickes & Turner, 1983).
- **Commitment:** Commitment is a person's "enduring adherence" to the team and the team's adherence to its members (Kelley, 1983). The key factor that affects commitment is the alternatives that are available to the individual and the team. For example, if a team has its choice of several, highly qualified candidates, its level of commitment to any one candidate is less than if a team does not have as many alternatives.
- **Role transition:** A person usually moves through a progression of membership in the team, going from nonmember to quasi member to full member. One key to

gaining full member status is to be evaluated positively by the team and to gain the team's commitment. This can often (but not always) be achieved by learning through direct experience with the team, and also through observations of others in the team. Indeed, newcomers in teams feel a strong need to obtain information about what is expected of them (Louis, 1980; Van Maanen, 1977; Wanous, 1980); simultaneously, teams communicate this knowledge through formal and informal indoctrination sessions (Gauron & Rawlings, 1975; Jacobs & Campbell, 1961; Zurcher, 1965, 1970). However, newcomers may not learn crucial information they need to perform their jobs, such as information about the preferences of supervisors or administrative procedures, until they are trusted by their coworkers (Feldman, 1977).

What are some key strategies that managers and team leaders can use to best increase the likelihood of a favorable match between an individual and a team? The following strategies are especially useful for integrating new members into teams:

Upper Management and Leaders: Make It Clear Why the New Member is Joining the Team

Many times, the introduction of a new team member is threatening for individuals, when it need not be. The manager should not assume that everyone is fully aware of why the newcomer is joining the team. Simple, clear, straightforward statements about how upper management sees the relationship between the individual and the team are needed early on, before an unnecessary cycle of paranoia is set in motion.

Existing Team Members: Explain What You Regard to Be the Strengths and Weaknesses of the Team

It can be very revealing for existing team members to talk about their strengths and weaknesses when a new member joins. First, the new member can "see" the team through the eyes of each team member.

New Members: Understand the Team's Goals and Processes

Existing members often expect newcomers to be anxious, passive, dependent, and conforming. Further, new members who take on those characteristics are more likely to be accepted by old-timers (Moreland & Levine, 1989). What newcomers may not realize, however, is that they inevitably pose some threat to the team. This is often because newcomers have a fresh and relatively objective view of the team, which causes them to ask questions or express opinions that are unsettling. New members can take initiative by demonstrating an interest in learning about the team. Remember that the team may be hypersensitive about past failures. Therefore, it is often a good idea to deflect defensive reactions by noting the team's positive qualities.

Role Negotiation

In all teams, task-management and people-management skills are required. Task-related roles focus on getting the work done and accomplishing the task at hand; interpersonal roles focus on how the work gets done and satisfying the emotional needs of team members. However, unlike traditional functional roles, such as finance, sales, and manufacturing, the roles of task management and people management are not necessarily played by one particular person. That is, these roles are more fluid and dynamic than are functional roles.

We do not discuss leadership until chapter 10, but here we want to distinguish two different kinds of leadership: *Task* versus *people*. In virtually all teams, a person or set of persons will take on the role of managing the team in terms of getting the work done. This person is often called the leader. Another role in most teams is that of managing the people aspects of the team—this role may be taken on by the task leader, but not necessarily. In manager-led teams, the manager or supervisor often takes on these roles in some form. However, even in manager-led groups, there can be implicit role renegotiation, whereby team members attempt to demonstrate skill in these areas.

Over time, through the process of role negotiation, various roles emerge (Bettenhausen & Murnighan, 1985). Most often these roles and the negotiations for them are not talked about in an explicit fashion; rather, people engage in actions designed to take on that role, which are either accepted or rejected by other members of the team. What should the manager expect in terms of role negotiation?

First, there is no one set of ideal roles for any particular team. In fact, roles are unique to each team. However, some roles are more common than others. **Action plan:** It might be a good idea to ask the team members, either at the outset or after a few meetings, what roles are helpful to have in the team. (Provide them the list in Table 4-2 as a starting point.)

Second, few people can simultaneously fulfill both the task and interpersonal needs of the team (Bales, 1955, 1958; Parsons, Bales, & Shils, 1953). When taskmasters move troops toward their goals, they often appear domineering, controlling, and unsympathetic. These actions may be conducive to goal attainment, but team members may react negatively. Because team members believe the task specialist is the source of the tension, someone other than the task leader must often assume a role aimed at reducing interpersonal hostilities and frustrations (Burke, 1967). The diplomat who intervenes to restore harmony and cohesion is the *socioemotional master*. An example of this interplay on a corporate scale is provided by the management styles of the former and current Chairman and CEO of AMR Corp. (parent of American Airlines), Robert Crandall and Donald Carty. Although they each assumed the same task-related role as Chairman and CEO, their management styles allowed them to play very different socioemotional roles. Crandall was known for his often abrasive and formal demeanor, whereas Carty is known as a soft-spoken, casual leader. Crandall's socioemotional role may have been to push for results from his employees; Carty takes a more coaxing role.

Third, role negotiation may take the form of **status competition** in the team. Status competition is the process by which people acquire the authority and legitimacy to be the taskmaster or the relationship coordinator of the team. Even in teams with established status roles, status competition can emerge as certain members attempt to compete with the leader. How does status competition work in a team and what can the manager do to capitalize on the process so as to improve overall team functioning?

Team members intuitively take note of one another's personal qualities they think are indicative of ability or prestige (years on the job, relevant connections, etc.). People take two types of cues or information into consideration: Real status characteristics and pseudostatus characteristics. **Real status** characteristics are qualities that are relevant to the task at hand (e.g., previous experience with the decision domain). **Pseudostatus** characteristics include factors such as sex, age, ethnicity, status in other groups, and cultural background. Typically, pseudostatus characteristics are those that are highly visible.

Pseudostatus characteristics, of course, have little to do with ability but people act as if they do.

Status systems develop very quickly, often within minutes after most teams are formed (Barchas & Fisek, 1984). Soon after meeting one another, team members form expectations about each person's probable contributions to the achievement of the team's goals (Berger, Rosenholtz, & Zelditch, 1980). These expectations are based on personal characteristics that people purposely reveal to one another (real status characteristics such as intelligence, background, and education) or that are readily apparent (pseudostatus characteristics such as sex, age, race, demeanor, size, musculature, and facial expression; Mazur, 1985). Personal characteristics that are more relevant to the achievement of team goals have more impact on expectations, but even irrelevant factors are evaluated. People who possess more valuable characteristics evoke more positive expectations and are thus assigned higher status in the team. **Action plan:** A manager who suspects that pseudostatus characteristics may supplant more relevant qualifications should provide clear information to team members about others' qualifications well in advance of the team meeting (e.g., circulating members' resumes). In addition to this, the leader should structure the first meeting of the team so as to ensure that relevant factors are made known to all members (e.g., a round-robin discussion in which members review their experiences).

Team Norms: Development and Enforcement

Just as role negotiation and status competition occur early on in the development of groups, so do norms, or the ideas and expectations that guide appropriate behavior for members. Norms differ from formal rules in that they are not written down. Norms are critical for team and organizational performance. Because norms are expectations about appropriate behavior, they embody information about what people should do under various conditions. This makes it easier for people to respond appropriately under new or stressful conditions and helps ensure that everyone is working towards the same goal. Thus, norms reduce threats to productivity and, in particular, they reduce coordination problems. Precious time is not lost while staff members brainstorm about what to do. For example, at Nordstrom, it is well known by employees as well as shoppers that customer service is the number one priority. In the case of any uncertainty about what needs to be done, the customer service dictum provides direction.

Many norms develop within the first few minutes of a team's first meeting—such as whether it is appropriate to come a few minutes late, seating arrangements, and so on (Bettenhausen & Murnighan, 1985; Gersick, 1988; Schein, 1988). As a general principle, however, this is not a very desirable state of affairs: When norms are left strictly to natural processes and interaction patterns among members, those individuals who are most disruptive and least self-conscious may set unfavorable norms. This is because people who are the most outspoken and the least self-conscious do the most talking. What is the best way to counteract these undesirable norms? One of the best mechanisms is to introduce some kind of structure to the team early on (see appendix 1 on meeting management); structure is the opposite of free-form interaction, where anything goes.

Adding structure to a team can mean that the team makes a commitment to do what the members value. For example, at Intel Corporation, there is a notion of constructive confrontation, which advocates that people challenge others in a productive fashion, rather than stand idly by and agree just to avoid conflict or hurt feelings. Still other norms may focus on improving group cohesion (e.g., team members regularly arriving with specialty coffee and breakfast items to share with others, technical engineers bringing their dogs to work at companies in Silicon Valley, office birthday parties, and casual Fridays).

Although some level of agreement is necessary for an expectation to be a norm, this does not mean that norms may not be in conflict. For example, in one hospital, nurses might think that the amount of work administrators expect the nurses to do is about right, whereas in another, nurses might think administrators expect the nurses to do too much paperwork (Argote, 1989). It may be that the norm within one department of a company will allow its employees to take time during the workday to handle personal matters, as long as the time is made up later, but this is not considered acceptable behavior in another department within the same company.

Like rules, norms may often be broken. What are the consequences of norm violation in a team? Contrary to naive intuition, the first response of a team to a norm violator is not exclusion, but rather to persuade that person to change. When regularity is interrupted, or violated, the "injured" parties frequently attempt to regain regularity by appealing to the norm (e.g., "Why didn't you circulate the report—we always do that!"). When a team member repeatedly violates a norm, there are serious repercussions, even if the behavior in question is useful for the organization. Consider, for example, the studies conducted at the Hawthorne Plant in the 1940s. Strong norms developed among work group members concerning the rate of acceptable productivity. That is, members in a particular work group developed a pace at which to work, that was just enough to produce the desired output requested by the supervisor, but not enough to overly tax group members. Consequently, when members of the work group failed to produce at the level displayed by their peers, they were sharply reprimanded. Furthermore, when members of the group overproduced (worked harder than other members of the group), they were harshly punished. In the Hawthorne Plant, a behavior called "binging" was observed, in which the "rate buster" (i.e., the overproducer) was given a sharp blow to the arm so as to reprimand the employee and decrease the level of output.

Certainly, not all cases of norm violation in organizational work groups are met with physical aggression. The first response of a team is usually to attempt to correct the misbehavior with some reminding. Teams will often persist in this kind of corrective activity for a long period of time before they move to more drastic measures of norm enforcement. Indeed, there are other forms of punishment and aggression that are perhaps even more detrimental to individual and organizational well-being, such as **ostracism,** in which people are excluded from certain social or professional activities (Williams, in press). Ostracism can have negative repercussions for the company as well if the isolated individual is not given sufficient information to effectively do the job.

Once established, norms are not easily changed. Norms are often maintained over several "generations" during which old members gradually leave the team and new members join (Jacobs & Campbell, 1961; Weick & Gilfillan, 1971). Teams' efforts to transmit their norms are particularly strong when newcomers are involved (Levine & Moreland, 1991; Moreland & Levine, 1989). Teams are highly motivated to provide newcomers with the knowledge, ability, and motivation they will need to play the role of a full member. Consequently, newcomers are usually receptive to these influence attempts because they feel a strong need to learn what is expected of them (Louis, 1980; Van Maanen, 1977).

Cohesion: Team Bonding

Most people who have been a part of a team will claim that there is a critical quality of teams that is difficult to capture, but yet is ever-present and very powerful, that goes beyond norms. When asked to describe what this quality is, managers will use words such as *camaraderie, fellow-feeling, energy, rapport, we-feeling,* and *good vibrations.* Intuitively, people on teams seem to know when these positive feelings are present and also when they are absent.

Cohesion—or solidarity, morale, community, and fellow-feeling—is the invisible binding material of teams. Cohesion makes people feel better, and it is a crucial ingredient for team viability.

What does a cohesive team look like? Members of cohesive teams sit closer together, focus more attention on one another, show signs of mutual affection, and display coordinated patterns of behavior. Furthermore, members of cohesive teams who have a close relationship are more likely to give due credit to their partners in contrast, those who do not have a close relationship are more likely to take credit for successes and blame others for failure (Sedekides, Campbell, Reeder, & Elliot, 1998). Cohesive groups are easier to maintain: Members of cohesive teams are more likely to participate in team activities, stay on the team and convince others to join, and resist attempts to disrupt the team (Brawley, Carron, & Widmeyer, 1988; Carron, Widmeyer, & Brawley, 1988). Cohesion increases conformity to team norms (O'Reilly & Caldwell, 1985; Rutkowski, Gruder, & Romer, 1983). This effect can be helpful when deviance endangers the team or harmful when innovation is required. Cohesive teams are more likely to serve team rather than individual interests (Thompson, Kray, & Lind, 1998). Most important, members of cohesive teams are more productive on a variety of tasks than are members of noncohesive groups (Dion & Evans, 1992; Michel & Hambrick, 1992).

However, *the relationship between team cohesion and performance is primarily correlational rather than causal.* Stated simply, cohesive teams are more productive than are less cohesive teams, but it could very well be that (1) more productive teams become more cohesive, (2) something other than cohesion is responsible for increased productivity, or (3) both of the above. The link of cohesion with performance may depend on team norms: Cohesion amplifies norms favoring both high and low production (Stogdill, 1972). There are many ways to promote cohesion (see Sidebar 4-3 for some interesting examples).

Sidebar 4-3. Notes from the Field

There are two companies based in Boulder, Colorado, that advocate writing poetry or banging on drums to help teams build cohesion. According to a participant in one of Kandome Percussion Workshop's sessions: "It builds a rhythm through the company." A brochure for CorPoet asserts that its method "reveals and anthologizes the heart and soul of your business" (LeJeune, 1997).

Building Cohesion in Groups

What is the best way to increase cohesion in teams? Actually, building cohesion is often (but not always) easier than most managers think.

- *Help the team build identity.* Simply assembling people into a team is enough to produce some cohesion (Hogg, 1987), and the more time people spend together, the more cohesive they become (Manning & Fullerton, 1988). When team members think about their identity (i.e., what they stand for) and what they have in common, they become more cohesive (Prentice, Miller, & Lightdale, 1994).
- *Make it easy for the team to be close together.* Physical proximity and real or perceived similarity strengthen team cohesion (e.g., Ruder & Gill, 1982; Stokes, 1983; Sundstrom & Sundstrom, 1986).
- *Focus on similarities among team members.* Team members feel more cohesive when they focus on their similarities, rather than their differences.
- *Put a positive spin on the team's performance.* Teams are more cohesive when they succeed rather than fail, though some teams can preserve (if not strengthen) cohesion even when they fail (Brawley et al., 1988).
- *Challenge the team.* External pressure (Glickman et al., 1987) and rewards for team performance also increase team cohesion (Shea & Guzzo, 1987a).

Warning: Many of the factors that produce greater cohesion in teams are in contradiction to those that promote diversity. We suggest that the manager first consider strategies for building diversity, and then focus on building cohesion.

Trust

Trust is the confidence one person places in another that the other will honor all commitments, including those that are difficult to define or specify in advance, especially when it is difficult to monitor or otherwise observe the other person's behavior after the fact. Trust is built on previous experience, on an understanding of the other party's interests, motives, and ideas, as well as more subtle factors, such as a willingness to believe a commitment. Thus, trust is two-sided, depending partly on the believability of the other party and partly on the willingness to believe. Many things can affect either of these, and abridgments to either can compromise teamwork.

Trust or Faith?

Business is built on relationships of all sorts and almost nothing is truly guaranteed in writing. No contract can be so complete as to specify, for instance, what an employee must actually do at a given time on a given day in a particular instance, especially since at some level, just about every situation is unique. Faith in other team members' integrity to do things that cannot be specified in a contract or monitored after the fact is an essential feature of a successful team—or for that matter, any business relationship. It is the integrity of the individual team members, and the members' trust in this integrity, that allows for successful teamwork.

The absence of a positive, trusting relationship can undermine any team activity, and so fostering trust is one of the most important tasks of a manager. Contractual relationships (such as when a consulting firm is hired for a project) come with the understanding that they will be evaluated, at least in part, by how fairly they used their time; that is, basically, how trustworthy they are in their billing practices. However, this is not a normal part of the relationship between coworkers, who are presumed to be working toward the same common goal. Moreover, what to do in cases when it seems like coworkers are furthering their own interests at the expense of the firm is less certain than it is with an outside contractor who, at the least, can be excluded from further work with the firm.

Many other forms of trust are also essential inside the firm, such as trust in the abilities or knowledge of other workers. Moreover, the absence of trust need not be associated with anything malicious; a lack of trust can stem, for instance, from a lack of experience working with others, such as when a cross-functional team is put together to establish firmwide policy or to hire key executives to lead the company. The next few sections elaborate on the issue of trust—how to get a better understanding of it and its role in working relationships and, most important, where and when to find it.

Calculated Trust

Calculated trust involves designing incentives to minimize breaches of trust. When an arrangement, such as a contract, is made on favorable terms for the other party, it is easier to trust that they will fulfill their end of the deal. Firms often pay bonuses, in fact, to ensure just this kind of outcome. For instance, contracts often include provisions for bonuses depending upon when a job gets done. Why pay extra for something that you could pay less for? The idea is that by providing incentives to the other party to do things that match your objectives, you can trust that they will be more likely to get things done the way that you want them done. Bonuses are only one mechanism that can be used to ensure this alignment.

Developing Trusting Relationships

As we noted in chapter 2, free riding is a frequent problem for teams and a major threat to team performance. The accomplishments of a team cannot often be traced to particular individuals. Free riding can undermine the trust in a team and prevent other, "cooperative" members from working, if they believe others are trying to benefit from their work without contributing their fair share. Thus, because individuals cannot be separately evaluated, they have an incentive to shirk. One of the key challenges for any team is to maintain an ongoing process of monitoring and evaluating the activities of team members to overcome the free-riding problem. (For an example of free riding in teams, see Sidebar 4-4.)

Sidebar 4-4. Free Riding in Teams

An example of free riding in teams can be easily constructed. Imagine that the efforts of each individual on a five-person team consist of choosing a dollar amount to contribute to a joint investment. The investment returns a certain 5 percent; so, for each dollar contributed, the investment returns $1.05. To make this a team story, let's set up the problem this way: Every person contributes anonymously to a team account (so, no one can observe whether or how much any one person contributes—all that can be observed is the net amount of funds collected), and the returns from the investment are distributed to all team members equally. Thus, if all five people contribute $1 apiece, they each receive $1.05 back in return; if four people contribute $1 and one person contributes $6, they each receive $2.10. The decision problem faced by individual team members is how much to contribute. Clearly, everyone is better off the higher the total contribution. However, payoffs cannot be separated based on individual contributions, so each team member receives only 21 cents in return directly as a consequence of their contribution (do you see why this is true?). Hence, from an individual point of view, a contribution costs more than it returns. On the other hand, everyone receives a share of the total pie regardless of whether or not they contribute. If four people contribute $1 and the fifth person contributes nothing, they each get back 84 cents. This is bad for the four people who pitched in, but great for the person who put in nothing. What will team members do in this instance? If their objective is to maximize return, they will each contribute nothing. Thus, despite the fact that high contribution levels are good for the team *as a whole* (total contributions are a public good), the free-riding effect prevents anyone from contributing, and so the worst outcome is achieved.

The problem in this example is that individual contributions cannot be monitored. Hence, people can hide behind the anonymity offered by the team structure to mask their lack of effort. If there were a way to remove anonymity, for instance, by having a taxing structure that collected $1 from everyone, or by somehow installing a monitoring system that could directly observe contributions, this would prevent the free-riding problem, because everyone could get back their fair share attributable to their efforts.

(A final note: Don't get caught up in the artificial details of this example. The structure of the example is meant to capture the fact that putting effort into teamwork is costly and difficult to monitor and that results from teamwork are generally attributed to the entire group, not allocated according to individual efforts.)

It is hard to completely overcome the free-riding problem. The key is to somehow find a way to monitor and evaluate individuals based on their efforts—not just on the outcome of the team. Thus, individual feedback and team review of individual contributions can have an important effect. They foster team spirit and cohesion and help to assure others that individuals are not free riding on them and that individual team members can be trusted.

Trust Based on Similarity

Oftentimes, trust can develop based on commonalities, such as being alumni of the same school, belonging to the same religious institution, or having kids who play on the same Little League team. People who are similar to one another in beliefs, attitudes, and interests tend to like each other more. It seems natural that we are attracted to those who are similar to us, and we are more likely to help and trust them. This principle explains why successful salespeople are trained to find immediate common ground with others: "Hi, Mrs. Jones! I have the same aluminum siding. How do you like it? Would you like to change your long-distance service?" Of course, the dark side of this is that people have lower trust in people who are less similar (more diverse).

Trust Based on Social Networks

Trusting relationships in organizations are often based upon social networks. *Social embeddedness* refers to the idea that transactions and opportunities take place as a result of social relationships that exist between organizational actors (Uzzi, 1997). This is conducive to organizational teamwork in that trust and shared norms of reciprocal compliance have beneficial governance properties for the people involved. In short, embedding commercial exchange in social attachments creates a basis for trust that, if accepted and returned, crystallizes through reciprocal coinvestment and self-enforcement for use in future transactions. Trust based on social networks offers several advantages (Uzzi, 1997). According to Uzzi, "embedded ties" reduce the time needed to reach and enforce agreements. Second, the expectations and trust associated with embedded ties increases risk taking and coinvestments in advanced technology. Third, the transfer of proprietary information through embedded ties leads to more win-win types of arrangements. Finally, embedded ties promote cooperation, even when groups will not work together very long.

Implicit Trust

Sometimes, we put our trust in others even in the absence of any rational reason or obvious similarity. We might trust someone on the basis of a short interaction. Trust, in this sense, is based upon highly superficial cues. In every social interaction, there are subtle signals that we attend to even though we are not aware of their influence. They operate below our conscious awareness. Here are some examples:

Instant Attitudes   These are near-immediate, intense likes or dislikes for a novel object based on a first encounter with it (Greenwald & Banaji, 1995).

Mere Exposure: "He Grew on Me"   The more we see someone, the more we like them (Zajonc, 1968). This even goes for people that we initially do not like. However, most people do not realize that they are affected by being exposed to someone. This **mere exposure** principle is the cornerstone of advertising and sales. It is particularly effective because people are not aware that they are influenced merely by the number of times they have been exposed to someone.

Schmoozing: "Let's Have Lunch Sometime"   Small talk often seems to serve no obvious function. The exchange of pleasantries about the weather or our favorite basketball team seems to be purposeless, except for conforming to social etiquette. However, on a *preconscious* level, schmoozing has a dramatic impact on our liking and trust of others. For example, even a short exchange can lead people to develop considerably more trust in others than in the absence of interaction.

Mimicking: "Monkey See; Monkey Do"   People involved in a face-to-face interaction tend to mirror one another in posture, facial expression, tone of voice, and mannerisms. This phenomenon, known as **social contagion,** is the basis for the development of rapport between people (Drolet, Larrick, & Morris, 1998). On the surface, it might seem that mimicking others would be extremely annoying—almost like a form of mocking. However, the type of mimicry that is involved in everyday social encounters is quite subtle, but definitely powerful. When two people are mimicking one another, their movements become almost like a choreographed dance. In this sense, people's behavior becomes synchronized. To the extent that our behaviors are synchronized with those of others, we feel more rapport, and this increases our trust in them.

"Flattery Can Get You Anywhere"   We like people who appreciate us and admire us. This means that we will tend to trust people more who like us. Many people believe that for flattery to be effective in engendering trust, it must be perceived as genuine. However, even if people suspect that the flatterer has ulterior motives, this can still increase liking and trust under some conditions (Jones, Stires, Shaver, & Harris, 1968).

Face-to-Face Contact   We are more likely to trust other people in a face-to-face encounter than when communicating via another medium, such as phone or fax machine. Perhaps this is why people often choose to travel thousands of miles for a short, face-to-face meeting when it would be more efficient to communicate via phone, fax, or mail.

CONCLUSIONS

We have focused on some of the important dimensions of creating and managing teams in a direct fashion. Much planning needs to precede the construction of teams and, once constructed, teams need fairly continuous maintenance. To the extent that the teams are manager-led, this work is the purview of the leader or manager; the more self-directing the team becomes, the more the team will do this for itself. When the team is built—in terms of the task, the people, and their relationships—the leader's work does not stop. During this time, the leader needs to also assess the physical, material, economic, and staffing resources necessary for performing the work to be done. The focus of the leader should not be to presume that everything is fine, but rather to coach the team to work through the issues of task, people, and relationships systematically.

CHAPTER 5

Sharpening the Team Mind: Communication and Collective Intelligence

In 1988, Iran Air Flight 665 took off from Bandar Abbas Airport and headed across the Persian Gulf en route to Dubai. Seven minutes into the flight, Captain William Rogers of the USS Vincennes, *judging the airliner to be a hostile fighter plane, destroyed it with two missiles. Captain Rogers had approximately 3 minutes in which to process information from several of his support staff and make the decision as to whether to shoot the (misidentified) Iranian airbus and protect his crew. Although the decision was militarily correct, 290 civilians died and questions were raised regarding the inadequacy of our scientific knowledge concerning team decision making and decision support systems in this setting.*

In 1989, an Avianca Airlines flight crashed in New York while awaiting clearance for landing, critically low on fuel. Ground control misinterpreted the Colombian pilot's urgent message regarding his fuel shortage and assumed that a fuel emergency had not been reached. More than 270 people died.

In 1990, Martin Marietta deployed a satellite into the wrong orbit when engineers instructed the computer programmers to open the bay door to the hatch containing the satellite. The programmers opened the "wrong door," although they had followed the instructions correctly (Associated Press, *1990). Today, $150 million sits dead in orbit around the earth. The total cost of the miscommunication: $500 million.*

In each of these examples, otherwise highly skilled and competent team members failed to adequately communicate with others in their organization. In each of the cases, an obvious mistake was made—but the mistake could not be attributed to any single individual. In other words, there was a failure of collective intelligence. Whether organizations make fighter airplanes or cookies, effective decision making and behavior rely upon effective communication and common understanding. Thus, to be effective, teams must not only be able to transmit and receive ideas from other group members accurately; they must also have a shared understanding of what the information means. This is especially critical in teams because members rely on the judgments of others to make important decisions.

This chapter examines how members of teams communicate and develop team intelligence. We begin by discussing communication within teams and the possible problems that can occur and how to effectively treat them. Then, we describe the information-dependence problem—the fact that team members are dependent upon one another for critical information. After this, we build a model of team-level collective intelligence. We suggest that teams implicitly develop mental models, which are causal structures that spell out how a team solves problems and does its work together. We then explore the team mind in depth and the nature of transactive memory systems, which are the ways in which teams encode, store, and retrieve critical information necessary for doing their work. Next, we undertake a case analysis of the effects of different types of training on transactive memory systems. Finally, we make some recommendations for team development and review some evidence pointing to the effects of group longevity, particularly in creative teams.

TEAM COMMUNICATION

Most people take communication for granted in their interactions with team members. The tragic events described in the opening examples suggest this can be a mistake. Communication among people and between teams is subject to biases that afflict even the most rational of human beings with the best of intentions.

In a perfect communication system, a sender transmits or sends a message that is accurately received by a recipient. There are at least three points of possible error: The sender may fail to send a message; the message may be sent, but is inaccurate or distorted; or, an accurate message is sent, but it is distorted or not received by the recipient. In a team environment, the complexity grows when teams of senders transmit messages and teams of recipients receive them. Here, we examine some of these biases and then take up the question of how to effectively deal with their existence.

Message Tuning

There are infinite possibilities of how to send any one message. **Message tuning** refers to how senders tailor messages for specific recipients. People who send messages (e.g., "I have no fuel"; "I did not receive the attached file") will edit their messages in a way that they think best suits the recipient. For example, individuals give longer and more elaborate street directions and instructions to people whom they presume to be non-natives or unfamiliar with a city (Krauss & Fussell, 1991). Also, senders capitalize on the knowledge that they believe the recipient to already hold (e.g., "Turn right when you see that big tree that the city pruned last week"). For this reason, members of teams and groups may send shorter, less complete messages to one another because they believe that they can capitalize on an existing shared knowledge base. However, team members often overestimate the commonality of information they share with others. Consequently, the messages they send become less clear (e.g., in the previous example, the other person may not know the location of the tree that was pruned by the city last week).

Message Distortion

Message senders have a bias to present information that they believe will be favorably received by the recipient and will, therefore, distort messages (Higgins, 1999). For example, when people present a message to an audience whom they believe is either pro- or anti- a particular topic, they err in the direction of adopting the audience's point of view. It is as if they know that the messenger who brings unwelcome news is endangered—so one way of dealing with this is to modify the news. Unfortunately, message distortion can play havoc for effective teamwork.

Biased Interpretation

Senders are not the only ones who distort messages. Receivers often hear what they want to hear when receiving messages, especially ambiguous ones. For example, when people are given neutral information about a product, they tend to interpret it in a way that is favorable toward their own position. Furthermore, they selectively pay attention to information in a report that favors their initial point of view and ignore or misinterpret information that contradicts their position.

Perspective-Taking Failures

People are remarkably poor at taking the perspective of others. For example, people who are privy to information and knowledge that they know others are not aware of still tend to act as if others are aware of it, even though it would be impossible for the receiver to have this knowledge (Keysar, 1998). This problem is known as the **curse of knowledge** (Camerer, Loewenstein, & Weber, 1989). For example, in a simulation, traders who possessed privileged information that could have been used to their advantage behaved as if their trading partners also had access to the privileged information. Perspective-taking deficiencies also explain why some instructors who understand an idea perfectly are unable to teach students the same idea. They are unable to put themselves in their students' shoes to explain the idea in a way the students can understand. Perspective-taking deficiencies explain why teams fail, even though every team member really wants to succeed. It is as if people are saying after the fact, "I thought I was clear . . ." or "I thought you knew that . . ." Thus, we tend to overestimate the commonality or overlap between our own knowledge base and that of others.

Transparency Illusion

People believe that their thoughts, attitudes, and reasons are much more transparent—that is, obvious to others—than is actually the case (Gilovich, Savitsky, & Medvec, 1998). For example, members of teams often have no idea what their leaders are thinking, but the leaders believe they are being perfectly clear. Part of the reason for the transparency illusion is that people find it impossible to put themselves in the position of the receiver. For example, when people are told to "tap out with their fingers" famous songs such as "Happy Birthday," they significantly overestimate the likelihood that a listener will understand which song they are tapping—but the listeners hardly ever do! (Griffin & Ross, 1991).

Indirect Speech Acts

Each statement one person makes to another has an intended meaning that is couched in casual conversation. **Indirect speech acts** are the ways in which people ask others to do things—but in indirect ways. For example, consider the various ways of requesting that a person shut a door (see Table 5-1). Each statement can serve as a request to perform that act although (except for "close the door") the sentence forms are not requests but assertions and questions. Thus, statements 2 through 9 are indirect speech acts; a listener's understanding of the intention behind a communicator's intention requires an extra cognitive step or two—and can often fail, especially in cases of stress.

Indirect speech acts are a function of the magnitude of the request being made (i.e., trivial requests, such as asking someone for the time of day, are easy to accommodate; asking someone if you can have a job is much more difficult to accommodate), the

TABLE 5-1 Different Ways to Make a Request That Require Progressively More Inferences and Assumed Common Knowledge on the Part of the Receiver

1. Close the door.
2. Can you close the door?
3. Would you close the door?
4. It might help to close the door.
5. Would you mind awfully if I asked you to close the door?
6. Did you forget the door?
7. How about a little less breeze?
8. It's getting cold in here.
9. I really don't want the cats to get out of the house.

Sources: Adapted from Krauss, R. M., & Fussell, S. R. 1996. "Social Psychological Models of Interpersonal Communication." In E. T. Higgins, & A. W. Kruglanski (Eds.), *Social Psychology: Handbook of Basic Principles* (pp. 655–701). New York: Guilford; Levinson, S. C. 1983. *Pragmatics* (p. 264). Cambridge, England: Cambridge University Press.

power the recipient has over the sender, and the social distance in the culture (Brown & Levinson, 1987). Thus, as the magnitude of requests increases, the power distance increases, and the social distance increases, requests made by team members will become more indirect. Of course, indirectness can be disastrous for effective communication.

THE INFORMATION DEPENDENCE PROBLEM

Teams presumably have access to a broader range of decision-making resources and, hence, should be better equipped to make high-quality decisions than any single person could alone. By pooling their different backgrounds, training, and experience, team members have at least the potential to work in a more informed fashion than would be the case were the decision left to any single person. The fact that team members are dependent upon one another for information is the **information dependence problem.** As an example of information dependence in groups and the dire consequences it can have, consider the case in Box 5-1.

When the team consists of members who come from different functional areas—with different areas of expertise, different information, different priorities, and different perceptions of problems and opportunities—the information dependence problem is even more pronounced. The challenge is finding a way to quickly and efficiently pool all the relevant information in a coordinated fashion. Thus, a central issue facing any group charged with making a collective decision is how to get the ideas, information, and expertise in each person's head onto the table for all to see.

Common Knowledge Effect

Pooling unique information in a team is valuable. Rehashing commonly known information or "stating the obvious" is largely a waste of time. Unfortunately, unique information does not readily emerge in team interaction; rather, teams tend to discuss what everyone already knows. This team fallacy is known as the **common information effect** (Gigone & Hastie, 1997). Consider a typical group decision-making task in the ABC Company. A three-member top-executive committee, Allen, Booz, and Catz, is charged

---

BOX 5-1

Information Dependence

"In 1955, the Centers for Disease Control took the responsibility of evaluating the polio vaccine developed by Jonas Salk. In late 1954, six vaccine manufacturers met with the Division of Biological Standards, with Jonas Salk, and others. Some of them had been having problems with inactivation of the virus during the process of vaccine manufacture. While one of the manufacturers was explaining that his company had been more efficient and successful at inactivating the virus, a representative from one of the other manufacturers had a telephone call, left the room, and came back after the discussion. Within two weeks after the beginning of the nationwide vaccination program, in April 1955 CDC began to get reports of polio. What was significant was that these children had received the vaccine 6–8 days earlier and had developed polio, almost invariably in the arm or leg where they received the shot. Of the six reported cases, the vaccine contaminated with the live virus was manufactured by the laboratory whose representative took the phone call during the discussion on inactivating the virus" (Larson & LaFasto, 1989, p. 46).

---

with the task of hiring a new manager for an important division within the ABC firm. The firm has determined that six pieces of information are critical to evaluate in a candidate for this position:

- Previous experience (A)
- Academic grades (B)
- Standardized test scores (C)
- Performance in round 1 interview (D)
- Cultural and international experience (E)
- Letters of recommendation (F)

Allen, Booz, and Catz have narrowed the competition down to three candidates: Kate, Ken, and Kerry. As is standard practice in the firm, members of the hiring committee specialize in obtaining partial information about each candidate. Stated another way, each member of the hiring committee has *some* of the facts about each candidate, but not *all* of the facts. Thus, Allen, Booz, and Catz are information dependent upon one another.

What will happen when they discuss various candidates for the job? Consider three possible distributions of information (see Figure 5-1):

- **Nonoverlapping case:** Each partner, Allen, Booz, and Catz, has unique information about each candidate.
- **Distributed, partial overlap:** Each partner knows something about each candidate that others also know (common information), but also knows some unique information.
- **Fully shared case:** Each partner knows full information about each candidate. In this sense, the partners are **informational clones** of one another.

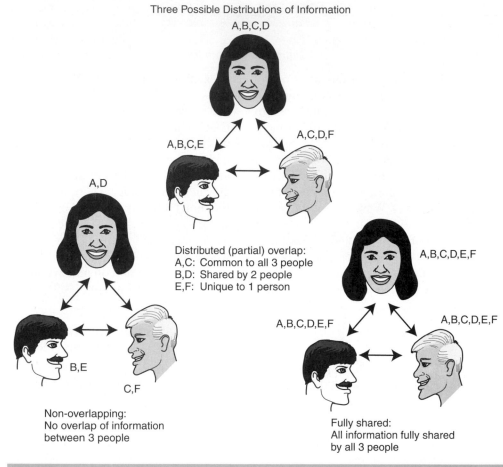

Three Possible Distributions of Information

A,B,C,D

A,B,C,E

A,C,D,F

A,D

Distributed (partial) overlap:
A,C: Common to all 3 people
B,D: Shared by 2 people
E,F: Unique to 1 person

A,B,C,D,E,F

A,B,C,D,E,F

A,B,C,D,E,F

B,E

C,F

Non-overlapping:
No overlap of information
between 3 people

Fully shared:
All information fully shared
by all 3 people

FIGURE 5-1   The Common Knowledge Effect

The only difference among these three cases is the **information redundancy,** or how equally the information is distributed among decision makers. The collective intelligence of the partners is the same in all three cases. Does the distribution of information affect the way the partners make decisions? In a rational world, it should not, but in real teams, it does.

The impact of information on the aggregate decision of the team is directly related to the number of members of the team who know the information prior to making a group decision. Stated simply: *Information held by more members before team discussion has more influence on team judgments than information held by fewer members, independent of the validity of the information.*

This means that even though (in an objective sense) the six pieces of information are really equally important, the top management group will tend to overemphasize information (such as A & C in the distributed case) more than is warranted.

The common information effect has several important consequences. First, team members are more likely to discuss information that everyone knows, as opposed to unique information that each may have. As a consequence, decisions will be biased in the direction of whatever information happens to be commonly shared. This often means that technical information (which is often not fully shared) is not given the weight that experts believe it should have. Information that people have in common is not only more likely to be discussed, it gets discussed for a longer period of time, and this too can exert a significant bias on the integrity of decision making.

The bottom line is that teams often fail to make the decision that would be supported if all the team members had full information about the choices.

Hidden Profile

A **hidden profile** is a superior decision alternative, but its superiority is hidden from group members because each member has only a portion of the information that supports this superior alternative (Stasser, 1988). Stated another way, the information held in common by group members favors a particular choice, whereas the unshared information contradicts the choice.

Let's consider an executive meeting, in which three different candidates (Alva, Jane, and Bill) are being considered for promotion to partner in the firm—obviously, an extremely important decision. Each of the three potential candidates has been with the firm for some number of years; each has made a different number and type of accomplishments. The executive group can only promote one person for the position at this time.

In theory, the executive group can benefit the organization by pooling individual members' information so as to gain a complete picture of the qualifications of each candidate. This is particularly important when individual members of the decision-making team are biased by virtue of their own agendas.

However, free-style discussion may be an ineffective way of disseminating information, because information that is known to only one or a few members will often be omitted from discussion (Stasser & Titus, 1985). Team members are not only more likely to mention information if it was known to all before discussion, but are also more likely to bring it up repeatedly and dwell on it throughout the discussion. Thus, the team decision will often reflect the common knowledge shared by members before discussion rather than the diverse knowledge emanating from their unique perspectives and experiences.

Consider the scenario in Figure 5-2. In this situation, the initial bias favors Bill. At the outset of the meeting, each team member has more information about him (five pieces of information). The information the team has about Bill is fully shared, meaning that all team members are apprised of this candidate's qualifications prior to the meeting. Obviously, Bill has done an excellent job of marketing his own achievements within the firm!

However, consider Alva, who has a combined total of eight pieces of favorable information supporting his candidacy for the partnership. However, each member of the executive team is privy only to three pieces of information about this candidate, and the information is not redundant. In an objective sense, Alva is by far the most qualified; yet his accomplishments are not fully shared among the top-management team—a factor that will not be corrected with discussion (at least unstructured discussion).

FIGURE 5-2 Hidden Profiles

If this team were immune to the common information effect, and optimally combined and pooled their unique information, a hidden profile would emerge. *A hidden profile is a conclusion that is only apparent after team members have fully shared information.* In this case, Alva, would prevail.

Common information also affects people's memory for team discussions. People recall fewer unshared arguments from team discussion (Stasser & Titus, 1985, 1987). Moreover, analysis of tape-recorded discussions reveals that unshared arguments are less likely to be expressed (Stasser, Taylor, & Hanna, 1989).

The reliance on previously shared information is not an optimal use of team resources because uniquely held or previously unshared information may be most enlightening for the team as a whole. Unstructured, free-style discussion, even among trained professionals who have every motivation to make an accurate diagnosis, is insufficient for ensuring the quality of outcomes. (For an illustration of the inability of professionals to share relevant information, see Box 5-2.)

BOX 5-2

Hidden Profiles in Medical Diagnosis

Professional teams are created for a number of important reasons. For example, in medicine, the use of teaching rounds, interdisciplinary consults, and case conferences serves both clinical and educational functions. Collaborative efforts of this sort are designed to ensure that relevant information is brought to bear on important clinical decisions, to facilitate the coordinated action of experts toward appropriate treatment goals, and to train novices. Consider how clinical teams composed of a resident, intern, and third-year medical student arrive at patient diagnoses on the basis of case information (Christensen et al., 1998). (For example, the management of a seriously ill geriatric patient may require input from specialties and subspecialties such as internal medicine, pulmonology, and oncology, as well as from nurses and nutritionists.) Prior to discussion, team members may individually review different versions of a videotaped interview with a patient actor. Each videotape contains some information that is present in all three versions (shared information) and some that is present in only that version

(unique information). In addition, some patient case profiles are constructed so that unique information that appeared in only one tape was crucial for a correct diagnosis (i.e., "hidden profile" situation). After viewing the tapes, the team members meet to discuss the case and develop a differential diagnosis for the patient.

These medical specialists were not immune to the common information effect: Shared information about the patient was mentioned more often (67 percent) than was unique information (46 percent). More disconcerting, teams offered incorrect diagnoses substantially more often for the "hidden profile" patient case than for the "standard" patient cases: Overall, 17 of the 24 hidden profile cases were diagnosed correctly (a hit rate of about 70 percent), whereas all of the shared information cases were correctly diagnosed. Clearly, the medical teams' overreliance on previously shared information and the inability to appropriately utilize unique information were detrimental when a correct diagnosis demanded the inclusion of such information.

Practices to Put in Place

There are ways to avoid the biases induced by the common information effect and hidden profiles. We want to point out first, however, some "obvious" solutions that do not work, either because they actually reinforce the problem or do not address the problem adequately.

Things That Don't Work

Increasing the Amount of Discussion

It would seem that, if teams had more time to discuss a matter or issue, they would eventually discuss what they do not know. However, even when teams are explicitly told to spend more time discussing information, they still fall prey to the common information effect (Parks & Cowlin, 1996).

Separating Review and Decisions

It would seem reasonable to structure the group discussion by dividing deliberations into two parts: Review the information available in the first phase and then make decisions and judgments in the second phase. However, this is not effective; teams simply discuss what they already know during the first phase. For example, in one investigation, team members were given instructions intended to curb the common information effect (Stasser et al., 1989). Team members avoided stating their initial preferences and were encouraged to review all relevant facts. These instructions did increase the *amount* of discussion that occurred, but the discussion primarily favored those facts initially shared by team members (67 percent of all shared facts were discussed in contrast to 23 percent of unshared facts).

Increasing the Size of the Team

As team size increases, but the distribution of information stays the same, the tendency to discuss common information increases. For example, the bias is more pronounced in six-person groups than three-person groups. In a typical three-person group, 46 percent of shared information is mentioned, in contrast to only 18 percent of unshared information. This difference is even larger for six-person groups (Stasser et al., 1989).

Increasing Information Load

If members of the team are given additional information, but the relative distribution of information remains the same, the common information effect still plagues the team (Stasser, 1992). In fact, the bias to discuss shared information is most likely to occur when there is a large number of "shared" facts to discuss.

Accountability

Accountability refers to the extent to which people and teams feel responsible for their actions and decisions. Surprisingly, accountable teams are *less* likely to focus on unshared information than groups that are not held accountable (Stewart, Billings, & Stasser, 1998). For example, the medical teams described in Box 5-2 were videotaped and told to come up with a correct diagnosis that would be evaluated; yet they still demonstrated an overreliance on previously shared information and a tendency to misdiagnose the case. Why doesn't accountability help? The problem is that accountable teams focus on the wrong thing—shared information.

Effective Interventions

Fortunately, there are ways to successfully combat the common information effect. They have one thing in common: They put the team leader in the position of an **information manager.** In fact, having a leader in the team can be an advantage in itself: Team leaders are consistently more likely than are other members to ask questions and repeat unshared (as well as shared) information (Larson, Christensen, Franz, & Abbott, 1998). Leaders can play an important information management role during team discussion by focusing the team's attention, facilitating communication, stimulating member contributions, and ensuring that critical information brought out during discussion is "kept alive" and factored into the team's final decision. The *type* of leader is also important. Directive leaders are more likely than participative leaders to repeat unshared information and, consequently, identify the best options (Larson, Foster-Fishman, & Franz, 1998). Leaders with more experience are also more effective (Wittenbaum, in press). The common information effect can be substantially reduced when the leader actively does the following:

Redirects and Maintains the Focus of the Discussion to Unshared (Unique) Information

The leader should be aware that some information is common to all members, whereas other information is not. The leader should be persistent in directing the focus of the discussion to unique information. The leader must work against the natural tendency of the team to retreat to the comfortable by discussing and rediscussing what they already know. Furthermore, the leader must reintroduce noncommon information after it has been dismissed.

Labels the Task As a "Problem" to Be Solved, Not a "Judgment" to Be Made

Subtle differences in wording of the team's goal dramatically affect the way people think and process information. Leaders can take a proactive role in this process by labeling the task as a "problem" to be solved with "demonstrable evidence" and explicitly state that they are not interested in personal opinion and judgment. Teams are less prone to overlook unshared information if they believe that their task has a demonstrably correct answer (Laughlin, 1980; Stasser & Stewart, 1992).

As an example, consider the instructions given to a panel of jurors: Members of the jury are explicitly told to pay attention to the facts and evidence of the case. They are cautioned that the lawyers representing the parties in the case are not witnesses but rather, are attempting to sway members of the jury to adopt a particular belief. It is precisely for this reason that trial lawyers have an opportunity to dismiss potential jurors who are regarded as unable to consider the facts because their mind is already made up—that is, they enter the courtroom with a particular bias or belief.

Ranks Rather Than Chooses

When teams are instructed to "rank" candidates or alternatives, they are more likely to make the best decision than when they are simply told to "choose" (Hollingshead, 1996). The reason is that when teams are asked to choose, people make comparisons among candidates and if the best candidate is a hidden profile, teams are likely to choose the wrong candidate. If teams can move away from choosing among candidates to estimating or predicting the performance of each individual candidate, an accurate, or data-based, choice is more likely (Gigone & Hastie, 1997).

Considers the Decision Alternatives One at a Time

Leaders should make sure their team discusses one alternative before turning to the next (Larson, Foster-Fishman, & Keys, 1994). Otherwise, hidden profile alternatives may be prematurely rejected.

Heightens Team Members' Awareness of the Types of Information Likely to Be Possessed by Different Individuals

When team members are publicly identified, the likelihood that unshared clues will be mentioned during discussion increases (Stasser, Stewart, & Wittenbaum, 1995). For example, when team members know who has expertise in specific knowledge domains, the amount of unshared information discussed increases significantly (Stasser, 1988; Stasser, Stewart, & Wittenbaum, 1995). This creates important metaknowledge for the team (Larson & Christensen, 1993). However, the metaknowledge must be accurate.

Suspends Initial Judgment

Probably one of the most effective strategies for avoiding the common knowledge effect is to caution team members against arriving at a judgment prior to the team discussion of the candidates. Indeed, the common information effect is a direct result of the biases that people bring to discussion, not the team discussion itself (Gigone & Hastie, 1993).

Builds Trust and Familiarity among Team Members

Although it seems obvious, the practical implications are profound: Teams that trust one another more are more likely to make use of nonredundant types of information. Team members who are familiar with one another are less likely to make poor decisions resulting from the common knowledge problem than are teams whose members are unacquainted (Gruenfeld, Mannix, Williams, & Neale, 1996).

Communicates Confidence

The communication of confidence is a subjective measure of how sure team members are about what they are saying. Teams whose members are encouraged to express confidence about their decisions and judgments perform more effectively and learn significantly more from their interaction than do teams whose ability to communicate confidence during interaction is reduced (Bloomfield, Libby, & Nelson, 1996).

COLLECTIVE INTELLIGENCE

Team Mental Models

Mental models are mental representations of the world that allow people to understand, predict, and solve problems in a given situation (Gentner & Gentner, 1983; Johnson-Laird, 1980; Rouse & Morris, 1986). Mental models reflect people's experiences and expectations and guide their behaviors in different situations. Mental models organize information and knowledge about a problem and influence how people interpret information. Mental models can represent many different problems and systems. On the one hand, they can be models of a simple physical system, such as the trajectory of a thrown object; on the other hand, mental models can represent a complex social system, such as an organization or financial system. Mental models are not always accurate. Yet, mental models influence the process by which people and teams go about solving particular problems—what information they seek, how they combine it, how they formulate plans, and how they enact them.

A **team mental model** is a common understanding that members of a group or team share about how something works (Klimoski & Mohammed, 1997). From this, members form expectations about what others will do in a given situation. Team members do not come equipped with hardwired mental models; they are acquired by learning and experience. Team members not only have mental models about the operation of their team, they also have mental models about the work they do. Consider, for example, the mental models that team members might have for how their team functions:

- **Manufactured product model:** Some people understand teams as manufactured products, such that well-made ones "last" and "work" and poorly constructed ones "fall apart" and "break."
- **Journey:** Some people reason that teamwork is like an ongoing journey in which team members "travel" through good times and bad times.
- **Sports model:** Some people understand teamwork to be a sport such that they need to practice, compete, score, and win.
- **Marriage model:** Some people understand teamwork to be like a marriage vow, in which they make commitments to one another that last through time.

These models of teamwork are neither right nor wrong; the important point is that they can influence how team members try to deal with problems in the team, conflict, and a host of other internal dynamics. If team members have different (and perhaps conflicting) mental models about their team, this can lead to conflict.

There are two key considerations in terms of the mental models that members have about their actual work: The *accuracy* of the model and the degree of *correspondence* (or noncorrespondence) between members' models.

Accuracy

As an illustration of what we mean by accuracy, suppose that you are asked to explain how the thermostat in your house operates (Kempton, 1986, 1987). According to one (erroneous) model, the "valve" model, the thermostat works much like the accelerator in a car. People who hold a valve mental model of a thermostat reason that just as greater depression of the accelerator causes the car's speed to increase at a faster rate, turning the thermostat setting to high temperatures causes the room temperature to increase at a faster rate.

A different (and correct) mental model is the "threshold" model, in which the heat is either on or off and the thermostat setting determines the duration for which the heat is on. The greater the discrepancy between the current room temperature and the thermostat setting, the longer the heat will be on. These two models have different implications for how people set the thermostat in their homes. People with valve models will continuously adjust their thermostat setting in an effort to reach a comfortable room temperature. In contrast, those with threshold models will determine at what temperature they are comfortable and set the thermostat to only one or two settings per day, a nighttime setting and a daytime setting. Indeed, after interviewing people to determine the mental models they use to understand the operation of a thermostat, Kempton revisited thermostat records and showed that people's models of how thermostats operate predicted the stability of their actual thermostat settings.

This simple analogy illustrates an important aspect of the use of mental models in problem solving: The use of an incorrect mental model can result in inefficient or undesirable outcomes. People with an incorrect mental representation of a thermostat as a valve will spend greater time and effort adjusting the thermostat setting. In addition, they will be perpetually uncomfortable because they will either be too warm or too cold.

There are several implications for teamwork. If team members hold erroneous mental models concerning the task at hand (either because they lack technical training or communicate poorly), their well-intentioned behaviors could produce disastrous results.

Correspondence

Let's now turn to the question of correspondence between members' models. Effective teams are able to adapt to external demands and anticipate other members' information needs because of shared or compatible knowledge structures or team mental models. For example, when novel or unexpected events are encountered (such as when an airplane enters another's airspace), teams that cannot strategize overtly must rely on preexisting knowledge and expectations about how the team must perform in order to cope with task demands. The greater the overlap or commonality among team members' mental models, the greater the likelihood that team members will predict the needs of the task and team, adapt to changing demands, and coordinate activity with one another successfully (Cannon-Bowers, Salas, & Converse, 1993; Cannon-Bowers, Tannenbaum, Salas, & Converse, 1991). For example, the negative effects of fatigue on air crew performance can be overcome when crews develop interaction patterns over time (Foushee, Lauber, Baetge, & Comb, 1986).

The following example, taken from Perrow's (1984) book on normal accidents, illustrates the concepts of accuracy and correspondence:

> On a beautiful night in October, 1978, in the Chesapeake Bay, two vessels sighted one another visually and on radar. On one of them, the Coast Guard cutter training vessel *Cuyahoga,* the captain (a chief warrant officer) saw the other ship up ahead as a small object on the radar, and visually he saw two lights, indicating that it was proceeding in the same direction as his own ship. He thought it possibly was a fishing vessel. The first mate saw the lights, but saw three, and estimated (correctly) that it was a ship proceeding toward them. He had no responsibility to inform the captain, nor did he think he needed to. Since the two ships drew together so rapidly, the captain decided that it must be a very slow fishing boat that he was about to overtake. This reinforced his incorrect interpretation. The lookout knew the captain was aware of the ship, so did not comment further as it got quite close and seemed to be nearly on a collision course. Since both ships were traveling full speed, the closing came fast. The other ship, a large cargo ship, did not establish any bridge-to-bridge communication, because the passing was routine. But at the last moment, the captain of the *Cuyahoga* realized that in overtaking the supposed fishing boat, which he assumed was on a near parallel course, he would cut off that boat's ability to turn as both of them approached the Potomac River. So he ordered a turn to the port. (p. 215)

The two ships collided, killing 11 sailors on the Coast Guard vessel. Clearly, the captain's mental model was incorrect. In addition, there was a lack of correspondence between the captain and the first mate's mental models.

The Team Mind: Transactive Memory Systems

As capable as the human information-processing system is, it is insufficient for most organizational work. For this reason, people rely on others for the information they need. Thus, many people supplement their own memories, which are known to be highly limited and unreliable, with various external aids. For example, objects such as address or appointment books allow us to store and retrieve important information externally rather than in our own long-term memory. Similarly, other people (e.g., friends, family, coworkers, and teammates) also function as external memory aids.

Transactive memory systems (TMS) are group-level information-processing systems that are an extension of the human information-processing system: Shared systems for attending to, encoding, storing, processing, and retrieving information (Wegner, 1986; Wegner, Giuliano, & Hertel, 1995). Think of transactive memory systems as a division of mental labor. The key to an effective TMS is a shared knowledge base. In short, when each person learns in some general way what the other persons on the team may know in detail, team members can share detailed memories. In essence, each team member cultivates the other members as external memory and, in doing so, they become part of a larger system. TMS develop implicitly in many teams to ensure that important information is not forgotten. TMS are a combination of two things: *Knowledge* possessed by particular team members and *awareness* of who knows what. In this way, a TMS serves as an external storage device, such as a library or computer that can be visited to retrieve otherwise unavailable information. Teams that have a TMS have access to more and better information than any single group member does alone.

To see how a TMS might work within a team, consider a team composed of a finance, marketing, and production manager. The team members would expect that the person from finance would remember details concerning costs or profitability; the person from marketing would remember the results of a study concerning how customers responded to test marketing; and the production person would remember details about the mechanics of making the product. In other words, the other members of the team instinctively expect that the "experts" on the team will remember the details most closely associated with their area of expertise. Even when the experts are not so clearly defined, people still seem to specialize in remembering certain kinds of information, and it is generally understood by all members of the team (although often implicitly) which person is to remember what. This way of processing information provides an advantage to teams because they can collectively remember and utilize more information than can individuals acting on their own—even the same number of individuals considered separately.

The main disadvantage is that team members are dependent upon one another for knowledge and information. Teams who have been working together for years find it nearly impossible to reconstruct interactions with clients and other shared experiences without the other team members present.

What does a TMS do for teams? How does it affect productivity in terms of the key dimensions of performance criteria? More important, how can the manager best capitalize on the strengths of a TMS while minimizing the liabilities?

Tacit Coordination

Tacit coordination is the synchronization of members' actions based on assumptions about what others on the team are likely to do. This is important because task-oriented groups rarely discuss plans for how to perform their tasks unless they are explicitly instructed to do so (Hackman & Morris, 1975). Team members' attempts to coordinate tacitly begin prior to interaction. Evaluating the competence of other team members can be difficult, however. Claims of personal competence by coworkers cannot always be trusted, because they may reflect members' desires to impress one another (Gardner, 1992). Accepting coworkers' evaluations of one another's competence can be risky as well because these secondhand evaluations are often based on limited information (Gilovich, 1987) and may reflect impression-management efforts by the people who provide them (Cialdini, 1989). Knowing who is good at what is valuable for a team because it can improve the team's performance in several ways; for instance, it becomes easier to plan activities so that the people most suited for a particular task actually become responsible for that task. Similarly, coordinating actions and dealing with unexpected problems is easier when team members know who is good at what.

TMS and Team Performance

Teams that have TMS generally perform better than teams that do not in tasks that require memory and retrieval of information. TMS eliminate a lot of the coordination loss that can plague team effectiveness (Moreland, Argote, & Krishnan, 1998). Teams that have a transactive memory structure because its members are familiar with one another are less likely to fall prey to the common knowledge problem as compared to teams composed of previously unacquainted persons (Gruenfeld et al., 1996). Thus, the key question for the manager is how to ensure that teams develop an accurate TMS.

Probably the most straightforward way is to simply ask members of the team to indicate what knowledge bases the other members of the group possess. If there is high intrateam agreement, the TMS is higher than if there is low agreement about who knows what.

Developing TMS in Teams

TMS naturally seem to develop when a team works together over time. However, it may take quite a bit of time for a team to realize each member's strengths and to learn how to capitalize on those strengths in a coordinated fashion. Training is one of the most effective ways of ensuring that groups quickly and accurately develop a TMS.

TMS and Training

The development of a team TMS begins with training. Training is widely used in organizations. U.S. companies spend $30 billion to $100 billion annually on training (Baldwin & Ford, 1988; "Labor Letter," 1991). This figure is likely to increase as a result of changes in the nature of work and characteristics of the workforce (Goldstein, 1989, 1991; "Labor Letter," 1992; Webb & Smith, 1991). A fundamental question that companies face is whether to train individuals independently or as part of a team. As a guiding principle, there should be a high degree of correspondence between workers' experiences during training and their experiences on the job. The key reason is that similar conditions will facilitate the transfer of knowledge learned in training to how individuals actually carry out their job. This type of state-dependent learning can be a strength of teamwork. Too often, learning is decontextualized from the work teams are doing.

People perform their work differently when they are working in teams than when they are alone. This means that individuals require different kinds of training when they work in teams than when they work alone or apart. People that will work together as a team should train together, because (among other reasons) even during training, TMS will ensure that the right structure of information sharing and responsibility will develop. Training can be specifically geared toward developing specific TMS structures. For example, teams can plan who will be responsible for what types of information; they can also make explicit efforts to discern expertise and then make that information known to members. Transactive memory training may be especially important when team members will only work together for a single project or when the team interacts with several other teams across the organization. It is important to align the unit of work—for example; individual, small team, large group—with the unit that is being trained. Therefore, when small teams will be working together, they should be trained together; when large groups will be working together, they should train together; when individuals will be working alone, it may be best to train them as individuals.

Recall that in the last chapter, we reviewed three types of competencies for team members: Technical skills, task-related skills, and interpersonal skills. If a company has limited resources for training, it is far better to ensure that employees who will work together receive their technical training together. If that is not feasible, the training that they do undergo together should be directly connected to the work they will do together. Merely having workers undergo interpersonal skills training together that is largely divorced from the real work they will do together can undermine performance.

A reasonable counterargument may be that even if people do not train together (and therefore do not develop a TMS and underperform initially), after working together for a while, they will inevitably develop a TMS. However, it should be recalled that the key to effective learning in most situations is the receipt of timely and effective feedback, so that workers can best recalibrate how they are doing their work. With some notable exceptions, clear feedback is not necessarily forthcoming to all newly minted teams. In fact, core teams may be pulled together for a single project that might last for several months; ideally, they should do some training together at the outset so as to better prepare them for the work they will do together in the future.

Example of Training in Work Groups

As an illustration of the power of TMS to affect performance, simulated work groups were asked to assemble AM radios as part of a training experience (Moreland, Argote, & Krishnan, 1996). There were two ways in which the training was organized: (1) individually based training (as is common in many companies); and (2) group training, in which groups of three people worked together. In the training phase, all individuals and groups received identical information. Groups were not given any instructions in terms of how they should organize themselves. The *only* difference was whether people were trained alone or as part of a group.

Exactly 1 week later, the participants were asked to assemble the radios again. This was more difficult, because no written instructions were provided, as had been the case in the training phase. In this part of the investigation, everyone was placed into a three-person team, given the parts of the radio, and asked to assemble it from memory. This meant that some of the groups were composed of people who had trained individually and others were composed of people who had trained with a team. Thus, any difference in performance between the two types of groups would be attributable to the differences in training.

Not surprisingly, the groups that had trained together did dramatically better. They were more likely to successfully complete the assembly and did so with fewer errors. The intact groups performed better than did the ad hoc groups because they were able to tap into the TMS that had spontaneously developed during training.

TMS and an emphasis on team training are most relevant to tactical teams (i.e., teams that carry out a procedure) as opposed to creative or problem-solving teams. Thus, if a team is assembling radio parts, operating machinery in a coal mine, flying a jetliner, or doing heart surgery, it helps a lot for the members to have trained together on the job. However, as we saw in the last chapter, teams do more than perform routinized procedures; sometimes teams need to solve problems or create things. For example, consider a firm like Johnson and Johnson, dealing with a public relations nightmare: Someone has tampered with a bottle of Tylenol and people have died. Many things have to take place quickly, both to ensure the health and safety of customers as well as to preserve the company's image and reputation as a quality firm concerned with the well-being of its customers. Obviously, this team cannot take the time to train together, but it probably does help if the people on the emergency task force have worked together and have a sense of each other's competence in particular areas. (See Box 5-3 for a case analysis of training effectiveness.)

Recommendations for Team Development

What are the ways to maximize team performance through TMS? We present five fundamentals.

Work Planning   Teams whose members will work together should plan their work. Teams spend a disproportionate amount of their time together doing the task, rather than deciding how it should be done. Team tasks, unlike individual tasks, require coordination of effort and planning. There is a strong bias in teams to get down to work immediately and to get busy, if for no other reason than to signal to relevant organizational authorities that they are hard at work. Team members often wish they would have spent more time thinking about how they should do their work together before jumping into it.

Optimizing Human Resources   Teams should assess relevant areas of expertise among team members. Teams perform better when their members know who is good at what (Stasser et al., 1995). For example, when bank loan officers review the financial profiles of various companies and predict whether each company will go bankrupt, diversity in expertise and the ability of groups to recognize expertise lead to more accurate predictions (Libby, Trotman, & Zimmer, 1987). Unexpected problems can be solved more quickly and easily when members know who is good at what (Moreland & Levine, 1992). Such knowledge allows team members to match problems with the people most likely to solve them.

Anticipation in Addition to Reaction   Teams should learn to anticipate problems, not just react to them. They are better able to do this if they know one another's strengths and weaknesses.

BOX 5-3

Case Analysis of Different Types of Training Effectiveness

PRELIMINARY INVESTIGATION

At a certain factory that assembles radios, a consultant was called in to assess variations in performance. To create healthy within-company competition, workers were organized into self-managing teams. There were four such teams in the plant, but performance varied dramatically across the four teams. What was the problem?

The consultant began her investigation by asking for information about how the different teams were trained. She uncovered four distinct training programs used by each of the teams. Upon interviewing each team in the plant, she found that each team was convinced that its method was the best one. When the consultant confronted teams with the evidence pointing to clear differences in performance, the team pointed to a number of countervailing factors that could have affected their performance. The managers were particularly concerned because the company was about to hire and train four new plant teams and they did not know which method would be best. The consultant devised the following test using the radio assembly task previously described (based upon Liang, Moreland, & Argote, 1995). Everyone in the entire plant received identical technical training and ultimately performed in a three-person group. However, certain aspects of the training were systematically varied. The consultant tracked the following teams:

- **Red team:** Members of the red team were trained individually for 1 day.
- **Blue team:** Members of the blue team were given individual training for 1 day and then, the entire team participated in a 2-day team-building workshop, designed to improve cohesion and communication.

- **Yellow team:** Members of the yellow team were given group training for 1 day but were reassigned to different teams on the test day.
- **Green team:** Members of the green team were given group training for 1 day and remained in the same team on test day.

TEST DAY

On test day, the consultant wanted to capture the four key measures of team performance outlined in chapter 2. Whereas the hiring organization seemed primarily interested in productivity—as measured by number of units successfully completed—the consultant was also interested in assessing other signs of team performance, such as team satisfaction, individual growth, and organizational gains.

The consultant first asked each team to recall as much as they could about the training. In short, each team was asked to reconstruct the assembly instructions from memory. The consultant used this as a measure of organizational memory.

The consultant then asked each team to assemble the radios without the benefit of any kind of written instructions. Thus, each team was forced to rely on the training principles they had learned and (hopefully) remembered. Results were timed so that each team could be evaluated with respect to both efficiency and how accurately they met specifications.

Then, the consultant asked each team member to evaluate other team members in terms of their task expertise. This was a measure of the tendency to specialize in remembering distinct aspects of the task as well as who was regarded by all team members as having a certain, relevant skill. The consultant videotaped each team during the critical test phase and documented how smoothly members worked together in terms of the principles of coordination (discussed in chapter 2). Specifically, did members drop things unintentionally on the floor? Lose parts? Bump elbows? Have to repeat questions and directions? Question each others' expertise and knowledge? Or, alternatively, did the team work together seamlessly?

The tapes revealed the level of team motivation and also allowed the consultant to document things like how close members of the team sat to one another and the tone of their conversation. Finally, the consultant recorded the "we-to-I" ratio, or the number of times team members said "we" versus "I"—an implicit measure of team identity and cohesion. What do you think happened?

OUTCOME

The green team outperformed all of the other teams in terms of accuracy of completion.

DEBRIEFING WITH MANAGERS

One of the managers found it difficult to believe that team training received by the blue team in the area of cohesion and interpersonal skills did not make an appreciable difference. "We spend a lot of money every year trying to build trust and cohesion in our teams. Is this going to waste?" The consultant then shared the information in Figure 5-3.

The results in Figure 5-3 directly compare teams with a total of 6 weeks of working intensively with one another on cohesion-building (non-technical-skill building) tasks with teams who are virtual strangers, with the exception of having trained together. As you can see, the fewest number of errors were made by groups who trained with one another and then worked with one another; having special training in cohesion on top of that does not seem to matter much.

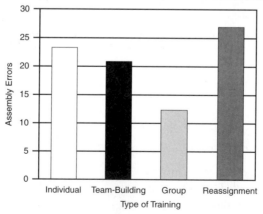

FIGURE 5-3   Effects of Various Training Methods on Assembly Errors

Adapted from: Moreland, R. L., Argote, L., & Krishnan, R. 1996. "Socially Shared Cognition at Work." In J. L. Nye & A. M. Brower (Eds.), In *What's Social about Social Cognition?* Thousand Oaks, CA: Sage. Reprinted with permission.

Teams That Will Work Together Should Train Together   Most organizations emphasize individual learning in their training programs. Participants in these programs work on their own, under the guidance of instructors, to learn how various tasks should be performed. The fact that they may later perform those tasks in teams is largely ignored. Some training programs include team activities, of course, but these often focus on general topics (Oddou, 1987; Silberman, 1990; Tetrault, Schriescheim, & Neider, 1988). Teams whose members work and train together perform better than teams whose members are equally skilled but do not train together (Littlepage, Robison, & Reddington, 1997). Team training increases performance by facilitating recognition and utilization of member expertise.

Some organizations train team members together; for example, General Motors, at its Saturn automobile manufacturing plant, or the U.S. Army unit personnel replacement system (Griffith, 1989). Airlines often provide team training for cockpit crews (Oberle, 1990). The importance of work group familiarity vis-à-vis training is hard to overestimate. For example, archival analysis of coal mine accidents and fatalities reveals that familiarity among team members is associated with fewer accidents among pairs of crew members working closely together (e.g., roof bolters and bolter helpers; Goodman & Garber, 1988). Although familiarity with the terrain has somewhat more impact than personnel similarity, the latter factor is clearly important, especially when teams work in less familiar terrain. Familiarity is associated with higher levels of crew productivity, even after labor, technology, and environment factors are taken into account (Goodman & Leyden, 1991).

Plan for Turnover   At some point, teams dissolve; a member leaves or is transferred and the team is left to find a replacement. Sometimes turnover is planned; other times it is unanticipated. Turnover can be a disruptive factor in teams, largely because newcomers and old-timers are unfamiliar with one another. However, much of the potential damage of turnover can be averted by strengthening team structure, such as assigning roles to members and prescribing work procedures (Devadas & Argote, 1995).

TEAM LONGEVITY: ROUTINIZATION VERSUS INNOVATION TRADE-OFFS

Teams whose members work together for longer periods of time are more likely to develop a TMS and will, therefore, be more productive. However, there is a countervailing force at work in teams that have been together for long periods of time; namely, routinization. That is, because a TMS is basically a set of expectations, certain working relationships may become entrenched over time. For example, Joe always handles the design aspects, so the team can (implicitly) trust him to ensure the product will look good; Sally always handles the technical aspects, so the team can trust that she will make sure the product works; and likewise for the channeling of information, and so on. This suggests that when delegation is optional (which a TMS does not ensure), and in a world in which the team's expectations about what is needed (e.g., consumer demand) are accurate, then more TMS should basically lead to more routinization of the task and, hence, to a more efficient channeling of efforts by team members (because there will be less coordination loss involved in figuring out each team member's role). Such expectations would seem to be best when there is little need for innovation. Thus, there is a precarious trade-off of sorts between *routinization* and *innovation.*

For much of the work that organizations do, routinization is a good thing; however, for a large part of what organizations do, innovation is desirable and necessary to meet the competitive challenges we outlined in chapter 1. Thus, a well-defined TMS could hinder the team's ability to be adaptive.

For these reasons, there may be significant problems associated with extended team longevity. As a case in point, let's examine an R&D facility of a large American corporation (Katz, 1982). The division, which included 345 engineers and scientific professionals, was geographically isolated from the rest of the organization. Katz examined 50 project groups in this division that varied greatly in terms of their longevity—that is, how long members of one group had worked with one another.

To keep informed about relevant developments outside the organization as well as new requirements within the organization, project groups must collect and process information from a variety of outside sources. The preferred means for obtaining such information for engineering professionals is interpersonal communication, rather than technical reports, publications, or other written documentation.

Therefore, for a period of 15 weeks, professionals kept records of their work-related communication; any time that a group member consulted or spoke with others, whether at the water cooler or in the parking lot, this was recorded.

As a final step, the department managers (a total of seven) and the two lab directors evaluated the performance of each project produced by each group with which they were technically familiar. Criteria that the managers considered included schedule, budget and cost performance, innovation, adaptability, and ability to cooperate. A consultant then computed a correlation between the longevity of teams and their performance. The results were startling.

As may be seen in Figure 5-4, the performance of these groups increased as they gained longevity, but only up to a point. After 5 years of working together, team project performance declined steeply, as well as intraproject communication, organizational communication, and external professional communication—basically all the types of communication that serve to bring fresh ideas to the group.

Four behavioral changes took place in groups that worked together for over 5 years:

- **Behavioral stability:** Project members interacting over a long time develop standard work patterns that are familiar and comfortable. This can happen very rapidly—for instance, the way people in a group tend to sit in the same places in meeting after meeting, even when there may be no logical reason for doing so. Over time, this behavioral stability leads to isolation from the outside. The group can grow increasingly complacent, ceasing to question the practices that shape their behavior.
- **Selective exposure:** There is a tendency for group members to communicate only with people whose ideas agree with their own. It is related to the homogeneity bias—the tendency to select new members who are like members in the existing group. Over time, project members learn to interact selectively to avoid messages and information that conflict with their established practices and disposition.
- **Group homogeneity:** Groups that are separated from the influence of others in the organization develop a homogeneous set of understandings about the group

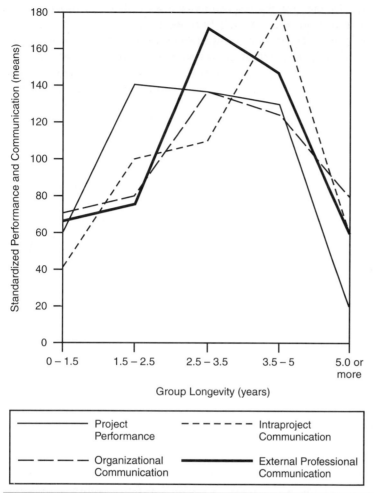

FIGURE 5-4 Group Longevity

Source: Katz, R. 1982. "The Effects of Group Longevity on Project Communication and Performance." *Administrative Science Quarterly, 27,* 81–104.

and its environment. The members of the group act as reinforcing agents for behaviors and practices of the group.

- **Role differentiation:** As we have seen in the analysis of the TMS groups, as groups work and train together, they become increasingly specialized in project competencies and roles. This results in greater role differentiation, which in turn results in less interaction among group members because the roles and expectations held by each are so well instantiated. Consequently, they lose access to much of the internal talent, and their ability to learn new ideas from one another is diminished.

Thus, in terms of actual task performance, as team longevity increases, certain social processes conspire to lower levels of project communication, which in turn decrease project performance. Project groups become increasingly isolated from key information sources both within and outside their organizations with increasing stability in their membership. Reductions in project communication adversely affect the technical performance of project groups. Variations in communication activities are more associated with the tenure composition of the project group than with the project tenures of the individual engineers. Stated another way, it is not the age of the employee that is of critical importance, but the age of the team. Furthermore, individual competence does not account for differences in performance. Thus, it is not the case that the older, less skilled members were working in teams that were of greater longevity. Furthermore, the longevity of project groups does not appear to be part of the mental models of the managers—virtually no one was aware of the tenure demographics of their project groups.

What does all of this mean for team longevity? A certain amount of familiarity is necessary for teams to work together in a productive fashion. The effect of working together tends to make team members grow more familiar with each other's relevant knowledge base and, hence, TMS can develop. TMS can be helpful in tasks where coordination losses need to be reduced and tactical precision is key. Although a certain amount of routinization is desirable in any team, the overly routinized team hinders communication and obstructs innovation. Unfortunately, we don't have a precise answer as to how long teams should work together on a particular task; it simply depends too much on the nature of the task and the membership of the team.

Looking at this question from a team design standpoint might offer some insights. It may be desirable, for example, to design some teams whose primary objective is to act as innovation experts for the creation and transfer of the organization's best practices.

CONCLUSIONS

When we revisit the team failures described in the opening of this chapter, it is clear that for teams to be effective in their work, they need to have a shared knowledge base. The knowledge base allows teams to more efficiently process and encode relevant information and then act upon it in a thoughtful and appropriate fashion. However, the shared knowledge base that governs a team is only as adequate as the team communication system. Communication among team members is a collaborative effort. Natural biases in communication can play havoc for effective teamwork, as it did in the *Vincennes* decision, the Avianca Airlines crash, and the Martin Marietta satellite deployment. In all three incidents, teams were operating within a faulty communication system. The answer in each of these cases is not to fault a particular team player, but rather to critically inspect the communication system. It is the responsibility of team leaders to ensure that successful communication occurs among team members. The development of accurate team mental models and transactive memory systems (TMS) can partially combat the threat of the common information effect and hidden profiles.

CHAPTER 6

Team Decision Making: Conformity, Pitfalls, and Solutions

"I ... grabbed the photographic evidence showing the hot gas blow-by comparisons from previous flights and placed it on the table in view of the managers and somewhat angered, admonished them to look at the photos and not ignore what they were telling us; namely, that low temperature indeed caused significantly more hot gas blow-by to occur in the joints. I received cold stares ... with looks as if to say, 'Go away and don't bother us with the facts.' No one in management wanted to discuss the facts; they just would not respond verbally to ... me. I felt totally helpless at that moment and that further argument was fruitless, so I, too, stopped pressing my case" (Boisjoly, 1987, p. 7).

We all know that decisions made by committees can be of the worst caliber. It might seem, because the downside potential is so great, that team decisions are not worth the risk. However, good team decisions can be outstanding—far better than those attainable by any individual. The key, of course, is doing it right, and doing it right is the topic of this chapter.

The space shuttle *Challenger* disaster may have resulted, in part, from a poor team decision process. The opening quote from Roger Boisjoly, an engineer who tried to halt the flight in 1986, led the Presidential Commission to conclude that the disaster was, indeed, the result of a "flawed decision-making process."[1] Another example from the business world is the American Medical Association's decision to allow Sunbeam to use the AMA name as a product endorsement. Because bad team decisions can have disastrous consequences, it is important to understand the particular kinds of faults that lead to faulty decision making, specifically in teams.

DECISION MAKING IN TEAMS

Decision making is an integrated sequence of activities that includes gathering, interpreting, and exchanging information; creating and identifying alternative courses of action; choosing among alternatives by integrating the often differing perspectives and opinions of team members; and implementing a choice and monitoring its consequences (Guzzo, Salas, & Associates, 1995). Decision making is a key activity that teams must do, no matter what their governance structure—self-managing, manager-led, or self-directing. This is true for tactical, problem-solving, and creative teams. In teams, information is often distributed unequally among members and must be integrated, and

---

[1]Committee on Science and Technology, House of Representatives, House Report 99-1016, "Investigation of the Challenger Accident," October 29, 1986.

the integration process may be complicated by uncertainty, status differences among members, failure of members to appreciate the significance of the information they hold or of the information not held by others, and so on.

This chapter focuses on four decision-making pitfalls that teams often encounter. For each, we describe the problem and then provide preventative measures. The first problem that we focus on is groupthink, the tendency to conform to the consensus viewpoint in group decision making. We then discuss escalation of commitment and the Abilene paradox. Finally, we discuss group polarization.

The quality of group decision making is impacted by conformity, and conformity can lead to any of the four main pitfalls of group decision making. We begin the chapter with an analysis of conformity and then discuss the four main group decision-making pitfalls.

CONFORMITY: WHY IT OCCURS AND HOW IT WORKS IN TEAMS

Suppose that you are meeting with your team. The question facing your team is a simple one: Which of the three lines in panel 2 is equal in length to the line in panel 1? (See Figure 6-1.)

The team leader seeks a group consensus. She begins by asking the colleague sitting to your left for his opinion. To your shock, your colleague chooses line 1; then, each of the other four team members selects line 1—even though line 2 is clearly correct. You begin to wonder whether you are losing your mind. Finally, it's your turn to decide. What do you do?

Most people who read this example find it nearly impossible to imagine that they would choose line 1, even if everyone else had. Yet 76 percent make an erroneous, conforming judgment (e.g., choose line 1) on at least one question; on average, people conform one-third of the time when others give the obviously incorrect answer (Asch, 1956).

The line experiment is a dramatic illustration of the power of conformity pressure. **Conformity** occurs when people bring their behavior into alignment with a group's expectations and beliefs. In this example, the people who give the wrong answer know that the answer is wrong; nevertheless, they feel compelled to provide an answer that will be acceptable to the group.

Although many people think their beliefs and behavior are based on their own free will, social behavior is strongly influenced by others. Why do people conform? There are two main reasons: They want to do the "right" thing and they want to be liked.

The Need to Be Right

Groups are presumed to have access to a broader range of decision-making resources and, hence, to be better equipped to make high-quality decisions than any person can alone. By pooling their different backgrounds, training, and experience, group members have at least the potential for working in a more informed fashion than would be the case were the decision left to any single individual. The implication of these two assertions is that individuals are **information dependent**—that is, they often lack information that another member has. Consequently, individuals look to the team to provide infor-

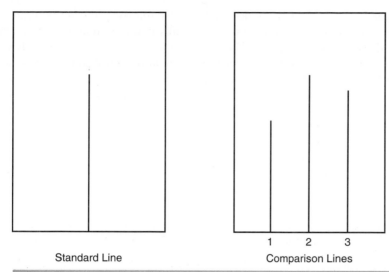

Standard Line   Comparison Lines

FIGURE 6-1 Conformity Pressure

Source: Adapted from Asch, S. E. 1956. "Studies of Independence and Conformity: A Minority of One against a Unanimous Majority." *Psychological Monographs, 70* (9, Whole No. 416).

mation that they do not know. On the one hand, this is an adaptive response. However, it can lead to problems when people treat others' opinions as facts and fail to question their validity. The need to be right, therefore, is the tendency to look to the group to define what reality is—and the more people who hold a particular opinion, the more right an answer appears to be. Whereas this information-seeking tendency would seem to be contradictory to the common information effect that we discussed in the previous chapter, the two processes are not inconsistent. The common information effect (and all of its undesirable consequences) are driven by a biased search for information. Conformity, or the adoption of group-level beliefs, is strongest when individuals feel unsure about their own position.

The Need to Be Liked

Most people have a fundamental need to be accepted and approved of by others. Conformity is often a ticket to group acceptance. There is good reason for this: Teams provide valuable resources. One of the most straightforward ways to gain immediate acceptance in a group is to express attitudes consistent with those of the group members. Stated another way, most people like others who conform to their own beliefs. This means that people in groups will become more extreme in the direction of the group's general opinion, because attitudes that are sympathetic toward the group are most likely to be positively rewarded. The need to be liked refers to the tendency for people to agree with a group so that they can feel more like a part of that group.

Conformity is greater when the judgment or opinion issue is difficult and when people are uncertain. People are especially likely to conform if they face an otherwise unanimous group consensus (Asch, 1956; Wilder & Allen, 1977). Conformity is greater when people value and admire their team—rejection from a desirable group is very threatening (Back, 1951). However, we do not want to paint the picture that managers lack integrity. People are more willing to take a stand when they feel confident about their expertise, have high social status (Harvey & Consalvi, 1960), are strongly committed to their initial view (Deutsch & Gerard, 1955), and do not like or respect the people trying to influence them (Hogg & Turner, 1987).

Coupled with the need to be liked is the desire not to be ostracized from one's team. There is good reason for concern, because individuals who deviate from their team's opinion are more harshly evaluated than are those who conform (Levine, 1989). A group may reject a deviant person even when they are not under pressure to reach complete consensus (Miller, Jackson, Mueller, & Schersching, 1987). Apparently, holding a different opinion is enough to trigger dislike even when it does not directly block the group's goals. For this reason, people are more likely to conform to the majority when they respond publicly (e.g., Deutsch & Gerard, 1955), anticipate future interaction with other group members (e.g., Lewis, Langan, & Hollander, 1972), are less confident (Allen, 1965), find the question under consideration to be ambiguous or difficult (Tajfel, 1978), and are interdependent concerning rewards (e.g., Deutsch & Gerard, 1955).

Most managers dramatically underestimate the conformity pressures that operate in groups. Perhaps this is because people like to think of themselves as individualists who are not afraid to speak their own minds. However, conformity pressures in groups are real and they affect the quality of team decision making. The key message for the manager is to anticipate conformity pressures in groups, to understand what drives it (i.e., the need to be liked and the desire to be right), and then to put into place group structures that will not allow conformity pressures to endanger the quality of group decision making. This leads us to the first of the decision-making problems that teams may encounter.

DECISION-MAKING PITFALL 1: GROUPTHINK

Groupthink occurs when team members place consensus above all other priorities—including using good judgment when the consensus reflects poor judgment, improper or immoral actions, and so on. Groupthink, at its core, involves a deterioration of mental efficiency, reality testing, and moral judgments as a result of group pressures toward conformity of opinion. For a list of groupthink decisions in the political and corporate world, see Box 6-1. The desire to agree can become so dominant that it can override the realistic appraisal of alternative courses of action (Janis, 1972, 1982). The reasons for groupthink may range from group pressures to conform to a sincere desire to incorporate and reflect the views of all team members. Such pressure may also come from management if the directive is to reach a decision that all can agree to, such as in cross-functional teams.

Conformity pressures can lead decision makers to censor their misgivings, ignore outside information, feel too confident, and adopt an attitude of invulnerability. The pressure for unanimity is thought to be a recipe for ineffective group decision making and explains how a group of otherwise intelligent and thoughtful people can make serious miscalculations that result in disastrous outcomes.

Symptoms of groupthink cannot be easily assessed by outside observers. Rather, most groupthink symptoms represent private feelings or beliefs held by group members or behaviors performed in private. There are three key symptoms of groupthink that take root and blossom in groups that succumb to pressures of reaching unanimity:

BOX 6-1

Instances of Groupthink in Politics and the Corporate World

EXAMPLES FROM POLITICS

- Neville Chamberlain's inner circle, whose members supported the policy of appeasement of Hitler during 1937 and 1938, despite repeated warnings and events that indicated it would have adverse consequences (Janis & Mann, 1977).

- President Truman's advisory group, whose members supported the decision to escalate the war in North Korea, despite firm warnings by the Chinese Communist government that U.S. entry into North Korea would be met with armed resistance from the Chinese (Janis & Mann, 1977).

- President Kennedy's inner circle, whose members supported the decision to launch the Bay of Pigs invasion of Cuba, despite the availability of information indicating that it would be an unsuccessful venture and would damage U.S. relations with other countries (Janis & Mann, 1977).

- President Johnson's close advisors, who supported the decision to escalate the war in Vietnam, despite intelligence reports and information indicating that this course of action would not defeat the Viet Cong or the North Vietnamese, and would generate unfavorable political consequences within the United States (Janis & Mann, 1977).

- The decision of the Reagan administration to exchange arms for hostages with Iran and to continue commitment to the Nicaraguan Contras in the face of several congressional amendments limiting or banning aid.

EXAMPLES FROM THE CORPORATE WORLD

- Gruenenthal Chemie's decision to market the drug thalidomide (Raven & Rubin, 1976).

- The price-fixing conspiracy involving the electrical manufacturing industry during the 1950s.

- The decision by Ford Motor Company to produce the Edsel (Huseman & Driver, 1979).

- The selling of millions of jars of "phony" apple juice by Beech-Nut, the second largest baby food producer in the United States.

- The involvement of E. F. Hutton in "check kiting," wherein a money manager at a Hutton branch office would write a check on an account in Bank A for more money than Hutton had in the account. Because of the time lag in the check-collection system, these overdrafts sometimes went undetected, and Hutton could deposit funds to cover the overdraft in the following day. The deposited money would start earning interest immediately. The scheme allowed Hutton to earn a day's interest on Bank A's account without having to pay anything for it—resulting in $250 million in free loans every day (*ABA Banking Journal*, 1985; Goleman, 1988).

- The illegal purchases by Salomon Brothers at U.S. Treasury auctions in the early 1990s (Sims, 1992).

- **Overestimation of the group:** Members of the group regard themselves as invulnerable and, at the same time, morally correct. This lethal combination can lead decision makers to believe they are above, and exempt from, standards.
- **Close-mindedness:** Members of the group engage in collective rationalization, often accompanied by stereotyping out-group members, a topic we discuss further in part III.
- **Pressures toward uniformity:** There is a strong intolerance in a groupthink situation for diversity of opinion. Dissenters are subject to enormous social pressure. This often leads group members to suppress their reservations. Thus, the group perceives itself to be unanimous.

Deficits arising from groupthink can lead to many shortcomings in the decision-making process. Consider, for example, the following lapses that often accompany groupthink:

- Incomplete survey of alternatives
- Incomplete survey of objectives
- Failure to reexamine alternatives
- Failure to examine preferred choices
- Selection bias
- Poor information search
- Failure to create contingency plans

Each of these behaviors thwarts the rational decision-making process we outlined at the beginning of this chapter.

Learning from History

Consider two decisions made by the same United States presidential cabinet—the Kennedy administration. The Kennedy cabinet was responsible for the Bay of Pigs operation and the Cuban Missile Crisis. The Bay of Pigs was a military operation concocted by the United States in an attempt to overthrow Fidel Castro, the leader of Cuba. The Bay of Pigs is often seen as one of the worst foreign policy mistakes in U.S. history. The operation was regarded as a disaster of epic proportions, resulting in the loss of lives and the disruption of foreign policy. It is also a kind of puzzle because the invasion, in retrospect, seems to have been so poorly planned and so poorly implemented—yet it was led by people whose individual talents seemed to make them eminently qualified to carry out an operation of this sort. What led capable people who should have known better to proceed with such a disastrous plan? In contrast, Kennedy's response to the Cuban Missile Crisis was regarded as a great foreign policy success. These examples, from the same organizational context and team, make an important point: Even smart and highly motivated people can make disastrous decisions under certain conditions. Kennedy's cabinet fell prey to groupthink in the Bay of Pigs decision, but not in the Cuban Missile Crisis. Why was the same cabinet so successful in one instance, but such a miserable failure in another?

A number of detailed historical analyses have been performed (Kramer, 1999; Peterson, Owens, Tetlock, Fan, & Martorana, 1998) comparing these two historical examples, as well as several others. Some sharp differences distinguish between groupthink and effective groups.

TABLE 6-1   Precipitating and Preventative Conditions for the Development of Groupthink

Conditions	Leader Behavior and Cognition	Team Behavior and Cognition
Precipitous conditions *(likely to lead to group-think)*	• Narrow, defective appraisal of options • Analysis of options in terms of political repercussions • Concern about image and reputation • Loss-avoidance strategy	• Rigidity • Conformity • View roles in political terms (protecting political capital and status) • Large team size • High sense of collective efficacy • Perceived threat to social identity
Preventative conditions *(likely to engender effective decision making)*	• Being explicit and direct about policy preferences allows the team to know immediately where the leader stands	• Task orientation • Intellectual flexibility • Less consciousness of crisis • Less pessimism • Less corruption (i.e., more concerned with observing correct rules and procedures) • Less centralization • Openness and candidness • Adjustment to failing policies in timely fashion • Genuine commitment to solving problems • Encouraging dissent • Acting decisively in emergencies • Attuned to changes in environment • Focus on shared goals • Realization that trade-offs are necessary • Ability to improvise solutions to unexpected events
Inconclusive conditions *(unlikely to make much of a difference)*	• Strong, opinionated leadership	• Risk taking • Cohesion • Internal debate

Table 6-1 summarizes three kinds of critical evidence: (1) factors that may lead to groupthink; (2) factors that may promote sound decision making; and (3) factors that do not seem to induce groupthink. We focus on two types of behavior: That of the leader and that of the rest of the group.

A number of factors may lead to groupthink. Leader behavior that is associated with too much concern for political ramifications, or the analysis of alternatives in terms of their political repercussions, is a key determinant of groupthink. The same is also true for group behavior; when groups are overly concerned with their political image, they may not make sound decisions.

In terms of preventative conditions, the behavior of the team has a greater impact on the development of groupthink than does leader behavior. Sound group decision making can be achieved through task orientation, flexibility, less centralization, norms of openness, encouraging dissent, focus on shared goals, and realizing that trade-offs are necessary.

How to Avoid Groupthink

In this section, we identify some specific steps managers can take to prevent groupthink. Prevention is predicated on two broad goals: The stimulation of constructive, intellectual conflict and the reduction of concerns about how the group is viewed by others—a kind of conformity pressure. We focus primarily on team design factors because those are the ones managers have the greatest control over. None of these can guarantee success, but they can be effective in encouraging vigilant decision making.

Monitor Team Size

Team size is positively correlated with groupthink, with larger teams more likely to fall prey to groupthink (McCauley, 1998). People grow more intimidated and hesitant as team size increases. This is related to the principle of performance anxiety, which we discussed in chapter 2. There is no magic number for team size, but with teams larger than 10, individual members may feel less personal responsibility for team outcomes and their behaviors may be too risky.

Get Buy-In from Organizational Authorities

Teams whose members are preoccupied with their political image are less effective than are teams whose members do not get caught up in their self-image. This should not be construed to mean that teams should be completely oblivious to organizational issues. It is obvious that teams, like individuals, are sensitive to how they are viewed by the organization and relevant organizational authorities. When teams believe that their decisions are important to organizational authorities, they are more likely to make sound decisions than if they believe that their decisions are unimportant (Thompson, Kray, & Lind, 1998).

Provide a Face-Saving Mechanism for Teams

A small team who has the respect and support of their organization would seem to be in an ideal position to make effective decisions. Yet often, they fail to do so. One reason is that they are concerned with how their decision, and its fallout, will be viewed by others. Many teams are afraid of being blamed for poor decisions—even decisions for which it would have been impossible to predict the outcome. Often, face-saving concerns keep people from changing course, even when the current course is clearly doubtful. For this reason, it can be useful to provide teams with a face-saving mechanism or a reason for why outcomes might appear to be poor. This basically amounts to giving teams an external attribution for poor performance. Indeed, teams that are given an excuse for poor performance before knowing the outcome of their decision are less likely to succumb to groupthink than teams that do not have an excuse (Turner, Probasco, Pratkanis, & Leve, 1992).

The Risk Technique

The risk technique is a structured discussion situation designed to reduce group members' fears about making decisions (Maier, 1952). The discussion is structured so that team members talk about the dangers or risks involved in a decision and delay discussion of any potential gains. Following this is a discussion of controls or mechanisms for dealing with the risks or dangers. This strategy may sound touchy-feely, but it basically amounts to creating an atmosphere in which team members can express doubts and raise criticisms without fear of rejection or hostility from the team. There are many ways to create such an atmosphere. One way is to have a facilitator play the role of devil's advocate for a particular decision. The mere expression of doubt about an idea or plan by one person may liberate others to raise doubts and concerns. A second method may be to have members privately convey their concerns or doubts and then post this information in an unidentifiable manner. Again, this liberates members to talk about their doubts.

Adopt Different Perspectives

In this technique, team members assume the perspective of other constituencies with a stake in the decision (Turner & Pratkanis, 1998). For example, in the *Challenger* incident, group members might have been asked to assume the roles of the federal government, local citizens, space crew families, astronomers, and so on. Although the *Challenger* disaster happened in large part because of a disastrously poor understanding of how to interpret statistical data, the key point of adopting different perspectives is to create a mechanism that will instigate thinking more carefully about problems, which could prompt these groups to reconsider evidence.

Debias Training Techniques

The goal of debiasing training techniques is to expose how human decision making can be faulty and based on limited information. For this reason, it is often helpful to have a decision expert work with a team and elaborate upon key decision biases, ideally through simulations and exercises. It is usually unhelpful to simply inform teams about biases, because they appear to be absurdly obvious after the fact. Rather, it is best to actively challenge teams with a realistic decision scenario and then use the team context to discuss the process of decision making and methods for improving its quality.

Structure Discussion Principles

The goal of structured discussion principles is to delay solution selection and to increase the problem-solving phase. This prevents premature closure on a solution and extends problem analysis and evaluation. For example, teams may be given guidelines that emphasize continued solicitations of solutions, protection of individuals from criticism, keeping the discussion problem-centered, and listing all solutions before evaluating them (Maier, 1952).

Establish Procedures for Protecting Alternative Viewpoints

Although teams can generate high-quality decision alternatives, they frequently fail to adopt them as preferred solutions (Janis, 1982; Turner et al., 1992). This means that most problems that teams face are not simple, "eureka" types of decisions, in which the correct answer is obvious once it is put on the table. Rather, team members must convince others about the correctness of their views. This is a difficult task when things like conformity pressure are operating and especially after individual team members have publicly committed to a particular course of action. For these reasons, it can be useful to instruct members to keep a log of all alternatives suggested during each meeting.

Second Solution

This technique requires teams to identify a second solution or decision recommendation as an alternative to their first choice. This enhances the problem-solving and idea generation phases as well as performance quality (Hoffman & Maier, 1966).

Beware of Time Pressure

Decisions involve idealistic considerations, such as moral principles and ideals, as well as practical considerations, such as difficulty, cost, or situational pressures. Therefore, it is undeniable that decision makers often make trade-offs. Moral principles are more likely to guide decisions for the distant future than for the immediate future, whereas difficulty, cost, and situational pressures are more likely to be important in near future decisions. In other words, managers are more likely to compromise their principles in decisions regarding near future actions compared with distant future actions (Liberman & Trope, 1998).

DECISION-MAKING PITFALL 2: ESCALATION OF COMMITMENT

It would seem that one remedy for groupthink would be clear feedback as to the effectiveness of the decision-making process. For example, the Coca-Cola Company's decision to introduce New Coke was eventually recognized as a mistake and reversed. Do such clear failures prompt teams to revisit their decision-making process and improve upon it? Not necessarily. In fact, under some conditions, teams will persist with a losing course of action, even in the face of clear evidence to the contrary. This type of situation is known as the **escalation of commitment** phenomenon.

Consider the decision-making problem in Box 6-2.

BOX 6-2

New-Product Investment Decision

As the president of an airline company, you have invested $10 million of the company's money into a research project. The purpose was to build a plane that would not be detected by conventional radar, in other words, a radar-blank plane. When the project is 90 percent completed, another firm begins marketing a plane that cannot be detected by radar. Also, it is apparent that their plane is much faster and far more economical than the plan your company is building. The question is: Should you invest the last 10 percent of the research funds to finish your radar-blank plane?

☐ Yes, invest the money.

☐ No, drop the project.

Next, consider the following decision situations.

- A senior marketing manager at a major pet food corporation continues to promote a specific brand, despite clear evidence that the brand is losing market share to its competitors.
- A company continues to invest in a manager who is known to have handled many situations poorly and receives consistently subpar 360-degree evaluations.
- Quaker Oats continued to push Snapple, even though its market share dropped staggeringly.
- When the stock market tide is running, wildly enthusiastic investors will bid up companies' stock prices to levels known to be too high, in the certainty that they can "only go up." Two years later, they dump these companies at any price, believing with equal certainty that they are becoming worthless (Train, 1995).
- A company continues to drill for oil, despite being unable to turn a profit on drilling efforts in the past 3 years.
- John R. Silber, previous president of Boston University, decided to invest in Seragen, a biotechnology company with a promising cancer drug. After investing $1.7 million over 6 years, the value is now $43,000 (Barboza, 1998).

In all of these situations, individuals and teams committed further resources to what eventually proved to be a failing course of action. The decision bias known as the escalation of commitment. In most cases, the situation does not turn into a problem for a while. The situation becomes an escalation dilemma when the persons involved in the decision would make a different decision if they had not been involved up until that point, or when other objective persons would not choose that course of action. Often, in escalation situations, a decision is made to commit further resources to "turn the situation around." This process may repeat and escalate several times as additional resources are invested. The bigger the investment and the more severe the possible loss, the more prone people are to try to turn things around. Consider the situation faced by Lyndon Johnson during the early stage of the Vietnam War. Johnson received the following memo from George Ball, then undersecretary of state:

> The decision you face now is crucial. Once large numbers of U.S. troops are committed to direct combat, they will begin to take heavy casualties in a war they are ill-equipped to fight in a noncooperative if not downright hostile countryside. Once we suffer large casualties, we will have started a well-nigh irreversible process. Our involvement will be so great that we cannot—without national humiliation—stop short of achieving our complete objectives. Of the two possibilities I think humiliation will be more likely than the achievement of our objectives—even after we have paid terrible costs. (Sheehan et al., 1971, p. 450).

The escalation of commitment process is illustrated in Figure 6-2. In the first stage of the escalation of commitment, a decision-making team is confronted with questionable or negative outcomes (e.g., a price drop, decreasing market share, poor performance evaluations, or a malfunction). This external event prompts a reexamination of the team's current course of action, in which the utility of continuing is weighed against the utility of withdrawing or changing course. This decision determines the team's commitment to its current course of action. If this commitment is low, the team may withdraw from the project and assume its losses. If this commitment is high, however, the

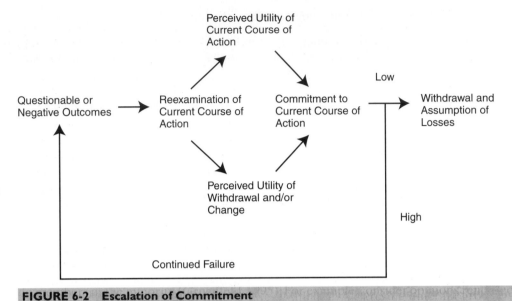

FIGURE 6-2 Escalation of Commitment

Source: Adapted from Ross, J., & Staw, B. M. 1993, August. "Organizational Escalation and Exit: Lessons from the Shoreham Nuclear Power Plant." *Academy of Management Journal,* 701–732.

team will continue commitment and continue to cycle through the decision stages. There are four key processes involved in the escalation of commitment cycle: Project-related determinants, psychological determinants, social determinants, and structural determinants (Ross & Staw, 1993).

Project Determinants

Project determinants are the objective features of the situation. Upon receiving negative feedback, team members ask whether the perceived setback is permanent or temporary (e.g., is reduced market share a meaningful trend or a simple perturbation in a noisy system?). If it is perceived to be temporary, there may appear to be little reason to reverse course. Then, when addressing questions like whether to increase investment in the project or to commit more time and energy to it, the team is essentially asking whether it wishes to escalate its commitment. Of course, this may often be the right choice, but it should be clear that such decisions also make it harder for the team to terminate that course of action if results continue to be poor.

Psychological Determinants

Psychological determinants refer to the cognitive and motivational factors that propel people to continue with a chosen course of action. When managers or teams receive indication that the outcomes of a project may be negative, they should ask themselves the following questions regarding their own involvement in the process:

What Are the Personal Rewards for Me in This Project?

In many cases, the *process* of the project itself, rather than the *outcome* of the project, becomes the reason for continuing the project. This leads to a self-perpetuating reinforcement trap, wherein the rewards for continuing are not aligned with the actual objectives of the project. Ironically, people who have high, rather than low, self-esteem are more likely to become victimized by psychological forces—people with high self-esteem have much more invested in their ego and its maintenance than do those with low self-esteem.

This advice may seem rather odd because it appears to be inconsistent with self-interest. That is, it would seem to be in a project manager's best interest to invest in the product, rather than to benefit the company as a whole. However, managers or teams who fall prey to escalation of commitment will ultimately end up losing because their product won't be successful, and they will have suffered more than if they simply cut off the project earlier on.

Is My Ego and the Team's Reputation on the Line?

"If I pull out of this project, would I feel stupid? Do I worry that other people would judge me to be stupid?" Ego protection often becomes a higher priority than the success of the project. When managers feel personally responsible for a decision, monetary allocations to the project increase at a much higher rate than when managers do not feel responsible for the initial decision (Staw, 1976).

In some sense, it does not seem too surprising that when managers personally oversee a project, they attempt to ensure that the project has every chance of success (e.g., by allocating more resources to it). After all, that is their job. A manager who works on a project through from beginning to end is going to know more about it and may be in a better position to judge it. Furthermore, personal commitment is essential for the success of many projects. Whereas it is certainly good to nurture projects so that they have their best chance of survival, it is nearly impossible for most managers to be completely objective about it. This is where it is important to have clear, unbiased criteria by which to evaluate the success of a project.

Are We Evaluating All of the Facts in an Unbiased Fashion?

The confirmation bias is the tendency for people to only see what they already believe to be true. When people are ego-invested in a project, the confirmation bias will even be stronger. It is striking how even upon the receipt of what appears to be unsupportive data, people who have fallen prey to the confirmation bias will maintain, and in some cases increase, their resolve. For example, the confirmation bias is related to the costly protraction of strike activity—a form of escalation of commitment. As a quick demonstration of the confirmation bias, take the test in Box 6-3.

Is the Glass Half-Empty or Half-Full?

If decision makers see themselves as trying to recover from a losing position, chances are they will engage in greater risk than if they see themselves as starting with a clean slate. Like the gambler in Las Vegas, decision makers who wait for their luck to turn around have fallen into the trap. For these reasons, decision makers who were initially responsible for the decision are likely to feel more compelled to continue to pursue the same course of action as compared to the successors of such managers. Escalation of commitment is partially responsible for some of the worst financial losses experienced by organizations. For example, from 1966 to 1989, the Long Island Lighting Company's investment in the

---

BOX 6-3

Card Test

Imagine that the following four cards are placed in front of you and are printed with the following symbols on one side:

Card 1	Card 2	Card 3	Card 4
E	K	4	7

Now, imagine you are told that a letter appears on one side of each card and a number on the other. Your task is to judge the validity of the following rule, which refers only to these four cards: "If a card has a vowel on one side, then it has an even number on the other side." Your task is to turn over only those cards that have to be turned over for the correctness of the rule to be judged. Which cards do you want to turn over? *(Stop here and decide which cards to turn over before reading on.)*

Averaging over a large number of investigations (Oaksford & Chater, 1994), 89 percent of people select E, which is a logically correct choice because an odd number on the other side would disconfirm the rule. However, 62 percent also choose to turn over the 4, which is not logically informative because neither a vowel nor a consonant on the other side would falsify the rule. Only 25 percent of people elect to turn over the 7, which is a logically informative choice because a vowel behind the 7 would falsify the rule. Only 16 percent elect to turn over K, which would not be an informative choice.

Thus, people display two types of logical errors in the task. First, they often turn over the 4, an example of the confirmation bias. However, even more striking is the failure to take the step of attempting to disconfirm what they believe is true—in other words, turning over the 7 (Wason & Johnson-Laird, 1972).

Shoreham Nuclear Power Plant escalated from $65 million to $5 billion, despite a steady flow of negative feedback. The plant was never opened (Ross & Staw, 1993).

Social Determinants

Most people want others to approve of them, accept them, and respect them. Consequently, they engage in actions and behaviors that they think will please most of the people most of the time, perhaps at the expense of doing the right thing, which may not be popular.

The need for approval and liking may be especially heightened among groups composed of friends. Indeed, groups of longtime friends are more likely to continue to invest in a losing course of action (41 percent) than groups composed of unacquainted persons (16 percent) when groups do not have buy-in from relevant organizational authorities. In contrast, when they are respected by their organization, groups of friends are extremely deft at extracting themselves from failing courses of action (Lind, Kray, & Thompson, 1998).

Structural Determinants

The same determinants that create groupthink on a team level also exist at the level of the institution. For instance, a project can itself become institutionalized, thereby removing it from critical evaluation. Instead, old-timers and newcomers learn to perceive the project as an integral part of the culture. It becomes impossible for these teams to consider removal or extinction of the project.

Often in organizations, political pressure can kill an otherwise viable project. Similarly, political support can keep a project alive that should be terminated. The escalation of commitment phenomenon implies that more often than not, teams will persevere with a losing course of action because of the psychological, social, and structural reinforcements in the situation. Teams become entrenched and committed to their positions and reluctant to move away from them.

Avoiding the Escalation of Commitment Problem

Most teams do not realize that they are in an escalation dilemma until it is too late. Complicating matters is the fact that, in most escalation dilemmas, the team might have some early "wins" or good signs that reinforce the initial decision. How can a team best get out of an escalation dilemma?

Unfortunately, there is no magical, overnight cure. The best advice is to adopt a policy of risk management: Be aware of the risks involved in the decision; learn how to best manage these risks; and set limits, effectively capping losses at a tolerable level. It is also important to find ways to get information and feedback on the project from a different perspective. More specifically:

Set Limits

Ideally, a team should determine at the outset what criteria and performance standards will be necessary to continue to invest in the project or program in question. These should be spelled out and distributed to all relevant personnel.

Avoid the Bystander Effect

In many situations, especially ambiguous ones, people quite frankly are not sure how to behave and, therefore, do nothing out of fear of acting foolishly. This dynamic explains the bystander effect, or the tendency to not help others who obviously need help in emergency situations (Latané & Darley, 1970). If team members have well-defined, predetermined limits, they need not try to interpret others' behavior; they can refer to their own judgment and act upon it.

Avoid Tunnel Vision

Get several perspectives on the problem. Ask people who are not personally involved in the situation for their appraisal. Be careful not to bias their evaluation with your own views, hopes, expectations, or other details, such as the cost of extricating the team from the situation, because that will only predispose them toward the team's point of view. This is not what you want—you want an honest, critical assessment.

Recognize Sunk Costs

Probably the most powerful way to escape escalation of commitment is to simply recognize and accept sunk costs. Sunk costs are basically water under the bridge: Money (or other commitments) previously spent that cannot be recovered. It is often helpful for teams to have built into their agenda a period in which they consider removal of the project, product, or program. In this way, the situation is redefined as one in which a decision will be made immediately about whether to invest or not; that is, if you were making the initial decision today, would you make the investment currently under consideration (as a continuing investment), or would you choose another course of action? If the decision is not one that you would choose anew, you might want to start thinking about how to terminate the project and move on to the next one.

External Review

In some cases, it is necessary to remove or replace the original decision makers from deliberations precisely because they are biased. One way to do this is with an external review of departments.

DECISION-MAKING PITFALL 3: THE ABILENE PARADOX

In the case of groupthink and escalation of commitment, teams pursue a course of action largely because they are personally involved; a decision to discontinue might involve admission of a poor earlier choice. There is another kind of behavior that can lead teams to make undesirable choices—choices, in fact, that none of the individuals would have made on their own. Known as the **Abilene paradox** (Harvey, 1974), it is a kind of consensus seeking that has its roots in the avoidance of conflict. The Abilene paradox is basically a form of **pluralistic ignorance:** Group members adopt a position because they feel other members desire it; team members don't challenge one another because they want to avoid conflict or achieve consensus. Although this is a kind of "expectational bubble"—a set of expectations about other people's expectations that could be burst if even one person expressed a contrary view—it can have a dramatic impact on the actual decision-making behavior of the team. The story in Box 6-4 illustrates the dilemma.

To the extent that team members are more interested in consensus than debate, they may end up in Abilene. Indeed, the mismanagement of agreement can be more problematic than the management of disagreement (Harvey, 1974). This may seem counterintuitive, but the consequences are very real.

It may seem strange to think that intelligent people who are in private agreement may somehow fail to realize the commonality of their beliefs and end up in Abilene. However, it is easy to see how this can happen if members fail to communicate their beliefs to each other.

Quandaries like the Abilene paradox may seem absurd, but they are easy to fall into. Strategies to avoid the situation include playing devil's advocate, careful questioning, and a commitment on the part of all team members to both fully air their opinions as well as respectfully listen to others. Note that none of these requires team members to abandon consensus seeking as a goal—if that is indeed their goal. However, it does require that consensus actually reflect the true beliefs of the team.

What factors lead to problems like the Abilene paradox? In general, if individual team members are intimidated or feel that their efforts will not be worthwhile, then they are less likely to air or defend their viewpoints. This is called *self-limiting behavior.*

BOX 6-4

The Abilene Paradox

The July afternoon in Coleman, Texas (population 5,607), was particularly hot—104 degrees as measured by the Walgreen's Rexall Ex-Lax temperature gauge. In addition, the wind was blowing fine-grained West Texas topsoil through the house. But the afternoon was still tolerable—even potentially enjoyable. There was a fan going on the back porch; there was cold lemonade; and finally, there was entertainment. Dominoes. Perfect for the conditions. The game required little more physical exertion than an occasional mumbled comment, "Shuffle 'em," and an unhurried movement of the arm to place the spots in the appropriate perspective on the table. All in all, it had the markings of an agreeable Sunday afternoon in Coleman—that is, it was until my father-in-law suddenly said, "Let's get in the car and go to Abilene and have dinner at the cafeteria."

I thought, "What, go to Abilene? Fifty-three miles? In this dust storm and heat? And in an un-air-conditioned 1958 Buick?"

But my wife chimed in with "Sounds like a great idea. I'd like to go. How about you, Jerry?" Since my own preferences were obviously out of step with the rest I replied, "Sounds good to me," and added, "I just hope your mother wants to go."

"Of course I want to go," said my mother-in-law. "I haven't been to Abilene in a long time."

So into the car and off to Abilene we went. My predictions were fulfilled. The heat was brutal. We were coated with a fine layer of dust that was cemented with perspiration by the time we arrived. The food at the cafeteria provided first-rate testimonial material for antacid commercials.

Some four hours and 106 miles later we returned to Coleman, hot and exhausted. We sat in front of the fan for a long time in silence. Then, both to be sociable and to break the silence, I said, "It was a great trip, wasn't it?"

No one spoke. Finally my mother-in-law said, with some irritation, "Well, to tell the truth, I really didn't enjoy it much and would rather have stayed here. I just went along because the three of you were so enthusiastic about going. I wouldn't have gone if you all hadn't pressured me into it."

I couldn't believe it. "What do you mean 'you all'?" I said. "Don't put me in the 'you all' group. I was delighted to be doing what we were doing. I didn't want to go. I only went to satisfy the rest of you. You're the culprits."

My wife looked shocked. "Don't call me a culprit. You and Daddy and Mama were the ones who wanted to go. I just went along to be sociable and to keep you happy. I would have had to be crazy to want to go out in heat like that."

Her father entered the conversation abruptly. "Hell!" he said.

He proceeded to expand on what was already absolutely clear. "Listen, I never wanted to go to Abilene. I just thought you might be bored. You visit so seldom I wanted to be sure you enjoyed it. I would have preferred to play another game of dominoes and eat the leftovers in the icebox."

After the outburst of recrimination we all sat back in silence. Here we were, four reasonably sensible people who, of our own volition, had just taken a 106-mile trip across a godforsaken desert in a furnace-like temperature through a cloud-like dust storm to eat unpalatable food at a hole-in-the-wall cafeteria in Abilene, when none of us had really wanted to go. In fact, to be more accurate, we'd done just the opposite of what we wanted to do. The whole situation simply didn't make sense (Harvey, 1974).

According to a survey of 569 managers by Mulvey, Veiga, & Elsass (1996), there are six key causes of self-limiting behavior in teams:

- **The presence of someone with expertise:** When team members perceive that another member of the team has expertise or is highly qualified to make a decision, they will self-limit. Members' perceptions of other teammates' competence play a key role, and these evaluations are formed quickly—often before a team meets for the first time.
- **The presentation of a compelling argument:** Frequently, the timing of a coherent argument influences decision making—such as when the decision is made after a lot of fruitless discussion.
- **A lack of confidence in one's ability to contribute:** If team members feel unsure about their ability to meaningfully contribute to the decision, they will be inclined to self-limit.
- **An unimportant or meaningless decision:** Unless the decision is seen as vital or important to the individual's well-being, there is a powerful tendency to adopt a "who cares" attitude.
- **Pressure from others to conform to the team's decision:** Roger Boisjoly reported that he felt incredible pressures to conform exerted by the management team.
- **A dysfunctional decision-making climate:** When team members believe that others are frustrated, indifferent, disorganized, or generally unwilling to commit themselves to making an effective decision, they are likely to self-limit. Such a climate can be created in the early stages of a decision by inadvertent remarks such as, "this is a ridiculous task," "nothing's going to change, so why bother," and so on.

How to Avoid the Abilene Paradox

The following suggestions are taken from Harvey (1974) and Mulvey et al. (1996).

Confront the Issue in a Team Setting

The most straightforward approach involves meeting with the organization members who are key figures in the problem and its solution. The first step is for the individual who proposes a solution to state it and then be open to any and all feedback. For example:

> I want to talk with you about the research project. Although I have previously said things to the contrary, I frankly don't think it will work and I am very anxious about it. I suspect that others may feel the same, but I don't know. Anyway, I am concerned that we may end up misleading one another, and if we aren't careful, we may continue to work on a problem that none of us wants and that might even bankrupt us. That's why I need to know where the rest of you stand. I would appreciate any of your thoughts about the project. Do you think it can succeed? (Harvey, 1974, p. 32).

Conduct a Private Vote

People often go along with what they think the team wants to do. Dissenting opinions are easier to express privately—pass out blank cards and ask team members to privately write their opinions. Guarantee them anonymity and then share the overall outcomes with the team.

Minimize Status Differences

High-status members are often at the center of communication, and lower status members are likely to feel pressures to conform more quickly. Although this can be difficult to avoid, reassurances by senior members about the importance of frank and honest discussion reinforced by the elimination of status symbols, like dress, meeting place, title, and so on, may be helpful.

Minimize the Size of the Team

As we have seen, teams that are too large often experience social loafing, free riding, and a diffusion of responsibility—all of which can contribute to making a trip to Abilene.

Frame the Task As a Decision to Be Made

Framing the task as a decision to be made, rather than a judgment (which suggests personal opinion), helps cast a tone of somber decision making, absent of the trappings of power or personal prestige. When team members are given a decision-making responsibility, they fundamentally approach the problem differently when the decision that needs to be made is framed as a *problem to be solved.* The typical approach is to view decisions as judgments, not problems. People typically view a problem as needing more analysis, such as pros and cons, and less opinion. Telling your team that you believe in "fact-based decision making" is a potentially helpful way of framing the decision.

Provide a Formal Forum for Controversial Views

This may be achieved by segmenting the discussion into pros and cons. Debate must be legitimized. Members should not have to worry about whether it is appropriate to bring up contrary views; it should be expected and encouraged.

Take Responsibility for Failure

It is important to create a climate where teams can make mistakes, own up to them, and then move on without fear of recrimination. Consider what happened to a three-man forge team, called the "Grumpy Old Men," at Eaton Corporation in the Forge Division plant. Through an assumption at the start of their shift, they made an error that resulted in about 1,200 pieces of scrap. It was not an inexpensive mistake, but it was not one that would close the plant. The team had jeopardized the plant's output to customers. The team came forward to the plant leadership, admitted their error, described its potential impact, and demanded to be allowed to take corrective action so that the problem could never occur again. They even took it a step further and demanded to be allowed to go before the entire workforce at the start of each of the three shifts and admit their error and describe what they were doing to make sure it would not happen again (Bergstrom, 1997).

DECISION-MAKING PITFALL 4: GROUP POLARIZATION

Consider the case in Box 6-5. Most people independently evaluating the problem state that the new company would need to have nearly a two-thirds probability of success before they would advise Mr. A. to leave his current job and accept a new position (Stoner, 1961). What do you think happens when the same people discuss Mr. A.'s situation and are instructed to reach consensus?

You might expect the outcome of the team to be the same as the average of the individuals considered separately. However, this is not what happens. The group advises Mr. A. to take the new job, even if it only has slightly better than a 50-50 chance of success! In other words, groups show a **risky shift.**

Now consider a situation in which a company is deciding the highest odds of an engine malfunction that could be tolerated on the release of a new vehicle. In this case, individual advisors are cautious, but when the same people are in a group, they collectively insist on even lower odds. Thus, they exhibit a **cautious shift.**

Why are teams both more risky and more cautious than are individuals, considering the identical situation? The reason for this apparent disparity has to do with some of the peculiarities of group dynamics. Teams are not inherently more risky or cautious than individuals; rather they are more *extreme* than individuals. **Group polarization** is the tendency for group discussion to intensify group opinion, producing more extreme judgment than might be obtained by pooling the individuals' views separately (see Figure 6-3).

Group polarization is not simply a case of social compliance or a bandwagon effect. The same individuals display the polarization effect when queried privately af-

---

BOX 6-5

Advice Question

Mr. A., an electrical engineer who is married and has one child, has been working for a large electronics corporation since graduating from college 5 years ago. He is assured of a lifetime job with a modest, though adequate, salary and liberal pension benefits upon retirement. On the other hand, it is very unlikely that his salary will increase much before he retires. While attending a convention, Mr. A. is offered a job with a small, newly founded company that has a highly uncer- *tain future. The new job would pay more to start and would offer the possibility of a share in the ownership if the company survived the competition with larger firms.*

Imagine that you are advising Mr. A. What is the lowest probability or odds of the new company proving financially sound that you would consider acceptable to make it worthwhile for Mr. A. to take the new job? Before reading on, indicate your response on a probability scale from zero to 100 percent.

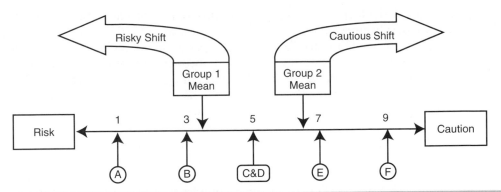

FIGURE 6-3 Group Polarization Processes. Imagine that Group 1 includes Person A (who chose 1), Person B (who chose 3), and Persons C and D (who both chose 5); the average of pregroup choices would be (1 + 3 + 5 + 5)/4, or 3.5. Because this mean is less than 5, a risky shift would probably occur in Group 1. If, in contrast, Group 2 contained persons C, D, E, and F, their pregroup average would be (5 + 5 + 7 + 9)/4 or 6.5. Because this mean is closer to the caution pole, a conservative shift would probably occur in the group.

Source: Adapted from Janis, I. L. 1982. *Victims of Groupthink* (2nd ed.). Boston: Houghton Mifflin.

ter group discussion. This means that people really believe the group's decision—they have conformed inwardly! The polarization effect does not happen in nominal groups. The polarization effect grows stronger with time, meaning that the same person who was in a group discussion 2 weeks earlier will be even more extreme in his or her judgment.

Two explanations for group polarization hearken back to our discussion of conformity at the beginning of the chapter: The need to be right and the need to be liked. Simply stated, people want to make the right decision and they want to be approved of by their team. Take the case concerning Mr. A., the electrical engineer. Most people are positively inclined when they agree to recommend to Mr. A. that he seriously consider a job change. However, they vary greatly in their reasons for why Mr. A. should change jobs. Someone in the group may feel that Mr. A. should leave the secure job because it does not represent a sufficient challenge; others may think that Mr. A. should leave the company because he should increase his standard of living. Thus, people feel that Mr. A. should consider a move, but they have different (yet complementary) reasons supporting their belief. This is the rational type of conformity we discussed earlier. At the same time, members of the team want to be accepted—part of the socialization process we outlined in chapter 4.

CONCLUSIONS

Teams make important decisions and some of them will not be good ones, despite the very best of intentions. It is unrealistic to suggest that poor decision making, or for that matter even disastrous decision making, is avoidable. The key message hearkens back to a point we made early in chapter 1, which has to do with creating an organization that can optimally learn from failure. Learning from failure is difficult when people suffer—especially innocent ones. As a case in point, consider the steps that were taken by NASA following the space shuttle *Challenger* accident, including the redesign of the joints and solid rocket booster, which went through hundreds of modifications; the institution of full hazard analysis for thousands of parts; certification of flight readiness, which includes verbal and video-recorded affirmation from a variety of NASA officials; the institution of a veto policy, in which anyone at any level can stop the process—a policy that has been exercised by NASA members; and creation of launch criteria, which occurs in the cool of the morning, rather than in the heat of the afternoon. Is there a downside to the creation and use of decision-making procedures and criteria that err on the side of safety? As Don McMonagle, manager of launch integration at NASA puts it: If every one of the hundreds of thousands of components on space vehicles were required to work perfectly, no one could ever launch and this would effectively paralyze the U.S. space program (personal communication, July 1998). The key for NASA and other decision-making teams within organizations is to develop and use decision-making procedures, such as veto policies and preestablished criteria to guide decision making. All of these decisions involve a certain level of risk, but that risk can be minimized.

CHAPTER 7

Conflict in Teams: Leveraging Differences to Create Opportunity

At Emap, the fast-growing media company, an extraordinary general meeting had to be called to expel two nonexecutive directors, Professor Ken Simmonds and Joe Cooke, from the board. Earlier the pair had called on the chairman, Sir John Hoskyns, to resign, and although the dispute was positioned by both sides as being purely about matters of corporate governance, it was difficult for impartial observers to escape the conclusion that the men involved simply did not want to have to sit around the same table any more (Lynn, 1997).

At Cable & Wireless (C&W), there was an even more spectacular clash at the close of 1995 between the company's chairman, Lord Young, and chief executive James Ross. Both men wanted to stay in ultimate command of the firm, and through weeks of public squabbling, the pair waged a bitter battle with one another. In the end, both turned out to be losers: The nonexecutives despaired of finding any workable solution to the painfully protracted conflict, and it was agreed that both men would simply have to go, while the company started merger talks with British Telecom (Lynn, 1997).

Our survey of executives and managers, presented in chapter 1 of this book, revealed that team conflict is one of the top three concerns of team management.[1] Conflict that is not properly managed may lead to hostility, performance deficits, and, in extreme cases, dissolution of the team. Most people regard conflict to be detrimental to effective teamwork and believe that differences between team members should be immediately eliminated. However, differences in interests, perception, information, and preference cannot be avoided, especially in teams that work together closely for extended periods of time. Moreover, conflict can be good for the team—when managed properly. The challenge for the manager is to transform conflict into opportunity. Conflict can have positive consequences, such as enhancing creativity or fostering integrative solutions reflecting many points of view. However, effective conflict management is not intuitive, as illustrated in Box 7-1.

This chapter begins by distinguishing between two types of conflict: Emotional conflict and cognitive conflict. We then discuss the team dilemma, which centers on the tension between one's own and the team's interests. Next, we describe voting and majority rule and when they are appropriate to use in teams. Finally, we discuss team negotiation and how to maximize mutual interests.

---

[1]Survey of Kellogg Executive Program's Team Building for Managers.

BOX 7-1

Check Your Intuition About Conflict

Our intuitions about conflict are not always accurate. Faulty information about the causes of conflict can have unintended consequences which can exacerbate, rather than reduce, conflict. Below are 10 observations pertaining to conflict in teams and organizations.

As you read each statement, note whether you think the observation is generally true or false (there will always be some qualifiers) and justify your answer. Do this first to avoid hindsight bias: The tendency to think the answer is obvious—once you know it.

_____ 1. You can weaken an opposing group's resolve (i.e., their motivation to continue conflict escalation) by using coercive, rather than conciliatory, strategies.

_____ 2. When people engage in competitive, as opposed to cooperative, strategies to resolve conflict, this stems from a basic need to take advantage of the situation—in short, one-upmanship.

_____ 3. Most people in the competitive business world will take advantage of others whenever and however they can.

_____ 4. The best method of reaching settlement and avoiding costly delays (such as strikes) is to get the other party to empathize with your position.

_____ 5. People who are friends are most likely to come up with creative solutions (i.e., win-win solutions) to conflict situations, as compared with nonacquaintances.

_____ 6. In conflict situations, giving both sides more and accurate information about the situation is an effective method of reducing conflict.

_____ 7. The more successful people (or teams) are in achieving their desired outcomes in conflict situations, the happier they are.

_____ 8. Conflict among team members hinders their productivity.

_____ 9. For the most part, the key to reaching win-win outcomes is to build trust between parties in conflict.

_____ 10. Voting, and in particular, majority rule, is the best way to resolve conflicts among team members.

After you have read this chapter, review the questions again and see whether your answers—or explanations—change. (If you can't wait, the answers are presented in Box 7-6 at the end of the chapter.)

TYPES OF CONFLICT

All conflict is not created equal. Many types of conflict can threaten teamwork. Before a manager launches into conflict management mode, it is important to accurately diagnose the type of conflict that plagues the team. There are two basic types.

Emotional conflict is personal, defensive, and resentful. Also known as **A-type conflict** or **affective conflict** (Guetzkow & Gyr, 1954), it is rooted in anger, personal friction, personality clashes, ego, and tension.

Cognitive conflict is largely depersonalized; also known as **C-type conflict,** it consists of argumentation about the merits of ideas, plans, and projects. Cognitive conflict

---

BOX 7-2

The Effects of A-Type Conflict

Amason (1996) interviewed 48 top-management teams in small and mid-sized food processing firms across the United States and 5 top-management teams in furniture manufacturing firms in the southeastern United States. Both CEOs and managers were asked about strategic decisions and team behavior. Questions to assess A-type conflict included: How much anger was there among the group over this decision? How much personal friction was there in the group during this discussion? How much were personality clashes between group members evident during the decision? How much tension was there in the group during this decision?

Questions to assess C-type conflict included: How many disagreements over different ideas about this decision were there? How many differences about the content of this decision did the group have to work through? How many differences of opinion were there within the group over this decision?

The results were striking: The presence of cognitive conflict was associated with higher decision-making quality, greater understanding, higher commitment, and more acceptance. In contrast, the presence of affective conflict significantly reduced decision quality, understanding, commitment, and affective acceptance.

---

is often effective in stimulating creativity because it forces people to rethink problems and arrive at outcomes that everyone can live with. This is why having divergent views in a team is beneficial for creativity and innovation. For example, when a majority of members in a team is confronted by the differing opinions of minorities, the majority is forced to think about why the minority disagrees. This thought process can instigate novel ideas (Levine & Moreland, 1985; Nemeth, 1995). As a general rule, A-type conflict threatens team productivity, whereas C-type conflict benefits team functioning.

Why is A-type conflict bad for team functioning? Affective conflict interferes with the effort people put into a task because members are preoccupied with reducing threats, increasing power, and attempting to build cohesion rather than working on the task. In contrast, C-type conflict can improve decision-making outcomes and team productivity by increasing decision quality through incorporating devil's advocacy roles, constructive criticism, and stimulation of discussion.

Clear evidence for the advantages to C-type conflict over A-type conflict is found in observations of actual organizational work teams. According to Jehn (1997), who investigated everyday conflicts in six organizational work teams, A-type conflict is detrimental to performance and satisfaction (two major indices of team productivity); furthermore, emotionality reduces team effectiveness. Groups that accept task (C-type) conflict but not A-type conflict are the most effective.

In Jehn's (1997) investigation, cognitive conflict was associated with higher decision-making quality, greater understanding, higher commitment, and more acceptance. In contrast, emotional conflict significantly reduced decision quality, understanding, commitment, and acceptance. (For another illustration of the deleterious effects of A-type conflict, see Box 7-2.)

Cognitive conflict is productive because when people are in conflict about ideas, they are forced to consider the ideas of others. For example, consider a debate between two managers concerning how to market a company's product. Although they have their own individual ideas, when they try to persuade the other by presenting a rationale for their approach, each is forced, on some level, to integrate the other's point of view. It is possible, of course, to completely reject the other's arguments, but this is inappropriate in a healthy working relationship. It would also represent A-type rather than C-type conflict.

Transforming A-Type into C-Type Conflict

The key, of course, for the manager is to learn how to turn A-type conflict into C-type conflict; or, ideally, design the team so that A-type conflict does not erupt and, instead, only healthy C-type conflict exists. It is interesting to note that teams of friends are better at applying effective conflict management strategies to suit the task at hand than are teams of strangers, whose conflict management approaches are less sophisticated (Shah & Jehn, 1993). Some specific strategies follow.

Agree on a Common Goal or Shared Vision

The importance of a common goal is summed up in a quote by Steve Jobs, who is associated with three high-profile Silicon Valley companies—Apple, NeXT, and Pixar: "It's okay to spend a lot of time arguing about which route to take to San Francisco when everyone wants to end up there, but a lot of time gets wasted in such arguments if one person wants to go to San Francisco and another secretly wants to go to San Diego" (Eisenhardt, Kahwajy, & Bourgeois, 1997, p. 80). Shared goals do not imply homogeneous thinking, but they do require everyone to share a vision. Steve Jobs is not alone in his thinking. Colin Sewell-Rutter, a director of The Results Partnership, a consultancy that specializes in improving board-level communications, concludes that "The single most important source of problems within the boardroom is the lack of a shared vision, and shared corporate goals . . . All the major difficulties ultimately stem from that" (Lynn, 1997, p. 31).

The 1993 departure of Ernest Mario as chief executive of pharmaceutical firm Glaxo (as it then was) illustrates how conflicts can also mask the fact that teams never fundamentally agreed on what the company is about. Mario was thought to have been preparing a takeover of American rival Warner-Lambert, even though the then chairman, Sir Paul Girolami, believed that the company should stick with its strategy of investing for organic growth. The result was a bitter conflict that culminated in Mario's departure with a $3 million payoff (it was only after Girolami retired that Glaxo made its first takeover in decades when it bid for Wellcome).

Create a Place for Conflict and Get It Out in the Open

Most people, even seasoned managers and executives, feel uncomfortable about conflict. It is much easier to capitalize on constructive conflict by creating a time and place for it to occur, rather than expecting it to naturally erupt. Furthermore, discussing the potential for conflict before it erupts is a lot more effective than trying to deal with it after the fact. As an example of how companies create a forum for conflict, see Box 7-3.

BOX 7-3

Creating a Forum for Conflict

Bovis Construction Corporation, which has worked on the renovation of Los Angeles City Hall and the construction of a football stadium in Nashville, deals with conflict in an open fashion. Prior to each project, Bovis construction teams hold a planning session in which team members openly address potential conflicts. These planning sessions are conducted by company facilitators who encourage the project owner, architects, contractors, and other players to map out processes they plan to follow to get the job done. During the session, participants draft and sign a "win-win agree-

ment," which includes a matrix that lays out what team members expect from one another. The first box in a matrix may detail the owner's responsibilities on the project, whereas the next box may look at the owner's expectations of the construction manager. Teams then use this matrix to review their progress on the project. Bovis managers agree that the process has not only decreased the adversity that is so prevalent on construction sites, but the firm has also saved millions of dollars and has completed projects on time (Oldham, 1998).

TEAM DILEMMA: GROUP VERSUS INDIVIDUAL INTERESTS

In most teams, members have both cooperative and competitive motives (Deutsch, 1973). Team members share a common objective when they work together—this is the cooperative aspect. Yet in many teams, individual members have an incentive to further their own interests. Team efforts are often subverted when individual agendas lead to competition between members, and members become preoccupied with what others are getting, relative to what they themselves are getting. Sometimes the way teams are set up can lead to these kinds of conflict. For example, when individuals are compensated according to team rather than individual performance, conflict may arise to the detriment of the team if members' skills, abilities, or effort vary to a significant degree.

In many team situations, members face a choice between furthering team-level interests or their own personal interests. For example, consider project teams composed of various members within a company. Each employee may be, at any time, a member of four or more project teams. Consequently, the team members have other projects vying for their attention and have an incentive to work on pet projects, letting the rest of the team carry them on the other project. However, if everyone does this, each project suffers. The choice between individual and group interests is a **team dilemma.** The hallmark features of a team dilemma are when members are *interdependent* with regard to resources, and each person has an *incentive to free ride* on the group's efforts. The resources may be tangible outcomes, such as salaries, office space, or equipment; or intangible outcomes, such as information, services, or social support (Foa & Foa, 1975).

Team members in this case must choose between the team and self-interest. Consider the following team dilemmas:

- A group of M.B.A. students is working on a class project that counts for 50 percent of their grade. Some take a higher course load than others; some are taking the course pass-fail; some are second-year students who already have jobs. How should the work be divided?
- Firms with significant R&D activities frequently use cross-functional teams. However, when the R&D is spread across different parts of the firm, members may want to retain control of the project in their own division, rather than collaborating with others across divisions, which might add substantial value.
- In large law firms, partners act as their own profit centers and, thus, have little incentive to provide knowledge to attorneys outside their group. Yet doing so improves the long-term viability of the firm in a competitive marketplace.

Team dilemmas pit individual incentives against group incentives in such a way that a poorer outcome for the firm is likely if each member acts in a self-interested way. The dilemma lies in the fact that members cannot simultaneously choose to cooperate and avoid exploitation by other members.

Strategies to Enhance Cooperation and Minimize Competition

In chapter 2, we offered some specific strategies to reduce free riding. Here, we add to the list.

Build Team Identity

The stronger a team's identity, the less sharply members distinguish between their self-interest and that of the group (Dawes, van de Kragt, & Orbell, 1990). There are several ways to increase team identity, such as linking individual outcomes (i.e., compensation) to team outcomes (i.e., performance). Recognition of individual efforts can also be effective. Sometimes, emphasizing team identity as being an integral part of a larger team effort, such as that of a plant, division, or firm, is effective, particularly when a conscious challenge is presented in which the team can either succeed or fail—for example, beating the competition to market with a new product. If the team has an identity or reputation of its own, that can also make members want to uphold their end of the work.

Certain things detract from team identity, the most important of which is whether members expect to work together in the future. If the cooperative effort is short-lived, individuals have less incentive to invest in the team. Hence, another way of enhancing team identity is to extend the length of time people expect to work as a team. Moreover, members who believe that other members will leave cooperate less than those who expect the team to remain intact (Mannix & Loewenstein, 1993). Therefore, preserving continuity in membership can also be important.

Make Pledges

To the extent that team members make pledges, cooperation is greatly enhanced (Chen, 1996). Pledges or social contracts come in all shapes and forms, the most common being the business handshake, or the simple statement "You have my word." Social contracts are sometimes explicit ("You can count on me") and sometimes implicit (such as a wink, a nod, or a handshake). Social contracts capitalize on a basic psychological need for commitment and consistency. The power of pledges cannot be underestimated. In many instances, team members who make specific pledges or commitments to their team will act in ways that benefit the group, even at the expense of self-interest.

Change the Incentive Structure

When it is more cost-effective for group members to cooperate rather than adopt self-interested behavior, cooperation increases. This is precisely why many organizations are moving toward team-based pay (as we examined in detail in chapter 3). However, team-based pay must be structured in such a way that everyone feels they are being treated fairly (so, for instance, there is no antagonism between members with different skill levels).

PERILS AND PITFALLS OF DEMOCRACY

In some teams, the choice facing members does not center upon a choice between the team and self-interest. Rather, members must agree on some course of action. This is particularly true when the decisions facing the team are complex. Consider, for example, team members who disagree about their weekly meeting time. This cannot be resolved by individual members simply deciding the time that is best for them. Effective conflict resolution requires coordination and consensus among members. Voting is one method for reducing conflict, in which members agree to adopt the choice preferred by the majority. Voting is commonly used in organizational hiring, promotion, and firing decisions. Team members who vote among alternatives acknowledge that conflict exists, but agree to accept the outcome of the vote. The key issue becomes how to develop and utilize a suitable voting scheme.

Voting Rules

There are several kinds of voting rules, and different rules are used in different situations. The objective of voting rules can be to find the alternative that the greatest number of team members prefer, the alternative the fewest members object to, or the choice that maximizes team welfare. Anything short of unanimity indicates disagreement or conflict within the team. In most cases, conflict will be reduced or eliminated following the conclusion of voting, although there are exceptions. For example, individuals who "lose" the vote may assert that the voting procedure was fraudulent or not carried out as agreed upon (Tyler & Smith, 1998).

Voting does not guarantee conflict resolution. First, members may not agree on a method for voting. For example, how is a winning choice to be determined? Some members may insist on unanimity, others on simple majority rule, and still others on a weighted majority rule. Second, even if a voting method is agreed on, it may not yield a decision (in the case of a tie, for instance) or may not yield a single decision. Finally, because voting does not eliminate conflicts of interest, but rather provides a way for members to live with conflict, such decisions may not be stable. In this sense, voting masks disagreement within teams, potentially threatening long-term group and organizational effectiveness.

Majority Rule

The most common voting procedure is majority rule. However, it presents several problems in the attainment of consensus. Despite its democratic appeal, majority rule does not reflect the strength of individual preferences. The vote of a person who feels strongly about an issue counts only as much as the vote of a person who is virtually indifferent. Consequently, majority rule does not promote creative trade-offs among issues. For example, groups that use unanimous rule reach more win-win outcomes (i.e., profitable outcomes for everyone involved) compared to groups that use majority rule (Mannix, Thompson, & Bazerman, 1989; Thompson, Mannix, & Bazerman, 1988). When groups use voting in combination with strict agendas (in which the order of issues is discussed sequentially, rather than simultaneously), outcomes for the team as a whole plummet. Why? One of the successful keys to conflict management is the ability to make trade-offs between issues under discussion (i.e., "I will do this for you if you do such-and-such for me"; Mannix et al., 1989; Thompson et al., 1988). In short, when teams discuss only one issue at a time and vote on outcomes under consideration, this results in less profitable outcomes than when teams discuss issues simultaneously and seek consensus.

Unanimous Decision Making

Although unanimous decision making is time-consuming, it encourages team members to consider creative alternatives to expand the size of the pie and satisfy the interests of all members. On the other hand, unanimous rule can present formidable obstacles, such as when members refuse to compromise. By holding out, these members can force decisions their way when considerations like timeliness are important. When a decision reached in these circumstances goes against what most members believe is right, it can lead to poor outcomes.

Drawbacks to Voting

Arrow Paradox

Consider the situation described in Box 7-4. The product development team members are victims of the **Arrow paradox**, in which the winners of majority rule elections change as a function of the order in which alternatives are proposed. In fact, any system of weighted voting (such as when members give three points to their first choice, two to their second, and one to their third) produces the same problem.

Impossibility Theorem

The unstable voting outcomes of the product development team illustrate the **impossibility theorem** (Arrow, 1963), which states that the derivation of team preference from individual preference is indeterminate. Simply put, there is no method of combining group members' preferences that guarantees that group preference has been maximized when groups have three or more members and there are three or more options.

The context of voting often involves people explaining the reasons for their preferences. Sometimes they persuade others with their arguments; other times, the holes in their arguments become illuminated. Therefore, aside from the mathematical complexities involved in voting rules, voting serves an important function. The process itself can lead to buy-in, if not downright consensus, by the time the vote is through.

BOX 7-4

When Voting Goes Awry

Suppose a three-person product development team (Raines, Warner, and Lassiter) is choosing among designs A, B, or C. Each manager's preference ordering is depicted below. As a way of resolving the conflict, Warner suggests voting between designs A and B. In that vote, A wins over B. Warner then proposes a vote between A and C. In that vote, C wins. Warner then declares design C the consensus choice—which Lassiter agrees to. However, Raines proposes a new vote, but this time starting with a contest between B and C. B wins this vote, eliminating C. Between A and B, A beats B, so Raines happily declares A the winner. Lassiter complains the whole voting process was fraudulent, but cannot explain why.

Manager	*Design A*	*Design B*	*Design C*
Raines	1	2	3
Warner	2	3	1
Lassiter	3	1	2

Note: Numbers represent rank-ordered choices.

Strategic Manipulation

Strategic manipulation further compounds the problem of indeterminacy of team choice (Chechile, 1984; Ordeshook, 1986; Plott, 1976; Plott & Levine, 1978). Consider a situation in which members do not vote for their first choice because by voting for another choice, some other, undesirable option is sure to lose. This is an example of strategic manipulation—people do not vote in accord with their true preferences. Furthermore, members may manipulate the order in which alternatives are voted on, because when the alternatives are voted on sequentially in pairs, those voted on later are more likely to win (May, 1982).

GROUP NEGOTIATION

Some situations call for team members to discuss issues and build consensus—for example, when a team of professionals must divide responsibilities among themselves, or members of a department must allocate funds. In both cases, members must arrive at a mutually satisfactory outcome although each may have different interests. This involves negotiation.

Negotiation occurs when interdependent parties make mutual decisions regarding the allocation of scarce resources (Bazerman, Mannix, & Thompson, 1988). Negotiation is necessary when no one can dictate a solution. Furthermore, team members must agree for any decision to be binding. Failure to reach consensus can be costly for the team if, for example, it cannot move forward because it fails to reach agreement, if opportunities are missed due to protracted negotiations, if costs of negotiation increase over time (such as if lawyers or arbitrators must be paid), or if the rights to decision making are lost and must instead be sent to a higher level. An example of opportunity lost due to impasse occurred at a prominent state university. A department had been granted special funds to create a badly-needed additional wing of a new building.

Unfortunately, department members could not agree on how to allocate the new space among themselves, preventing the drafting of final blueprints. Because no plans were forthcoming, the university withdrew the funding. This is an example of a **lose-lose outcome** (Thompson & Hrebec, 1996). When group members fail to reach consensus, it can be costly for everyone. In retrospect, the members of the department would have all been happier had the new wing been built, but at the time, they were absorbed in paralyzing conflict with one another.

What are some strategies that teams can use to avoid lose-lose outcomes and move toward mutual agreement? Most conflict situations contain the potential for joint gain, or integrative outcomes, although these may be obvious only after the fact. The following strategies are aimed at uncovering the win-win potential existing in most conflicts.

The BATNA Principle

Team consensus is only feasible if it represents an improvement over each member's **best alternative to a negotiated agreement,** or **BATNA** (Fisher & Ury, 1981). If members have better options outside the team (such as with another team or different company), then group dissolution is inevitable. Thus, for consensus to be viable, the outcome must be at least as attractive as each person's best available outside option. Knowing the BATNAs of the parties involved greatly enhances the ability to achieve consensus.

Avoid the Fixed-Pie Fallacy

The fixed-pie fallacy is the tendency of people in conflict to assume that their interests are completely opposed to those of others. The fixed-pie mentality can be extremely detrimental in negotiations (Thompson & Hastie, 1990). Although most negotiations contain potential for mutually beneficial agreements, the belief that the pie is fixed and successful negotiation means grabbing the biggest slice is so pervasive that most people fail to recognize opportunities for win-win agreements.

For example, Thompson and Hrebec (1996) found that about 50 percent of people fail to realize when they have interests that are completely compatible with others, and about 20 percent fail to reach optimal agreements even when their interests are completely compatible. A key reason for such breakdowns is that people in negotiations fail to exchange information about their interests, making it unlikely that faulty judgments will be challenged and corrected (Thompson, 1991). Furthermore, when people are provided with information about others' interests, they often overlook areas of common interest (Thompson & DeHarpport, 1994; Thompson & Hastie, 1990).

Build Trust and Share Information

Rapport between members of the team makes mutually beneficial agreement more likely (Moore, Kurtzberg, Thompson, & Morris, 1999). Rapport is usually established when people find points of similarity. Surprisingly, it does not take much to find something in common with another person. For example, in one investigation (Nadler, Thompson, & Morris, 1999), students from two highly competitive rival M.B.A. programs negotiated with one another via electronic mail. The bargaining zone was small and reputations were at stake. All buyer-seller pairs had exactly 8 days to reach some kind of settlement. Some of the negotiators were randomly selected to have a "get acquainted" phone call with their opponent immediately before getting down to the business of negotiation. Others just immediately commenced negotiations. The results were dramatic: The impasse rate was cut nearly in half when negotiators spent a few minutes on the phone with the other person—a strong testament to the power of rapport in building trust in negotiations. Furthermore, those who had the phone call were convinced that their opponent had been especially selected for them on the basis of similarity, when in actual effect, the opponent was chosen at random.

These results may suggest that the better two persons know one another, the stronger their rapport should be and, consequently, the better they should be at finding common ground. However, this is not always the case. In fact, when friends negotiate, they often do worse than complete strangers (Fry, Firestone, & Williams, 1983; Thompson & DeHarpport, 1998). Friends are often uncomfortable negotiating with each other, and so may make premature concessions; as a result, they may overlook opportunities for expanding the pie in their hurry to reach a deal. Friends may also presume they know each other's interests, when this may not be the case. However, it can be awkward trying to explain your side to someone who knows you. Strangers, by contrast, do not need a pretense to clarify their point of view. The key take-away message goes back to our earlier point: It is important to create a forum for C-type conflict.

Ask Questions

Integrative negotiation often requires that people have information about each other's preferences (Pruitt & Lewis, 1975; Thompson, 1991). Most people in negotiations neither provide nor seek the information necessary to reach such agreements. The most important question a team member can ask of another is: "What are your priorities in this situation?" (Thompson, 1991).

Provide Information

The distinction between this strategy and building trust and providing information has to do with bilateral versus unilateral strategies. In the earlier strategy, it was assumed that teammates were mutually engaged in a process of information exchange. However, if that strategy fails, then we encourage some degree of unilateral (i.e., one-sided) information sharing. It would seem that individuals should always reveal their interests to fellow team members. However, they may hesitate to do so if they feel this will place them in a strategically disadvantageous position. Consider a team negotiating the allocation of scarce resources (research money, secretarial assistance, and travel support) among its members. One member may feel that, of these scarce resources, research support is most important, although secretarial and travel support are also valuable. This person may reason that a mutually beneficial agreement is possible by "trading" secretarial support for research support. However, he may hesitate to reveal his priorities, fearing that other members will demand large concessions on the secretarial and travel support issues in exchange for conceding research support. There are several advantages of revealing information: It builds trust, convinces others of your sincerity in achieving the priorities you do reveal, encourages others to incorporate your priorities in their proposals, and leads to faster agreements.

Make Multiple Offers Simultaneously

In some cases, team members are frustrated when their attempts to provide and seek information are not effective. This happens most commonly in the face of high distrust and less than amicable relations. The strategy of multiple offers can be effective even with the most uncooperative of negotiators. The strategy involves presenting the other party with at least two (and preferably more) proposals of equal value to yourself. The other party is asked to indicate which of the proposals they prefer. This should reveal information about how the other side values trade-offs between different components of the negotiations. There are psychological benefits as well: When people believe they have more choices, they are more inclined to cooperate.

Avoid Sequential Discussion of Issues

There is a pervasive tendency in teams to discuss issues sequentially. This usually stems from the belief that making progress on some issues will grease the wheels of cooperation for more difficult ones. However, sequential discussion inhibits joint discussion of sets of issues, reducing the likelihood that team members will identify potentially beneficial trade-offs between issues (Mannix et al., 1989; Thompson et al., 1988; Weingart, Bennett, & Brett, 1993). Just as we saw in the Arrow paradox, it may not be possible to find the best outcome if trade-offs are only considered pairwise.

Team members who discuss issues simultaneously exchange more information and have greater insight into other members' interests (Weingart et al., 1993). Teams following sequential agendas under majority rule are less likely to reach integrative agreements. This may stem from the fact that coalitions often form, preventing information exchange and discussion of members' underlying interests. It may also be that the full set of trade-offs cannot be evaluated one pair at a time. For instance, you may prefer A over B and C over D, and so think that in a negotiation over four such possibilities, your position would be AC. However, you may also prefer AD over BC, and this could be a potential compromise that you would accept. If you proceed with pairwise trade-offs, this opportunity may never arise.

Construct Contingency Contracts and Leverage Differences

Team members differ in their forecasts about what they think will happen in the future. These different expectations may make negotiation difficult. For example, one member wants to protect against disaster stemming from a potentially bad investment; another may worry about how to spend the vast riches that are sure to follow. Each may have difficulty taking the other's position seriously, because each has very different expectations about what the consequences (and the value) of a decision may be. However, such differences in beliefs can actually improve the possibility of integrative agreements.

This is possible through the formation of **contingency contracts.** Consider the case of a cross-functional team in which a sales manager is more optimistic than the manufacturing manager about product sales. A contingent contract can be constructed, establishing that manufacturing will produce more products, but if sales fail to meet an agreed upon level, the sales department will cover all manufacturing costs.

In other situations, team members may agree on the probability of future events, but feel differently about taking risks. For example, two colleagues may undertake a collaborative project, such as writing a novel, for which they both agree that the probability of success is only moderate. The colleague with an established career can afford to be risk seeking; the struggling young novelist may be risk averse. The two may capitalize on their different risk-taking profiles with a contingent contract: The more risk-averse colleague receives the entire advance on the book; the risk-seeking colleague receives the majority of royalties after publication of the novel.

People may value the same event quite differently depending on when it occurs. If one party is more impatient than the other, mechanisms for sharing the consequences over time may be devised. Two partners in a joint venture might allocate the initial profits to the partner who has high costs for time, whereas the partner who can wait will achieve greater profits over a longer, delayed period.

Capitalizing on differences often entails contingency contracts, in which team members make bets based upon different possible outcomes. For contingency contracts to be effective, they should be easy to evaluate and leave no room for ambiguity of interpretation. Conditions and measurement techniques should be spelled out in advance.

Be Wary of Intuition

Many people make the mistake of relying on intuition to guide their negotiations. This is a mistake because they frequently make faulty assumptions about what the other person wants—an example of the fixed-pie perception. Furthermore, people are not very good at reading others' emotions in mixed-motive situations. In fact, intuition is almost completely unrelated to how well people actually do in negotiations. For example, an investigation examined M.B.A. students at Stanford University who engaged in simulated negotiations (Thompson, Valley, & Kramer, 1995). Prior to receiving feedback on how well they actually did, they were asked to indicate how "successful" they felt. Most students reported feeling extremely successful and confident about the quality of their negotiated settlements. However, these same students were often dismayed to learn that they failed to capitalize on a number of integrative opportunities.

In the absence of any objective indices of their performance, people rely on the emotional expressions and reactions of others to assess their own success at the bargaining table. People appear to follow a simple rule of thumb: "If the other party is happy, then I probably did not do so well; if the other party is disappointed, then I probably did pretty well." This rule of thumb is based upon a false heuristic—namely, the fixed-pie fallacy. If the situation is strictly fixed-pie in nature—meaning that whatever one person gains, the other loses—then whenever one person is happy about something, the other person should be disappointed.

Search for Postsettlement Settlements

Team members may decide to renegotiate after reaching a mutually agreeable settlement. It may seem counterintuitive or counterproductive to resume negotiations once an acceptable agreement has been reached, but the strategy of postsettlement settlements can be remarkably effective in improving the quality of negotiated agreements (Raiffa, 1982). In the postsettlement settlement, team members agree to explore other options with the goal of finding another that both prefer more than the current one. The current settlement becomes the new BATNA. The postsettlement settlement strategy is effective because it allows team members to reveal their preferences without fear of exploitation; they can safely revert to their previous agreement if the postsettlement settlement discussion does not prove fruitful. If better terms are found, parties can be more confident they have reached a truly integrative agreement. If no better agreement is found, the parties may be more confident that the current agreement is really a win-win outcome.

Use Team-on-Team Negotiation

Consider the following situations:

- A group of employees approaching management about wages and working conditions
- A small software company approaching a large software company concerning a joint venture
- A functional team approaching upper management about increasing resources

In each of these examples, a team needs to negotiate with another group. Is a team best advised to send one person to negotiate on their behalf or a team?

To answer the question of whether teams are more effective than solos at the bargaining table, Thompson, Peterson, and Brodt (1996) compared three types of negotiation configurations: Team versus team, team versus solo, and solo versus solo. The presence of at least one team at the bargaining table dramatically increased the quality of agreements reached. The question is, why? It turns out that people exchange much more critical information when at least one team is at the bargaining table than when two individuals negotiate (O'Connor, 1994; Rand & Carnevale, 1994; Thompson et al., 1996). Apparently, team members who negotiate as a team create kind of transactive memory system or shared mental model that forces them to be more explicit about what they know. The team effect (i.e., the ability of teams to expand the pie of value for everyone involved) is quite robust. It is not even necessary that members of teams privately caucus with one another to be effective (Thompson et al., 1996).

Avoid Majority Rule

Because team negotiation is so complex, members often use simplifying procedures to reach decisions (Bazerman et al., 1988). For example, teams may use majority rule as a decision heuristic because of its ease and familiarity (Hastie, Penrod, & Pennington, 1983; Ordeshook, 1986). However, as noted, majority rule ignores members' strength of preference for alternatives. Teams that use majority rule are less likely to reach mutually beneficial, integrative outcomes than are teams requiring unanimity (Thompson et al., 1988). Majority rule inhibits the discovery of integrative agreements because it discourages information exchange about preferences (Castore & Murnighan, 1978).

Beware of Coalitions

A **coalition** is a group of two or more members who join together to affect the outcome of a decision involving at least three parties (Komorita & Parks, 1994). Coalitions involve both cooperation and competition: Members of coalitions cooperate with one another in competition against other coalitions but compete within the coalition regarding the allocation of rewards the coalition obtains. Power is intimately involved in both the formation of coalitions and the allocation of resources among coalition members. In some cases, members of an organizational coalition might be relatively equal in power (e.g., all may be of the same rank); however, in other cases, there might be extreme differences in power (e.g., a team of senior executives and junior hires). Although members of a coalition cooperate in joining resources (e.g., a team might rally together in an organization to gain a greater budget), eventually, they need to allocate the resources they attain among themselves (e.g., individual team members may think they deserve a higher percentage of the budget).

Power imbalance among coalition members can lead to a number of detrimental consequences, including more defecting coalitions (Mannix, 1993), fewer integrative agreements (Mannix, 1993; McAlister, Bazerman, & Fader, 1986), greater likelihood of bargaining impasse (Mannix, 1993), and more competitive behavior (McClintock, Messick, Kuhlman & Campos, 1973).

Appeal to Norms of Justice

Team members in conflict who use objective appearing arguments are more effective than those who use subjective arguments. However, there are many different objective arguments. Consider the following:

- **Equity** (or contribution-based distribution) prescribes that benefits should be proportional to members' contributions (Adams, 1965).
- **Equality** (or blind justice) specifies that all team members should suffer or benefit equally (Messick, 1993).
- **Need** (or welfare-based justice) specifies that benefits should be proportional to members' needs (Deutsch, 1975).

Characteristics of Fairness-Based Arguments

The effectiveness of any given principle will be enhanced to the extent that it is simple, clear, justifiable, popular, and general. To be more specific, a fairness-based argument that has the following characteristics is more likely to win the support of team members and other relevant organizational actors (Messick, 1993):

- **Simplicity:** Team members should be able to articulate the procedure easily. This reduces the chances of misunderstanding and makes it easier to evaluate how accurately the procedure is being implemented.
- **Clarity:** The allocation procedure should be clear; if not, conflict may erupt concerning its interpretation.
- **Justifiability:** The procedure should be consistently applied across different individuals, time, and situations.
- **Consensus:** Team members should agree on the method of allocation. Team members often internalize effective social justice procedures, and such norms act as strong guidelines for decision making in teams. Because these norms often outlive current team members, new members are frequently indoctrinated with procedures the team found useful in the past (cf. Bettenhausen & Murnighan, 1985; Levine & Moreland, 1991, 1994).
- **Generality:** The procedure should be applicable to a wide variety of situations.

The Many Faces of Fairness

No matter how objective a fairness rule may appear, fairness is not an absolute construct. And, people's uses of fairness are for the most part self-enhancing. We do not wish to evaluate here what is really fair, but rather to stress the importance of arriving at an outcome that is perceived as fair by everyone concerned.

Reputations for fairness can be extremely important in business and employment relationships and often set the background against which a negotiation takes place. Generally speaking, people with a reputation for fairness will be trusted more than those who are viewed differently. We are not saying that being "fair" or "not fair" is the right or moral thing to do in every circumstance, simply that a reputation for fairness can be beneficial in many negotiating contexts. Moreover, an expectation of fairness as a splitting rule is pervasive—despite the emphasis in virtually every business publication, textbook, and so on, for competitive behavior.

WHAT TO DO WHEN CONFLICT ESCALATES?

Sometimes a firm will set up teams within the organization to compete with one another. The idea is to create a healthy competition to spur motivation. However, this can lead to escalating conflict and destructive outcomes that need special interventions. As an example, see Box 7-5.

Conflict often escalates because people believe that coercion is effective in reducing the resolve of others. Paradoxically, most people believe that when others use coercion on them, that it increases their resolve (Rothbart & Hallmark, 1988). The unfortunate consequence is that this perception encourages mutually aggressive behavior. (For an example of this in a military setting, see Sidebar 7-1.) What can be done to reduce the likelihood of strikes and get parties back to the bargaining table once a strike has begun?

BOX 7-5

Strike Behavior

To paraphrase a General Motors Corp. official, strikes hurt both the company and the workers and so are designed to put each of them in the mood to get together and compromise. However, bad blood can often escalate to a point where parties look beyond their own welfare to inflict punishment on the other party. Strikes are influenced by fairness perceptions; for instance, the likelihood and length of strikes is influenced by the difference in perceived fair wages between management and the union. That is, if management and the union have widely differing perceptions of what constitutes a fair settlement, a strike is more likely. Furthermore, teams on opposite sides of a conflict, such as management and union, hold biased perceptions about the strategies that will effectively settle conflict (Babcock & Olson, 1992; Thompson & Loewenstein, 1992).

Sidebar 7-1. We, but Not They, Would Rather Fight Than Switch

During World War II, the American journalist Edward R. Murrow made a nightly broadcast from London, reporting on the psychological and physical consequences of the Nazi bombing of British cities (Rothbart & Hallmark, 1988). Contrary to Nazi intent, the bombing did not move the British toward surrender. In fact, it had the opposite effect: It strengthened the British resolve to resist German domination. Shortly after the United States entered World War II, the Americans joined the British in launching costly bombing raids over Germany. In part, the intent was to decrease the German people's will to resist. Later research reported by the Office of Strategic Services that compared the lightly and heavily bombed areas found only minimal differences in civilians' will to resist.

The likelihood of protracted conflict is intimately linked to the beliefs each party holds about what they regard to be a fair settlement (Thompson & Loewenstein, 1992). People in conflict have different ideas about what is fair, and the most difficult conflicts are ones in which the parties' ideas of fairness are highly discrepant. In fact, the length of costly strikes can be directly predicted by the discrepancy between what the parties involved regard to be a fair outcome: The greater the discrepancy, the longer the strike—and both parties ultimately lose. Thus, to reduce conflict, it is critical to understand how to get parties to move away from egocentric perceptions of fair outcomes to more reasonable ones. The key problem is that most people regard themselves to be uniquely immune to bias and benevolent in their own motivations (Farwell & Weiner, 1996); they regard bias to be something that afflicts the other party in conflict. Most people involved in really difficult conflicts hold the following perceptions: (1) they are fairer than others; (2) the other party's view is egocentrically motivated (and, hence, unfair); and (3) there is only one correct (and fair) way to view the situation. This trilogy of beliefs is a recipe for disaster, unless something can be done to move parties away from one (and hopefully more) of these views.

Most people are not aware that their own perceptions of fairness are egocentrically biased. For example, van Avermaet (1974) asked team members to complete several questionnaires. These took either 45 or 90 minutes. The questionnaires were constructed so that, for each duration, some participants completed six questionnaires, while others completed only three. When asked to allocate monetary rewards, participants emphasized the dimension that favored them in the allocation procedure (those who worked longer emphasized time; questionnaire completion was emphasized by those who worked on more questionnaires).

It is not surprising, then, that members who contribute less prefer to divide resources equally, whereas those who contribute more prefer the equity rule (Allison & Messick, 1990). In groups containing members having different power or status levels, those with low power want equality, whereas those with high power desire equity (Komorita & Chertkoff, 1973; Shaw, 1981).

As a way of dealing with how to minimize egocentric perceptions of conflict it is probably most useful to first indicate which strategies seem like they would work, but usually don't. We are not saying that these strategies are doomed to failure, but rather that they have been tried and have not been shown to work, at least in simulated (yet realistic) conflict situations. It would seem that providing both parties with veridical information pertaining to the conflict situation (statistics on the labor supply, competitive analysis, etc.) would be helpful, at the very least serving as a reality check; however, this has not shown to be helpful. That is, when management and labor are provided with additional, unbiased information concerning disputes, this has the effect of further entrenching both parties more firmly in their own positions (Thompson & Loewenstein, 1992). To understand this backfire effect, it is important to recall our discussion of the confirmation bias. Parties interpret information in a way that is most favorable to their own position. Thus, they put their own spin on the facts in a way that gives them more confidence in their position.

It may seem that warning disputants about the existence of bias may be effective in reducing conflict and, at the very least, getting parties to perform a reality check of their own positions and beliefs supporting those positions. However, this does little to assuage biased perceptions (Babcock, Loewenstein, Issacharoff, & Camerer, 1995). Apparently, people regard bias as something that afflicts the "other guy"—not themselves. For similar reasons, taking the other person's point of view is generally not effective in reducing bias and conflict.

So much for what does *not* work; what *does* work to reduce egocentric perceptions of fairness? The key is to get parties to change their own perceptions about what is fair. Inducing parties to actively think about the weaknesses in their own position can be effective in reducing the length of costly strikes (Babcock et al., 1995). Furthermore, inviting a respected, neutral outsider to mediate can be effective (see Sidebar 7-2).

Sidebar 7-2. Team Therapy

We've all heard of group therapy. What about team therapy? Like families, there is a tendency for companies to hide conflict from the view of outsiders, coupled with a stoic tendency to want to work things out on their own. However, there is a lot of sense in calling in informed and skilled outsiders to deal with conflict. Indeed, there has been a recent development of therapist teams to work directly with companies to deal with unproductive conflicts.

CONCLUSIONS

Conflict in teams is unavoidable. However, it does not have to result in decreased productivity. Managed effectively, conflict can be key to leveraging differences of interest to arrive at creative solutions. However, many people intuitively respond to conflict in a defensive fashion, and this emotional type of conflict can threaten productivity. To the greatest extent possible, team members should depersonalize conflict. We have presented a variety of ways to achieve this. We have also cautioned against using majority rule, splitting the difference, and strict agendas, which might stifle the opportunity for team win-win gains.

BOX 7-6

Answers to Conflict Quiz

1. **False.** By using coercion, rather than conciliatory strategies, you increase the resolve of the opponent, thereby escalating conflict.

2. **False.** The large majority of people want outcomes to be fair; meaning that they do not want to deliberately take advantage of others and they want to get what they perceive to be equitable. However, because fairness has many definitions, people tend to focus on those that serve their own interests.

3. **False.** Even when people are faced with opportunities where they can take advantage of others, they frequently do not. There are several reasons for this: many people's self-identities are such that they do not want to take obvious and deliberate advantage of others. People also feel uncomfortable reneging on their promises. Lastly, most people realize treating others unfairly is generally a poor strategy in the long run.

4. **False.** In general, people have a hard time empathizing with others; a more effective strategy is for parties to list the weak points in their own position.

5. **False.** People who are friends are likely to compromise too quickly, failing to take advantage of mutually beneficial opportunities. Integrative agreements require parties to identify and focus on their priorities—and be willing to compromise on other, less important issues. If people compromise too quickly, they do not identify and take full advantage of this information.

6. **False.** Providing further information can exacerbate conflict because each person will interpret information as supporting their own position. A better strategy would be to have parties think about the weaknesses in their own position.

7. **False.** There is little relationship between objective measures of success in negotiation and self-appraisal. People's subjective assessment of success may be based on largely irrelevant cues, such as the emotional expression of the other party.

8. **False.** Conflict among team members can boost creativity within teams—if the conflict situation is properly structured. Constructive conflict is idea- and data-focused, not emotional.

9. **False.** Trust does not guarantee win-win outcomes. Instead, diagnostic information needs to be exchanged by providing information about priorities, asking questions, making multiple-issue offers, discussing issues simultaneously (rather than sequentially), and revisiting agreements after they are completed (postsettlement settlement strategy.).

10. **False.** Although it may seem that voting is a democratic and fair method of reconciling differences among team members, it often can lead to ineffective choices or choices that do not adequately reflect the interests of group members. However, more than producing paradoxical choice, voting hinders the discovery of members' interests.

CHAPTER 8

Creativity: Mastering Strategies for High Performance

A large group of microbiology laboratories were studied over a period of time. Each laboratory was staffed with trained scientists, and the goal of each lab was to make new discoveries. Over time, some labs distinguished themselves in terms of having more breakthrough discoveries. The laboratories that were more successful in terms of developing new ideas—as measured by the number of new patents, and so on—did not have a larger staff, nor were its scientists better paid or smarter. The key differences between the highly creative laboratories and the other labs were threefold: Diversity in staff member training and experience; paying attention to inconsistencies and failures; and the use of analogical reasoning. Thus, teams that were more heterogeneous in composition, learned from their failures, and freely drew from other domains to address problems were more likely to make breakthrough discoveries (based on Dunbar, 1997).

Most businesses are not exactly run like microbiology laboratories, but many businesses need managers and their teams to be creative to remain competitive. We distinguished three kinds of team tasks in chapter 4: Tactical, problem-solving, and creative (Larson & LaFasto, 1989). In this chapter, we deal with the creative challenges that teams face.

Just because the task facing a team is one that calls for creativity, however, is no guarantee that the team members will be creative. In fact, as we have seen in our discussion of decision-making biases, many factors inhibit the idea exchange process in groups. As we noted in chapter 2, groups often suffer from motivation and coordination problems, all of which may lead them to develop low performance standards.

Common wisdom holds that creativity in teams is lurking below the surface and that with the proper intervention or team design, it can be unleashed. This view of creativity as a latent or dormant force is not really accurate. In fact, if motivation and coordination losses are not managed carefully, individual creativity often exceeds that of most teams! However, if the situation is right, the combined efforts of team members exceed what is possible for each person to do independently. Unfortunately, this is rare; most often, the whole of team effort falls far short of the sum of the parts. The reasons have to do with the threats to performance that we discussed in chapter 2.

The objective of this chapter is to examine team processes and designs that hinder or facilitate creativity. First, we define creativity and discuss how it is measured. Next, we explain the differences between individual creativity and team creativity. Then, we describe several types of reasoning including analogical reasoning and convergent and divergent thinking. Finally, we examine brainstorming techniques and discuss the advantages and disadvantages of each technique.

WHAT EXACTLY IS CREATIVITY?

Creativity is the production of novel and useful ideas—the ability to form new concepts using existing knowledge. A creative act is *original* and *valuable*.

Measuring Creativity

To be considered creative, an idea must be highly original and useful. The last part is the challenge—many people can come up with totally bizarre but useless ideas. The key is for these ideas to be valuable. One common way of evaluating the creativity of a team's ideas is via three indices: Fluency, flexibility, and originality (Guilford, 1959, 1967).

- **Fluency:** The ability to generate *many solutions* that all fit some requirement.
- **Flexibility:** The ability to change approaches to a problem, such as being able to solve a series of tasks that each require a different strategy.
- **Originality:** The ability to generate unusual solutions, such as coming up with unique answers.

As a way of thinking about these three indices of creativity, do the following exercise: See how many possible uses you can think of for a cardboard box. (Give yourself about 10 minutes to do this.)

Now suppose that one person who completed this exercise, Geoff, generated two ideas: Using the box as a cage for a hamster and as a kennel for a dog. Geoff would receive two points for fluency of ideas because these are two different ideas, but only one point for flexibility because the ideas are of the same category (i.e., a home for animals). It seems likely that creative people would generate more novel and unusual ways to use a cardboard box.

Another person, Avi, generated these unusual ideas for a cardboard box: Using it as a god, using it as a telephone (e.g., two boxes and some string), and trading it as currency. Avi would get a score of three points for fluency and three points for flexibility, because there are three separate categories of ideas for use, involving religion, communication, and economics. In addition, Avi's ideas are extremely original.

Creativity through Categorization of Ideas and Team Diversity

It is easy to see how flexibility in thought—that is, thinking about different categories of use—can influence originality. Thus, one simple key for enhancing creativity is to *diversify the use of categories.* By listing possible categories of use for a cardboard box (containers, shelter, building material, therapy, religion, politics, weaponry, communication, etc.), a person's score on these three dimensions could increase dramatically. Thus, a key strategy is to think in terms of *categories* of ideas—not just *number* of ideas. This can often help teams break out of a narrow perspective on a problem and open up new opportunities for creative solutions.

There is a deeper message in this prescriptive advice: One way to enhance creativity is to diversify the members of the team. With different backgrounds, training, and perspectives, people are naturally going to bring different categories of thought and ways of looking at a problem to the team. The more heterogeneous the team is, the more likely it is that the team members will excel in all measures of creativity. Indeed, teams in which members are diverse, with regard to background and perspective, outperform teams with homogeneous members on tasks requiring creative problem solving and innovation (Jackson, 1992). This occurs when coworkers experience cognitive conflict (i.e., C-type conflict) in the absence of conformity pressures and respond by revising fundamental assumptions and generating novel insights (Levine, Resnick, & Higgins, 1993; Nemeth, 1994). As a result, teams with heterogeneous members generate more arguments (Smith, Tindale, & Dugoni, 1996), apply a greater number of strategies (Nemeth & Wachtler, 1983), detect more novel solutions (Nemeth & Kwan, 1987), and are better at integrating multiple perspectives (Gruenfeld, 1994, 1995; Peterson & Nemeth, 1996) than teams without conflicting perspectives.

Creativity through Cognitive Flexibility

One route to greater creativity in teams is to increase the flexibility of thought. Integrative complexity is a measure of the extent to which people exhibit (1) conceptual differentiation (recognition of multiple perspectives on a problem), and (2) conceptual integration (recognition of trade-offs among these perspectives). Intensive examinations of teams reveal that members in the majority exhibit greater integrative complexity than do members in the minority (Gruenfeld, 1995). For example, consider opinions rendered by the U.S. Supreme Court (Gruenfeld, 1995). The authors of majority opinions tend to concern themselves with specifying all imaginable contingencies under which the law should and should not apply to ensure the longevity of their precedent. In contrast, the authors of minority opinions often focus on arguments that could eventually facilitate the precedent's overruling. This suggests that people who are exposed to members who hold a majority view experience an increase in their own levels of integrative thought; in contrast, people exposed to minority opinions or unanimous groups actually experience a decrease in integrative thinking (Gruenfeld, Thomas-Hunt, & Kim, 1998).

Creativity and Context Dependence

Consider the *Mona Lisa,* Stephen Hawking's theory of the universe, and the development of the microcomputer. All of these are tremendously creative acts that seem to go above and beyond the simple measures of fluency, flexibility, and originality. These achievements are not only unique, but they are impressive because they were invented with limited resources and in the face of numerous obstacles. Furthermore, if someone today developed the microcomputer, it would not be regarded as a creative act—not just because it has already been done, but because of other advances in technology that already exist. Similarly, if an artist painted the *Mona Lisa* today—even if it had not already been done by Leonardo da Vinci—it probably would not be regarded as an especially creative act. Thus, surrounding all creative products is a context. Creative acts take place within a particular context and within a particular domain given a set of certain resources (Csikszentmihalyi, 1988). To a large extent, the timeliness of an idea is an index of its usefulness or value.

CREATIVE PEOPLE OR CREATIVE TEAMS?

Is creativity a characteristic of individuals or groups? The answer is both. There is little doubt that some people are more creative than others. However, creativity as a trait is highly correlated with intelligence, motivation, education, and other desirable personal qualities. In general, creative people are more intelligent, ambitious, successful, persistent, committed, and determined than are others.

Where do creative ideas come from? In contrast to popular belief, they rarely come out of the blue. Creative ideas, whether they be for new products, paintings, organizational theories, or inventions, often begin as a straightforward extension of earlier work that undergoes modification. For example, many of Thomas Edison's inventions developed through continuity with earlier inventions (Weisberg, 1993; see Sidebar 8-1).

> ### Sidebar 8-1. Analogy in Edison's Development of an Electric Lighting System
>
> After Edison invented the incandescent light, his next project was to develop an entire system whereby the invention could be made commercially successful. At the time, there were two in-place lighting systems (neither developed by Edison): Gas lights and electrical arc lights. Gas lights could be directly controlled for brightness; gas fuel was produced off-site and sent through buried gas mains. Arc lighting was produced by an electrical spark between carbon rods, was very hot, and produced fumes. The generating plant was located directly by the user. Edison's electric lighting system was based on the principles of gas lighting. Edison wrote in his workbooks that he completely imitated the gas system, replacing the gas with electricity. In Edison's electric system, the source of power was remote from the user, and the wires that brought the power were underground. Furthermore, the individual lights were turned on and off by the user. The lightbulb in Edison's system was called a burner and was designed to produce the same amount of light as a gas burner (Basalla, 1988; Weisberg, 1997).

The creative person is able to select the relevant information and ignore irrelevant information. An extended period of preparation is involved in most creative products and ideas. Indeed, creative people work very hard. For example, creative scientists typically work 70 to 80 hours a week. Think of it this way: It typically takes people at least 10 years to develop expertise in their domain, no matter what it is: Chess, tennis, astrophysics, or management. Skilled chess players undergo years of study before they become "masters" (DeGroot, 1966). No one composes outstanding music without at least 10 years of intensive musical preparation (Weisberg, 1986). Basically, if you have been working hard for years at something, think in terms of decades!

Team Creativity

In this chapter, we are interested in factors that can enhance creativity in teams. We call this **team creativity.** Team creativity is the opposite of threats to performance, which we discussed in chapter 2. Team creativity refers to the synergistic gains that teams can, but certainly do not always, experience. It is what people mean when they say that the teams whole is greater than the sum of its parts: The group as a whole achieved something that would not have been possible by merely combining the individual efforts of members.

Team creativity, as with all team endeavors, seeks to maximize synergies and minimize threats to performance. It refers to otherwise normal people doing incredible things in a team operating within a given external environment. Team creativity is the Holy Grail of organizational behavior: Everyone wants it, but very few people know where to look for it or how to set up the conditions to make it happen. This chapter examines how to design the team so as to make creativity more likely.

ANALOGICAL REASONING

Analogical reasoning is the act of applying one concept or idea from a particular domain to another domain. The simplest analogy might be something like this: *Green* is to *go* as *red* is to *stop*. A much more complex analogy that indicates creative genius is Kepler's application of concepts from light to develop a theory of the orbital motion of planets (Gentner, Brem, Ferguson, & Wolff, 1997).

As we saw in the example of microbiology labs, teams are often able to be creative by applying a concept useful in one domain to a new domain. To the extent that teams can recognize when a particular concept might be useful for solving a new problem, creativity can be enhanced. The problem is that it is not easy to transfer relevant information from one domain to another—humans tend to solve problems based upon their surface similarity to other situations, rather than their deep, structural similarity.

To see the difference between surface-level similarity and deep-level similarity, consider the problem presented in Box 8-1. The problem is how to use a ray to destroy a patient's tumor given that the ray at full strength will destroy the healthy tissue en route to the tumor. Only about 10 percent of people solve this problem. Now, consider the problem in Box 8-2. In this problem, a general needs to capture a fortress but is prevented from making a frontal attack by the entire army. How should he deal with this

---

BOX 8-1

The Tumor Problem

Suppose you are a doctor faced with a patient who has a malignant tumor in his stomach. It is impossible to operate on the patient, but unless the tumor is destroyed, the patient will die. There is a kind of ray that can be used to destroy the tumor. If the rays reach the tumor all at once at a sufficiently high intensity, the tumor will be destroyed. Unfortunately, at this intensity, the healthy tissue that the rays pass through on the way to the tumor will also be destroyed. At lower intensities, the rays are harmless to healthy tissue, but they will not affect the tumor either. What type of procedure might be used to destroy the tumor with the rays and, at the same time, avoid destroying the healthy tissue (Gick & Holyoak, 1980; adapted from Duncker, 1945)?

problem? One solution is to divide the army and converge on the fortress from many sides. An analogous solution is possible for the radiation problem: The doctor can converge on the tumor with low-strength rays from multiple sides. At a surface level, the problems seem to have little or nothing in common—one from the medical world and the other from a military decision. However, at a deeper level, the problems are highly analogous, as can be seen in Figure 8-1. What do you think happens when people are given the tumor problem prior to reading the fortress problem?

Even when given the tumor problem, at the most only 41 percent of people spontaneously apply the convergence solution to the radiation problem. Yet when simply told to "think about the earlier problem," solution rates rise to around 85 percent. If people are given a story about a doctor treating a brain tumor in a similar fashion, solution rates rise to 90 percent. This points up an important aspect of creativity and knowledge: *People usually have the knowledge they need to solve problems, but fail to access it because it comes from a different context.* Thus, a key limitation of managers is not that they are lacking information and knowledge, but that they do not have access to relevant aspects of their own experience when they need it. Thus, applying previously learned knowledge to new situations is surprisingly difficult for most managers.

BOX 8-2

The Fortress Story

A small country fell under the iron rule of a dictator. The dictator ruled the country from a strong fortress. The fortress was situated in the middle of the country, surrounded by farms and villages. Many roads radiated outward from the fortress like spokes on a wheel. A great general arose, who raised a large army at the border and vowed to capture the fortress and free the country of the dictator. The general knew that if his entire army could attack the fortress at once, it could be captured. His troops were poised at the head of one of the roads leading to the fortress, ready to attack. However, a spy brought the general a disturbing report. The ruthless dictator had planted mines on each of the roads. The mines were set so that small bodies of men could pass over them safely, since the dictator needed to be able to move troops and workers to and from the fortress. However, any large force would detonate the mines. Not only would this blow up the road and render it impassable, but the dictator would destroy many villages in retaliation. A full-scale direct attack on the fortress therefore appeared impossible.

The general, however, was undaunted. He divided his army up into small groups and dispatched each group to the head of a different road. When all was ready, he gave the signal, and each group charged down a different road. All of the small groups passed safely over the mines, and the army then attacked the fortress in full strength. In this way, the general was able to capture the fortress and overthrow the dictator (Gick & Holyoak, 1980; adapted from Duncker, 1945).

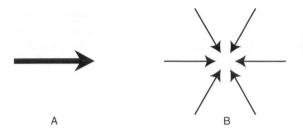

Source: Gick, M. L., & Holyoak, K. J. 1983. "Schema Induction and Analogical Transfer." *Cognitive Psychology, 15,* 1–38. Reprinted in Holyoak, K. J., & Thagard, P. 1995. *Mental Leaps: Analogy in Creative Thought.* Cambridge, MA: MIT Press.

The single large arrow (A) can be mapped to a single high-intensity ray; the multiple converging arrows (B) can be mapped to multiple converging low-intensity rays.

FIGURE 8-1   A Visual Analog of the Tumor Problem

How many of us have experienced the frustration of seeing a connection after it was pointed out to us, but not before? This is known as the **inert knowledge problem**—it means that people's ability to take full advantage of their prior experience is highly limited. Even when they possess the relevant experience necessary to deal with a novel problem, they often fail to do so when their previous experience comes from a different context.

When people encounter a new situation or problem, they are reminded not of prior problems with the same underlying deep structure (such as how the tumor problem is similar to the fortress problem), but of problems with the same surface features (Gentner, Rattermann, & Forbus, 1993). In fact, they recall problems that have surface similarity about 55 percent of the time and problems that are deeply relevant about 12 percent of the time. This points to an important fact about managerial information processing: The knowledge people gain from their daily experience is often not accessed, despite the fact that once it is called to their attention, they regard it to be helpful (Forbus, Gentner, & Law, 1995; Gentner & Landers, 1985; Gentner et al., 1993; Gick & Holyoak, 1980, 1983; Holyoak & Koh, 1987; Reeves & Weisberg, 1994; Ross, 1987).

Expertise

The key question is how to overcome the inert knowledge problem—how to *access* our relevant experience when we need it. One proven way of doing this is through expertise. For example, novices at physics categorize physics problems by their surface features (pulley problems, weight problems, etc.); in contrast, physics experts categorize the same problems according to laws of physics (Ross, 1987). Novices clearly show the surface similarity retrieval pattern. Although experts continue to experience surface retrieval, they also experience remindings based on underlying relational similarity. Expertise increases the likelihood that analogical transfer will ultimately occur successfully (Novick, 1988, Novick & Holyoak, 1991). Experts show an improvement in analogical transfer due to the consistency with which they represent problems, particularly through encoding relations uniformly across contexts (Forbus et al., 1995). The problem is that most managers and consultants do not have the time, inclination, or resources to become experts in all of the areas in which they must solve problems. So what can be done?

Comparison and Abstraction

There is another strategy that is remarkably cost-effective, quick, and extraordinarily effective. We call it *comparison and abstraction* (Gentner et al., 1997; Loewenstein, Thompson, & Gentner, in press; Thompson, Gentner, & Loewenstein, in press).

If **relational similarity** between the presenting problem and a manager's own knowledge base increases the likelihood of analogical transfer, a key element of successful transfer should be making the relational structure explicit during the original encoding. One method for doing this is to make a comparison. According to Gentner & Markman (1997), comparison entails a structural alignment and mapping process that highlights the similar aspects of the two examples. Focusing on shared aspects between examples promotes the abstraction of common relational structures that can then be stored as a schema. Such a schema is useful for the manager because it is uncluttered with irrelevant surface information. People seem to draw such abstractions readily in the process of making comparisons (e.g., Brown, 1989; Chen & Daehler, 1989; Crisafi & Brown, 1986; Gick & Holyoak, 1983; Kotovsky & Gentner, 1996; Loewenstein, 1997; Loewenstein & Gentner, in preparation). Thus, one way to promote encoding relational structure during the initial learning situation is to provide managers with a comparison. Comparison and abstraction fosters subsequent knowledge transfer.

For example, managers who are asked to compare two cases are much more likely to effectively transfer a relevant concept to a real-world problem (60 percent) than when they are exposed to the same two cases, but are asked to give advice (33 percent; Loewenstein et al., in press).

There are three conclusions to be drawn here: (1) comparison among a manager's own experiences can be illuminating; (2) potentially useful comparisons are easy to miss, even when the cases are juxtaposed in time and space; and (3) techniques that encourage comparison and analogical encoding can lead to better learning and analogical transfer (Thompson, Loewenstein & Gentner, in press).

DIVERGENT VERSUS CONVERGENT THINKING

There are two key skills involved in creative thinking: Divergent thinking and convergent thinking (Guilford, 1959, 1967). **Convergent thinking** is thinking that proceeds toward a single answer, such as the expected value of a 70% chance of earning $1,000 is obtained by multiplying $1,000 by .7 to reach $700. **Divergent thinking** moves outward from the problem in many possible directions and involves thinking without boundaries. It is related to the notion of flexibility of categories and originality of thought. Divergent thinking *is* out-of-the-box thinking.

Many of the factors that make up creative problem solving seem most closely related to divergent thinking. However, ideas eventually need to be evaluated and acted upon. This is where convergent thinking comes in. In convergent thinking, a team or person judges and evaluates the various ideas presented as to their feasibility, practicality, and overall merit.

C-type conflict can stimulate the generation of divergent thinking in teams (Nemeth, 1994). For example, teams in which a single member proposes unusual or even incorrect solutions have outperformed teams in which no such "deviance" occurred. Cognitive deviance of this sort leads to a greater number of problem-solving strategies, original arguments, and associations compared to teams that lack a vocal minority (Nemeth & Kwan, 1987). Furthermore, once a team has experienced this type of activity, these performance advantages generalize to subsequent, unrelated tasks, even when the vocal, cognitively deviant member is not present (Smith, Tindale, & Dugoni, 1996).

People working independently excel at divergent thinking because there are no cognitive or social pressures to constrain their thought. In short, there are no conformity pressures. In contrast, teams are much less proficient at divergent thinking. The key reasons have to do with conformity pressures. To avoid social censure, people assess the norms of the teams and conform to them. These factors are exactly what produces the common information effect and groupthink. In contrast, teams excel compared to individuals when in comes to convergent thinking. Teams are better at judging the quality of ideas. This suggests that an effective team design for promoting creativity involves separating the generation of ideas—leaving this to individual team members—and then evaluating and discussing the ideas as a team. Presumably, this is what an advertising executive named Alex Osborn had in mind when he developed the strategy of brainstorming.

GROUP BRAINSTORMING

Alex Osborn, an advertising executive in the 1950s, wanted to increase the creativity of organizations. He believed that one of the main blocks to organizational creativity was the premature evaluation of ideas. He was convinced that two heads were better than one when it came to generating ideas, but only if people could be trained to defer judgment of their own and others' ideas during the idea generation process. Therefore, Osborn developed the most widespread strategy used by organizations to encourage creative thought in teams: Brainstorming.

Brainstorming is a technique used by a large number of companies and organizations to unleash the creative group mind and avoid the negative impact of group dynamics on creativity. The goal of brainstorming is to maximize the *quantity* and *quality* of ideas. Osborn aptly noted that quantity is a good predictor of quality: A team is more likely to discover a really good idea if it has a lot of ideas to choose from. But there is even more to brainstorming than mere quantity. Osborn believed that the ideas generated by one person in a team could stimulate ideas in other people in a synergistic fashion.

Osborn believed that the group product could be greater than the sum of the individual parts if certain conditions were met. Hence, he developed rules for brainstorming. Contrary to popular corporate lore that brainstorming sessions are wild and crazy free-for-alls where anything goes, brainstorming has defined rules (Osborn, 1957, 1963). They are still widely used today and several companies post the brainstorming guidelines and roles prominently in their meeting rooms (see Table 8-1).

Some companies, like Silicon Valley's IDEO, live by these rules. Douglas Dayton of IDEO says that five rules govern every brainstorming session at IDEO: "Have one conversation at a time. Build upon the ideas of others. Defer judgment. Encourage wild ideas (not wild behavior). Stay focused on the subject" (Gendron, 1998, p. 9).

Brainstorming in companies caught on quickly. Osborn believed, as did others, that the four rules had the effect of enhancing motivation among team members by stimulating them to higher levels of productivity via establishment of a benchmark or via competitive rivalry to see who could generate the most ideas. Osborn also thought that the social reinforcement of fellow members increased motivation. Finally, Osborn believed in a "priming effect"; namely, that members would make mutual associations upon hearing the ideas presented by others.

Brainstorming on Trial

"But is it effective?" is the question that organizational psychologists and management theorists asked of the brainstorming technique. Controlled, scientific studies supported

TABLE 8-1 Rules for Brainstorming	
Expressiveness:	Group members should express any idea that comes to mind, no matter how strange, weird, or fanciful. Group members are encouraged not to be constrained nor timid. They should freewheel whenever possible.
Nonevaluation:	Do not criticize ideas. Group members should not evaluate any of the ideas in any way during the generation phase; all ideas should be considered valuable.
Quantity:	Group members should generate as many ideas as possible. Groups should strive for quantity, as the more ideas, the better. Quantity of ideas increases the probability of finding excellent solutions.
Building:	Because all of the ideas belong to the group, members should try to modify and extend the ideas suggested by other members whenever possible.

Source: Adapted from Osborn, A. F. 1957. *Applied Imagination* (rev. ed.). New York: Scribner.

Osborn's intuition: Brainstorming instructions enhance the generation of ideas within a team, in comparison to teams working without those instructions (Parnes & Meadow, 1959). Thus, following the brainstorming guidelines can help increase team creativity.

However, Osborn's most controversial claim was that group brainstorming would be more effective—"twice as productive," in his words— than **individual brainstorming,** where group members work independently (Osborn, 1957). The research evidence testing this assertion has found that the opposite is true: *Most studies have found that solitary brainstorming is much more productive than is group brainstorming,* in terms of both quality and quantity of ideas (Diehl & Stroebe, 1987; Mullen, Johnson, & Salas, 1991). In fact, virtually all of the empirical studies for group brainstorming are strongly (not just mildly) negative (Diehl & Stroebe, 1987; Mullen et al., 1991) of its effectiveness compared to solitary brainstorming. As a typical example, look at the statistics in Table 8-2, which are actual performance data of brainstorming groups and solitary groups in terms of quantity and quality of ideas.

On the basis of these results, which have been replicated several hundred times with a variety of teams brainstorming about all kinds of things, the same pattern emerges again and again. "It appears particularly difficult to justify brainstorming techniques in terms of any performance outcomes, and the long-lived popularity of brainstorming techniques is unequivocally and substantially misguided" (Mullen et al., 1991, p. 18).

TABLE 8-2 Performance Data of Brainstorming and Solitary Groups		
	Face-to-Face Brainstorming Group	*Same Number of People Working Independently (Solitary Brainstorming)*
Quantity: The number of ideas generated	28	74.5
Quality: Percentage of "good ideas" as judged by independent experts who did not know whose ideas they were evaluating	20.8%	79.2%

Source: Diehl, M., & Stroebe, W. 1987. "Productivity Loss in Brainstorming Groups: Toward a Solution of a Riddle." *Journal of Personality and Social Psychology, 53,* 497–509.

Thus, official rules of brainstorming, when followed, do enhance team performance, but brainstorming teams still generate fewer ideas than similar numbers of solitary brainstormers (nominal groups).

Why are brainstorming groups less effective than brainstorming individuals? How could the intuition of so many companies and managers be so wrong? There are at least three key things that go wrong in a group brainstorm and hinder idea generation: Social loafing, conformity pressures, and coordination problems.

First, in terms of **social loafing,** as the number of team members increases, each person engages in a type of free riding that we have discussed in previous chapters (Karau & Williams, 1993; Shepperd, 1993). It is as if members say to themselves, "I don't need to work really hard when thinking of ideas since everyone else is working too." This free-riding tendency may be especially true when members' outcomes cannot be individually identified or evaluated.

Second, in terms of **conformity,** people may be somewhat apprehensive about expressing their ideas because they are concerned about others judging and evaluating them (Mullen et al., 1991). This is the need to be liked, which we discussed in chapter 6 (decision making). Most people are highly concerned with presenting a positive image to others (Leary, 1995). This concern for "what others will think of me" may inhibit idea generation in teams (Camacho & Paulus, 1995). Many social conventions, even those in companies, suggest that in most settings, people should stay "on topic" and not present ideas that diverge greatly from the ones being discussed. Indeed, in interactive teams, there is much more of a tendency to stay on topic than with individual brainstorming. This convergent pattern limits the exchange of ideas that are relatively novel to the team and possibly have the most stimulation value.

Finally, **coordination problems** arise when team members have to take turns presenting their ideas. In contrast, individual brainstormers have the entire allotted time for themselves. A person who is working alone on a problem can enjoy an uninterrupted flow of thought. In contrast, participants in a face-to-face brainstorming group must not only think of ideas, but also listen to others' ideas. It is cognitively difficult to maintain a train of thought or remember ideas generated while others are talking (Diehl & Stroebe, 1987). Members of teams may be prevented from generating new ideas during a team discussion because they are distracted by hearing the contributions of other members while waiting for their turn to participate. During the waiting period, members may listen to others' contributions and, in the process, forget to rehearse the ideas they want to mention. Furthermore, the inability to express ideas or get floor time may be frustrating and depress motivation.

What Goes on During a Typical Group Brainstorming Session?

Social loafing, conformity pressures, and coordination problems combine to cause most brainstorming groups to generate ideas at a rather slow pace. When idea generation *does* occur, a number of interaction processes conspire to keep the performance level rather low: The need to develop a comfortable means of interacting may interfere with the focus on an efficient rate of idea generation in the early phases of group interaction. Furthermore, people get involved in rituals of interaction that may not be conducive to high levels of idea generation: They may give positive feedback, repeat ideas, and tell stories. This is the natural pattern of conversation. These activities take up time that could be spent generating ideas and processing information.

Social comparison processes may lead team members to converge their performance levels to one another (Jackson & Harkins, 1985). This performance level may set the benchmark for the team, in that it is seen as an appropriate or typical level of performance. For example, participants in interactive dyads or groups of four tend to be more similar in their rate of idea generation than noninteracting groups (Camacho & Paulus, 1995; Paulus & Dzindolet, 1993). Unfortunately, the least productive members of the team are often more influential in determining overall team performance than the high performers; and people conform more in groups. For example, word associations are more conventional and clichéd when produced by people in interacting groups than by similar people working alone.

As we have seen, the ideas generated by one member may block or hinder the idea generation of others. Furthermore, there is no evidence for any stimulating impact of unique or rare ideas in brainstorming (Connolly, Routhieaux, & Schneider, 1993).

Finally, unless there are strong competitive or individual accountability pressures, a downward comparison process may predominate: The least productive team performers may become the reference point for a social matching or convergence process. However, because the team members do not have a benchmark to evaluate their performance, they will be predisposed to evaluate their own performance, and the team's performance, favorably.

Brainstorming is simply not as effective as it was hoped to be. What can be done to restructure the design of brainstorming groups?

Trained Facilitators

A trained facilitator can bring the level of team performance to that of nominal groups (Offner, Kramer, & Winter, 1996; Oxley, Dzindolet, & Paulus, 1996). Furthermore, there are long-term benefits to this investment: Teams that are given several sessions in which they are guided by facilitators into productive idea generation patterns demonstrate high levels of productivity in subsequent sessions without the facilitators (Paulus, Putman, Coskun, Leggett, & Roland, 1996). Apparently, teams can become accustomed to sharing ideas without extensive social interaction or "filler" talk.

High Benchmarks

Brainstorming groups are often missing relevant benchmarks. Information about other members' activity levels may increase performance as long as the benchmark is not too discrepant (Seta, 1982). Providing brainstormers with high performance standards greatly increases the number of ideas generated (Paulus & Dzindolet, 1993). Even when members are working independently and announcing to others how many ideas they are generating every 5 minutes, the number of ideas generated by the team is enhanced (Paulus, Larey, Putman, Leggett, & Roland, 1996). Similarly, a facilitator can periodically call brainstormers' attention to a graph on the computer screen indicating how the team's performance compares with that of other teams—this significantly enhances the number of ideas generated by the group (Shepherd, Briggs, Reinig, Yen, & Nunamaker, 1995-1996). Even forewarning teams that they will see a display of all ideas at the end of the session increases the number of unique ideas generated (Roy, Gauvin, & Limayem, 1996). It is also helpful for members to record their own ideas after the brainstorm.

Two-Step Approach: Solitary and Group Ideation

A much better method of group brainstorming, proposed by Osborn himself, is to *prepare* for group brainstorming by having a prior session of **solitary writing.** An alternative is for teams to engage in periods of **brainwriting** during a brainstorming, wherein members write in the same room (Paulus, 1998). Alternating between team ideation and individual ideation is desirable because it allows teams to circumvent production blocking (coordination problems) and it also sets the stage for divergent thinking (Osborn, 1957).

This two-step technique requires a considerable number of conditions to be in place for optimal productivity in group brainstorming. Each member needs to take time out for solitary mediations. Similar benefits can be accomplished through preliminary writing sessions, quotas or deadlines, brief breaks, and the use of specific, simple, and subdivided problems. Thus, by working together, then alone, and then together, teams are more likely to achieve the best in creative thinking (Osborn, 1963).

At the very least, all talking should be stopped periodically to allow members to think silently; the more pauses and silences that occur during brainstorming, the higher the quality of the ideas. Giving members brief breaks, even if they don't write anything down, can help (Horn, 1993).

Nominal Group Technique

The **nominal group technique** separates the idea generation from idea evaluation phases. In the nominal group technique, it is useful to have a facilitator, but it is not necessary. The facilitator introduces a problem on the board or on a flipchart. Once members understand the topic or issue, they silently write ideas for 10 to 15 minutes. Members state their ideas in a round-robin fashion and each idea is given an identification number. Once ideas are all listed, the team discusses each item, focusing on clarification. Following this, members privately rank the five solutions or ideas they most prefer. The leader-facilitator collects the cards and averages the rating to yield a group decision (see also Box 8-3).

The advantage of the nominal group technique is that it maximizes information gain, ensures a democratic representation of all members' ideas (i.e., avoids the lumpy participation effect), and avoids production blocking. Yet members still have an opportunity for face-to-face discussion of issues. Although it might seem that the nominal group technique would run the risk of generating redundant ideas, they are no more common per number of total ideas than in real face-to-face groups. There are some disadvantages of the nominal group technique. It is less spontaneous and it may require a separate meeting for each topic.

Nominal groups that perform in the same room generate more ideas than those in separate rooms (Mullen et al., 1991). This technique, called brainwriting, can be tremendously effective (Paulus, 1998).

Stepladder Technique

The stepladder technique (Rogelberg, Barnes-Farrell, & Lowe, 1992) is a decision-making approach in which members are added one by one to a team. Step 1 of the technique involves the creation of a two-person subgroup (the core) that begins preliminary

---

BOX 8-3

Rotating Nominal Group Technique

A variation called the **rotating nominal group technique** involves members writing down their ideas on individual sheets of paper or notecards. The meeting facilitator collects the notecards, shuffles them, and redistributes them to individual group members who read the cards aloud or discuss in small groups. This variation creates greater acceptance of others' ideas and prevents individual members from championing their own ideas.

---

discussion of the group task. After a fixed time interval, another member joins the core group and presents his or her ideas concerning the task. The three-person group then discusses the task in a preliminary manner. The process continues in steps until all members have systematically joined the core group. When this occurs, the group arrives at a final solution. Each member must have sufficient time to think about the problem before entering into the core group. More important, the entering members must present their preliminary solutions before hearing the core group's preliminary solutions. A final decision cannot be reached until the group has formed in its entirety. Self-pacing stepladder groups (which proceed through the paces at a self-determined pace) produce significantly higher quality group decisions than conventional groups (Rogelberg & O'Connor, 1998). Members with the best individual decisions exert more influence in stepladder groups than in free interaction groups.

Delphi Technique

The Delphi technique is an extreme version of the nominal group technique. In the Delphi technique, group members do not interact in a face-to-face fashion at any point. This technique is ideally suited for teams whose members are geographically dispersed, making meetings difficult to attend, and for teams whose members experience such great conflict that it is difficult to get through a meeting. This technique requires a leader or facilitator who is trusted by team members. The entire process proceeds through questionnaires followed by feedback, which can be computerized. The leader distributes a topic or question to members and asks for responses from each team member. The leader then aggregates the responses, sends them back out to the team, and solicits feedback. This process is repeated until there is resolution on the issue in question.

The Delphi technique provides maximum structure, ensures equal input, and avoids production blocking—it is pretty easy to avoid coordination loss when team members never interact directly! The technique is a good alternative for teams whose members are physically separated but, nevertheless, need to make decisions. Because members respond independently, conformity pressures and evaluation apprehension are limited. One problem associated with this technique, which is not associated with regular brainstorming or nominal brainstorming, is that it can be quite time-consuming. Sessions can last several days, even weeks.

ELECTRONIC BRAINSTORMING

Electronic brainstorming (EBS) has recently been introduced into organizations as a means of generating ideas; it makes use of computers to allow members to interact and to exchange ideas. The ideas that are generated using EBS are anonymous and, thus, tend to be expressed more freely and in greater quantity.

EBS is used as part of a regular organizational meeting process. It gives organizations the opportunity to gather ideas efficiently, organize those ideas, and subsequently make decisions. It speeds up the meeting at which it is used, increases productivity, and allows the focus to remain on the ideas rather than on the people who spawned them. When members run out of ideas, they access the ideas produced by the team.

In EBS, people are usually not identified by their contributions. Typically, participants can view subsets of ideas generated by other team members on part of the screen at any time by using a keystroke. Ideas are projected on a large screen and people are asked to evaluate them. The team may eventually vote on the most preferred ideas. A facilitator guides both the idea generation and decision processes (Jessup & Valacich, 1993; Nunamaker, Briggs, & Mittleman, 1995). For an example of how one company uses EBS, see Sidebar 8-2.

Sidebar 8-2. An Implementation of Electronic Brainstorming

At Mattel Media, a division of Mattel Toys in El Segundo, California, a self-proclaimed "technographer" records team members' new-product ideas on a laptop—the entries appearing before the group either on 35-inch color monitors or projected onto the wall. Bernie DeKoven, whose title at Mattel is "Doctor Fun / staff designer," is an expert of meeting dynamics. No one at a new-product meeting is allowed to write, based upon the belief that if you are writing, you are not thinking. Thus, the note taker records everyone's ideas in front of the group. These ideas can be rated, evaluated, and eventually dumped. Furthermore, everyone leaves the meeting with a hard copy of the notes in hand—thus serving the organizational memory. In addition, DeKoven keeps a "boneyard," which is a file of ideas that are rejected in the meeting, in a separate section for the notes. Some of those dismissed notions often become valuable later on in the context of another project. For example, when Andy Rifkin, senior vice president of creative development for Mattel Media, was touring with toy buyers, he got repeated requests for activity-based toys for boys. Picking through the boneyard of a year-old meeting, he found a Hot Wheels CD-ROM concept for designing and decorating cars and printing licenses and tickets. The Hot Wheels Custom Car Designer has been a hot item in toy stores—all because of organizational memory (Grossmann, 1998).

Advantages of Electronic Brainstorming

The key advantages of EBS are that it addresses all the blocks to productivity that occur in traditional brainstorming—that is, the threats to performance that occur because people have to compete for floor time; because only one person can talk at one time while others listen; because members may feel inhibited making suggestions, especially if there exist status differences among the team members; because people have a difficult time staying focused on idea generation, as opposed to repeating or evaluating someone else's idea; and because the organizational memory for ideas can be cumbersome or incomplete. EBS elegantly circumvents most of these problems.

Parallel Entry of Ideas

Parallel entry of ideas, like brainwriting, means that all members of the team can generate ideas simultaneously. Although it might seem desirable to have members listen attentively to others' ideas, this, in fact, is highly inefficient. To be sure, EBS does not mean that members disregard or tune out the ideas of others; rather it means that they can both contribute and listen in a much more interactive and efficient fashion. The result is that most members regard the entire process to be more egalitarian and satisfying than a traditional brainstorming session, which can be dominated by one person or a subset of members and, consequently, highly frustrating for others.

Anonymity

In addition to finessing the floor competition that can take place in traditional brainstorming sessions, EBS also has the attractive feature of reducing many people's inhibitions and concerns about what others think of them. As we saw in chapter 2 (performance and productivity), performance pressure can lead to choking, and as we saw in chapter 6 (decision making), conformity pressures are extremely strong in teams, even whose members value independent thought. Because the ideas that are generated in EBS are anonymous, people can express themselves without having to worry about criticism, and the team, therefore, will be less conforming. This is especially true when teams are composed of members of differing status levels. K. C. Guinn, the CEO of Southwest Gas, commented on EBS, "Because the process is anonymous, the sky's the limit in terms of what you can say, and as a result it is more thought-provoking. As a CEO, you'll probably discover things you might not want to hear but need to be aware of" (Dennis, Nunamaker, Paranka, & Vogel, 1990, p. 38). In this sense, EBS can be a venue for the type of evaluations that we discussed in chapter 3 (paying for teamwork). That is, managers can get clear and full feedback on what others think of them or their ideas.

Size

Traditional brainstorming groups suffer greatly from coordination and communication problems as the team grows. In contrast, EBS can easily handle large teams. This can be an advantage for the organization, putting more minds to work on the problem and involving several people in the creative process. It also has the potential for improving organizational memory.

Proximity

An important way that EBS clearly dominates traditional brainstorming is that EBS groups can meet synchronously while being physically dispersed. The members do not have to be in the same place, or even in the same country, to interact.

Memory

As noted, the creation and utilization of organizational memory is greatly facilitated with EBS. The members, whether or not they attended the EBS, have the option of viewing the session via computer disk.

Refinement and Evaluation of Ideas

EBS allows the use of specialized software to help refine, organize, and evaluate ideas. Some software manufacturers have three types of components in their software: Presession planning, in-session management, and postsession organization. Collectively, these tools finesse much of the task-management skills that are needed in meetings. Instead of delegating a person to perform these activities, they are automated.

Equality

EBS places every participant on a level playing field. Practically, this means that no individual can dominate the meeting through rank, status, or raised voice. Thus, EBS ensures equality of input. Equality has many virtues in this type of teamwork. When members feel more equal, there is often more participation, which can increase productivity. For example, one company used traditional brainstorming to develop a 1-year and a 5-year plan (Dennis et al., 1990). The committee, composed of five members, spent 2 days trying to develop a mission statement. In the end, the statement was unacceptable to several key people in the company. When the same team used EBS, they developed a mission statement in 2 hours. Then they developed further objectives, goals, and strategies. This plan was accepted by the board, with no changes. The EBS session was more effective because each member of the team had input into the process.

Disadvantages of Electronic Brainstorming

EBS does have disadvantages. As with most new technologies, the unrealistic expectation is that it will solve all known problems and not create any new ones. Technology cannot replace thinking: Members must generate ideas and then evaluate them.

Small Teams

Smaller EBS groups do not generate as many ideas as do larger groups. For example, an 18-person EBS group generated more ideas than a 3-person EBS group (Gallupe, 1992). This is not really a disadvantage, but rather an admonition to EBS managers that larger teams will be more productive—something that is not true in traditional brainstorming. However, this in no way implies that EBS with small teams is less effective than face-to-face brainstorming. Quite the contrary!

Loss of Social Interaction

Probably the most notable disadvantage is that EBS prevents members from interacting socially. Although we have seen that natural social interaction leads to inefficiencies in performance, social interaction does do other (positive) things for teams. Nonverbal communication, such as facial expressions, laughing, and intonation, is important for building feelings of rapport and trust between members. Furthermore, when people do not interact directly, greater misunderstanding and miscommunication can result. What's more, there is some concern that EBS may actually promote antisocial behavior, with people being more judgmental, pointed, and abrupt in their communications—something we discuss more in chapter 12 on virtual teamwork. These drawbacks may leave team members less satisfied than when traditional brainstorming is used. There may be a dissociation between two measures of productivity: Actual productivity (quantity and quality of ideas produced) and team satisfaction. The manager (and team) may have to make some hard choices about which objective to prioritize.

Loss of Power

Paralleling the greater equality that EBS creates in the organizations that use it is a resultant loss of power for individuals higher in status. Quite frankly, anonymity and equality of input may very well be regarded to be a disadvantage for managers accustomed to having their own ideas implemented. Thus, there could be a backlash of sorts, with organizational members accustomed to greater power attempting to return to traditional status hierarchies.

No Credit

The downside of the anonymity aspect of EBS is that members who generate ideas don't receive credit for them. As we saw in chapter 3, recognition is often the most powerful form of reward. Because EBS is anonymous, this means that members are not accountable for generating and evaluating ideas. This means that some members may work hard and others may do nothing or free ride on the efforts of others (Diehl & Stroebe, 1987). Furthermore, EBS participants may feel that their contribution to the team will not make a difference. In contrast, people in traditional brainstorming groups are keenly aware of the contributions of others, which may promote high levels of participation.

It is important to note that EBS has not proven to be more successful than the nominal group technique. In summary, EBS is extraordinarily useful for managing the discussions of large, physically separated teams. EBS limits the demands of social synchronization—that is, coordination loss—and allows flexibility in accessing one's own, or others', ideas. It also creates a transactive memory system by using an external storage system that may limit the potentially debilitating effects of keeping track of ideas generated during the exchange of ideas (Nagasundaram & Dennis, 1993).

Capstone on Brainstorming

There is no evidence that conventional brainstorming teams can exceed the performance of people working alone. The various inhibitory social and cognitive factors in teams simply outweigh the potential positive effects of social and cognitive stimulation (Paulus et al., 1998).

Why then, with all of its faults, is face-to-face group brainstorming so pervasive in companies? Part of the reason is that the evidence that brainstorming is not effective is not taken well by companies. Indeed, upon finding out that there is virtually no research that supports its effectiveness, managers and executives refuse to give up the belief that brainstorming—in its traditional form—is effective. Brainstorming groups, and the managers who use them, are their own worst enemy: They fall prey to the illusion that they function very effectively (Paulus, Larey, & Ortega, 1995). Brainstorming groups fall victim to the illusion of invulnerability, collective rationalization, belief in the morality of the group, and stereotyping of outgroups. In fact, the illusion is so self-serving that most people take credit for the ideas generated by others (Stroebe, Diehl, & Abakoumkin, 1992). Furthermore, most managers severely underestimate the process loss in teams—that is, the inhibitory cognitive and social factors such as social loafing, production blocking, coordination loss, task irrelevant behaviors, and filler talk—because they lack a relevant benchmark.

It is not uncommon for teams to cite advantages of brainstorming, such as increasing cohesion and building morale. They may suggest that productivity is a rather narrow basis for evaluating the effectiveness of idea-generating techniques like group brainstorming (Kramer, Kuo, & Dailey, 1997; Sutton & Hargadon, 1996). They suggest that group brainstorming can have a number of positive side benefits, such as increased morale and a generally more effective work environment. Consider, for example, IDEO in Palo Alto, founded in 1978 by David Kelley. IDEO is the largest product design consulting firm in the United States and uses brainstorming on a regular basis. Convinced that IDEO was not just spinning its wheels when brainstorming, organizational psychologists performed an extensive case study of IDEO's brainstorming (Sutton & Hargadon, 1996). The productivity of the design engineers working in real groups was not compared to that of nominal groups—or any other variation on the process. Instead, the design engineers themselves were asked to speak to the benefits of brainstorming. One of the key benefits they cited was the development of an organizational memory of design solutions. For example, one brainstorming session at IDEO with 10 engineers present means that 20 percent of the engineers in Palo Alto are exposed to the ideas. IDEO is serious about creating organizational memory: Brainstormers are commonly videotaped and shown as reruns for stimulation. Other benefits cited by engineers included providing skill variety for designers and setting organizational norms regarding asking for help. Brainstorming at IDEO purportedly creates a status auction among designers, whose reputations are shaped during brainstorms. Finally, impressing clients and providing income for the firm were also cited as benefits of brainstorming.

With some simple changes, the productivity of teams can increase dramatically. The positive perspective on brainstorming stems from the validation that people receive when interacting in teams, especially those with cooperative goals, such as in brainstorming. For this reason, it is not at all surprising that brainstorming maintains a high degree of popularity in organizations (Grossman, Rodgers, & Moore, 1989; Rickards, 1993). Unfortunately, this belief does not square with reality.

CONCLUSIONS

Creativity is the Holy Grail of teamwork. This is certainly true for creative teams, but also true for problem-solving and tactical teams. However, many of our intuitions about creativity are incorrect. We see this most clearly in the case of face-to-face brainstorming. The process of generating novel and useful ideas is often blocked in teams. Most creative ideas are applications or transfers of concepts, ideas, and processes from one domain to another. This may sound easy or straightforward, but most people under most conditions do not transfer ideas across domains, even when it would be useful. Johannes Kepler's analogy of the sun and planets as magnets; conceiving the heart as a pump; or comparing the human mind to a computer may seem obvious in hindsight, but it is the getting there that is the hard part. The techniques described in this chapter—comparison and abstraction, maximizing flexibility of categorizing, brainwriting, and so on—are the keys to promoting creative teamwork.

CHAPTER 9

Managing the External Environment

Eastman Chemical Company is the only chemical corporation to have received a Malcolm Baldrige National Quality Award. The award was bestowed in 1993 following vast quality improvements in its manufacturing operations and dramatic sales growth of over 84 percent in 10 years. One secret to the winning strategy is the use of teams within the organization. In 1984, Eastman Chemical faced quality issues, declining sales, and diminished profitability, and committed to change through teamwork and a team-driven organization. Over the next few years, Eastman Chemical employees formed over 1,000 interlocking teams to improve the communication and break down the barriers between functions in the company. Much of the success the firm achieved can be attributed to the cross-functional coordination of the teams; that is, functional teams were networked to other teams in different functions via a supervisor who coordinated their activities. The supervisor's role was crucial. She encouraged communication among different functional as well as geographical units. Russel Justic, a technical associate in quality management, compares interlocking teams to conducting an orchestra: The conductor understands the part each performer plays in the whole and works to align the efforts of all performers to accomplish the composer's objectives. Therefore, each performer is linked to the composition through the conductor. As a case in point, in one program, the linkage among teams was symbolized by taking photographs of each team and linking them graphically on a prominent wall-sized poster at all headquarters. A videotape of each team's symbolic link on the wall was sent to all remote locations to emphasize the worldwide effort by all teams involved (Milliken, 1996).

We saw in part II that the manager must focus on internal team processes. However, there is more to creating and sustaining a successful team than supporting its internal activities. Team members interact with one another in the context of a larger environment. A team's environment includes the organization to which the team belongs and the clients they serve. This chapter focuses on the team's relationship to the larger organization. This is essential because, among other reasons, team productivity is often judged by those who consume the group's services; namely, its customers.

Defined in this way, the environment is both a cause and effect of team behavior: It influences internal team dynamics and is influenced by them. Managers often make the mistake of only focusing on internal team dynamics. However, to be effective, managers must also develop the external relationships of the team. These external relationships are increasingly important as firms diversify the traditional organizational structure of the company's activities. Organizations call upon teams to span traditional boundaries both inside firms, where they might provide a closer coupling between functional units, and outside firms, where they might provide links to customers, suppliers, or competitors (Clark & Fujimoto, 1987; von Hippel, 1988).

In this chapter, we first discuss what we mean by team boundaries. Then, we describe four prototypical teams in organizations in terms of how they manage their team boundaries and the trade-offs associated with each. Next, we focus on the external roles that team members play. We then discuss networking within the organization and contrast clique networks to entrepreneurial networks and strategies for increasing team effectiveness. Finally, we take up the issue of physical space and time: Namely, how the physical setting affects teamwork and how team members manage time constraints.

TEAM BOUNDARIES

In the minds of the team members and the organization, an identifiable boundary exists between the team and the other parts of the organization. This, in fact, was one of the key defining characteristics of a team, as indicated in chapter 1. In this chapter, we examine the in- and outflow of information, resources, and people across this border.

Team boundaries differentiate one work group from another and affect knowledge transfer and distribution of resources. In some cases, boundaries are well defined, but in other cases, boundaries are more ambiguous. If the boundary becomes too open or indistinct, the team risks becoming overwhelmed and losing its identity. If its boundary is too exclusive, the team might become isolated and lose touch with suppliers, managers, peers, or customers (Alderfer, 1977). Thus, teams can be **underbounded**—having many external ties but an inability to coalesce and motivate members to pull together; or **overbounded**—having high internal loyalty and a complex set of internal dynamics but an inability to integrate with others when needed. There is a trade-off between internal cohesion and external ties—more cohesive teams are less likely to engage in necessary external initiatives (Alderfer, 1976; Sherif, 1966). Although there is no perfect answer for how to deal with the tension between internal cohesion and the external environment, we offer in this chapter a combination of consciousness-raising about key issues and strategies for arranging the team environment so as to be maximally productive.

Leaders play an integral role in connecting a team with the external environment. Some leaders focus all of their energies on the internal functioning of the team through classic coaching; other leaders spend most of their efforts on promoting the team within the organization. These are two extremes that are equally ineffective. In this section, we try to be more specific in pinpointing the choices leaders have in managing the interface between their team and the greater environment, and, most important, considering the effects on team productivity and performance.

The choices that a leader has, in terms of managing the interface, parallel the choices for control outlined in chapter 1. Recall our analysis of manager-led, self-managing, self-designing, and self-governing teams. In the case of the leader managing the team within its environment, the relationship of interest is between the team and the environment. Table 9-1 outlines four types of teams in terms of their relationship to the environment: Insulating teams, broadcasting teams, marketing teams, and surveying teams (see Ancona, 1990). Of course, these are four *pure* strategies, and *blends* may exist. It is useful to try to identify which style best characterizes a particular team.

TABLE 9-1 Prototypical Relationships Teams May Have with Their Environment

Team's Relationship with Environment	*Key Focus and Activities*	*Advantages*	*Disadvantages*
Insulating	Team is isolated from other parts of organization or its customers; team concentrates solely on internal functioning; usually highly goal driven	• Less likely to compromise ideals and objectives • Especially facilitative for creative teams	• Disconnected from rest of organization • May develop groupthink or overconfidence
Broadcasting	Team concentrates on internal team processes until the team is ready to inform outsiders of its intentions	• Control over negative information • Broadcasting is relatively inexpensive	• May fail to sense true needs of customers • May fail to develop customer buy-in
Marketing	Team concentrates on getting buy-in from outsiders through advertising, self-promotion, lobbying	• High visibility often is helpful for team	• May fail to meet true needs of customers • Marketing costs can be high
Surveying	Team concentrates on diagnosing needs of customers, experimenting with solutions, revising their knowledge, initiating programs, and collecting data	• Greatest potential customer satisfaction • Understand outsiders' demands • Rated by outsiders as higher performers (Ancona, 1990)	• Often extremely costly and time-consuming • May surface latent conflict within the organization • Possible low cohesion (due to divergent views created by surveying) • Possible dissatisfaction

Insulating Teams

Insulating teams are, for the most part, sequestered from the environment. This may be a deliberate choice by the manager or leader; other times, the team may be ostracized by the organization. Managers often want to isolate their teams for security reasons (e.g., the Los Alamos team that developed the Atomic bomb) or intellectual reasons (e.g., the Xerox Park team that developed the computer). The greatest threat to the effectiveness of insulating teams is dissociation from the organization. Insulating teams may fail to develop a viable product or service because they are out of touch with the rest of the organization and industry; or, they may have a great product, but lack the buy-in they need for success.

Broadcasting Teams

Broadcasting teams concentrate on their internal processes and simply inform others what they are doing. More often than not, the broadcasting team has little outside contact; it makes decisions about how to serve its customers from within. The team members let others outside the team know what they are doing after they have already made decisions.

Marketing Teams

When we refer to *marketing teams,* we do not rely on the traditional, functional definition. Marketing teams promote their objectives, products, services, and culture actively within their organization. Often, their objective is to get buy-in from above and receive recognition. They differ from broadcasting teams in that they actively tailor their communication to suit the perceived needs, interests, and objectives of the organization. To use an analogy, the broadcasting team is like a news report; the marketing team is like an advertisement.

Surveying Teams

Surveying teams try to put their finger on the pulse of the organization, their clients, and customers. The downside, of course, is that the team may spend an undue amount of time and resources surveying instead of engaging in the task at hand. In this sense, a surveying team is really a sort of task force. At some point, the surveying team has to make critical decisions about when to stop collecting and probing for information and develop a product or service for its customers.

It is rare for teams to be self-sufficient, and it is their dependence on others for economic, social, and political support that drives many of the strategies for interacting with the environment. Xerox Park is an example wherein an insulated team used its insulation to advantage in developing essentially all the technology used in today's modern computer age. However, the team members were unsuccessful in selling their ideas to their own management (because virtually no broadcasting or marketing had been done). Therefore, Xerox did not obtain the benefits of its own special research group.

We have been looking at the team's relationship with its environment as a deliberate and purposeful decision made by the team's manager at the outset of team activity. However, this is rarely the case. The relationship a team has with its environment evolves—sometimes from direct managerial intervention, but more often from organizational norms, culture, and situational constraints. For example, if the physical facilities within an organization make interaction difficult between different units, teams will be more likely to adopt insulating or broadcasting strategies.

Our discussion of team management vis-à-vis the external environment may seem to be overly politicized. Indeed, there is a trade-off between the team members actually doing their work and their efforts at influencing management and other relevant external entities. In some sense, this is a hidden cost to the organization, similar to hiring lawyers or writing contracts—a form of team red tape. If so, the organization should try to find ways to avoid this. There are two messages here. One is for the team leader: If you fail to effectively manage the relationship between your team and the external environment, your team may be regarded as ineffective, regardless of its actual productivity. The other message is for the organization: By placing constraints and barriers upon the team's ability to control and gain access to resources, such as education, knowledge, and economic resources, team effectiveness may be hindered.

The interaction between a team and the organization is similar to the interaction between the members and the team itself in that there are struggles for power, status, and roles (Ancona, 1990). Just as members often spend time during the formation of a team to determine what role they will play and which members will have power, so, too, do teams play out these same issues with other organizational entities. For example, top management may set constraints and provide direction. Teams may react in a variety of ways; some welcome the direction, some try to shape the new directives, and others reject direction.

TEAM IDENTITY

Just as people develop reputations and make impressions on others in the organization within the first few months of their arrival, so do teams. Early on, teams are labeled, and on the basis of this initial impression, a negative or positive escalating cycle in terms of both team reputation and team performance begins. Initial reputations may remain intact for quite some time, despite efforts to change them. Teams that do not overcome a negative initial evaluation may be perceived as failures—even if they eventually achieve their goals. "The inability to influence top management early on can be devastating to a team since they control resources and rewards. In short, labeling creates self-fulfilling prophecies" (Ancona, 1993, p. 233). Often, teams want to get down to work and not waste time navigating external relations issues. However, these very issues—if ignored early on—can haunt the team in the future. Therefore, even though teams must fulfill both internal and external activities, the point in time at which they undertake those activities is not trivial. Obtaining support from the environment is critical if a team is to enter a positive escalation cycle (Ancona, 1993).

EXTERNAL ROLES OF TEAM MEMBERS

Just as members develop roles for the internal functioning of a team, they develop roles for the external functioning of a team (Ancona, 1990). Identifying and understanding the roles that team members play vis-à-vis the in- and outflow of information to the team is an important predictor of team productivity and performance.

Roles are not formally assigned; rather, through an implicit process of team negotiation, roles are taken on by members of the group. Members quickly size up others' abilities, and tasks are often delegated on the basis of demonstrated performance in these areas.

Although it would be impossible to list an exhaustive set of roles, Box 9-1 lists some of the most common and important roles that have been observed in work groups (see Ancona, 1990; Ancona & Caldwell, 1987, 1988, 1991, 1992).

Not all of these roles are identifiable in all teams. Because the boundary-spanning role has been studied in detail and can significantly affect the course of individuals' career paths within the organization (see Burt, 1999), we discuss it in more detail in the following section.

NETWORKING: A KEY TO SUCCESSFUL TEAMWORK

The shift away from top-down management and bureaucratic structures means that more than ever, team members are in control of their own movement within the organization. This can bring opportunity for the team, the organization, and its members, but only if this task is handled optimally. The heart of this task involves management of relationships. In this section, we describe the key issues that managers should know when building the relationship between their team and the organization.

BOX 9-1

Common Roles in Work Groups

- The **boundary spanner** acts as a bridge between units or people in an organization who would not otherwise interact. Boundary spanners are exposed to more ideas than members who do not interact with other groups. Indeed, boundary spanners who spend time with different groups exhibit greater integrative complexity in their thinking (a form of creativity) than people who don't boundary span (Gruenfeld & Fan, 1999).

- The **bufferer** protects the team from bad or disappointing news that might cause morale to suffer and volunteers to absorb pressure or criticism from others.

- The **interpreter** shapes the collective understanding of the team. This is important because in many cases, the messages that teams receive from others are ambiguous and open to interpretation.

- The **advisor** informs the team about which options they should consider and what approach they should take in dealing with changing events.

- The **gatekeeper** controls the flow of information to and from a team.

- The **lobbyist** is an extremely critical role, especially for new-product groups. By providing meanings about what the team is doing and how successful it is to people outside the team, the lobbyist controls the interpretation of what the team is perceived to be doing. For example, Tom West, the leader of a team at IBM designing a computer, presented his computer differently to various groups (from Kidder, 1981). By presenting it as "insurance" (we will have it in case the other one designed by another team in the company does not work) to top management, he was allowed to set up a team that competed with another team in the company. By presenting it as a "technical challenge" to engineers, he was able to attract the best ones. By not saying anything at all to external competitors, he protected his company (Ancona, 1987).

- The **negotiator** or **mediator** is empowered by the team to negotiate on behalf of the group. This person has extraordinary power in terms of garnering resources, defining options, and so on. This person may act as a mediator in cases where the team is in conflict with others.

- The **spokesperson** is the voice of the team. This position is determined in two ways: By the group members themselves, e.g., "Talk to Bob if you want to find out what happened in Lois's promotion decision"; and by the members of the external environment who have their choice in terms of contacting group members.

- The **strategist**, like the negotiator, plans how to approach management for resources and deal with threats and other negative information.

- The **coordinator** arranges formal or informal communication with other people or units outside the team.

Perfect and Imperfect Markets

In an ideal organizational environment, there would be perfect communication among the different functional and geographical units. Among other things, such communication would have the advantage of quickly dispersing innovation, reducing unnecessary duplication of effort, moving toward the implementation of best practices, and a variety of other advantages. However, the reality of organizational communication is a far cry from the ideal. Communication among different functional and geographically dispersed units does not occur as frequently as it should.

Thus, most organizations are **imperfect markets,** in which communication is incomplete and information is not ubiquitously dispersed throughout the company. In a company, information may be controlled or held only by certain people, as opposed to being directly accessible to everyone in the organization.

Human Capital and Social Capital

Why is it that some people are singled out and seem to advance faster through their organizations than other team members? Why is it that some teams are singled out and seem to advance faster through their organizations than other teams? The typical explanation centers upon **human capital:** Inequalities result from differences in human individual ability. People who are more intelligent, educated, and experienced rise to the top of their firm; those who are less qualified do not.

However, there is another, perhaps more plausible, explanation that accounts for the existence of inequality. **Social capital** is the value managers adds to their teams and organizations through their ties to other people (Coleman, 1988). Social capital is the value that comes from knowing who, when, and how to coordinate through various contacts within and beyond the firm. Whereas human capital refers to individual ability; social capital refers to opportunity created through the interactions of people. Managers with more social capital get higher returns on their human capital because they are positioned to identify and develop more rewarding opportunities (Burt, 1992). Stated simply, certain managers are connected to certain others, trust certain others, feel obligated to support certain others, and are dependent on exchange and reciprocity with certain others, above and beyond those in their immediate functional unit.

To understand the value of social capital within the firm and how it affects team performance, it is necessary to consider the larger organizational environment. Organizational charts are rather crude depictions that reveal the chain of command and reporting relationships. However, as many managers can attest, the way that work gets done and information gets spread within an organization is a far cry from published organizational charts. Instead, informal systems of connections and relationships, developed over time, guide the flow of information between people and teams. Let's explore these informal networks in detail.

Consider Figure 9-1, which is a somewhat crude depiction of two organizational environments. The dots represent certain managers. The lines that connect the dots are the communication networks between people in the organization—simply, who talks with whom. To be sure, members of a given department or functional unit are more interconnected than are members of completely different functional units. However, even within particular departments, there can be a high degree of variation in communication patterns. Moreover, there is high variation among organizational

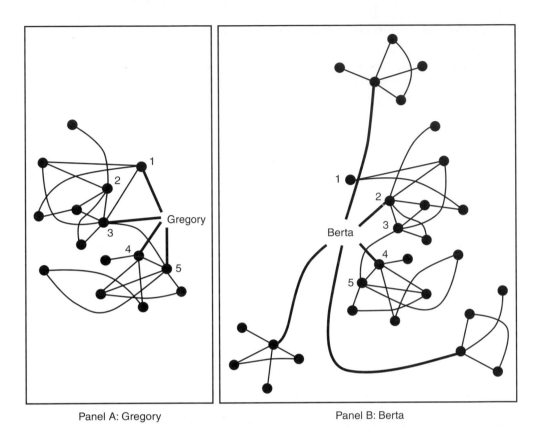

Panel A: Gregory   Panel B: Berta

FIGURE 9-1 Communication Networks of Two Managers within the Same Company

Source: Adapted from Burt, R. S. 1999. "Entrepreneurs, Distrust, and Third Parties: A Strategic Look at the Dark Side of Dense Networks." In L. Thompson, J. Levine, & D. Messick (Eds.), *Shared Cognition in Organizations: The Management of Knowledge.* Mahwah, NJ: Lawrence Erlbaum & Associates.

members in terms of who reaches beyond the walls of the functional teams and communicates with others.

Consider the two different panels in Figure 9-1. Panel 9-1a depicts the network (or communication) structure of a manager, Gregory, who has a network of relatively close colleagues—most likely from the same functional unit. This type of close-knit, self-contained network is a **clique network,** and is reminiscent of the traditional family unit. In the clique network, groups of people, all of whom know one another quite well, share largely redundant communication structures. At the extreme, members of clique networks are only aware of others with whom they have direct contact.

When we contrast Gregory's communication network to Berta's in panel 9-1b, we notice some striking differences. First, Berta's network is much less tightly knit than is Gregory's network. Second, Berta's network spans what appears to be more functional units than does Gregory's network. In a sense, Berta knows more people—perhaps less well—than does Gregory, who knows fewer people on a much tighter basis. Third, Berta's network is structurally more unique than is Gregory's network. Simply stated,

Gregory's network is highly identical to all the other people in his clique. In contrast, Berta's network does not look like anyone else's, in terms of the connections she has. Before reading further, how do you think these differing network structures affect the performance of the team, the individuals involved, and the larger organization?

Boundary Spanning and Structural Holes

Individuals (and teams) who are able to span across organizational divides and integrate the knowledge, innovation, and best practices from different areas of the organization (who otherwise have little incentive to do so) are extremely valuable for the organization. These people are known as **boundary spanners.** Boundary spanners bridge the functional gaps, or the **structural holes,** that exist in organizations. Structural holes are what separates nonredundant social contacts in the organization. A person who bridges or spans a structural hole fills a unique spot in the organizational network: Bringing together people, knowledge, and information that would otherwise not be brought together. This, of course, is critical for maximizing diversity of ideas and setting the stage for creative thinking in the organization—not to mention avoiding duplication of effort and speeding along organizational innovations to relevant units. Indeed, teams whose members have access to different social networks, independent of their individual knowledge and skills, may be more likely to learn through interaction than teams whose members' social ties are redundant (Granovetter, 1973). The value of a boundary spanner is the ability to capitalize on the social structure of the organization which, as we have seen, is structurally imperfect.

When we again compare the networks of Gregory and Berta, we see that Gregory has a network that spans one structural hole (i.e., the relatively weak connection between a cluster reached through contacts 1, 2, and 3 versus the other cluster that is reached through contacts 4 and 5). In contrast, Berta preserves the connections with both clusters in Gregory's network, but expands the network to a more diverse set of contacts. Berta's network, adding three new clusters of people, spans 10 structural holes.

These structural holes that exist between people, functional units, and teams are *entrepreneurial* opportunities for teams and their leaders. Boundary spanners can broker the flow of information between people on opposite ends of a structural hole, and control the form of projects that bring people together on opposite ends of the structural hole. For example, Eastman Chemical's interlocking teams spanned many of the company's structural holes and aided in dismantling the imperfect flow of information between different functions. Not only were the teams individually productive, but their combined productivity separated the organization from others in the industry. In this way, the structure of a network is a competitive advantage for certain people and certain teams in the organization.

Quite frankly, managers with contact networks rich in structural holes are the people who know about, have a hand in, and exercise more control over rewarding opportunities. They have broader access to information because of their diverse contacts. This means that they are more often aware of new opportunities and have easier access to these opportunities than do their peers—even their peers of equivalent or greater human capital! For this reason, they are also more likely to be discussed as suitable candidates for inclusion in new opportunities. They are also likely to have sharpened and displayed their capabilities because they have more control over the substance of their work defined by relationships with subordinates, superiors, and colleagues.

Types of Networks

Consider once again two people in a typical organization: Gregory and Berta. Gregory is in a tightly constructed, dense clique network. In contrast, Berta's network does not follow functional or organizational charts. It is much less dense, more unique, and more varied. Which person would a manager want to recruit for a team? Gregory or Berta? Let's consider their ability to add value.

Gregory is a member of a **clique network,** a tightly knit, exclusive, and cohesive group. Members of clique networks consider one another to be their closest contacts, and because they focus their efforts at primarily internal communications, they are often sequestered away from the larger organization.

In contrast, Berta's is an **entrepreneur network,** a less tightly knit group, with contacts in a variety of disparate organizational areas. In fact, Berta does not appear to be housed in any particular network. On the surface it might seem that Gregory would feel more secure, nestled in his cohesive group, and, hence, be more successful on the whole. Berta is a boundary spanner, a link between different subgroups and functional units that without her would not be connected. For this reason, Berta occupies a unique position in her network, as she single-handedly bridges these separate groups. In this sense, Berta is an **information broker,** because she alone is at the critical junction between these networks and serves the important role of brokering information. Stated another way, the people in Berta's functional group are more information dependent upon Berta than upon Gregory. In a very crude sense, Gregory is an organizational clone—expendable—at least on a sociostructural level. In contrast, Berta is a critical player; remove her and the organization may suffer serious consequences and lost opportunities. Berta serves an important team and organizational function by garnering information that would otherwise be unavailable to the team or to the organization.

Is there anything *wrong* with Gregory's situation? He is in a highly cohesive group, which can be advantageous when it comes to managing the internal team environment. The problem is that Gregory does not really learn anything new by interacting with the members of his group. In contrast, because Berta's contacts do not know one another and, therefore, cannot apply social pressure on each other—as they can in clique networks—Berta is potentially privy to a greater amount of accurate and nonredundant information. Berta's position as a structural hole is an indicator that people on either side of the hole circulate in different flows of information. The structural hole between two clusters (or teams) does not mean that people in the two clusters are unaware of one another. Rather, people are so focused on their own activities that they have little time to attend to the activities of people in the other cluster.

In comparing Gregory's and Berta's networks, the information benefits in Berta's network are enhanced in several important ways that go a long way toward furthering individual, team, and organizational goals—the very things that we outlined in chapter 2 to be critical measures of performance. First, from Berta's view, there is more benefit reaped because more contacts are included in the network. The diversity of contacts enhances the quality of benefits, because each cluster of contacts is an independent source of information. One cluster (e.g., a team), no matter how numerous its members, is only one source of information because people connected to one another know about the same things at approximately the same time. Because nonredundant contacts are only linked through the leader at the center of the network, the leader is assured of being the first to see new opportunities created by the need of one team that could be served by skills in another team. Berta has the opportunity of bringing together otherwise disconnected individuals where it will be rewarding. Furthermore, having more diverse contacts means that the manager is more likely to be among the people discussed as suitable candidates for inclusion in new opportunities. Because people communicate through Berta, she can adjust her image with each contact—much like Tom West did in his strategy for IBM. Berta is able to monitor information more effectively than is possible with typical bureaucratic control. Berta is highly mobile relative to bureaucracy.

People like Berta also are advantageous from the perspective of the team and the larger organization. For example, teams in several plants operated by a Midwest manufacturing firm were evaluated in the early 1990s by the firm's quality control officers (Rosenthal, 1996). There was a striking association between team performance and team members' network structures: The more successful teams were composed of people with networks richer in structural holes (see also Sidebar 9-1).

Sidebar 9-1. Minority Managers

"Fast-track" minority managers develop networks that are well connected to both minority and white informal circles. In contrast, high-potential whites and non-fast-track minorities have few, if any, network ties with minorities. Ironically, many non-fast-track minorities feel that networking with members of their racial group is detrimental to their careers. Yet the more successful minorities consistently stress the value of same-race contacts in helping them to develop and implement strategies for career success (Ibarra, 1995). Minority fast-trackers develop networks that span a much broader set of social and corporate circles than the non-fast-trackers.

Advice for the Manager

In comparison with others who are equal in human capital, people like Berta tend to have more successful careers. Managers with larger networks of more disconnected contacts get promoted earlier than comparable managers with smaller networks of more interconnected contacts (Burt, 1992; Podolny & Baron, 1997; Sparrowe & Popielarz, 1995). For example, in an investigation of 3,000 senior managers in a high-technology firm with over 100,000 employees, those promoted early had more social capital—as determined by their social network analysis (Burt, 1992). The network structure of team members affects how much information they share in common with others in a team. For this reason, we can say that boundary spanners are more cognitively central (i.e., aware of what other people know) than are non–boundary spanners. This affects their ability to influence the team. The more information team members share with others, the more cognitively central they are in the team. Also, cognitively central members acquire pivotal power in a team and exert more influence on consensus than members who are not cognitively central (Kameda, Ohtsubo, & Takezawa, 1997). Thus, those who are "tapped in" are more influential.

How can managers best try to expand their network and link their team within the organization? As the previous discussion argues, strategic network expansion involves

Network Expansion

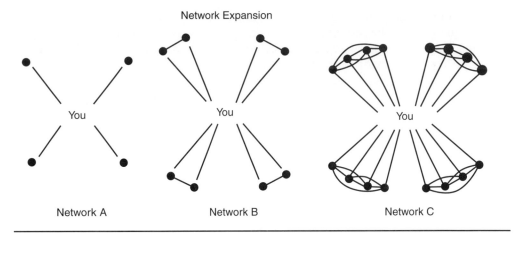

Strategic Network Expansion

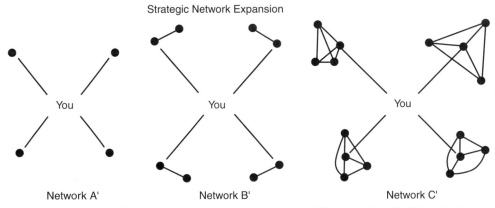

FIGURE 9-2 **Strategic Network Expansion**

Source: Burt, R. S. 1992. *The Social Structure of Competition.* Cambridge, MA: Harvard University Press. Copyright © 1992 by the President and Fellows of Harvard College. Reprinted with permission.

connecting to people and teams in such a way that the manager (and the team) is filling a structural hole. To see the difference between typical network expansion and strategic network expansion, see Figure 9-2.

Structural Positioning

The reaction of many people to our analysis of social capital, structural holes, and entrepreneurial activity within the firm is that it seems very self-promotional, which, of course, is antithetical to traditional notions of teamwork. It is somehow disconcerting to realize that relationships among people within an organization hurt or facilitate one's chances of advancing. We advocate a team-based view of structural positioning within the organization. That is, teams are more likely to achieve their goals and stay in touch with the needs of the organization if they have connections with others within the organization. Thus, the structural positioning of an entrepreneurial, as opposed to clique-like, network has benefits for individual team members, the team, and the organization.

From the point of view of the employee, organizational benefits are maximized in a large network of nonredundant contacts. It is better to know a lot of people who don't know one another. The opportunity is there because most people are too busy to keep in touch directly. Furthermore, people in organizations display a type of **functional ethnocentrism:** Believing that their own functional area is of key importance and that the other units do not matter as much. Entrepreneurs, like Berta, take advantage of functional ethnocentrism and act as critical go-betweens to bring individuals, teams, and units together in ways that are profitable to themselves and the organization.

What are some practical steps that individuals, teams, and organizations can take to build more connections across functional groups? Consider the following strategies.

Expand the Size of the Network

This does not mean increasing the size of the team, but rather, increasing the number of people that the manager and the team come into contact with.

Recognize the Limitations of Clique Networks

Clique networks contain a number of disadvantages for the organization and the team. People in clique networks fall prey to the homogeneity bias. For example, men in clique networks include significantly fewer women among their contacts (Burt, 1992). This can stifle creativity, propagate prejudice, and hinder the benefits of diversity.

Recognize Key Scripts

Quite often, business opportunities are conducted in the context of social relationships (Uzzi, 1997). Many social relationships are common and therefore highly scripted or routinized, such as conducting a business meeting on the golf course. According to Uzzi and Gillespie (1999), these scripts are significant because they define the conditions under which networks are most effective. For this reason, it is difficult to form close relationships across gender lines if they are built through socializing activities such as playing golf, going to the theater, or evening dinner gatherings because these practices often have a different meaning between men and women than they do between persons of the same gender (Etzkowitz, Kemelgor, & Uzzi, 1999). (See Box 9-2 for an examination of women's and men's networks.)

Diversify Networks

As we have seen, the homogeneity bias pulls people toward developing cliques of like-minded people—which is exactly the wrong type of network to foster. It may be more comfortable in the short run, but it will have negative, long-term consequences for the individual, the team, and the organization. A better alternative is to develop a diversified network, which means crossing organizational boundaries and functional areas. Uzzi (1997) distinguishes between embedded ties (social ties) and arm's-length (nonsocial, purely business) ties. According to Uzzi (1997), at the network level, the optimal composition of ties is achieved when a network has an integrated mix of embedded and arm's-length ties. This is because embedded ties and arm's-length ties can offer complementary benefits when combined, just as the overall value of a portfolio increases when it is composed of complementary assets that offset each other's inherent weaknesses and strengths. Networks dominated by one type of tie produce fewer benefits, which partly accounts for the negative effects of overly embedded (e.g., "old-boy") networks, or overly

---

BOX 9-2

Social Capital and Gender

Etzkowitz, Kemelgor, and Uzzi (1999) investigated why women scientists with human capital equal to, or better than, their male counterparts do poorer in graduate school and are thereafter disadvantaged by a lack of contacts to the resources and tacit information important for identifying, developing, and following through on leading-edge research projects. The differential performance of women follows from their disadvantaged position in a social structure of relations, not their human capital endowments. By actively managing social networks, key barriers to the advancement of women in science can be overcome.

---

disembedded exchange networks (e.g., whipsawing of suppliers by large manufacturers; Uzzi, 1997).

Build Hierarchical Networks
In bureaucratic organizations, boundary spanners need to network not only laterally, but also hierarchically.

Integrate across Teams
Networking across structural holes is not limited to informal, individual activity. Teams can introduce structural strategies for integrating with other teams. Table 9-2 reviews seven structural solutions for integrating across teams within an organization. Three of the strategies focus on integrating between teams. Four of the strategies focus on integrating across multiple teams and components of a business unit.

None of these strategies is flawless. In fact, even though boundary spanning has the effect of increasing cognitive growth, teams often exhibit a cognitive territoriality in response to the presence of others. For example, old-timers in teams use a greater number of their own ideas *after* newcomers arrive than before (Gruenfeld & Fan, 1999; for more details, see Box 9-3).

Greater integration is important to achieving the four major goals of productivity outlined in chapter 2: Achieving team goals, fostering team spirit, enhancing individual development, and furthering organizational objectives. In many cases, though, integration is not a choice—it is an absolute necessity for organizations. Consider, for example, the challenges that face Microsoft Corporation in managing large software development teams (Cusumano, 1997). Many software project managers prefer very small product teams of 12 or fewer programmers. This largely derives from a culture in the early days of programming, when two or three people built a new product. For example, initial versions of Microsoft's MS-DOS, Word, and Excel from the early 1980s had programming teams of 6 to 10 developers and consisted of just a few tens of thousands of lines of code. However, in the development of larger systems, with more memory-

TABLE 9-2 Integrating across Teams: Formal Structural Solutions						
Integration between Teams			*Integration across Multiple Teams and Components of a Business Unit (Tighter Integration)*			
Liaison roles	Overlapping membership	Cross-team integrating teams	Management teams	Representative integrating teams	Individual integrating teams	Improvement teams

Liaison roles	One boundary spanner is formally a member of one team, but sits in on meetings of another team to share and gather information (e.g., a day shift worker sits in on night shift)
Overlapping membership	Several employees are members of two groups simultaneously or in sequence
Cross-team integrating teams	Team composed of several members from other teams with integration needs, responsible for documenting and communicating changes in a timely manner
Management teams	Forge strategy and direction for multiple teams in business unit; make resource trade-offs among teams that are consistent with strategy, manage team performance
Representative integrating teams	Nonmanagement team with authority to make decisions that affect system or context in which teams are embedded, composed of peers of team members
Individual integrating roles	Individuals in specific function provide integration with more flexibility than a team (e.g., a salesperson pulls together team for specific customer or project)
Improvement teams	Teams that initiate changes in how parts of business unit work together to improve business unit performance; must have legitimacy from the level of the organization at which their changes will be enacted; often not a full-time assignment but must be managed as an official project team

Sources: Gruenfeld, D.H. (1997). Integrating across teams: Formal structural solutions. Presentation at J.L. Kellogg School, May 1997, Evanston, IL; also based on Mohrman, S.A., Cohen, S.G., & Mohrman, A.M. 1995. *Designing Team-Based Organizations.* San Francisco: Jossey-Bass.

intensive graphical interfaces and complex functions, product development teams are forced to be larger. For example, the first version of Windows NT, introduced in 1993, consisted of 4.5 million lines of code and had a development team of about 450 people. Windows 95, introduced in 1995, consisted of 11 million lines of code. A team of about 300 people built the core components of Microsoft's Internet Explorer browser, introduced in 1996, with more people involved in creating various modular features. Given that the complexity and magnitude of the task drives the teams to be larger and integrated, what is the best way to optimize integration among teams?

The teamwork integration process is especially difficult in software because it is so easy to change components and then extremely difficult to predict the effects on other components in the debugging and testing process. Software programmers do not work in an assembly-line fashion, receiving work passed down to them. The parallel processing environment invites iteration or innovation constantly. Furthermore, there is also the problem of technical and management education. University computer science departments and management schools generally do not teach students how to design large-scale systems or manage large-scale products and work in teams of hundreds of people. For Microsoft, the key is to allow many small teams enough freedom to work in parallel, but to be able to function as one large team in terms of the overall picture. For

---

BOX 9-3

An Investigation of Itinerant and Indigenous Team Members

Gruenfeld, Martorana, and Fan (1999) ingeniously investigated the consequences of temporary membership changes for itinerant members (i.e., members who leave their core group to visit a foreign work team and then, subsequently, return) and indigenous members of those foreign and origin groups. Although it would seem that itinerant members would learn new ideas that would transfer back to their core group once they returned, this was not always the case. In fact, members of all groups produced more unique ideas after itinerant members returned to their core group than before they left or during the temporary change period, but the ideas produced by the itinerant members were significantly less likely to be included in a group project designed to draw on knowledge of the work team than the ideas of indigenous members. After their return, itinerant members were perceived as highly involved in the group activity, but they were also perceived as more argumentative than they were before leaving, and although they produced more unique ideas than indigenous members, their contributions to the team project were perceived as less valuable. As a result, itinerant group members had less direct influence after their boundary-spanning stint than they did prior to it!

---

example, at Microsoft, the core group for each team is generally one program manager and three to eight developers, including a development team leader. The extended team includes a parallel feature-testing team. Microsoft gives each team and each person within the team considerable autonomy and responsibility. Autonomy and responsibility allow each team to work relatively independently and "own" their features.

It is worth noting that this type of integration, which effectively allows small teams to work as one large team, may only work well when teams have been given responsibility. For example, Microsoft gives each team and each individual considerable autonomy and responsibility, which also allows teams to work relatively independently. Individual and feature teams set and maintain their own schedules, and relatively few rules are required for changes.

DISTANCE

Even more encompassing than the social structure of an organization is its physical structure. Indeed, the physical layout of an organization can exert powerful effects on team productivity.

For better or for worse, teams operate within the physical constraints set by the organization. In terms of physical space, there is a direct, nearly perfect negative correlation between distance (as measured in feet) between employees' offices or workspaces and the interaction patterns between them. People form relationships, both personal and professional, to others who are close to them. Obviously, these processes feed on each other. Being physically close leads people to like and work with each other. People choose to be near those whom they like and want to work with. For example, even when students are seated alphabetically in a classroom, friendships are significantly more likely to form between those whose last names begin with the same or a nearby letter (Segal, 1974). This is what is called the **propinquity effect.** This may not seem important until you consider the fact that you may meet some of your closest colleagues, and perhaps even a future business partner, merely because of an instructor's seating chart! Similarly, those people given a corner seat, or an office at the end of a corridor, make fewer friends in the organization (Maisonneuve, Palmade, & Fourment, 1952). If an instructor changes seat assignments once or twice during the semester, each student becomes acquainted with additional colleagues (Byrne, 1961). To further see the power of the propinquity effect, consider the entering class of the Maryland State Police Training Academy (Segal, 1974). Trainees were assigned to their classroom seats and to their dormitory rooms by the alphabetical order of their last names. Some time thereafter, trainees were asked to name their three best friends in the group; their choices followed the rules of alphabetization almost exactly. Larsons were friends with Lees, not with Abromowitzes or Xiernickes, even though they were separated by only a few yards! (Byrne, 1961; Kipnis, 1957).

As another example, consider friendship formation among couples in apartment buildings. In this particular case, residents had been assigned to their apartments at random as vacancies opened up, and nearly all of them were strangers when they moved in. When asked to name their three closest friends in the entire housing project, 65 percent named friends in the same building. Of those living in the same building, the propinquity effect was in play: 41 percent of next-door neighbors indicated they were close friends, compared to only 22 percent who lived two doors apart, and only 10 percent who lived on the opposite ends of the hall.

The propinquity effect has an impact on **functional distance:** Certain aspects of architectural design make it more likely that some people will come into contact with each other more often than with others, even though physically, the distances might be the same. For example, more friendships were made with people on the same floor than on another floor, presumably because having to climb stairs to go visiting required more effort than just walking down the hall.

The point is clear: What appear to be trivial aspects of the physical environment shape the pattern of communication and relationships in organizations and how the work gets done. Corporate responses to these issues have led to the development of more open work plans and flexible, project-based seating as ways to increase interaction, collegiality, and productivity in teams. For example, consider the Mars, Inc. company. There are no executive offices, only partitions in a large, open space. No one has a reserved parking spot, and executives' desks are out in the open. According to Mars' executives, this facilitates communication and cuts down on the need for many meetings. Similarly, McCaskey (1995) describes a company that created a special space for a new product development team on a separate floor from the rest of the company. The group was allocated a large space and was left on its own to arrange desks, common space, and so on. The result was an exceptionally high-functioning and productive team. A key reason for the success of the team was the fact that the spatial arrangement allowed team members to interact informally and frequently, yet at the same time, maintain some degree of personal space for independent thinking—exactly the same ingredients we discussed in chapter 8 on creativity.

TIME

Another contextual factor is time and the organization's norms of marking time—in particular, deadlines. How much time should a group devote to completing its work? A typical response might be "as long as it takes." This answer is neither good nor practical. When a work group is given a specific amount of time to do a job, its members adjust their behavior to "fit" whatever time is available. When time is scarce, team members work harder, worry less about the quality of their output, and focus on the task rather than social or emotional issues. However, if more time becomes available, these employees continue to work as though time was still scarce, rather than relaxing. It is important to properly manage how teams are initially introduced to their tasks.

Consider a telling example in which three groups were evaluated according to their ability to solve puzzles (McGrath, Kelly, & Machatka, 1984). Each group had a different task load (completing 20, 40, or 80 anagrams), time limit (5, 10, or 20 minutes), and group size (one, two, or four persons). The situation was designed so that each group had three work periods. The task load remained the same for all periods for any given group, but the time interval either increased, decreased, or remained constant. Groups of any size, and over all possible time intervals, solved more anagrams per member-minute the *higher* the assigned task load; groups of any size and for any given task load solved more anagrams per member-minute the *shorter* the time limit; and for any given load and time limit, productivity was higher the *smaller* the size of the group. Thus, the more the work load per member-minute, the more work gets done. The point is clear: Teams adapt themselves to the constraints presented to them, such as the amount of time they have to perform a task.

Not only is team performance susceptible to arbitrary "norming" cues, but team communication and interaction and some aspects of product quality are also affected by these factors (Kelly & McGrath, 1985; Kelly, Futoran, & McGrath, 1990). For example, short time limits on an initial task induce teams to spend more time on task-oriented behaviors and less time on interpersonal interaction; whereas teams with a longer time period engage in more interpersonal interactions.

Kelly et al. (1990) outlined two different kinds of problems related to this issue: Capacity problems and capability problems. *Capacity* problems occur when there is not enough time to do all of the required tasks, although each task is easy. *Capability* problems occur when the task is difficult, even though there is plenty of time in which to do it. Capacity problems lead to a faster rate of task activity on subsequent trials, regardless of the actual time limits set for those later trials; capability problems lead to more extensive processing of information, hence a slower rate of production on subsequent trials, regardless of the actual time limits set for those trials.

CONCLUSIONS

Teams are not independent entities within the organization. There is a critical tension between the internal relations of a team and the external ties. Both are necessary; neither is sufficient to ensure long-term survival of the team. Depending upon the nature of the task that the team is working on, structural solutions should be put into place to ensure that the team is integrated with other individuals and teams within the organization. This activity itself requires that some members of the team act as boundary spanners and gatekeepers to bring needed information to the team, as well as distributing knowledge outside the team.

Managing the internal and external dynamics in a team is a difficult task, requiring constantly changing focus. The frequency of external communication may come at the expense of attention to internal processes (the ability to set goals, coordinate members' strategies, maintain cohesion, etc.; Ancona & Caldwell, 1991). Given that managing the internal team process and the external environment are somewhat opposing processes, how can managers optimize the probability of successful teamwork? An important first step is to talk with team members about the need to engage in these activities. A second step is to assign roles or talk about how to manage the dual processes of internal dynamics and external relations. This can go a long way toward minimizing the diffusion of responsibility problem that often haunts teams. A third step is to identify goals and indices of team success at the outset; this largely avoids rationalizing behavior after the fact. A final step is to develop a team contract—a document written by all members that focuses on internal and external management issues.

CHAPTER 10

Leadership: Managing the Paradox

In 1989, J.D. Bryant was perfectly content overseeing a staff of 15 circuit-board assemblers at the Texas Instruments Forest Lane defense plant in Dallas. "Then one day I heard the company was moving to teams and that I was going to become a facilitator. I'm supposed to teach the teams everything I know and then let them make their own decisions." Not sure if something good or bad had happened, Bryant pressed his supervisor for more information: " 'This is career enhancing?' He said, 'Oh yes. You won't have to do performance reviews any more. The team will take them on.' " Later the supervisor followed with: "Since you won't be a supervisor anymore, you'll have to take a 5% pay cut" (Caminiti, 1995, p. 93).

THE TEAM PARADOX

Teamwork, to those in power in command-and-control organizations, is not necessarily a good thing. A major investigation of first-line supervisors to employee involvement programs revealed that 72 percent of supervisors view participative management as good for their company and 60 percent view it as good for employees, but only 31 percent view it as beneficial for themselves (Klein, 1984). Yet companies often expect middle managers to metamorphose into stellar team leaders, ready to coach, motivate, and empower. The problem is that few people understand how to make this transformational process and many probably have an incentive to see it unravel. For example, in one plant, resistance to participative management programs took the form of supervisors keeping "hands off" as newly formed semiautonomous work teams attempted to solve problems. When questions arose that teams were unable to handle, supervisors replied, "That's not my job; it's the team's problem." In essence, the supervisors were undermining the teams so they could resume their traditional position of authority (Klein, 1984).

Leaders who have successfully made the transformation comment that they learned something that they did not realize at the outset. For example, Eric Doremus, of Honeywell's defense avionics division in Albuquerque, reflects, "My most important task was not trying to figure out everybody else's job. It was to help this team feel as if they owned the project by getting them whatever information, financial or otherwise, they needed. I knew that if we could all charge up the hill together, we would be successful" (Caminiti, 1995, p. 94).

In the best of circumstances, teams are empowered groups of people who collaborate in a mutually beneficial fashion to enact positive change. Leadership—or one person taking the helm of the group's efforts—seems antithetical to teamwork. Yet leaders are often necessary for effective teamwork—to shape goals, coordinate effort, and motivate members. We call this the **team paradox:** The fact that leaders often are necessary for teamwork, but that their very existence threatens teamwork, and vice versa. Traditional notions of leadership—that is, top-down, command-and-control approaches—may be ineffective in the new team environment. Leadership is perhaps easier to reconcile with effective teamwork when we realize that leadership comes in many forms. For example, a team may have a manager, administrator, supervisor, facilitator, director, coordinator, spokesperson, or chairperson. Leaders can also serve a vital role coordinating team members, resolving disputes or disagreements, motivating individuals, monitoring performance, and maintaining the goals and focus of the group.

This chapter addresses how people can be trained to become leaders and what techniques will enable these leaders to be more effective. We describe two theories of leadership—the Great Person theory and the Great Opportunity theory—and explain why the Great Opportunity theory better describes how leadership is developed. We examine approaches to influencing people, and we elaborate on several methods to create an effective participative team environment. Finally, we demonstrate that not all decisions require large amounts of team participation and offer a model to help determine how much participation is appropriate for a leader to use in various situations.

LEADERS AND THE NATURE-NURTURE DEBATE: GREAT PERSON VERSUS GREAT OPPORTUNITY

There are two theories about where effective leaders come from. The Great Person theory asserts that leaders are born, not made; whereas the Great Opportunity theory claims that leadership can be learned as a skill. Strict proponents of the Great Person theory claim that people are either born leaders or born followers: They either have it or they don't. If they do have it, they dictate, command, and control. If they don't have it, they follow those who do have it. "The cowboy riding the range is the stereotypical American, and that has carried over into business" (Hequet, 1994, p. 7). This Great Person theory of leadership is unidirectional—from the top down, with leaders imparting truth, wisdom, and directives to those beneath them.

If the Great Person theory is true, it would seem likely that we would be able to identify personality traits that make someone a great leader. Psychologists, political scientists, and historians have studied the personality of leaders in governmental, business, and educational organizations to see what common threads can be found. However, decades of research have failed to yield an agreed upon list of key traits shared by all leaders (Yukl, 1981). It seems clear that there is little or no evidence to support connections between personality and leadership. For example, Simonton (1987) gathered information about 100 personal attributes of all U.S. presidents, such as their family backgrounds, educational experiences, occupations, and personalities. Only three of these variables—height, family size, and number of books published before taking office—correlated with how effective the presidents were in office. The other 97 characteristics, including personality traits, were not related to leadership effectiveness at all. By chance, 5 percent—five out of the 100—would be significant!

Nevertheless, the Great Person theory is still used as a basis for recruitment and selection, and many companies and institutions routinely assess leadership potential with paper and pencil tests. Do these tests accurately predict leadership? The conclusion of decades of research is that there is no single test that can measure leadership. Even when leadership is measured, its relationship to the kinds of performance measures we would expect to see is largely inconclusive. It is rather fruitless to attempt to identify stable characteristics that will predict leadership. Even if it were possible (which we highly doubt), this kind of knowledge does not provide organizations or managers with much control over their own or another's behavior. Therefore, in a very important sense, trying to identify stable characteristics of leaders is ill-fated.

If the Great Person theory of leadership is flawed, then why do so many people seem to believe that personality can predict leadership? The **fundamental attribution error** is the tendency to overemphasize the impact of a stable personality and dispositional traits on a person's behavior and underemphasize the impact of the *situation* on people's behavior (Ross, 1977). In fact, more temporary, situational characteristics can usually explain a great deal of human behavior.

Why do people err on the side of attributing behavior to dispositions instead of more transient (and controllable) factors? The key reason is associated with the human need to predict and control. To the extent that people can predict the behavior of others, their chances for survival increase. For example, the ability to predict whether someone is trustworthy is highly adaptive. When people's behavior can be attributed to stable, dispositional characteristics, it is possible to more accurately predict their actions in various situations. Conversely, when people's behavior is attributed to temporary, environmental factors, it is more difficult to predict their behavior. Thus, the bias toward dispositional explanation is driven by the human need to control.

The Great Opportunity approach focuses on how leaders do two things vis-à-vis teamwork in their organizations. First, it focuses on how leaders directly interact with their teams. The second thing these leaders do is to structure the external environment so the team can best achieve its goals. In both of these tasks, leadership is bidirectional, with leaders learning from their team just as often as they provide direction for their team. These leaders maintain the relationship between the group and organization to ensure that organizational objectives are being pursued. Leaders also coordinate team members, resolve disputes or disagreements, motivate individuals, monitor performance, and establish the goals and focus of the group.

As we have seen in chapters 4 and 9, leadership in a team-based organization requires leaders not just to lead the team, but to interface between the organization and the team. In this sense, the leader is an important boundary spanner. No manager has all of the requisite skills required for effective leadership, but the effective manager knows where to go to get these skills and resources.

GREAT OPPORTUNITY: SOME EVIDENCE

A great deal of evidence indicates that leadership has more to do with designing the environment than personality. In this section, we cite a few of the most compelling examples. (Just a warning: Not all of the examples are what may be called "benevolent" leadership. In fact, a lot can be learned about leadership in cases where people seem to work against self-interest and collective well-being.)

Obedience to Authority

Do you think you would follow the direction of a leader even if it meant hurting or possibly killing someone? Most people say that they, personally, would never succumb to this. However, they fail to account for the powerful forces present in many situations that influence their behavior.

In a dramatic illustration of this, a Yale psychologist named Stanley Milgram recruited students and businesspersons to participate in a "study of learning" (Milgram, 1963). The learning study, under the auspices of Yale University, involved the principles of reinforcement and punishment on people's ability to learn. Accordingly, during each session, one person was selected to "teach" another person. The teacher's goal was to teach the other participant a list of word pairs (blue-box, nice-day, etc.) and then test the learner. The learner in this organization was always a male, in his late forties, overweight, and good-natured. The key learning strategy involved delivering an electric shock to the learner each time he made a mistake. The teacher was instructed how to use a "shock generator" containing 30 switches, labeled "Slight Shock" to "Danger: Severe Shock" to "XXX." The supervisor informed all trainees that they should deliver a shock of 15 volts (the smallest amount) the first time the learner made a mistake and then increase to the next highest switch for each subsequent mistake. After a few minutes, the learner made a mistake and was given a shock. This continued until the 75-volt level and his screams were heard from across the room. The "teachers" were concerned and asked the supervisor what to do. The supervisor instructed the teachers to continue—and they did.

A group of prominent psychiatrists estimated that only about 1 percent of the population would continue to the maximum amount of 450 volts. However, nearly 63 percent of the participants delivered the 450-volt shock amidst the agonizing screams and pleas of the learner to stop. Milgram (1963) described a typical participant's response in the teacher role:

> I observed a mature and initially poised businessman enter the laboratory smiling and confident. Within 20 minutes, he was reduced to a twitching, stuttering wreck, who was rapidly approaching a point of nervous collapse. He constantly pulled his earlobe, and twisted his hands. At one point, he pushed his fist into his forehead and muttered, "Oh God; let's stop it." And yet he continued to respond to every word of the experimenter and obeyed to the end. (p. 377)

In actuality, the learner was not hurt; he was an accomplice of the supervisor. However, in virtually all cases, the people recruited for the teacher role believed that the learner was actually being harmed, yet they continued to shock him. Most people have a difficult time accepting the reality of these results, believing themselves to be immune to such situational pressure to conform to the organizational practices. However, in reality, this investigation points up the extreme, yet subtle, power of the situation as an influence on human behavior. Perhaps the supervisor in this situation would not be regarded as a model leader, yet he created the perfect conditions by which to maximize effort and compliance by his trainees.

Blind Faith

Great leaders often get people to follow them and the goals they define, even when the odds are extremely doubtful for success. Unlike the obedience to authority principle, blind faith is often engendered in followers through a process of *self-rationalization.* In such situations, leaders are successful in creating environments where they lead people to believe that they have made their own choices. Consider the following examples:

- **Case 1:** The People's Temple was a cultlike organization based in San Francisco that primarily attracted poor residents. In 1977, the Reverend Jim Jones, who was the group's political, social, and spiritual leader, moved the membership with him to a jungle settlement in Guyana, South America. On November 18, 1978, Congressman Leo R. Ryan of California, who traveled to Guyana to investigate the cult, three members of Ryan's task force, and a cult defector were murdered as they tried to leave Jonestown by plane. Convinced that he would be arrested and implicated in the murder, which would inevitably lead to the demise of the People's Temple, Jones gathered the entire community around him and issued a call for each person's death, to be achieved in a unified act of self-destruction. In November 1978, 910 people compliantly drank, and died from, a vat of poison-laced Kool-Aid.

- **Case 2:** Marian Keech was a middle-aged woman who started a small cult group in the 1950s (Festinger, Riecken, & Schachter, 1956). The group met regularly, primarily to receive messages from spacemen "guardians," located on other planets, who communicated through Mrs. Keech. Convinced that a great flood would destroy all life on earth, Mrs. Keech told group members that they needed to give up all of their earthly possessions so that they could embark on the spaceship, which would safely transport them from the earth to another planet. Members of the group—including mothers, college students, high school students, a publisher, a physician, a hardware store clerk and his mother—gave up all of their possessions, including their homes, jobs, and personal belongings, to travel on the spaceship that Mrs. Keech was convinced would come at exactly 12:00 midnight. When the hour passed without event, the group's belief system was severely shaken. Within 5 hours, however, Mrs. Keech—in an act of brilliant leadership—pronounced that the group had been able to avert the flood by demonstrating faith and that they should now recruit new members. Thus, despite the obvious failure, the group's belief system was stronger than ever!

- **Case 3:** Army reservists were asked to eat fried grasshoppers as part of a research project on survival foods. Reservists who ate grasshoppers at the request of a stern, unpleasant officer increased their liking for grasshoppers far more than those who ate grasshoppers at the request of a well-liked pleasant officer (Zimbardo, Weisenberg, Firestone, & Levy, 1965).

In all three of these cases, the behavior of people seems to be exactly the opposite of common sense. Yet all of these cases are based upon real events that illustrate the power of self-rationalization.

Most attempts to analyze the Jonestown incident focus too much on the personal qualities of Jim Jones. The power he wielded came less from his personal style and more from his understanding of fundamental psychological principles. People willingly drank the poison drink in Guyana because up until that point they had put their complete faith in the cult; to reject the Reverend and his teachings at that point would have been an admission of inconsistency in their beliefs. In the case of Mrs. Keech, the participants themselves when interviewed indicated the power of their own actions in influencing their subsequent beliefs: "I have to believe the flood is coming on the twenty-first because I've spent all of my money. I quit my job. I quit computer school . . . I have to be-

lieve" (from the mother of a 3-year old; Festinger et al., 1956, p. 80). In tl
Army reservists, those who complied with the unfriendly officer's request
ternal justification for their actions. As a rule they adopted more positive
ward eating grasshoppers so as to justify their otherwise strange behavior.
principle involved is the **need for consistency:** People have a strong, almost overpow-
ering need to behave in a way that is consistent. In short, they want their actions to reflect their beliefs and vice versa.

Good Samaritans

The preceding examples all point to the darker side of leadership. Now, let's look at
some cases of humanitarian leadership. The biblical story of the Good Samaritan (Luke
10:25–37) who stops to help a stranger in trouble is the quintessential example of proactive, humanitarian leadership. Consider the following scenario: Suppose there is a person slumped in a doorway, obviously unconscious, and in need of help. Imagine that
someone is walking by this person—in one case, the person walking by is a seminary
student (enrolled in an intensive religious study program) and in the other case, the person walking by is a regular student. Who is more likely to help the person in need? If
you are like most people, you predict that the seminary student is most likely to act as
the Good Samaritan.

However, in a simulation of this exact scenario, seminary students were no more
likely to help the victim than were nonseminary students. The key factor that predicted helping behavior was whether the student had witnessed an example of helping in the immediate past. Students who had witnessed someone else helping in a similar kind of situation (e.g., someone donating blood, giving street directions, or picking
up trash) were much more likely to go out of their way to help the victim (Darley &
Batson, 1973).

The take-away message is clear: Immediate, available examples of organizational
citizenship are much greater predictors of behavior than are personality traits—
another powerful testament to the power of the situation and the importance of psychology for effective leadership. Thus, the manager-leader should endorse and promote examples of the kinds of behavior that are regarded to be important for achieving team goals.

Self-Fulfilling Prophecy

The mark of a great leader is to bring out the best in people. Wouldn't it be great if by
merely believing in their followers or employees, leaders could bring out the best in
them? The power of expectations can and does dramatically influence behavior. Consider the following examples from actual situations:

Pygmalion in the Classroom

In 1968, a pair of investigators gave IQ tests to children from several elementary
schools and then shared the results with the children's teachers (Rosenthal & Jacobson,
1968). They identified several children who could be expected to show substantial IQ
gains in the current school year. During the year, those children, as predicted, spoke
more, were more responsive, and scored higher on scholastic aptitude tests. All of these
were objective measures of performance. Thus, the children did perform in a more stellar way. So far, this sounds like a Great Person theory; that is, some children are more

CHAPTER 10 Leadership: Managing the Paradox

naturally gifted than are others—it only stands to reason that they will excel in class-room settings.

However, there is an important twist to this real-life story. The children who were predicted to be gifted were, in fact, randomly selected—that is, they were not of higher aptitude. However, the teachers did not know this. The children were in every way identical to those not targeted, but over the course of a year, they blossomed. How could this be? Before reading further, what do you think is going on? (Be specific about the process.)

Job Interviewing

The typical job interview is a stressful situation. Consider the observed performance between black and white applicants during job interviews: Black applicants are less articulate, less friendly, less social, more awkward, more hesitant, more aggressive, and less fluent than are white applicants when interviewing with white employees (Word, Zanna, & Cooper, 1974). Most of us would agree that is pretty disturbing. More careful analyses will reveal these differences in performance to be traceable to a *biased interview process*—not a difference in the attitude or quality of candidates.

To expose this bias, and ultimately restructure the interview method, let's consider what happens during the interview itself. Consider two cases: A white person interviewing an African American and the same white person interviewing a Caucasian (Word et al., 1974). Further, let's imagine that the two candidates are equally qualified: They have identical degrees, standardized test scores, previous work experience, skills, education, and training. Suppose we secretly videotape each interview; when we do so, we'll learn that the white interviewer does the following:

- Displays discomfort and lack of interest when interviewing the black applicant
- Sits further away from the black applicant
- Stammers when talking to the black applicant
- Terminates interview far sooner with the black applicant

As a consequence of this differential interpersonal treatment, is it any surprise that the two candidates perform differently during the interview?

Now, suppose that when white interviewers are trained to use one of the two interviewing "styles," white applicants perform more poorly when they receive the style previously used with blacks than when they receive the style previously used with whites. Specifically, when white candidates are treated the way black candidates are when they are interviewed, white applicants are judged to be more nervous, less effective, and less competent. Thus, when blacks are interviewed by whites, they are placed at a disadvantage and are likely to perform more poorly than their white counterparts.

Physical Attractiveness Bias

People, in general, expect more attractive people to be more successful, and attractive people generally are more successful regardless of their innate ability. Like it or not, there are benefits that accompany physical attractiveness that begin at a very young age and spill over into just about every important aspect of life—from marriage partners to job interviewing to court judgments. Most people would readily acknowledge, however, that beauty is only skin deep and that it should not affect organizational success. Why then, are attractive toddlers punished less severely by their teachers than less attractive youngsters (Dion, 1972)? Attractive people are presumed to be happier, more sociable and extroverted, less deviant, and more likely to be successful professionally (Hatfield & Sprecher, 1986). Less attractive female authors' written work was evaluated as lower in quality than identical work submitted by attractive women (Landy & Sigall, 1974).

So far, this does not sound like a self-fulfilling prophecy, but instead, a strong prejudice to reward attractive people and punish unattractive people. However, consider the behavioral implications of receiving steady, consistent treatment on the basis of your appearance. For attractive people, this would mean that others give you the benefit of the doubt, express praise, and show high interest; for unattractive people, this means a constant diet of rejection, disinterest, and skepticism. Indeed, when unattractive people are treated the way attractive people are, they behave in a more personally engaging, friendly, and likeable fashion! (Snyder, Tanke, & Berscheid, 1977).

All three of these cases illustrate an important principle of human behavior: The self-fulfilling prophecy, which is the tendency of people to come to behave in a manner consistent with how they are viewed and treated by others.

The Power of Labels

A person's behavior in any particular situation is much more influenced by temporary aspects of the situation than by enduring personality characteristics. As an example of this, consider a situation in which M.B.A. students are assessed in terms of their cooperativeness and competitiveness by their peers, who know them quite well. Then, imagine that these people are put into a game-playing situation in which they can choose to either behave in a cooperative, trusting fashion or in a competitive, self-interested fashion with some of their peers. Imagine further that in all cases wherein the M.B.A. students are playing the game, the situation is described slightly differently: In one case, the game is called the "Wall Street Game"; in the other case, it is called the "Community Game" (from Ross & Samuels, 1993). Otherwise, the game, the payoffs, and the choices are identical. Whereas the Great Person theory would predict that those students who are natural cooperators would choose to cooperate and the natural competitors would behave competitively, this is not at all what happens: The incidence of competition is determined by the label used to describe the situation. In fact, the incidence of cooperation is three times as high in the Community Game than in the Wall Street Game!

Head of the Table Effect

Seemingly trivial situational factors like seating arrangements can affect leadership in groups. In general, the person who grabs the chalk (or another recording device) is in a position of great influence. When a group sits at a table, the person at the head of the table has a greater probability of emerging as the leader, even when seating is randomly determined. For example, people appointed to lead small discussion groups tend to select seats at the head of the table (Sommer, 1969). People who sit at the head of the table talk more frequently, dominate, and influence more (Strodtbeck & Hook, 1961). This finding does not negate the possibility that some people do have an innate drive to lead others. The person who picks up the chalk on some occasions may, in fact, have a predisposition toward leading the group. To correct for this possibility, the seating experiment has been conducted with randomly selected people with randomly selected seating arrangements. If an innate drive was determining who led the group, it would be expected that the seat of the leader would vary; however, repeatedly, the person who sits at the head of the table (as opposed to sides) has more influence over others, which lends credence to the fact that the opportunity of sitting at the head of the table takes precedence over the Great Person approach (Nemeth & Wachtler, 1974; Riess, 1982; Riess & Rosenfeld, 1980).

For example, consider a group of consultants who arranged for five-person groups to hold a discussion while seated at a rectangular table (Howells & Becker, 1962). They had two people sit on one side of the table and three on the other side. Although no one sat in the end seat, the consultants made specific predictions about who should emerge as the leader if eye contact and control of communication were important causal factors. Whereas those seated on the two-person side of the table could maintain easy eye contact with three of the group members, those on the three-person side could best focus their attention on only two members. Therefore, those on the two-person side should be able to influence others more and, hence, are more likely to become leaders. Indeed, 70 percent of the leaders came from the two-person side; only 30 percent came from the three-person side!

Further evidence of the power of seating comes from an analysis of minority influence. In this situation, a person who was told to advocate a minority view was either seated at the head of the table or some other, nondominant position (Nemeth & Wachtler, 1974). The minority member systematically disagreed with the majority of the group members on the topic under discussion, and the extent to which the other group members altered their opinions to agree with the minority member was assessed. The minorities succeeded in influencing others only when they had freely chosen to sit in the head chair. Apparently, disagreeing with other group members at less powerful locations was viewed as disruptive deviancy, whereas those who had selected to sit at the head of the table were viewed more as leaders (Riess, 1982; Riess & Rosenfeld, 1980).

Random Selection of Leaders

Intuition tells us that leaders should be systematically selected. Organizations spend millions each year carefully selecting leaders. However, evidence suggests that selected leaders may hinder effective team performance. In an investigation of team performance, teams with randomly selected leaders performed better on an organizational decision-making task than did teams whose leaders were systematically selected (Haslam et al., 1998). Moreover, teams with a random leader also performed better than did teams with no appointed leader and team members adhered more strongly to the group decision. The key reason seems to be that systematically-selected leaders often undermine group goals because they assert their personal superiority at the expense of developing a sense of shared team identity.

Each of the previous stories attests to the power of the situation in influencing people. To the extent that managers are aware of how psychological factors are constantly operating in teams, they can use them more responsibly and effectively.

LEADERSHIP BEHAVIOR: ROUTES TO INFLUENCE

Leadership is the ability to influence people in such a way as to achieve desired objectives. The objectives might be those as defined by the leader (e.g., a manager-led team) or those defined by the team (e.g., a self-managed or self-designing team). The ability to influence others is a form of power. There are many types of influence: Some involve coercive tactics; others rely on cooperative tactics.

Much of what we argue in this section is based upon empirical psychological research (i.e., not case studies or casual observation). Each of the principles we derive here has been replicated and is, therefore, known to be a robust phenomenon. Some leaders may find it peculiar that we draw upon psychology to study leadership. In fact, leadership is really about applying psychological principles. However, psychology is often not intuitive, so it is important to understand something about human behavior and cognition. To the extent that leaders appreciate psychological principles, they are in a position to use these to accomplish their objectives.

Vivid Information

People are persuaded by clear facts and objective evidence. If a leader can provide new reasons for embarking on a particular course of action, members are more likely to be persuaded than if the leader merely reinforces what team members already know.

However, not all types of information are created equal. Single case studies are much more persuasive than is aggregated data—even though they are objectively less informative (Tversky & Kahneman, 1973). Consider, for example, consumers' car choices—one vivid story about a neighbor who owned a Volvo that ran like a clock is more influential than are the thousands of data points presented in consumer reports about the same car, even though consumer reports are more valid because they are based upon more observations.

Leaders should know that different presentation formats of the same data can produce different levels of accuracy in those that interpret the data. Conventional wisdom has it that graphic displays make it easier for a person to assimilate information and make a judgment than does a textual format, but empirical evidence suggests that this is not the case. Specifically, when people receive information in textual form, whether short descriptions or longer biographical stories, they make more accurate judgments than those who receive information in graphic or tabular form (Sanfey & Hastie, 1998). Thus, to be more effective, leaders should present clear, vivid data in textual form.

Gains and Losses

People intuitively perform cost-benefit analyses when considering different courses of action. However, they do not treat gains commensurately with losses (Tversky & Kahneman, 1974). People tend to overweight costs (or losses) relative to gains. In short, people are risk averse for gains and risk seeking for losses. As a simple demonstration of this psychological phenomenon, imagine that you have your choice of the following:

A. Receiving a cashier's check for $5,000; or
B. Playing a lottery-type game in which there is a 50 percent chance of winning a $10,000 cashier's check and a 50 percent chance of winning nothing.

Under these circumstances, the great majority of people choose option A—the sure thing. Note that the expected value of each choice is $5,000. However, the choice of A over B reflects a fundamental principle of human psychology: Risk aversion.

Now, imagine yourself facing the following unenviable choice:

C. Having to pay $5,000 for an unexpected expense; or
D. Playing a lottery-type game in which there is a 50 percent chance of paying nothing and a 50 percent chance of paying $10,000.

Most people find it more difficult to choose among C and D because these choices are undesirable—an avoidance-avoidance conflict. However, when forced to make a decision, a majority choose option D, which represents the risky alternative. The choice of D over C in this case reflects a fundamental principle of human psychology: Risk-seeking behavior.

At first it might seem to be a contradiction that people are both risk averse and risk seeking, but by understanding how people frame their decisions, leaders can present options in ways that encourage their followers to act in a particular way. The critical message for the leader is to know what pushes people toward risk aversion or risk-seeking behavior in any given situation. The answer is whether people are choosing between gains or losses: People are risk averse for gains and risk seeking when it comes to losses. A **reference point** defines what a person considers to be the status quo from which gains and losses are evaluated. Savvy leaders know that if they want to maintain the status quo—that is, induce risk aversion or conservatism in their group—they must present options as gains relative to a reference point. Similarly, if they want to induce change, they frame choices as losses.

Primacy

Leaders should present the most influential evidence first. This is because people tend to overweight information that they receive first, even though it may not be more diagnostic than information that follows. For example, primacy effects influence evaluations of other people: The first pieces of information people learn about others are more influential. Even when people have identical traits, others' impressions of them differ depending on which information they learn first (Jones, Stires, Shaver, & Harris, 1968).

Self-Identity and Self-Affirmation

Leaders draw an important part of their legitimacy and acceptance from their social relationships with team members. Thus, effective leadership depends on a leader's ability to identify with the team. People care about how they are treated by authorities (Tyler, 1997), and they want to have good feelings about themselves. Thus, team members interact with other members and leaders, not just to exchange resources, but to define and develop their own identities. If people feel valued and respected, they are more likely to support leaders. In general, people's self-identities are composed of many different things—their perceived strengths, skills, beliefs, relationships, and so on. Their experiences in the organization either affirm or threaten their self-identity. When self-identity is affirmed, everything is fine. However, when self-identity is threatened, individuals are in a psychologically precarious position (e.g., the young consultant who is ripped apart by his client or a senior partner). Consequently, they need to reaffirm their identity. In some cases, they may reject the person or thing that has threatened their identity (e.g., the consultant may regard the client to be crazy or unreasonable). In other cases, this may not be possible (e.g., the client has a reputation for honesty and solid judgment). In such instances, people attempt to focus on another key aspect of themselves that they want to promote (e.g., an accountant may take comfort in the fact that his skills are highly regarded by others).

What does all of this have to do with leadership and influence? Leaders are in a position of shaping and monitoring other people's self-identities. Members of a team are interested in the intrinsic aspects of their work and expect their leader to be as well. This even affects performance: People who are taught skills by extrinsically motivated leaders are less interested in learning and enjoy what they are doing less than people taught by an intrinsically motivated leader—even when the lessons and learning are identical (Wild, Enzle, Nix, & Deci, 1997). This means that leaders need to provide the people on their team with opportunities by which they can affirm their own organizationally relevant identities. Perhaps even more important, leaders need to provide a mechanism by which to help restore identities that may be threatened. Teams will suffer setbacks. When team members' identities are on the line (and they usually are in highly motivated groups), the leader must provide ways that team members can regroup, but not lose sight of team goals. In these times, the leader should focus on what the team does right. Perhaps it is for these reasons that leaders who are regarded to be most like team members are evaluated to be more effective than leaders who are seen as not very similar to their team (Hains, Hogg, & Duck, 1997).

Mere Exposure

The more people are exposed to someone, or someone's ideas, the more they like them (Zajonc, 1968). For example, imagine that you are viewing several hundred resumés or business proposals. You will like the ones that you see more often, independent of the actual quality of the proposal or resumé! The mere exposure effect does not depend on people's *awareness* that they have seen the person or idea before—actually, mere exposure effects are more likely to work when exposure is subtle. The mere exposure effect is so powerful that it also occurs for people and ideas that are *disliked* initially. Perhaps you are wondering why mere exposure leads a person to like someone or something more. The reason rests on a principle of human behavior called *familiarity*—to the extent that something seems familiar, people are more attracted to it. This is why companies print their name and logo on letterhead and everything else—to make their name more familiar and, therefore, more likeable.

Behavioral Synchrony

In social and business encounters, face-to-face or otherwise, people attempt to get in sync with one another. On a behavioral level, this means that people adjust their frequency of speech, content of their speech, posture, speaking distance, facial expression, and a host of other postural, verbal, and nonverbal indicators to those of the person with whom they are interacting. On an emotional level, this means that people's moods in groups tend to be linked (Totterdell, Kellett, Teuchmann, & Briner, 1998). For example, nurses who work in teams show significant associations between their own moods and the collective mood of their teammates, independent of shared hassles. Similarly, in an investigation of teams of accountants, individually reported moods were significantly associated with the collective mood of teammates. Thus, an employee's mood at work is linked to the mood of teammates, even though the employee is not necessarily aware of this. Why? The simple answer is that it is easier to conduct business if people feel comfortable with each other; and part of feeling rapport is feeling the same way. People are more receptive to ideas, more agreeable, and more accepting when they feel they have rapport with others. Thus, an important route to influence is knowing how to build rapport. Adopting a similar body posture as the person with whom you are speaking, following the rhythm of the person's speech patterns, and nodding at the right time can go a long way toward building immediate rapport and setting the stage for influence. For example, when people are undergoing one-on-one training, those pairs whose movements are in greatest synchrony feel the most rapport (Goleman, 1991).

We have reviewed a number of strategies by which leaders may gain influence by capitalizing on people's motivational needs and cognitive abilities. Our point is not to provide strategies for leaders to use to wield self-interest on unsuspecting team members. Most people are too smart to be duped. Rather, the point is to present some key facts about human behavior that can either present obstacles or be used as points of leverage. This leads us to the paradox we raised at the beginning of this chapter.

LEADERSHIP AND TEAMWORK: ADDRESSING THE PARADOX

Some managers believe that power and control should remain in the hands of a few high-level executives. This model of leadership assumes that the leader has all of the answers, knowledge, and ideas in the organization. This view, however, is being challenged by a model of leadership that delegates authority downward, toward individuals and groups. In this model, leadership is more equally shared by members as teams develop over time. Leadership style does make a difference. When teams have to learn a new task requiring coordination, leadership style (participative versus authoritative) makes a difference in the development and implementation of effective tactics. Teams led by a "coordinator," in which all team members share equal responsibility for determining the team strategy and directing its activities, implement better tactics than commander-led teams (Durham, Knight, & Locke, 1997). In the remainder of this chapter, we provide mechanisms by which organizations and leaders can move power downward and use more participative management strategies.

Just because leaders want to move in the direction of participation and empowerment, however, does not mean that this can be done by merely changing their own behavior and style, independent of other organizational forces. Leadership style and strategy must be integrated into the organizational context (as indicated in Sidebar 10-1).

> **Sidebar 10-1. Organizational Culture and Commitment**
> "People hear senior management talk about empowerment, teamwork, and service. What they get are paternalistic pats on the head, motivation programs, and blame for not using the systems, processes, and technology dropped on them and their customers. The problem stems from the expanding gulf between rising expectations and the reality of the organization's traditional culture" (Clemmer, 1995, p. 62).

Consider two types of organizations: Bureaucratic and commitment organizations. **Bureaucratic organizations** are the traditional, hierarchical style of leadership; information, rewards, knowledge, and power are concentrated at the top of the organization. In the classic bureaucratic organization, teams do not exist or at least are not acknowledged. Furthermore, when they do emerge, they are often ignored, suppressed, contained, or neglected (Walton & Hackman, 1986). **Commitment organizations** are the opposite extreme: Teams are expected and encouraged to form; power is not hierarchical; the organization has a deliberate flat structure. For an example that illustrates the difference between bureaucratic and commitment organizations, see Box 10-1.

BOX 10-1

Going from Bureaucracy to Commitment

An example that illustrates the difference between bureaucratic and commitment organizations is the hierarchical leadership style of General Motors during the early 1980s (long lead time to react to market pressures, poor manufacturing quality, and dissatisfaction in the workforce) and the new Saturn division, where the guiding principle is focused on the empowerment of people (Keller & McGahan, 1994). General Motors was a bureaucratic corporation. It took the company twice as long as its Japanese counterparts to respond to outside market forces (i.e., introducing new models) and to build competitive cars. The company's executives blamed this inefficiency on high labor costs. According to one su-

pervisor, the way to regain competitiveness was "to go down the line and knock some heads off." This antagonism between management and the workers made the workers less willing to work with management to jointly solve problems and exacerbated the high labor costs. On the other hand, when GM launched the Saturn project, the company was able to share with its new hires the common vision of building an affordable and dependable car in a short time frame. They succeeded by delegating important decisions downward and by forming teams led by various charter team members. The Saturn plant does not suffer from long cycle times or abnormally high labor costs.

DECISION ANALYSIS MODEL: HOW PARTICIPATIVE DO YOU WANT TO BE?

Leaders will be more effective if they understand that not every decision requires the input of their entire team. The amount of team participation varies along a continuum from zero to total involvement. How much participation is ideal? It is simply not practical to canvass and consult with the team on every organizational issue, but where to draw the line is unclear. The decision analysis model of Vroom and Yetton (1973) provides a useful mechanism for the manager to consider.

As can be seen in Figure 10-1, the key questions facing the leader concern the *quality* of the decision to be made (e.g., is it necessary to find the best outcome, given time and budget constraints, or are most outcomes basically sufficient?) and the *acceptance* needed for the decision (e.g., how much does the ultimate outcome need to be accepted by the organization?). The model prompts leaders to be more deliberate in the decision-making process. This has the effect of increasing the consistency of their behavior, and consistency is the key principle by which leaders are evaluated. This model of leadership focuses on matching the leader and the situational requirements (Vroom & Jago, 1988; Vroom & Yetton, 1973).

Decision Styles

Vroom & Jago (1988) considered four different decision methods available to the leader. The first is **autocratic**, in which the leader makes the decision with little or no involvement of other team members. The second method, the **consultative approach**, involves different degrees of consultation with team members; however, the leader is still the final decision maker. The third method, **consensus building**, involves extensive consultation and consensus building with the team. Here, the leader shares a problem with team members and together, they try to reach consensus. The leader essentially is another member of the team, and has no more or less influence than any other member. The final method involves total **delegation** of decision making to the team. The team makes the decision without the leader. The leader gives the problem to the team and lets the team determine the best course of action with virtually no additional input.

Problem Identification

The leader must also determine the right questions and the right order in which to ask them. This also influences the best decision style in a particular context. For example, consider a situation in which a high-quality decision is crucial (the stakes are high), the leader has enough information or expertise to make the decision alone, and acceptance by subordinates is not crucial—that is, the decision will work even without their support. In this case, a relatively autocratic style of decision is best. It is efficient, and getting the decision implemented will cost very little. In contrast, consider a situation in which a high-quality decision is necessary, the leader has enough information to make the decision alone, but acceptance by subordinates is crucial—that is, the decision will not work without their active support. Here, a more participative style would be preferable. Indeed, leaders who adapt their style of decision making to existing conditions are generally more successful than those who are either uniformly autocratic or participative in style (Vroom & Jago,

AI	Leader makes the decision alone.
AII	Leader asks for information from the team but makes the decision alone. The team may or may not be told about what the problem is.
CI	Leader shares the problem with the team and asks for information and evaluations from them. Meetings take place with each member separately, not as a group, and the leader makes the decision.
CII	Leader and team meet as a group to discuss the problem, but the leader makes the decision.
GII	Leader and team meet as a group to discuss the problem, and the team as a whole makes the decision.

Note: A = alone, C = consultation, G = group.

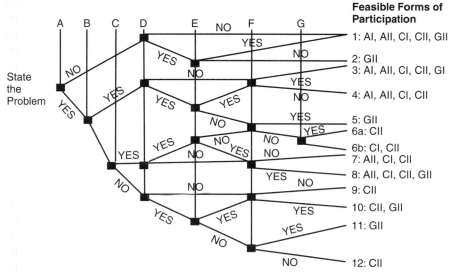

Feasible Forms of Participation

1: AI, AII, CI, CII, GII
2: GII
3: AI, AII, CI, CII, GI
4: AI, AII, CI, CII
5: GII
6a: CII
6b: CI, CII
7: AII, CI, CII
8: AII, CI, CII, GII
9: CII
10: CII, GII
11: GII
12: CII

A: Does the problem possess a quality requirement?

B: Do I have sufficient information to make a high-quality decision?

C: Is the problem structured?

D: Is acceptance of the decision by the team important for effective implementation?

E: If I were to make the decision by myself, am I reasonably certain that it would be accepted by my team?

F: Does the team share the organizational goals to be attained by solving this problem?

G: Is conflict among team members likely in preferred solutions?

FIGURE 10-1   Decision Analysis Model

Source: Adapted from Vroom, V.H., & Yetton, P.W. 1973. *Leadership and Decision-Making.* Pittsburgh, PA: University of Pittsburgh Press. Reprinted with permission.

1978). However, most team members prefer a participative approach by their leader, even under conditions where the decision model recommends an autocratic style (Heilman, Hornstein, Cage, & Herschlag, 1984). This means, of course, that the perceived effectiveness of decisions among leaders may very well differ from that perceived by their team (Field & House, 1990). Teams have strong aversion to autocratic decision-making strategies, even when these are predicted by the model to be most effective. Thus, the decision-making model is a useful device for helping the leader to be a consistent decision maker, but team members generally prefer participation.

Decision Tree Model

The decision tree model is one in which all of these questions and alternatives are put together to formulate a sound decision, as illustrated in Figure 10-1. A fundamental assumption in this model is that consultation with teams and individuals is inefficient because it requires time; therefore, the model is conservative in that it tends to push the leader toward autocratic or independent decision making. However, in cases where the model recommends a relatively autocratic or individual control strategy, the leader must not let people think that they have control when they actually do not.

STRATEGIES FOR ENCOURAGING PARTICIPATIVE MANAGEMENT

Once management has considered the potential benefits of a more employee-empowering leadership style, management must determine how to best implement this new structure. In the following paragraphs, we provide several strategies to make a smooth transition from a bureaucratic to a commitment organization. *Empowerment, participative management,* and *self-managing teams* are popular buzzwords. However, they don't happen overnight—even when upper management has made a public commitment to creating an empowered workforce. Many companies that want to become more participatory in their management styles don't know how to begin. What are some down-to-earth, concrete steps for moving power downward in the organization—that is, into the hands of team members?

The variety of approaches to inviting participation in the workforce can be clustered into four types of approaches: Task delegation, parallel suggestion involvement, job involvement, and organizational involvement (Lawler, 1988).

Task Delegation

The idea behind task delegation is that leaders delegate meaningful tasks and responsibilities to others. The spirit of task delegation is multifold: To invite others to have a share in the performance of work; to have leaders do other, more important things; and to mentor. This not only serves the interests of the employees, who presumably want to have a greater hand in the work and operations of the company, but it also serves the interests of the leader and the organization in creating more efficient uses of time. Many people have a somewhat old-fashioned view of leadership that holds that a leader is responsible not only for creating and defining the vision of the organization, but must handle all of the details, manage all of the personal relationships, and determine the process. Many managers mistakenly think that every task requires their constant attention from beginning to end. These statements are supported by the experiences of two innovative leaders, Phil Carroll of Shell Oil and Rich Teerlink of Harley-Davidson

Key Guidelines for Successful Delegation (Hall, 1997)

Use delegation to develop, not dump. As people become more concerned about time management, there has been a tendency to think that this means getting rid of unwanted tasks. Be sure that you and your subordinates discuss the task in terms of what is in it for them. Don't just pass the buck. Pass on challenge, responsibility, and a chance to learn new skills or aspects of the organization.

Set specific goals with subordinates. This includes a review of the task, especially the results expected, and a timetable for getting things done and reviewing progress. Don't assume that they understand what you expect and/or need. Be specific and check for understanding.

Discuss the meaning of the assignment in terms of its value within the larger organizational picture.

Provide for autonomy. Make it clear that subordinates have the authority and resources and are free to "run with the ball," but reassure them that you will be there to provide support.

Elicit questions from the subordinate. Test for understanding of the talk.

Get additional ideas or other inputs from the subordinate.

Provide feedback. Your subordinates need to know how they are doing. This is helpful for taking corrective action before a deadline. It is especially reinforcing after a goal is accomplished.

Provide times for follow-up. Don't just delegate and expect the results to just happen. Plan to meet, review preliminary results, discuss problems, and so forth.

Select the most motivated person.

Delegate only once, and to only one person, group, or team. Nothing is more demoralizing for subordinates than to find out that other people are working on a project that they thought had been delegated solely to them.

(Senge, 1996). Phil Carroll recalls: "When I first came in as CEO, everyone thought, 'Phil will tell us what he wants us to do.' But I didn't have a clue, and if I had, it would have been a disaster" (p. 43). Likewise, Rich Teerlink says, "Anyone who thinks the CEO can drive this kind of change is wrong. They succeeded by delegation" (p. 43).

Leadership, if it is to be effective, requires delegation. **Delegation** is the handing over of the responsibility and authority required to accomplish a task without relinquishing final accountability. This means that leaders are still accountable for their delegates as well as for themselves. Delegation is much easier said than done, however. There are right and wrong ways to delegate that depend on things such as team members' skill levels and the nature of the work. Box 10-2 outlines guidelines for successful delegation.

The inability to delegate effectively creates two negative consequences for the organization: Overloaded executives and underutilized subordinates. Each of these conditions is associated with work-related stress and burnout—not to mention many different forms of underperformance. By giving meaningful responsibility to subordinates, managers give them the opportunity to perform their jobs well, demonstrate ability, experience success, be visible within the organization, develop skills, and experience new challenges.

Parallel Suggestion Involvement

The idea behind parallel suggestion involvement is to invite employees and team members to make suggestions about organizational procedures and processes. Thus, employees are given opportunities and are actively encouraged to recommend different tactics for increasing sales, minimizing production costs, increasing customer satisfaction, and so on. The classic example of parallel suggestion involvement is the suggestion box, which is not even limited to employees—customers can be asked to make recommendations as well. Quality circles also invite workers to share ideas about improving production and products. The parallel suggestion strategy is cost-effective; providing a venue to solicit suggestions can be relatively inexpensive, but can potentially have huge payoffs in terms of improving organizational functioning. What's more, parallel suggestion involvement can significantly reduce turnover and absenteeism because employees who feel that their interests, concerns, and ideas are valued are more motivated. This was true for Delta Credit Union, which in early 1991 planned to upgrade customer service by moving some of the eight branches to more expensive and larger locations (Clemmer, 1995). However, when managers shared some of their plans with customer focus groups, they learned they were completely off-target. Customers wanted improvements in existing branch services—reduced waiting and more of a family feeling. In short, by listening to their customers, Delta experienced asset growth of 25 percent in the following 2 years.

Job Involvement

Job involvement entails restructuring the tasks performed by employees to make them more rewarding, enriching, and, in the case of teams, more autonomous. When people are challenged with interesting tasks, they perform more effectively and creatively. There are a variety of ways by which this may be achieved, such as providing employees with feedback from customers, restructuring tasks so that employees complete a whole and meaningful piece of work, and training employees with new skills and knowledge so that their job scope increases. With job involvement, employees at the lowest levels get new information, power, and skills, and they may be rewarded differently. For example, individuals may be rewarded for team effort and group-level productivity. Unlike parallel suggestion involvement, job involvement affects the daily work activities of employees. For this reason, job involvement is considerably more costly than is parallel suggestion involvement because of the high start-up costs of reconfiguring job descriptions, training, and, in many cases, the physical reconfiguration of the workplace. A good example of greater job involvement comes from Levi Strauss & Company. Tommye Jo Daves, a plant manager at Levi's in Blue Ridge, Georgia, has embraced participative management, yet acknowledges that things do not always work smoothly. She states that "Sometimes it's real hard for me [not to push back at the team] and say 'you do this, and you do that, and you do this.' Now [with the new structure], I have to say 'How do you want to do this?' I have to realize that their ideas may not be the way to go, but I have to let them learn that for themselves" (Huey, 1994, p. 48).

Organizational Involvement

Organizational involvement, or the commitment approach, restructures the organization so that employees at the lowest level will have a sense of involvement (commitment) in not just how they do their own jobs (as in the job involvement approach), but in the performance of the entire organization. Organizational involvement strategies invite employees to contribute to higher order strategy decisions. The McGregor method and Theory Y (McGregor, 1960) are examples of high-involvement strategies in which employees make decisions about work activities as well as organizational direction. Organizational involvement is based on the argument that if employees are going to care about the performance of their organization, they need to know about it, be able to influence it, be rewarded for it, and have the knowledge and skills to contribute to it.

A key difference between parallel suggestion involvement and organizational involvement is that employees not only make recommendations about how to improve organizational functioning, but are able to implement their suggestions. Thus, employees and team members have **implementation power.** This disadvantage of the organizational involvement strategy is that it is very difficult to know which employee-suggested strategies are, in fact, worthwhile to implement. Moreover, there are very few company examples of high-involvement organizations. Dana Corporation, a manufacturer of products for the automobile and truck industry, is a good example of a high-involvement organization that is structured on a product basis—each of its relatively small divisions can serve customers autonomously, with substantial ownership over a product from beginning to end (Lawler, 1992).

FREEING THE CAGED BIRD: EFFECTS OF EMPOWERMENT

It would seem that empowerment and greater employee participation would be the preferred mode in most companies—certainly, at least, from the view of the employees. However, humans have a fundamental need for structure and order, and new employees are often uncomfortable in the absence of clear structures, guidelines, and constraints. For example, newly matriculated M.B.A. students frequently lobby for instructor-assigned, rather than free-forming, study groups. What is the effect of empowerment and the ambiguity it brings to the individual, the team, and the organization?

When an organization removes existing structures to provide empowerment in a more democratic fashion, it may find the ambiguity associated with the new structure uncomfortable, and so respond by imposing a more controlling and bureaucratic structure than the one it sought to replace. This highly rational, but powerfully oppressive bureaucracy is known as the **iron cage** (Weber, 1958). Out of a desire for order, people continually rationalize their bureaucratic relationships, making them less negotiated (i.e., less based upon commitment) and more structural (Weber, 1978). As a case in point, see Sidebar 10-2.

> **Sidebar 10-2. ISE Communications**
> ISE Communications is a small manufacturing company in a mountain state, located in a metropolitan area (Barker, 1993). ISE manufactures voice and data transmission circuit boards for the telecommunications industry. ISE employs a total of 150 employees, 90 of whom are in manufacturing. Originally, ISE was a division of a large telecommunications firm. The ISE management team bought it outright in 1984, although the large firm still remains ISE's largest customer. ISE has traditional

manufacturing, engineering, sales, marketing, human resources, and executive staffs. ISE converted from traditional manufacturing into self-managing teams in 1988.

In 1988, the CEO of ISE made a commitment to restructure the organization into self-managing teams. Literally overnight he reconfigured the physical workspace and created several work teams called Red, Blue, Green, Orange, and so on. Before the change, the structure of ISE was such that three levels of managerial hierarchy existed between the vice president and the manufacturing workers. Line and shift supervisors formed the first managerial link. The assembly line in manufacturing organized the plant, with workers manufacturing circuit boards according to their place on the line. Workers had little input into work-related decisions (i.e., not even parallel suggestion involvement). Management disciplined all workers and interviewed and hired all new workers.

After the change, the managerial hierarchy extended directly from the new manufacturing teams to the vice president. Team work areas replaced the old assembly lines. Teams were responsible for all aspects of the product: Complete fabrication, testing, packaging, and so on. Team members took on management issues within each team, electing someone to coordinate information, and to discipline, interview, hire, and terminate members. When workers reported to the plant on the next business day, there was mass confusion and chaos. What happened in the ensuing months was surprising.

ISE is an example of a company in which upper management moved from bureaucratic control to participative management. However, many of the effects were not intended. Three distinct phases were observed over a 4-year period of change.

In the first phase, the challenge for the teams was to learn how to work together and supervise themselves functionally; that is, how to get a customer's order manufactured and out the door.

In the second phase, the teams had to deal with the socialization processes that had shaped the norms of the group. The company prospered and a large number of new workers had to be integrated into the teams; workers were unfamiliar with the existing teams' value consensus and they posed an immediate challenge to the power relationships that the older employees had formed.

In the third phase, the company began to stabilize and turn a profit; teams' normative rules became more and more rationalized; simple norms (e.g., we all need to be at work on time) became highly objective rules similar to ISE's old bureaucratic structure (e.g., if you are more than five minutes late, you're docked a day's pay). The social rules were more rigid. The senior group members took on the role of leader within each team. Not surprisingly, many employees were frustrated and confused. It is a bitter irony that some looked back fondly on the days in which there was greater bureaucratic control.

TEAM EMPOWERMENT

Just what does an "empowered" team do? Many managers claim that their team is empowered when, in fact, it is not. Figure 10-2 depicts a continuum of team empowerment. Level 1 teams have the least power; they are often new teams, perhaps lacking the skills,

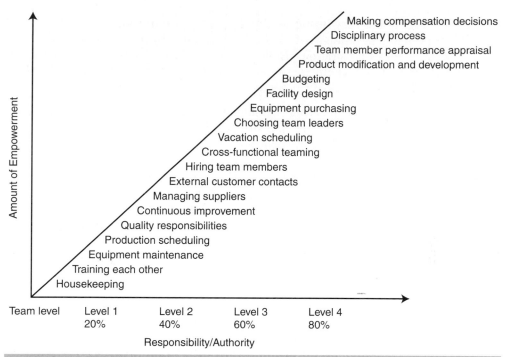

FIGURE 10-2   Team Empowerment Continuum

Source: Wellins, R.S., Byham, W.C., & Wilson, J.M. 1991. *Empowered Teams* (p. 26). San Francisco: Jossey-Bass Inc., Publishers.

experience, or training to implement more control. Perhaps this is why many successful self-directed organizations intentionally devote 20 percent of the team members' and leaders' time to training in the first year (Wellins, 1992). Job skill training is necessary to give team members the depth and breadth they need to effectively carry out the broadened range of activities that self-directed teams perform.

It is precisely for reasons of greater empowerment and the benefits of creativity that many organizations turn to teams rather than a single individual for leadership at the top. Among other advantages, top-management teams, as opposed to individuals, are more likely to represent the wide range of interests of the people and groups in the organization and provide valuable development experiences for its members (Beer, Eisenstat, & Spector, 1990). Leadership via top-management teams challenges the traditional view of leadership because it moves away from the image of the leader as the autonomous, prophetic, and omniscient, and toward the idea that leadership is a team process. It is unfortunate, however, that *top-management team (TMT)* is actually a misnomer for the teams that exist at the apex of many firms, because they have few "team" properties. Many TMTs are simply constellations of executive talent—individuals who rarely come together (and usually only for perfunctory information exchange), who rarely collaborate, and who focus almost entirely on their own pieces of the enterprise (Hambrick, 1997). For some suggestions on getting top executives to function like a real team, see Sidebar 10-3.

Sidebar 10-3. Overcoming Senior Team Fragmentation

The potential advantages of TMTs are threatened by fragmentation, which is basically a lack of integration, vision, purpose, and coordination of effort and talent (Hambrick, 1997). There are five key steps that a CEO can take to deal with fragmentation and pull a TMT together (Hambrick, 1995, 1997):

- **Team identity:** The group should have a clear identity. Even simple things like identifying a team name, sharing a vision, or engaging in collaborative activities can build team identity.
- **Teamwork:** The team should do "real work" together, not just exchanging updates and reviewing others' work. Real work involves fact-finding, analysis, and problem solving. On a practical level, this can be achieved by (a) convening the team together several times a year, including at least an in-depth, off-site meeting; and (b) establishing constructive norms, especially of openness, informality, and collegiality; even mundane matters such as attendance, punctuality, and preparation are critically important.
- **Team composition and roles:** Line executives should be given additional responsibilities for companywide endeavors. These "overlay" assignments can be temporary (such as leading a key task force) or more continuous (overseeing a staff or support unit). The team should strive for gradual, staggered turnover within the team, and attempt to avoid the extremes of uniformly long tenures and wholesale turnovers (which cause tumult and erratic relations). One strategy is to selectively rotate executives or, at least, appoint senior executives with multiunit experience in the company.
- **Team incentives:** At least one-third of every executive's target incentive compensation should be tied to overall company performance, and at least one-third of every executive's incentive reward should be paid out in restricted stock grants or stock options.
- **The CEO's team leadership:** The CEO must personally convey and reinforce openness and constructive candor; there can be no hidden agendas, no off-line deals. The CEO must also convey and reinforce mutual trust; disagreement and minority views must not be penalized; debate must stay on business issues, not on personal issues.

The opposite of fragmentation is organizational coherence. Even though most CEOs recognize the importance of coherence, few know how to carry this awareness into the design and process of their TMTs. Corporate coherence must emanate from the top of the firm, with the executive group thinking and acting as a team.

RED FLAGS ON THE WAY TO GREATER INVOLVEMENT

As we saw in the ISE example, understanding existing social and structural factors is critical to successfully forming empowered work teams. Probably the most regrettable state of affairs in the organization is when employees feel powerless. Feelings of powerlessness lead to depression and organizational decline. Part of a team "well visit" should include a check on four factors, listed in Table 10-1, that can lead to a state of

TABLE 10-1 Context Factors Leading to a Potential State of Powerlessness	
Context Factor Leading to State of Powerlessness	*Condition*
Organizational factors	• Significant organizational change/transitions • Start-up ventures • Excessive, competitive pressures • Impersonal, bureaucratic climate • Poor communications and limited network-forming systems • Highly centralized organizational resources
Supervisory style	• Authoritarian (high control) • Negativism (emphasis on failures) • Lack of reason for actions/consequences
Reward systems	• Noncontingency (arbitrary reward allocations) • Low incentive value of rewards • Lack of competence-based work • Lack of innovation-based rewards
Job design	• Lack of role clarity • Lack of training and technical support • Unrealistic goals • Lack of appropriate authority/discretion • Low task variety • Limited participation in programs, meetings, and decisions that have a direct impact on job performance • Lack of appropriate/necessary resources • Lack of network-forming opportunities • Highly established work routines • Too many rules and guidelines • Low advancement opportunities • Lack of meaningful goals/tasks • Limited contact with senior management

Source: Conger, J. 1989. "The Art of Empowering Others." *Academy of Management Executive, 3*(1), 17–24. Reprinted with permission.

powerlessness in the organization: Organizational factors, the leader's supervisory style, the organizational reward system, and job design. Furthermore, instead of the leader performing this check, the team members should do it themselves.

CONCLUSIONS

Most of us have been socialized in bureaucratic organizations. In these organizations, participative management of the sort we have described seems antimanagement or an admission of failure at one's own job. One senior-level banker from an international banking firm put it this way: "If I do the kind of things you are describing here—inviting other people who are supposed to be under me to make suggestions about how to accomplish my division's objectives—I am going to work myself out of a job." This bank official was worried about others doing his job better than he could. This is perhaps the most often cited reason against participative management. The irony of this example is that the company would probably be better off if all of its employees invited participation. Traditional leadership may no longer be the right image of leadership in a corporate world placing an ever-heavier emphasis on team-based work units. A new image of leadership is necessary, one that is associated with being a leader among equals, rather than a leader of followers. Teams (or at least some teams) are often composed of talented individuals selected for their specific knowledge or skills to fit a particular role; in this case, the leader as director is not the right image. The leader as coordinator or assembler may be a better image. When this is true, the leader functions better, activities are performed better, teams work better, and the organization is more successful. The key idea is that it is in the interests of both leaders and organizations to move in this direction.

CHAPTER 11

Interteam Relations: Competition and Stereotyping

On June 7, 1998, in Jasper, Texas, three white supremacists captured an African American man, beat him, and then dragged him to his death on the back of a pickup truck in a ghastly and horrid display of racial hatred and violence.

At a company party at the Bell Atlantic Corporation, Willie Bennett, an African American 27-year veteran of the company, was shocked when his white coworkers showed him a video they made, in which a white coworker wearing an Afro wig pretended to be Bennett and portrayed him getting his job because of his basketball-playing skills. Derrick Williams, a 23-year veteran of Bell Atlantic, is haunted by the memory of finding a fake and crudely racist job application in the copy machine, which asked questions such as "Name of father (if known)," whether the applicant was born in a "charity hospital" or a "back alley," and how many words the candidate could "jive" per minute (Grimsley, 1997).

It is a shocking fact that as we approach the next millennium, the fires of racial hatred and crippling prejudice are rampant and widespread. What's more is that acts of racial discrimination are not confined to small towns and lower-class organizations. They exist in corporate America, even in the Fortune 500. No one should take any comfort in the fact that racial prejudice, stereotyping, and discrimination are widely frowned upon. How can it be that blatant acts of racism and discrimination exist in corporations when it is clearly against the law to discriminate? What can the manager do to avoid creating a hostile work environment and to build solidarity and respect between groups?

OVERVIEW

Displays of racism in the corporate world are shocking because it is not often that such blatant racial slurs are heard in a work environment. Many people believe that there are no such problems in their workplace. What type of corporate culture leads to this obviously inappropriate behavior, hostile work environment, and poor use of corporate time and energy? What role do teams play in perpetuating or curtailing this behavior? This is the focus of the chapter.

The preceding evidence makes a sobering point: Bias and prejudice are common in organizations and adversely affect the ability of teams and organizations to accomplish their goals. In the following list, we draw distinctions between various kinds of prejudiced thoughts, actions, and reactions.

- **Bias** is any patterned deviation from a standard (e.g., Mark, a senior member of the firm, never evaluates anyone as being "above average"; in contrast, his partner, Lura, consistently evaluates everyone as being "above average"). Each executive, then, displays a bias.

213

- **Prejudice** is the evaluative or emotional aspect of stereotyping: The tendency to evaluate members of other groups less favorably than members of one's own group (e.g., a white manager is prejudiced when he regards a white male to be more worthy of promotion than a black female, despite their identical objective measures of performance).

- **Stereotyping** is the cognitive aspect of bias: The tendency to assume that members of a particular group also have attributes stereotypical of that group (e.g., an executive manager assumes that the female middle manager likes fashion magazines and soap operas, that the black supervisor is fond of barbecue and watermelon, and that the Asian intern has a camera affinity). Stereotypes are cognitive generalizations about the qualities and characteristics of the members of a particular group or social category. In many ways, stereotypes function as useful labor-saving devices by helping people to make rapid judgments about others based on their category memberships (McCauley, Stitt, & Segal, 1980; Miller, 1982). Stereotypes come with built-in biases, for they usually paint a picture of people that is too simplistic, too extreme, and too uniform.

- **Discrimination** is the behavioral aspect of stereotyping: The tendency for people to change their behavior as a function of assumptions they make about others (e.g., a manager doesn't hire a female whom he believes to be interested in starting a family; a supervisor doesn't promote a Hispanic male whom she regards to be less intelligent).

In the corporate world, people exist in teams, and for this reason it is not too surprising that people identify themselves in terms of their group memberships. On a preconscious level, humans categorize themselves and others into groups. This categorization is advantageous in the respect that it can mean an efficient division of labor, and team affiliations provide people with a greater sense of belonging. Furthermore, the division of people into different groups and teams can create a healthy competition between teams. However, much of this can backfire, such as when healthy competition erupts into sabotage and discrimination. The mere categorization of people into different groups sows the seeds of prejudice, discrimination, and stereotyping. Perhaps even more disturbing is the fact that most people are completely unaware that their behavior is affected by how they categorize others. Furthermore, intrateam harmony does not guarantee peaceful interteam relations and, in fact, may very well exacerbate conflict between groups.

Conflict between groups does not always arise from competition over scarce resources, such as full-time employees, facilities, budgets, and promotions. Much conflict in organizations does not seem to have its roots in resource scarcity, but rather stems from fundamental differences in values. Thus, we distinguish **realistic group conflict** from **symbolic conflict** (Bobo, 1983).

Realistic group conflict involves competition between groups for the same scarce resources (e.g., groups that compete over new hires, office space, assignments, territory, information, contacts, and, of course, remuneration). Naturally, groups in organizations prefer to be the "haves" rather than the "have-nots," so they take steps to achieve two interrelated outcomes: (1) attain the desired resources; and (2) prevent other groups from reaching their goals (Campbell, 1965; LeVine & Campbell, 1972). As competition persists, groups come to perceive each other in increasingly negative ways. Even worse, competition often leads to direct and open conflict. Consider, for example, the relationship between the number of lynchings of black people in 14 states in the American South and two indices of economic conditions: Farm value of cotton and acre value of cotton. The data over a 49-year period were clear: The more negative economic conditions (i.e., the lower the price of cotton), the more lynchings. As another example, consider the conflict between Andersen Consulting and Arthur Andersen. Each group feels justified in claiming a greater share of the profit stream. Andersen Consulting, the smaller of the two groups, is highly profitable and feels justified in demanding more resources; Arthur Andersen, the founding company, sees the situation quite differently and argues that the opportunities they provide entitle them to a greater share of the joint profits.

As a general principle, groups of people are much more competitive than are individuals (Carnevale, Pruitt, & Seilheimmer, 1981; Insko et al., 1987; McCallum et al., 1985; van Oostrum & Rabbie, 1995). As an illustration of this, consider the team dilemma game that we reviewed in chapter 7. When individuals play against each other, in a one-on-one fashion, they are not particularly competitive—averaging only 6.6 percent competitive responses over the course of the game. However, when a group of individuals plays against another group, competition rises to 53.5 percent of all moves (Insko et al., 1987). This suggests that even though most people may prefer to cooperate, when they are in groups, a competitive orientation takes over.

The conflicts we have described emanate from the allocation of scarce resources. However, it is not always the case that economic motivations are at the root of all conflicts. Sometimes, groups and teams are not trying to garner more resources, but hold conflicting values. Symbolic conflict involves clashes of values and fundamental beliefs. Consider, for example, the strong protests made against busing by people whose lives are not affected by it (Sears & Allen, 1984). Presumably, people who do not have children or grandchildren are not affected by busing. However, they tend to have strong feelings about it. Busing does not represent an economic issue to them, but rather, a symbolic issue.

GROUP MEMBERSHIP: THE LOCUS OF HUMAN IDENTITY

People naturally seek out group affiliations, and the reputation and accomplishments of the groups people belong to are a critical source of their self-esteem. To a large extent, feeling good about ourselves is dependent upon feeling that our groups are adequate or superior (Tajfel & Turner, 1986). Group affiliations also provide people with a buffer against threats and setbacks: When their self-esteem is shaken by personal setbacks, their groups provide them with reassurance and identity (Meindl & Lerner, 1984).

Although there is no limit to the ways in which people might identify themselves and others, the following categories of group identity are common in organizations:

- Gender groups
- Position, level, class (e.g., rank, how many people supervised)
- Functional unit (e.g., marketing, sales)
- Regional unit (e.g., Midwestern, Northeastern)
- Ethnicity and race

In short, these five categories are key when people interact with others in the organization.

Need for Categorization

Categorization is inevitable. Just as people categorize furniture into tables and chairs, they categorize each other into men or women, black or white, rich or poor, educated or not. From the first few microseconds of perception, latent stereotypes shape what people see. The tendency to use stereotypes as a basis of categorization leads people to view others as more similar to the stereotype than they actually are. Furthermore, even when given an opportunity to consider both stereotypical and nonstereotypical information about a person, people preferentially attend to stereotype confirming rather than disconfirming information. When people can question a person directly, they often seek to confirm their stereotypical beliefs (Snyder, 1984).

The most basic type of categorization is the classification of people into in-groups and out-groups. That is, even though there are any number of categories that people might use, they primarily use two basic social categorizations: In-groups and out-groups (Jones, 1983; Wilder, 1986a, 1986b). People consider in-groups to be people who are like themselves or who belong to the same group; out-groups are people who are not in their group or who are members of competitor groups.

What are the consequences of in-group and out-group categorization? There is a good deal of *subjectivity* in the boundaries that people draw around groups and the groups with which they identify. Categorization is highly influenced by rather arbitrary aspects of the situation. For example, take the case of Lorna W. Lorna is more likely to be categorized (i.e., pegged) by her colleagues because as the only female Hispanic American on the team, she attracts attention. As a consequence of the greater attention she gets, people evaluate her more extremely. This cuts both ways: In the case where Lorna is exceptional in her performance, she will be evaluated even more favorably. However, in the case where Lorna is not performing well or performing at an average level, she will be evaluated more negatively than a man or a Caucasian engaging in the same activities. The take-away message is clear: People who stand out in terms of their membership in gender, racial, or ethnic categories are scrutinized and evaluated more extremely. In short, they are in the spotlight.

How Categorization Affects Behavior

When it comes to predicting behavior in a particular situation, group affiliations are a more powerful determinant than is personal identity. For example, social activism is better predicted by feelings of fraternal deprivation (i.e., the perception that one's group is disadvantaged relative to other groups) than by feelings of personal deprivation (i.e., the perception that one is personally disadvantaged; Dubé & Guimond, 1986; Vanneman & Pettigrew, 1972). Furthermore, individual members of disadvantaged groups frequently perceive higher levels of discrimination directed against their groups than they report against themselves personally (Taylor, Wright, Moghaddam, & Lalonde, 1990). And it is fraternal, or group-level, discrimination that motivates participation in collective action (Taylor, Moghaddam, Gamble, & Zellerer, 1987; Wright, Taylor, & Moghaddam, 1990).

In terms of behavior within organizations, how people categorize themselves vis-à-vis the organization is a key determinant of behavior. Consider the following example. Don is a member of a large organization, that is divided into separate units that center around different product lines. Each division in Don's company is encouraged to act as

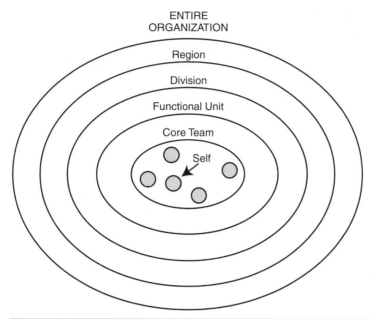

FIGURE 11-1   Levels of Identification in an Organization

its own profit center. Don takes this very seriously. In contrast, Terry, a member of the same organization who also belongs to Don's division, has more job responsibilities that bring her into contact with other units. Whereas she is well aware that each division is mandated to act as its own profit center, she is keenly concerned with the prosperity of the company as a whole. In short, Don's primary level of group identification is more narrowly defined than is Terry's (see Figure 11-1). As a consequence, Don is more likely to behave competitively to further the interest of his own division, at the expense of the company as a whole. The key is to try to get Don to identify with the company, rather than just his own division.

The take-away message is clear: People can identify at different levels within their organization (e.g., person, group, department, or unit). However, their behavior is influenced by the nature of their contacts and experiences within the firm. The more narrowly defined their groups are, the more competitive and self-serving their behavior is. Conversely, when they focus on the larger collective, they are more cooperative. The challenge for the team leader is to know how to focus on higher-order group affiliations.

"Us" versus "Them": The Psychology of In-Groups and Out-Groups

The very processes that allow people to build relationships with each other are the ones that may cause alienation, discrimination, and stereotyping. In short, social categorization sows the seeds for discrimination and prejudice by creating an "us" and "them."

Unfortunately, people are trigger-happy when it comes to categorizing people as members of in-groups or out-groups. The basis for inclusion and exclusion constantly fluctuates as a function of largely irrelevant aspects of the situation. Consider what happens in situations that on the surface do not seem to contain any meaningful basis of categorization:

- **Case 1:** In a room of adults who do not know one another, a box is passed around with two kinds of letters in it: One labeled "alphas," the other labeled "betas." Each person randomly draws a card from the box. Two groups are formed on the basis of an obviously arbitrary procedure. Members of each do not speak or communicate in any form with the members of the other group, nor do they talk among themselves. They are a group in name only. Nevertheless, in a subsequent evaluation period, members of each group rate the members of their own group as superior on a number of dimensions relative to members of the other group (Brewer, 1979; Tajfel, 1982; Tajfel & Turner, 1986).
- **Case 2:** In a room of adults who do not know one another, each person is presented with a page containing several dots and then asked to make an estimate of the total number of dots on the page. Two groups are then formed: Those who allegedly underestimate the actual number of dots on the page and those who overestimate the dots (Bettencourt, Brewer, Croak, & Miller, 1992). When group members are subsequently asked to evaluate the competence, intelligence, creativity, and personal qualities of both groups, they favor their own group—even though they have not communicated with the other members of their group and dot estimation is nondiagnostic.
- **Case 3:** In simulated negotiations between Stanford and Cornell M.B.A. students, each group awards the other significantly fewer stock options when given the opportunity (Thompson, Valley, & Kramer, 1995). Furthermore, group members reject options that would pay both teams extremely well; instead, team members seemed more intent on creating large payment differences, rather than maximizing their own welfare.

In all of the preceding examples, when people categorize the world into two or more groups and then face the task of evaluating or judging these groups, they uniformly favor their own group. There is a nearly universal tendency to rate one's own group as superior to an out-group, even on the basis of little or no information. In cases 1 and 2, members of groups never interacted; the personal identities of the in-group and out-group members were unknown, and no one gained personally by discriminating against the alleged out-group. If there is no incentive to derogate others, why does it occur? Because people identify with groups, they are psychologically invested in maintaining the illusion that their group is worthwhile and deserving. This raises a thorny paradox for the team manager: The very process of creating cohesion and group identity may fuel the fires of prejudice, stereotyping, and discrimination.

"We're Better Than They Are": In-Group Supremacy and Entitlement

Humans don't just segment the world into in-group and out-group members; once they categorize others, they view members of their own group more favorably than members of the out-group. When this occurs at the group level, it is called **in-group bias;** among larger groups, such as ethnic categories, nations, and regions, this is **ethnocentrism** (Sumner, 1906). Ethnocentrism, or the universal strong liking of one's own group and the simultaneous negative evaluation of out-groups, generates a set of universal reciprocal stereotypes in which each group sees itself as good and the out-group as bad, even when both groups engage in the same behaviors. Whereas the behavior may be similar, the in-

BOX 11-1

In-Group Bias in Response to an Organizational Merger

Employees from two hospitals were studied during the period of planning for a merger (Terry & Callan, 1998). One hospital was higher in status than the other hospital—a common issue that occurs when firms merge. How did the proposed merger affect intergroup relations between the two hospitals? A merger between two previously independent organizations made employees' premerger group membership more salient, and the unequal status issues meant an accentuation of intergroup status differences. There was clear evidence of an in-group ("we are better than they are") bias, particularly among the low-status employees. Why? Employees of the lower-status organization may have been particularly threatened by the merger situation and, therefore, more likely to engage in a high level of in-group bias—a form of identity protection.

High-status employees rated the in-group far better than the low-status hospital on status-relevant dimensions (high prestige in the community, challenging job opportunities, and high variety in patient type). In contrast, the low-status

employees engaged in greater in-group bias on the status-irrelevant dimensions (degree of industrial unrest, good relations between staff, good communication by management, relaxed work environment, and modern patient accommodations). The question is, why? High-status employees were motivated to acknowledge their position of relatively high status. In contrast, the low-status employees, motivated by a desire to attain positive social identity, focused on dimensions that did not highlight the status differential that existed between the hospitals. Indeed, low-status employees recognized the superior status of the high-status hospital, and high-status employees were especially generous when evaluating the low-status group on dimensions that are irrelevant to status. Yet the amount of in-group bias that the low-status employees exhibited on the status-irrelevant dimensions exceeded the extent to which the high-status employees were willing to acknowledge the strengths of the low-status employees on these dimensions.

terpretation is not: "We are loyal; they are clannish; we are brave and willing to defend our rights; they are hostile and arrogant." The negative effects of in-group bias may be heightened when companies merge (see Box 11-1).

"They All Look Alike": The Out-Group Homogeneity Effect

One unfortunate by-product of social categorization is the tendency to view out-group members as interchangeable, faceless, stereotypical caricatures.

Suppose that white managers watch a videotape of a discussion among members of a mixed-race group: Three African American men and three Caucasian men. After watching the videotape, the managers are presented with the actual text of the conversation and are asked to indicate who said what. They are told they will be evaluated based upon the accuracy of their memory. They are accurate at remembering whether a black or white person made a particular comment, and are fairly accurate in distinguishing among the three white males' comments, but their accuracy in terms of differentiating which African American male said what is abysmal (Linville, Fischer, & Salovey, 1989). Thus, within-race errors are more prevalent than between-race errors, because people categorize members of out-groups not as individuals, but simply as "black men."

The faulty memory of the manager illustrates a pervasive tendency for people to assume much greater homogeneity of opinion, belief, expression, and interest among members of the out-group than among members of their own group (Judd & Park, 1988; Katz & Braly, 1933; Park & Rothbart, 1982). This is another way of saying that most people believe that members of their own group are individuals and, consequently, should be evaluated upon their own merits, whereas members of out-groups are mere clones of one another, with no distinct identity.

The managerial implications of the "they all look alike" effect are very serious. Consider, for example, a police lineup in which a victim is asked to identify an assailant. A white victim is more likely to falsely identify a black perpetrator than a white one (Knight-Ridder Newspapers, 1991). Consider, also, the implications of a mixed-sex task force in a corporation.

Minority Groups

Members of minority groups are particularly likely to be targets of prejudice and discrimination in the organization. The reason is related to the principle of social categorization that we introduced earlier. As an example, consider a young, female manager on an otherwise all-male team:

- She is more likely to be severely judged than is the man. This cuts two ways: If she is excellent, she will be judged more favorably; if she is below average, she is judged more harshly. (Principle: Most people judge members of minority groups more harshly than others.)
- Her behavior in general will be viewed as more stereotypically "female" than if she were a member of a more gender-balanced group.
- Her own performance will be subverted to the extent that she is made to feel that women are at a disadvantage. (Principle: Believing that others ascribe to a stereotype can lead to self-handicapping behavior and worsened performance.)
- She holds lower expectations about her career than do the men; she expects to receive lower starting and peak salaries (Jackson, Gardner, & Sullivan, 1992), and she views these lower salaries as being fair (Jackson & Grabski, 1988).
- She expresses lower self-confidence than the men.
- If she succeeds at the task and attains the same level of performance as a man, it is assumed by relevant others that she was "lucky" or "fortunate" or had extra help; in contrast, the man's performance is attributed to effort and ability (Deaux, 1985; Nieva & Gutek, 1981).

Women continue to occupy a relatively disadvantaged position in most societies in a number of respects; they are concentrated in low-paying, low-status jobs, and their average salary remains lower than that of men.

When selecting applicants for jobs, especially high-level ones, organizations seek a good match: They want to hire people whose characteristics most closely resemble those that they view as necessary for effective performance (O'Reilly, Chatman, & Caldwell, 1991). This is a reasonable hiring strategy, but in the context of gender stereotypes, it may be highly damaging to women. The traits that are assumed to be necessary for success in high-level jobs are closer to the content of male gender stereotypes than to female gender stereotypes. Leaders are almost uniformly desired to be bold, assertive, tough, and decisive—all traits traditionally viewed as masculine in nature. In contrast, few companies want or expect leaders to be kind, sensitive, emotional, and nurturing—the typical female stereotype. To the extent that females are subject to traditional gender stereotypes, they may face a difficult struggle in their efforts to launch and advance their careers.

As a case in point, consider how male and female members of employment selection boards in the Netherlands interviewed applicants for high-level scientific and technical jobs (Van Vianen & Willemsen, 1992). They completed two questionnaires: One on which they rated the attributes of "ideal" candidates and another on which they rated the perceived qualities of each actual job applicant. Descriptions of ideal candidates included mainly traits present in the masculine gender stereotype. The candidates recommended for the job were rated as possessing more masculine attributes than the candidates they rejected. Finally, accepted female candidates were much closer to the description of the ideal candidate than rejected ones—that is, more masculine.

In another demonstration of the severity effect, Caucasian people were shown ambiguous pictures of African Americans and Caucasians interacting with one another (Allport & Postman, 1947). The observers were asked to make up a story about the pictures they had seen. Prejudiced individuals' stories often suggested that the Caucasians and African Americans were arguing or fighting with each other, and they usually blamed the African American for starting the dispute. When observers viewed a film depicting a staged argument between an African American and a Caucasian in which one person shoved the other, they described the push as "violent" when the perpetrator was African American, but "playing" or "dramatizing" when the perpetrator was Caucasian (Duncan, 1976).

Self-handicapping (also known as fear of success) is the tendency of people to sabotage their own likelihood of success, such as not getting enough sleep the night before an exam, watching TV instead of preparing for a report, and so on. Why would anyone want to sabotage their own performance? If they suspect that other, relevant superiors expect their behavior to be negatively affected by their own lack of innate ability, then they often attempt to justify poor performance as being caused by temporary factors. Consider the following situation: An African American female, who would like to be admitted to a competitive M.B.A. program, signs up to take a standardized test, the GMAT, because it is required for admission to all programs. On test day, she is asked to provide various demographic information about herself, including her racial identity. Then, she takes the test. Is her performance on the test better or worse than if she had not been asked to indicate her racial identity? (Before reading further, stop and indicate whether her performance is better, worse, or the same and specify your reasons for thinking so.)

In fact, her performance is worse (Steele, 1997). Certainly her aptitude has not changed in the flash of a moment. What has gone on in this situation? The test form itself has activated a **latent stereotype**—a cultural stereotype that this woman knows on a cognitive, rational level to be false, but that nevertheless once called to mind inter-feres with her ability to perform. The test form in this situation has instigated a self-fulfilling prophecy. That is, because she was asked to indicate her racial identity, she assumes that racial identity plays a role in success on this test. This is a form of **self-stereotyping,** in which a person negatively internalizes aspects of a culturally held stereotype.

Performance Evaluation

Imagine the following scenario: A young, African American male is apprehended by se-curity when he is caught removing a computer from an office. What does your first im-pression of this situation tell you? If you are like most people, you feel that more cul-pability is involved on the part of the African American male than you would if the person who left the building was a young woman. This simple example makes an im-portant point: When members of an out-group (in this case, African American men) be-have in what appears to be a suspicious fashion (removing equipment from private property), most people evaluate their behavior as a manifestation of their underlying personality or disposition—in this case, the black male is viewed as a criminal. In con-trast, the same action taken by a member of the in-group is usually attributed to benign situational factors (e.g., "She was taking it to a store to get it repaired").

In contrast, when the action in question is one that is positive (e.g., making a dona-tion to charity, volunteering for an additional assignment, or completing the report a day early), the opposite phenomenon occurs. That is, commendable actions by in-group members are regarded as reflecting their impeccable character, whereas the same act by a member of a stereotyped group is brushed off as the result of temporary, fleeting circumstances.

Extremism

Inevitably, conflicts occur between groups, teams, and factions. Groups on opposite sides of a conflict tend to see the other, opposing side as being extremist. Members of teams exaggerate the degree of conflict they actually have with other teams and groups—opposing groups typically assume that the difference between the two sides' attitudes is 1.5 to 4 times greater than the actual difference. This means, of course, that escalation of interteam conflict is often more illusion than reality. As an example, con-sider the Western Canon debate—a factious dispute over the choice of books in intro-ductory civilization and literature courses that has divided faculty and students within many universities, such as Stanford, Michigan, and Berkeley. There are two sides in the debate: Traditionalists and revisionists. Traditionalists advocate preserving the promi-nence of the traditional canon; revisionists advocate teaching more works by female and minority authors.

To measure the degree of conflict between traditionalists and revisionists, English teachers in California were asked to select 15 books from a list of 50 for their own course and to indicate which books they believed the "other side" would want. Traditionalists pre-dicted that they would have no books in common. In actuality, traditionalists and revision-ists had almost 50 percent—or seven books—in common! (Robinson & Keltner, 1996).

Careful inspection of group members' perceptions, however, reveals a striking asymmetry in the accuracy of misperception: The status quo, or the group in power, is much less accurate than is a group that is not in power. Traditionalists predicted no overlap in book choices; whereas revisionists predicted a six-book overlap. Why is this?

Majority group members typically enjoy benefits of greater power. They are prone to exaggerate the views of their own and the other side. Minority group members are perceived by both sides to be more extremist than majority group members. For example, high-status social group members judge the personality and emotion of other members less accurately than do low-status group members (Gruenfeld, Keltner, & Anderson, 1998). In contrast, high-status members' emotions are more accurately judged by both low- and high-status members.

Overt and Covert Racism

The reported racial attitudes of white Americans have changed dramatically in the past 50 years (Schuman, Steeh, & Bobo, 1985). For example, the percentage of whites willing to vote for a black presidential candidate rose from 37 percent in 1958 to 81 percent in 1983; and the percentage rejecting laws against cross-racial intermarriage rose from 38 percent in 1963 to 66 percent in 1982. Yet subtle indicators of prejudice remain intact (Crosby, Bromley, & Saxe, 1980). Given the opportunity to help a black person or a white person, whites give less help to a black person; in studies of "sanctioned aggression" (e.g., the white participant in the role of a "teacher" must punish the black student's apparently wrong answer), whites are more aggressive toward blacks than whites (e.g., administer more intense shocks as punishment); furthermore, subtle, nonverbal behaviors, such as tone of voice, indicate less positive feelings of whites toward blacks. These unobtrusive measures suggest that the true attitudes of whites toward blacks remain quite negative.

Most people in the corporate world do not regard themselves to be racists or white supremacists. In the contemporary United States, most people know that it is wrong to be prejudiced. Consequently, they mask prejudice or negative behavior toward blacks, women, and other minorities. In short, people suppress their prejudiced tendencies.

Thus, there is a contradiction of sorts between people's public attitudes and their more telling overt behaviors. Similar contradictions have been found in men's attitudes toward women. The modern racist or sexist is not filled with hatred toward blacks and women, but rather is attached to the status quo and defends traditional, conventional values. Modern norms against overt racism make people's own racist attitudes intolerable to them, so they find it difficult to admit this to themselves. Even well-intentioned people who do not think of themselves as racist may have rapid, automatic, racially biased associations that they would be averse to if they were consciously aware of them.

Most people regard the decline of overt or old-fashioned racism to be a positive aspect of modern organizational life. However, under the thin veneer of politically correct organizational actors lurks a more venomous racial monster. The type of racism that runs rampant through the modern corporation is much more insidious, and is known as **covert racism** (Gaertner & Dovidio, 1986; Greenwald & Banaji, 1995).

Just what is covert racism? Consider the following examples:

- Attractive men and women are judged to be kinder, more interesting, more sociable, happier, stronger, of better character, and more likely to hold prestigious jobs than those who are less attractive (Dion, Berscheid, & Walster, 1972).
- A black Ivy League professor takes the bus every day to work; white patrons never sit in the seat next to his when there is a choice of sitting by a white person.

- A Jewish manager prepares an important report for his company; he only cites other Jewish people in the report as important contributors, even though he was at liberty to mention other non-Jewish contributors (Greenwald & Banaji, 1995).
- A group of executives judging the quality of written essays judge those allegedly written by males to be of higher quality than those written by females, even though the essays are identical (Goldberg, 1968).
- Essays attributed to female students are judged by male students to be of higher quality when accompanied by a photo that shows the author to be physically attractive, rather than unattractive (Landy & Sigall, 1974).
- Sports teams who wear black uniforms are judged to be more aggressive (Frank & Gilovich, 1988).

In each of the preceding examples, people are arguably acting on the basis of stereotypical beliefs—for example, bus riders regard black men to be dangerous, so they don't sit by them. However, none of the people in the examples broke any law with their actions. Furthermore, when questioned, each person vehemently denies the operation of any racial or discriminatory intentions. Yet each of the actions is undesirable, not only from the point of view of the person who is discriminated against, but from the approach to teamwork we have outlined here. The question for the manager is: Should we worry about unconscious racism and, if so, how should we address it?

Unconscious Discrimination at Work

Covert, or implicit, racism operates at an unconscious level of awareness. For this reason, covert racists do not regard themselves to be prejudiced. In some cases, people are aware of prejudiced thoughts and vow that they do not act on them. Just as it is (currently) perfectly all right to smoke in your own home, it is all right for people to harbor racist attitudes in the recesses of their unconscious.

However, there is disturbing evidence that unconscious racism does affect behavior in the corporation. To demonstrate how and why, consider the following evidence:

When white students are placed into an experimental situation that involves administering shock for the purpose of facilitating learning, white students administer less shock to African Americans than to whites. When white people provide performance evaluations to African Americans, they exhibit a clear positivity bias; they give more positive feedback (Harber, 1998). Presumably, whites consciously want to minimize aggression toward African Americans. However, these same people administer far more shock when angered by an African American student than when angered by a white person (Rogers & Prentice-Dunn, 1981). This **retaliation effect** is preconscious. That is, when white managers believe that their anger is justified, this triggers the inherent bias toward out-group members that is often masked or repressed in other circumstances (Dollard, Doob, Miller, Mowrer, & Sears, 1939). Although most organizational employees are not in the practice of administering shocks, they are in the practice of administering a number of equally painful organizational burdens, as well as attractive organizational benefits. To the extent that the manager feels that negative feelings are justified, unconscious prejudice may be turned loose. Covert racists experience a conflict between their feelings and beliefs associated with a sincerely egalitarian value system and unacknowledged negative feelings and beliefs about African Americans (Gaertner & Dovidio, 1986).

As a further illustration, consider what happens to people whose unconscious thought processes are "primed" with racist ideas. (A prime is an unconscious influence, such as the subliminal advertising messages that advertisers use to get consumers to buy their products.) In an organization, a prime might be pornographic material pasted on walls or a coworker's computer screen saver. (Although this is hardly subliminal, on a day-to-day basis—even when they are not gazing directly at the material—it can affect employees' behavior.) Suppose, for example, that people in an organization are exposed to racist (or sexist) ideas in a manner that they do not consciously notice. For example, many commuters are unaware of the messages they see on billboards. What do you suppose happens when words are flashed very quickly on a computer screen at so fast a rate that people are not aware that they even saw a word (rather, it just seems that a white flash appears)? When Caucasians are subliminally exposed to a series of words that are stereotypically associated with African Americans (e.g., *poor, jazz, slavery, Harlem, busing*), they judge a race-unspecified male to be more hostile than those who are not exposed to the words (Bargh, Chen, & Burrows, 1996; Devine, 1989).

A similar phenomenon happens with the female stereotype: People who are exposed to ideas that signify "dependence" subsequently judge a female to be more dependent than when they are not exposed to these unconscious ideas (Banaji, Hardin, & Rothman, 1993).

The key take-away message is that the mere activation of a gender or racial stereotype, whether people cognitively endorse it or not, causes them to act in a way that is consistent with the stereotype (Bargh et al., 1996). This means that managers will treat older people with less dignity, women as sexual objects, and black people as ignorant or lazy if cultural stereotypes are primed.

STRATEGIES FOR REDUCING PREJUDICE

We have made the point that prejudice, discrimination, and stereotyping are pervasive in organizations today. It is a leader's job to deal effectively with these issues, which can seriously hinder individual, group, and organizational effectiveness. The responsible manager and team leader needs to scan the environment for factors that contribute to bias and try to put into place practices that will minimize discrimination. Once intergroup hostility becomes established, it is no simple matter to reduce it. Fortunately, many companies have dealt successfully with issues of discrimination on an organizational level. Companies that are equal opportunity employers make a public assertion that they wish to avoid bias. These are good things. However, eliminating bias from the organization is not easy. Some good faith efforts may even backfire. This section considers a number of strategies to effectively deal with discrimination and stereotyping.

Blinding

Blinding denies a decision maker access to potentially biasing information. For example, in several major consulting firms, applicants are requested *not* to enclose a picture. In principle, blinding would seem to be a foolproof method of avoiding unintended discrimination. However, because almost any socially stigmatizing attribute tends to be correlated with other characteristics that cannot be removed by blinding, effective blinding is often not achievable. For example, stereotypes can be triggered by surnames, speech accents, and dialects, especially over the telephone when no visual features are present (Wegner & Bargh, 1998). The biggest disadvantage with blinding is that it can result in the reestablishment of ethnic segregation (Schofield, 1986). For example, disadvantaged groups can be excluded from career opportunities (Blanchard & Crosby, 1989; Glasser, 1988). Denial of categorical information in connection with performance evaluations can result in less favorable judgments of minority group members. For example, consider a situation in which a videotape of a Hispanic manager is presented to non-Hispanic managers (Ferdman, 1989). Managers evaluating the Hispanic manager give him higher performance evaluations when he comments on the importance of his ethnicity to himself and his organization.

Consciousness-Raising ("Don't Be Prejudiced")

Consciousness-raising is the opposite of blinding; it encourages the decision maker to have a heightened awareness of the potential cues that could elicit discrimination. The idea of consciousness-raising is to educate people about the tendency to be biased and that employees of the corporation have a responsibility to guard their own behavior carefully. Consciousness-raising, however, may have some negative, unintended boomerang effects.

As a case in point, consider the following actual empirical demonstration (Bodenhausen, Macrae, & Milne, 1998). People were informed about the dangers and limitations of stereotyping and prejudice. In short, they were told that unless people actively work against it, prejudice can bias human judgment and result in unfair discrimination. People who were given this seemingly sage advice would seem to be the most likely to monitor their own behavior and actions in a way that would minimize discriminatory reactions. However, these people expressed even more intergroup bias than did those who were not told to avoid stereotyping. Even more disturbing, the prejudiced people were unaware that their actions were biased.

Why does this seemingly good faith effort to reduce prejudice backfire? The ironic situation arises because of fundamental properties of human control, or how people try to control how they think (Wegner, 1994). To avoid stereotypical reactions, people must monitor their thoughts and behavioral intentions to make sure that they are free of unwanted bias. The problem is that to make sure there is no stereotypical content in one's reactions. People must keep in mind what such reactions would be; thus, in searching for unwanted stereotypes, one must necessarily be aware of them. This heightened accessibility of stereotypical concepts can ironically produce greater discrimination, especially if the person is mentally preoccupied or the motivation to avoid bias dissipates over time (see Bodenhausen et al., 1998).

Similarly, when people are asked to suppress their stereotypical thoughts in imagining the life of a target person belonging to a stereotyped group (e.g., a "skinhead") and later write down their impressions of this group, they form more stereotypical impressions than those who are exposed to the same information but are not told to suppress their stereotypical thoughts (Macrae, Bodenhausen, Milne, & Jetten, 1994). Furthermore, when people are told to suppress stereotypical thoughts about a certain person, they subsequently choose to sit a greater distance from that person (Macrae et al., 1994)! Similar phenomena happen with the mental control of sexism (Erber, Wegner, & Bowman, 1996).

The boomerang effect tends to be worse when people are fatigued and tired. Presumably, consciousness-raising has the effect of activating suppressed stereotypes. When people are tired or stressed, their defense systems are not working as well, and stereotypical thoughts pop up to the surface. Thus, consciousness-raising often operates as a prime for activating negative beliefs.

Obviously, companies and programs that advocate consciousness-raising have the best of intentions. This evidence could potentially be used as an excuse for companies to not caution their employees about the dangers of discrimination. We do not advocate silence on these issues. A more effective approach is to also use affirmative action.

Contact

The "mere contact" strategy is based on the principle that greater contact among members of diverse groups increases cooperation between group members. Unfortunately, contact in and of itself does not lead to better intergroup relations, and in some cases may even exacerbate negative relations between groups. For example, contact between African Americans and Caucasians in desegregated schools does not reduce racial prejudice (Gerard, 1983; Schofield, 1986); there is little relationship between interdepartmental contact and conflict in organizations (Brown, Condor, Mathew, Wade, & Williams, 1986); and college students studying in foreign countries become increasingly negative toward their host countries the longer they remain in them (Stroebe, Lenkert, & Jonas, 1988).

Several conditions need to be in place before contact can have its desired effects of reducing prejudice:

- **Social and institutional support:** For contact to work, there should be a framework of social and institutional support. That is, people in positions of authority should be unambiguous in their endorsement of the goals of the integration policies. This fosters the development of a new social climate in which more tolerant norms can emerge.
- **Acquaintance potential:** A second condition for successful contact is that it be of sufficient frequency, duration, and closeness to permit the development of meaningful relationships between members of the groups concerned. Infrequent, short, and casual interaction will do little to foster more favorable attitudes and may even make them worse (Brewer & Brown, 1998). This type of close interaction will lead to the discovery of similarities and disconfirm negative stereotypes.
- **Equal status:** The third condition necessary for contact to be successful is that participants have equal status. Many stereotypes of out-groups comprise beliefs about the inferior ability of out-group members to perform various tasks. If the contact situation involves an unequal-status relationship between men and women, for example, with women in the subordinate role (e.g., taking notes, acting as secretaries), stereotypes are likely to be reinforced rather than weakened (Bradford & Cohen, 1984). If, however, the group members work on equal footing, prejudiced beliefs become hard to sustain in the face of repeated experience of task competence by the out-group member.
- **Shared goal:** When members of different groups depend on each other for the achievement of a jointly desired objective, they have instrumental reasons to develop better relationships. The importance of an overriding, clear, shared group goal is a key determinant of intergroup relations. Sometimes a common enemy is a catalyst for bonding among diverse people and groups. For example, by "waging

a war against cancer," members of different medical groups and laboratories can work together.

- **Cross-group friendships:** Sometimes it is not necessary for groups to have real contact with one another to improve intergroup relations. If group members know that another member of their own group has a friendship or relationship with a member of the out-group, or a cross-group friendship, in-group members have less negative attitudes toward the out-group (Wright, Aron, McLaughlin-Volpe, & Ropp, 1997). It is not necessary that all members of a group have cross-group friendships; merely knowing that one member of the group does can go a long way toward reducing negative out-group attitudes.

Many of these strategies are preventative in their approach warding off unhealthy, destructive, type A competition between groups. What steps can a manager take to deal with conflict after it has erupted?

GRIT and Bear It

The GRIT model, or Graduated and Reciprocal Initiative in Tension Reduction, is a model of conflict reduction for warring groups. Originally developed as a program for international disarmament negotiations, it can be used to deescalate intergroup problems on a smaller, domestic scale as well (Osgood, 1979). The goals of this strategy are to increase communication and reciprocity between groups while reducing mistrust, thereby allowing for deescalation of hostility and creation of a greater array of possible outcomes. The model prescribes a series of steps that call for specific communication between groups in the hope of establishing the "rules of the game." Other stages are designed to increase trust between the two groups as the consistency in each group's responses demonstrates credibility and honesty. Some steps are necessary only in extremely intense conflict situations in which the breakdown of intergroup relations implies a danger for the group members.

Mikhail Gorbachev's decisions in the period from 1986 to 1989 closely resemble the GRIT model (Barron, Kerr, & Miller, 1992). Gorbachev made a number of unilateral concessions that resulted in serious deescalation of world tensions in this period. On two occasions, the Soviets stalled resumption of atmospheric nuclear testing despite their inability to extend the prior treaty with the Reagan administration. They then agreed twice to summit meetings despite the Reagan administration's refusal to discuss the Star Wars defense system. They then agreed to the Intermediate and Strategic Range Nuclear Missile (INF) Treaty (exceeding the United States' requests for verification) with continued refusal by the United States to bargain about Star Wars. Next came agreements on the Berlin Wall and the unification of Germany. Eventually, even the staunchly anti-Communist/anti-Soviet Reagan-Bush regime had to take notice. This led to a period of mellowing tensions between these two superpowers (see Table 11-1).

Although the GRIT model may seem overly elaborate and therefore inapplicable to most organizational conflicts, the model clarifies the difficulties inherent in establishing mutual trust between parties that have been involved in prolonged conflict. Although some of the stages are not applicable to all conflicts, the importance of clearly announcing intentions, making promised concessions, and matching reciprocation are relevant to all but the most transitory conflicts.

TABLE 11-1   GRIT Strategy

1. Announce your general intentions to deescalate tensions and your specific intention to make an initial concession.
2. Execute the initial concession unilaterally, completely, and, of course, publicly. Provide as much verification as possible.
3. Invite reciprocity from the out-group. Expect the out-group to react to these steps with mistrust and skepticism. To overcome this, continued concessions should be made.
4. Match any reciprocal concessions made by the out-group and invite more.
5. Diversify the nature of your concessions.
6. Maintain your ability to retaliate if the out-group escalates tension. Any such retaliation should be carefully calibrated to match the intensity of the out-group's transgression.

Source: Barron, R. S., Kerr, N. L., & Miller, N. 1992. *Group Process, Group Decision, Group Action* (p. 151). Pacific Grove, CA: Brooks/Cole.

Stress and Fatigue Reduction

When people are under stress and feel fatigued, they are more likely to be biased than when they are not stressed. In a dramatic illustration of this, people were asked to classify themselves as either "morning people" or "night people" (most people claim to be at their best early in the morning or late at night; Bodenhausen, 1990). Theoretically, people are more stressed and fatigued when they operate in that part of the day in which they do not excel—that is, morning people are more fatigued in the evening; night people do not function properly in the morning. Most people display more prejudice and stereotyping during the part of the day in which they are least productive (Bodenhausen, 1990).

When people are distracted and are under lots of pressure, it is more difficult for them to monitor their own thoughts and behaviors. In a telling demonstration of this, people were asked to make judgments of people of obvious racial and gender identity. Some people making the judgments were somewhat distracted by having to simultaneously count numbers and do multiplication tables at the same time. When people were distracted in this fashion, their judgments were more racially biased than when they were not under cognitive load.

When people are emotionally aroused, such as with fear or embarrassment, they are more likely to judge others primarily on the basis of stereotypical information (category memberships) rather than on the basis of their actual behavior. For example, a smart juror embedded in an unintelligent jury is more likely to be labeled as unintelligent by emotionally aroused observers than by calm people (Wilder & Shapiro, 1989).

Affirmative Action

Affirmative action involves a deliberate compensatory component; an attribute that is known to be responsible for adverse discrimination is treated instead as if it were a positive qualification for the decision in question. The controversy surrounding affirmative action is noted by its common denotation as "reverse discrimination." Even members of disadvantaged groups may abhor affirmative action. Yet unintended discrimination may only be avoided through deliberate compensation strategies. Consider the case of

American symphony orchestras (Allmendinger & Hackman, 1993). American symphony orchestras have a long tradition of predominantly male membership. Alerted to the possibility of discrimination, orchestras routinely have candidates for vacant positions perform from behind a partition, removing all cues other than the sound of the performance (as an example of blinding). However, if past experience has benefited the performers, the men will maintain relative success.

Affirmative action programs are controversial. Minority group scholars argue that the very presence of affirmative action reinforces the perception that minority groups are inferior and, thus, require special assistance to succeed. Some research evidence indicates that the existence of affirmative action for a group can cause less favorable perception of, and attitudes toward, the group (Maio & Esses, 1998). However, many groups will not achieve fair representation in valuable positions in organizations without affirmative action; eliminating affirmative action guarantees that certain groups will remain unequal. The existence of affirmative action provides a mechanism, at least, to improve the status of these groups.

CONCLUSIONS

People in organizations have a fundamental need to categorize people into groups. This categorization process is automatic and nonconscious. The mere act of categorization creates in-groups and out-groups. Partly for these reasons, conflict between groups and teams in organizations is an inevitable aspect of organizational existence. Not surprisingly, people treat members of in-groups better than members of out-groups, even when the basis for group categorization is completely arbitrary and when the person does not stand to gain from discriminatory behavior. Thus, contrary to popular belief, conflicts among groups in organizations are not always rooted in competition for scarce resources; groups can be in conflict over values—what we call symbolic conflict. All organizational members—leaders, managers, and teams—have a responsibility to work against prejudice and discrimination. Blinding, consciousness-raising, egalitarian contact, tension reduction, and affirmative action are important tools. None is perfect, but used with care and knowledge, they can be effective.

CHAPTER 12

Teamwork via Information Technology: Challenges and Opportunities

"The VeriFone sales rep knew his big sale of the quarter was unraveling when he left the offices of an Athens bank at 4:30 P.M. A competitor had raised doubts about whether VeriFone could deliver a new payment-service technology, one that had not been used extensively in Greece. In fact, VeriFone was the main supplier of that technology in the United States and many other countries, with more than half a million installations and many satisfied customers. But the rep didn't have any particulars about those users to be able to make a rebuttal. He scouted out the nearest phone and hooked up his laptop to it. Then he sent an S.O.S. e-mail to all VeriFone sales, marketing, and technical-support staff worldwide. That e-mail launched a process that would create a virtual team to gather customers' testimonials and other data to make his case while he slept. In San Francisco, an international marketing staffer who was on duty to monitor such S.O.S. calls got the message at home when he checked his e-mail at 6:30 A.M. He organized a conference call with two other marketing staffers, one in Atlanta and one in Hong Kong, where it was 9:30 A.M. and 10:30 P.M., respectively. Together, they decided how to handle the data coming in from everyone who'd received the post. A few hours later, the two U.S. team members spoke on the phone again while they used the company's wide area network to fine-tune a sales presentation that the San Francisco team leader had drafted. Before leaving for the day, the leader passed the presentation on to the Hong Kong team member so he could add Asian information to the detailed account of experiences and references when he arrived at work. The Greek sales rep awakened a few hours later. He retrieved the presentation from the network, got to the bank by 8 A.M., and showed the customer the data on his laptop. Impressed by the speedy response to get business, the customer reasoned that VeriFone would also respond as fast to keep business. He placed the order" (Pape, 1997, p. 29).

A group of top managers at a progressive Silicon Valley company hated their weekly meetings, but enjoyed e-mail because it is quick, direct, and to the point. They thought meetings were "gassy, bloated, and a waste of time." So they decided to cancel their regular meetings and meet only when confronted with problems just too tough to handle over the network. Three months later, the same people resumed their regularly scheduled face-to-face meetings. They discovered that they had created a "morale-busting, network-generated nightmare." When the managers did get together, the meetings were unpleasant and unproductive. Precisely because they could use e-mail to reach consensus on easy issues, arguing the thorny issues face-to-face turned their "big problem" meetings into combat zones. E-mail interaction had eliminated the opportunity for casual agreement and social niceties that make meetings enjoyable. Even the e-mail communication

231

became most hostile as participants maneuvered themselves in anticipation of the big-problem meetings (Schrage, 1995).

In some cases, technology works, whereas in others, it doesn't—as illustrated in the previous examples. In the rush to go global, corporations are requiring their managers to be effective across distances and cultures never before mastered. Teams of managers armed with laptop computers, fax modems, e-mail, voice mail, videoconferencing, interactive databases, and frequent-flyer memberships are being charged with conducting business in the global arena. Virtual teams can efficiently harness the knowledge of company employees regardless of their location, thereby enabling the company to respond faster to increased competition. The VeriFone example is a testament to the power of information technology to bring together teams of people who would otherwise not be able to interact. As we saw in our analysis of group brainstorming, information technology offers the potential for improving information access and information-processing capability. Furthermore, information technology, in transcending time and place, offers the potential for members to participate without regard to temporal and spatial impediments.

However, as the Silicon Valley company example illustrates, not all virtual teamwork proceeds seamlessly. Managers responsible for leading virtual teams have found that distance is a formidable obstacle, despite electronic media and jet travel. A decision made in one country elicits an unexpected reaction from team members in another country. Remote offices fight for influence with the head office. Telephone conferences find distant members struggling to get onto the same page, literally and figuratively, in terms of shared viewpoint or strategy. Conflicts escalate strangely between distributed groups. Group members at sites separated by even a few kilometers begin to talk in the language of "us" and "them" (Armstrong & Cole, 1995). Thus, there is considerable debate among managers as to whether technology fosters or hinders teamwork in the workplace at the global, and even local, level.

This chapter examines the impact of information technology on teamwork at the global and local levels. We begin by describing a simple model of social interaction called the place-time model. This model will give us a framework through which we can evaluate the various forms of information technology and how they apply to team interaction. The model focuses on teams whose members either work in the same or different physical *location* and at the same or different *time.* For each of these cases, we describe what to expect and ways to deal with the limitations of that communication mode. Then, we move to a discussion of virtual teams, making the point that whenever teams must work together in a non-face-to-face fashion, this constitutes a virtual team. We describe strategies to help virtual teams do their work better. We then discuss transnational teams; we describe what transnational teams do and what it takes to get there. Obviously, transnational teams and global teamwork involve the diversity issues that we dealt with in chapter 4. We follow this discussion with a section on how information technology affects human behavior. We do not attempt to provide a state-of-the-art review on types of information technology; our purpose is to identify the considerations that managers must wrestle with when attempting to bring together groups of people who are not in the same place.

PLACE-TIME MODEL OF SOCIAL INTERACTION

The **place-time model** is based on the options that teams have when working across different locations and times. It is useful to conceptualize teams in terms of their geographic location (together versus separated) and in terms of their temporal relationship (interacting in real time versus asynchronously). For any team meeting, there are four possibilities as depicted in the place-time model in Table 12-1. As might be suspected, communication and teamwork unfold differently face-to-face than they do via electronic media.

Richness is the potential information-carrying capacity of the communications medium. Communication media may be ordered on a continuum of richness, with face-to-face communication being at the relatively "rich" end, and formal written messages, such as memos, being at the relatively "lean" or modality-constricted end (Daft & Lengel, 1984; Daft, Lengel, & Trevino, 1987; see Figure 12-1). Face-to-face communication conveys the richest information because it allows the simultaneous observation of multiple cues, including body language, facial expression, and tone of voice, providing people with a greater awareness of context. In contrast, formal, numerical documentation conveys the least rich information, providing few clues about the context. Depending upon the space and time relationships that characterize a team, groups are often constrained in their choice of communication medium.

Let's consider each of the four types of communication in the place-time model.

Face-to-Face Communication

Face-to-face interaction is the clear preference of most managers and executives; and rightly so. Face-to-face contact is crucial in the initiation of relationships and collaborations, and people are more cooperative when interacting face-to-face than via other forms of communication. Personal, face-to-face contact is the lubricant of the business engine. Without it, things don't move very well and relationships between businesspersons are often strained and contentious.

Face-to-face meetings are ideal when teams must wrestle with complex problems. For example, researchers need regular face-to-face contact to be confident that they accurately understand each other's work, particularly if it involves innovative ideas. The half-life of confidence decays over time as researchers communicate through telephone and computer conferences; face-to-face contact is required to renew trust in their mutual comprehension (DeMeyer, 1991, 1993). Face-to-face team meetings are particularly important when a group forms, when commitments to key decisions are needed,

TABLE 12-1 Place-Time Model of Interaction		
	Same Place	*Different Place*
Same Time	Face-to-face	Telephone
		Videoconference
Different Time	Single text editing	E-mail
	Shift work	Voice mail

Source: Thompson, L. 1998. *The Mind and Heart of the Negotiator.* Upper Saddle River, NJ: Prentice Hall.

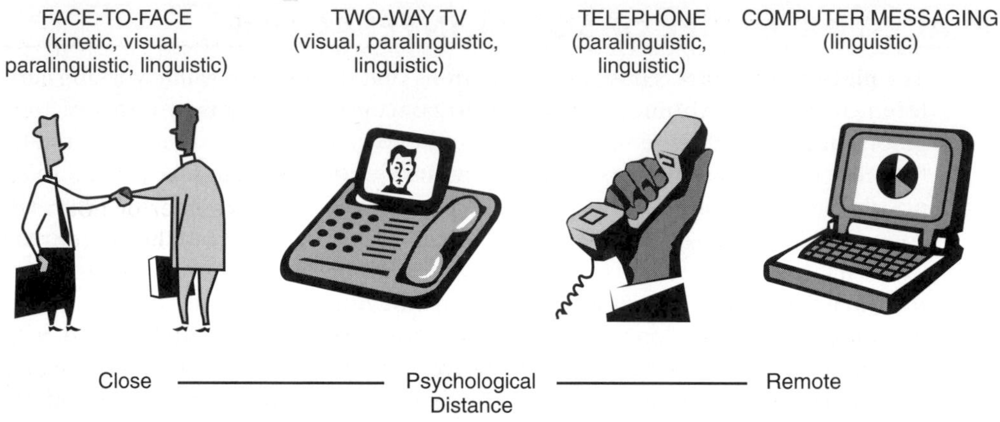

FACE-TO-FACE
(kinetic, visual,
paralinguistic, linguistic)

TWO-WAY TV
(visual, paralinguistic,
linguistic)

TELEPHONE
(paralinguistic,
linguistic)

COMPUTER MESSAGING
(linguistic)

Close ———————— Psychological ———————— Remote
Distance

FIGURE 12-1   Psychological Distancing Model

Source: Adapted from Wellens, A. R. 1989, September. "Effects of Telecommunication Media upon Information Sharing and Team Performance: Some Theoretical and Empirical Findings." *IEEE AES Magazine,* 14.

and when major conflicts among members must be resolved (DeMeyer, 1991; Galegher, Kraut, & Egido, 1990; Sproull & Keisler, 1991). Work groups form more slowly, and perhaps never fully, when they don't have face-to-face contact (DeMeyer, 1991; Galegher et al., 1990).

In most companies, the incidence and frequency of face-to-face communication is almost perfectly predicted by how closely people are located to one another: Employees who work in the same office or on the same floor communicate much more frequently than those located on different floors or in different buildings. The incidence of communication literally comes down to feet—even a few steps can have a huge impact. For example, communication frequency between R&D researchers drops off logarithmically after only 5 to 10 meters of distance between offices (Allen, 1977). In a study of molecular biologists, MacKenzie, Cambrosio, and Keating (1988) found that critical techniques for producing monoclonal antibodies were not reported in journals, but were passed from scientist to scientist at the lab bench. Workers in adjacent offices communicate twice as often as those in offices on the same floor, including via e-mail and telephone transmissions (Galegher et al., 1990).

Just what cues do people get out of face-to-face contact that makes it so important for interaction and productivity? Primarily, two things: First, *face-to-face communication is easier and, therefore, more likely to occur* than are other forms of communication. Simply stated, most people need a reason to walk up the stairs or to make a phone call. They underestimate how much information they get from chance encounters—which never happen in any mode but face-to-face because of this perceived effort. Second, although it is seldom consciously realized, *people primarily rely on nonverbal signals to help them conduct social interactions.* One estimate is that 93 percent of the meaning of messages is contained in the nonverbal part of communication, such as voice intonation (Meherabian, 1971). Perhaps this is why business executives will endure the inconveniences of travel across thousands of miles and several time zones so that they can have face-to-face contact with others, even if it is only for a short period of time.

The emphasis on the human factor is not just old-fashioned business superstition. Important behavioral, cognitive, and emotional processes are set into motion when people meet face-to-face. However, unless people are specially trained, they don't know what exactly it is about face-to-face interaction that facilitates teamwork—they just know that things go smoother.

Face-to-face interaction allows people to develop rapport—the feeling of being "in sync" or "on the same wavelength" with another person. Whether or not people feel rapport is a powerful determinant of whether they develop trust. The degree of rapport determines the efficiency and the quality of progress toward goal achievement, and whether the goal is ever achieved (Tickle-Degnen & Rosenthal, 1987).

Nonverbal (body orientation, gesture, eye contact, head-nodding) and paraverbal behavior (speech fluency, use of "uh-huhs," etc.) is the key to building rapport. When the person we are interacting with sits at a greater distance, with an indirect body orientation, backward lean, crossed arms, and low eye contact, we feel less rapport than when the same person sits with a forward lean, an open body posture, nods, and maintains steady eye contact. These nonverbal and paraverbal cues affect the way people work and the quality of their work as a team.

However, face-to-face communication is not the best modality for all teamwork. As a clear case in point, we saw in our discussion of creativity and brainstorming (chapter 8) that face-to-face brainstorming is less productive compared to other, less rich forms of interaction.

Same Time, Different Place

The same-time, different-place mode, in which people communicate in real time but are not physically in the same place, is often the alternative to face-to-face teamwork. The most common means is via telephone; videoconferencing is another example. Team members often rely on the telephone, but they do not always reach their party; up to 70 percent of initial telephone attempts fail to reach the intended party (Philip & Young, 1987). In telephone conversations, people lack facial cues; in videoconferencing, they lack real-time social cues, such as pauses, mutual gaze, and another person's immediate nonverbal response to what is being said (e.g., looking away or down). Yet at the same time, electronic interaction, such as in brainstorming groups, can greatly increase team productivity.

When technology tries to replace the dynamics of face-to-face interaction, it often falls short. The technology designed to make groups feel as though they are face-to-face does not lead to more and better communication. As a case in point, consider an engineering work group, located in two offices 1,000 kilometers apart, that experimented with an omnipresent video wall and cameras in all offices to link the sites together (Abel, 1990). Generally, the engineers interacted across the distance as one cohesive group, but there were some key exceptions: Video links were not very effective in generating new relationships or in resolving divisive differences, and miscommunication was treated as rudeness. Members of a design team were unable to listen to each other's ideas until they met face-to-face for 3 days, where they reached effective consensus.

What are the major ways in which group members who are physically distant from one another suffer because of their physical separation? There are several effects of physical separation of the team, some of which might not be immediately obvious (Armstrong & Cole, 1995).

Loss of Informal Communication

Probably the most-felt impact is the inability to chat informally in the hall, inside offices, and so on. The impromptu and casual conversations that employees have by the water cooler and the coffee machine are often where the most difficult problems are solved, and the most important interpersonal issues are addressed. Beyond a very short distance, people miss out on spontaneous exchanges that occur outside of formal meetings. Remote group members feel cut off from key conversations that occur over lunch and in the hall. Vince Anderson, director of environmental programs for Whirlpool Corp.'s North American Appliance Group in Evansville, Indiana, oversaw a 2-year project using a virtual team that developed a chlorofluorocarbon-free refrigerator, involving the United States, Brazil, and Italy. The team met approximately every 4 months to discuss the project and it was these informal meetings—a backyard cookout and a volleyball game—that were the most valuable for the project (Geber, 1995).

Separation of Feedback

Another negative impact of physical separation is feedback; greater distance tends to block the corrective feedback loops provided by chance encounters. One manager contrasted how employees who worked in his home office related to his decisions, compared with employees 15 kilometers away (Armstrong & Cole, 1995). Engineers in the home office would drop by and catch him in the hall or at lunch. "I heard you were planning to change project X," they would say. "Let me tell you why that would be stupid." The manager would listen to their points, clarify some details, and all would part better informed. In contrast, employees at the remote site would greet his weekly visits with formally prepared group objections, which took much longer to discuss and were rarely resolved as completely as the more informal hallway discussions. In short, groups working remotely do not get the coincidental chances to detect and correct problems on a casual basis. Managers tend to think of their home group as the people they sit beside at work. Geographic sites promote an informal, spontaneous group identity, reinforced by close physical proximity and the dense communication it promotes. Those working in an office all tend to have friends in nearby companies or groups, hear the same industry rumors, and share similar beliefs about technological trends. Thus, any distance—whether it be 15 miles or 15,000 miles—is problematic in this regard.

Loss of Informal Modeling

Another impact is the loss of informal modeling and observational learning. Distance tends to block casual observation, which is often invaluable to monitoring and mentoring performance, especially for one-on-one team coaching. The inability of remote employees to watch successful project managers enact their roles, along with the inability to observe the learned employee, is a barrier to effective coaching of task and interpersonal-related skills.

Out-of-the-Loop Employees

Another problem is that distant employees tend to be left out of discussions or forgotten. In a sense, they are "out of sight, out of mind." The default behavior is to ignore the person on the speakerphone. This is especially magnified when the person or group with less status is on the phone.

Time differences amplify the effects of physical distance. Distributed group members face the challenge of finding each other at the same time while they are living in different time zones. Furthermore, time differences sometimes highlight cultural differences. However, teams can try to overcome these cultural barriers. One group based in the United States and in Italy celebrated a project milestone in their weekly video-conference by sharing foods on the video screen and fax. The East Coast U.S. team, at 9 A.M., sent images of bagels and coffee. The Italian team, at 3 P.M. in their time zone, sent images of champagne and cookies.

Conflicts are expressed, recognized, and addressed more quickly if group members work in close proximity. A manager can spot a problem, "nip it in the bud," and solve the problem quickly. In geographically separated groups, the issues are more likely to just get dropped and go unresolved, contributing to a slow buildup in aggravation. People complain to their coworkers, reinforcing local perceptions of events, but do not complain to the distant leaders until feelings reach extremely high levels.

Although there are many disadvantages of distance, it is not always a liability for teams. The formality of a scheduled phone meeting can compel each party to better prepare for the meeting and to address the issues more efficiently. In addition, distance can reduce micromanagement. Some managers hinder their employees' performance by monitoring them too closely and demanding frequent updates. Distance can mitigate this problem. Most notably, groups can often be much more creative when interacting via information technology.

Different Time, Same Place

In the different-time, same-place mode, team members interact asynchronously, but share the same work space. An example might be shift workers who pick up the task left for them by the previous shift or collaborators working on the same electronic document. After one partner finishes working on the document, it goes to the other partner, who will further edit and develop it.

Although people may not realize it, they rely a lot on their physical environments for important information and cues. Remember the concept of transactive memory systems that we introduced in chapter 5: People often supplement their own memories and information-processing systems—which are fallible—with systems located in the environment. We discussed at length in chapter 5 how people use other team members as information storage, retrieval, and processing devices. The same is true for the physical environment. A Post-it note on the back of a chair, or a report placed in a certain bin can symbolize an entire procedural system (e.g., how to make a long-distance conference call). Just as people become information dependent on other people, they also can become information dependent upon aspects of the physical environment in order to do their work. At the extreme, this type of dependence can be a limitation for groups that find it impossible to work outside the idiosyncratic confines of their workspace. Information and workspace dependence can negatively affect the productivity and motivation of a team.

The productivity of any team, and organizational effectiveness in general, is a joint function of the technical and the social system (Emery & Trist, 1973). The structure of a group, both internally and externally, and the technology the group works with are products of an active adaptation process, in which the technology is shaped by the organization or its subunits, as well as being a factor in shaping the organization. For example, consider the introduction of a new technology, CT scanners, in two hospitals (Barley, 1996). The introduction of the CT scanners increased uncertainty and upset the distribution of expertise and the division of labor in the hospital units. Both hospital units became more decentralized with the introduction of the CT scanners and the associated increase in uncertainty.

Different Place, Different Time

In the different-place, different-time model, interactants communicate asynchronously in different places. The most pervasive means is e-mail. Asynchronous, distributed communication seems to be growing at a faster rate of popularity than are other forms of communication, such as the telephone and videoconferencing. The telephone has been around for 120 years, but less than half of the people on the planet have ever made a phone call. In contrast, the Internet is only about 30 years old, and it is expected that by the year 2000, there will be anywhere between 200 million to 1 billion Internet users.

Yet e-mail changes the nature of behavior and team dynamics. Because it is easy to send a message, and social norms are not present when sending e-mail, people often are more risk taking. Furthermore, there is virtually no competition to attain and hold the floor, so people are at liberty to send frequent and long messages. Some people receive several hundred electronic messages each day.

There is an etiquette to sending e-mail. You can check your e-mail savvy by reviewing Box 12-1, which indicates keys to successful e-mail collaboration.

Is e-mail effective for learning? In the fall of 1996, an experiment was carried out in which 33 students enrolled in a social statistics course at California State University at Northridge. The students were randomly divided into two groups—one taught in a traditional classroom and the other taught virtually on the World Wide Web (Schutte, 1996). Text, lectures, and exams were standardized for both classes; the virtual class scored an average of 20 percent higher than the traditional class on examinations. Furthermore, the virtual class had significantly higher peer contact, more time spent on class work, a perception of more flexibility, better understanding of the material, and a greater liking for math than the traditional class. The virtual students seemed more frustrated, but not from the technology. Instead, their inability to ask questions of the professor in a face-to-face environment led paradoxically to greater involvement among classmates, who formed study groups to "pick up the slack of not having a real classroom." Thus, the key performance differences here are most likely attributable to the collaboration among students instigated by the technology. It appears that the lack of rich communication in the virtual class led to the improved performance of students, who were sparked by the inadequacies of the virtual medium.

Information technology (in particular, the World Wide Web and the Internet) has led to the formation of new groups of people and communities. With over 40 million people on the Web, up from 1 million in December of 1994, these communities have been called the "colonizing of cyberspace." According to Andrew Busey, chairman and chief technology officer of ichat Inc., an internet start-up organization in Austin, Texas, that makes software for on-line chats, "Community and communica-

BOX 12-1

Keys to Successful E-Mail Collaboration

Given that you've got an international team that must communicate via information technology, how can you best achieve group goals? The following prescriptions are important (Thompson, 1998):

Make your messages concise and clear. Most people overestimate the ability of others to make sense out of what they mean (Keysar, 1994). People have a hard enough time deciphering our messages in face-to-face interactions; accuracy decreases dramatically in e-mail exchanges. Many people assume that longer means clearer. It doesn't. People have a short attention span and often dislike long e-mail messages, or perhaps even stop reading them if they begin to fall off of the screen. Most people are capable of only retaining seven, plus-or-minus two, ideas in their head at any one time. As a general rule of thumb, most e-mail messages should fit on a single screen. **Screen loading,** or the tendency to write very long messages, can annoy the recipients, especially if they are busy. Teams perform better when they exchange a greater number of shorter e-mails, rather than fewer but longer e-mails. Increasing the rate of e-mail exchange prevents misunderstanding because misperceptions can be quickly rectified. This also builds reciprocity in exchange.

Responding to e-mail. The asynchronous nature of e-mail provides people with the dubious luxury of not having to immediately receive or respond to e-mail messages. However, the sender of e-mail messages often expects a timely response. Not responding to e-mail may be perceived as rejection or disinterest. Newer forms of software allow senders to ascertain whether recipients have read their e-mail. Failure to provide a timely response to e-mail is akin to giving the "silent treatment" to someone. Suspicion and hostility increase as the communication between parties diminishes.

Metacommunication. **Metacommunication** is communication about communication. This boils down to people talking about how they should communicate. This is of critical importance in electronic interaction because the norms of turn-taking and conversation are not clear. In any electronic communication, it is important to let team members know how often you check your e-mail, whether you or someone else reads and responds to your e-mail, and whether you forward your e-mail to others.

Light of day test. The golden rule of e-mail is the **light of day test**—is what you're saying in the e-mail suitable to be rcad by your mother, supervisor, or jury? Could it appear on the front page of the newspaper? If not, it's probably not a good idea to send it.

Watch your temper. **Flaming** refers to the insults, criticisms, and character assassinations that people hurl over e-mail. Flaming remarks make fun of grammar, are patronizing (e.g., "I would recommend that you more closely read my first transmission prior to responding"), and include labeling and accusations (e.g., "That is completely ridiculous"; "Your idea is ludicrous"), character attacks, backhanded compliments ("I'm glad to see that you've come around to my point of view"), and blunt statements (e.g., "Why don't we stop treating each other as fools and start talking seriously?"). Flaming and other negative interpersonal behaviors that are found among computer-mediated communicaton system users stem from feelings of isolation (Keisler, Zubrow, Moses, & Gellar, 1985). In contrast, face-to-face groups have mechanisms and norms, such as conformity pressure, that largely prevent flaming (Rhoades & O'Connor, 1996).

People react to each other with less politeness, empathy, or inhibition if they cannot sense the other's social presence (Short, Williams, & Christie, 1976). People are much more likely to issue threats when communicating via information technology.

There is more uncertainty, doubt, and ambiguity in electronic mail exchanges. This stems from the asynchronous nature of communication. As a consequence, people become frustrated and seek to control the exchange by issuing threats (e.g., "I am not going to read my e-mail again"; "if I don't hear from you by 5 P.M., I will assume that the specifications are acceptable"). Along these lines, don't chastise or deliver negative feedback via e-mail; face-to-face (or telephone) communication is more appropriate.

tions is the next big wave on the internet" (Hof, Browder, & Elstrom, 1997). The Web is not just a meeting place for young people; 67 percent are 30 years of age or older, including 19 percent over age 50. Women account for a bigger portion of the Internet population than ever before—41 percent, up from 21 percent a year and a half ago.

Some even argue that these technologies are redefining individuals' identities as they explore the boundaries of their personalities, adopt multiple selves, and form on-line relationships that can be more intense than real ones (Turkle, 1995). Internet communities such as Women's Wire, Talk City, Parent Soup, Geocities, and Tripod are composed of various "netizens" who find they are spending more and more of their existence communicating in a virtual, as opposed to real, fashion (Hof et al., 1997).

It might seem that this type of community interaction is a far cry from the business world of information technology, but that is just the point: It is becoming harder to separate the personal lives of people and the communities to which they belong from their professional or business lives. The Internet does not make the clear distinction between work and home; the traditional distinction arises from physical separation, which is not the case on the Internet.

INFORMATION TECHNOLOGY AND SOCIAL BEHAVIOR

Information technology has extremely powerful effects on social behavior (Keisler & Sproull, 1992). Many people are surprised at how they behave when communicating via e-mail. What are the key things to expect when interacting with teammates via information technology?

Status and Power: The "Weak Get Strong" Effect

In face-to-face interactions, people do not contribute to conversation equally. One person or one clique usually dominates the discussion. In general, those with the higher status tend to talk more, even if they are not experts on the subject. Not surprisingly, managers speak more than subordinates and men speak more than women.

However, an odd thing happens on the way to the information technology forum: The traditional static cues are missing and the dynamic cues are distinctly less impactive. This has a dramatic effect on social behavior: Power and status differences are weakened. Decision making occurs on the basis of task expertise, rather than status (Eveland & Bikson, 1989). People who are in weak positions in face-to-face encounters become more powerful because status cues are harder to read in non-face-to-face interaction (Sproull & Keisler, 1991). Traditional, static cues, like position and title, are not as obvious on e-mail. It is often impossible to tell whether you are communicating with a president or clerk because traditional e-mail simply lists the person's name, not a title. In most networks, when people send e-mail, the only signs of position and personal attributes are names and addresses. Addresses are often shortened and may be difficult to comprehend. Even when they can be deciphered, addresses identify the organization, but not the subunit, job title, social importance, or level in the organization of the sender. Dynamic status cues, such as dress, mannerisms, age, and gender, are also missing in e-mail. In this sense, e-mail acts as an equalizer because it is difficult for high-status people to dominate discussions (see Sidebar 12-1).

Sidebar 12-1. Technology Can Be Empowering for Women

When a group of executives meet face-to-face, the men in these groups are five times more likely than the women to make the first decision proposal. When the same groups meet via computer, women make the first proposal as often as do men (McGuire, Keisler, & Siegel, 1987).

Additionally, when interacting via e-mail, an interesting dynamic happens: People respond more openly and conform less to social norms and other people. They focus more on the content of the task and less on the direction of high-status opinion leaders. E-mail and other forms of computer-mediated communication (CMC) are becoming increasingly prevalent. CMC is more democratic and less hierarchical in this way, with bad news conveyed upward to superiors with less delay (Sproull & Keisler, 1991). At the same time, there is less awareness of the needs of the group or its members (McGrath, 1990). With more rudeness and less inhibition, conflicts in CMC are sharper and escalate more quickly. Consensus on complex, nontechnical issues is more difficult to reach (Hiltz, Johnson, & Turoff, 1986).

The Impact of Technology on Social Networks

As we saw in chapter 9, social networks are the circulatory system of an organization. We also saw that people with entrepreneurial networks are more likely to advance in their organizations than those with clique networks. The types of networks that characterize and shape organizational life change dramatically when information technology enters the picture as a form of communication.

Technology Can Lead to Face-to-Face Meetings

An important value of information technology may come from the ability to generate face-to-face meetings that simply would not have occurred otherwise. For example, Boeing used a high-level computer-aided engineering network to manage the development of its new 777 passenger jet. This software network has the ability to alert Boeing engineers whenever their proposed modifications in subassemblies interfere with other subassemblies—for example, when a hydraulic system modification might interfere with an electrical system. Boeing management discovered that its engineers were deliberately making modifications in the plans that interfered with other systems. What appeared to be a form of software sabotage was actually Boeing engineers taking advantage of the network to find out who was working on the other systems. That way, they could get together to talk about their designs. In other words, the network created the opportunity for productive collaboration around the 777 that Boeing's own management structure could not (Schrage, 1995).

Increased Speed of Information Exchange

E-mail networks, or connections between people who communicate via electronic mail, increase the information resources of low-network people. When people need assistance (e.g., information or resources), they often turn to their immediate social network. When such help is not available, they use weak ties, such as relationships with acquaintances or strangers, to seek help that is unavailable from friends or colleagues. However, there is a problem: In the absence of personal relationships or the expectation of direct reciprocity, help from weak ties might not be forthcoming or could be of low quality.

Some companies, particularly global companies and those in the fields of information technology and communications, need to rely on e-mail and employees within the company forming connections with each other on the basis of no physical contact. The incentives for taking the time to assist someone who is dealing with a problem and is located in a different part of the world are pretty minuscule.

Tandem Corporation is a global computer manufacturer that has a highly geographically dispersed organization (Sproull & Keisler, 1991). Managers in the Tandem Corporation need technical advice to solve problems, but they cannot always get useful advice from their local colleagues. Simply stated, the local networks are often not sufficient to solve problems. What can be done?

One possibility is to catalogue or store information in some easily accessible database. In a technical company, this would mean published reports and scientific manuals. However, engineers and managers do not like to consult technical reports to obtain needed information; most of the information they use to solve their problems is obtained through face-to-face discussions. People in organizations usually prefer to exchange help through strong collegial ties, which develop through physical proximity, similarity, and familiarity.

An investigation of Tandem's e-mail revealed some startling and encouraging findings (Sproull & Keisler, 1991): Managers who put out a request for technical assistance received an average of 7.8 replies per request. All of the replies were serious and respondents spent 9 minutes per reply. The replies solved the problem 50 percent of the time. Information providers gave useful advice and solved the problems of information seekers, despite their lack of a personal connection with the person requesting information.

Risk Taking

Recall from chapter 6 that people intuitively perform cost-benefit analyses when considering different courses of action and, consequently, do not treat gains commensurately with losses. However, electronic interaction has an effect on risk-taking behavior. Consider the following choices:

A. Return of $20,000 over 2 years
B. 50 percent chance of gaining $40,000; 50 percent of gaining nothing

Option A is the safer investment; option B is riskier. However, these two options are mathematically identical, meaning that in an objective sense, people should not favor one option over the other. When posed with these choices, most managers are risk averse, meaning that they select the option that has the sure payoff as opposed to holding out for the chance to win big (or, equally as likely, not win at all). However, consider what happens when the following choice is proposed:

C. Sure loss of $20,000 over 2 years
D. 50 percent chance of losing $40,000; 50 percent of losing nothing

Most managers are risk seeking and choose option D. Why? According to the **framing effect** (Kahneman & Tversky, 1979), people are risk averse for gains and risk seeking for losses. This can lead to self-contradictory, quirky behavior. By manipulating the reference point, a person's fiscal policy choices can change.

We saw in chapter 6 that groups tend to make riskier decisions than do individuals in the same situation. Thus, risk seeking is greatly exaggerated in groups that meet face-to-face. Paradoxically, groups that make decisions via electronic communication are risk seeking for both gains and losses (McGuire, Keisler, & Siegel, 1987). Furthermore, executives are just as confident of their decisions whether they are made through electronic communication or face-to-face communication.

Social Norms

As mentioned previously, when social context cues are missing or weak, people feel distant from others and somewhat anonymous. They are less concerned about making a good appearance, and humor tends to fall apart or to be misinterpreted. Additionally, the expression of negative emotion is no longer minimized because factors that keep people from acting out negative emotions are not in place when they communicate via information technology. Simply, in the absence of social norms that prescribe the expression of positive emotion, people are more likely to express negative emotion. When people communicate via e-mail, they are more likely to negatively confront others. Conventional behavior, such as politeness rituals and acknowledgment of others' views, decreases; rude, impulsive behavior, such as flaming, increases. People are eight times more likely to flame in electronic discussions than in face-to-face discussions (Dubrovsky, Keisler, & Sethna, 1991).

Task Performance

Are people more effective when they communicate via information technology? We saw in chapter 8 that in terms of brainstorming and generating new ideas, face-to-face interaction is less effective than are some other forms of mediated communication.

It takes longer to write than it does to speak; hence, communicating via information technology is slower. It takes four times as long for a three-person group to make a decision in a real-time computer conference as in a face-to-face meeting (Siegel, Dubrovsky, Keisler, & McGuire, 1986). It takes as much as 10 times as long in a four-person computer-conference group that lacks time restrictions (Dubrovsky et al., 1991). This is especially true when the technology is new.

All of the team configurations discussed in this chapter, with the exception of the same-time, same-place teams, are virtual teams, and as such, face special challenges. In the sections that follow, we consider strategies for enhancing rapport and teamwork in local teams and in remotely distributed teams.

ENHANCING LOCAL TEAMWORK: REDESIGNING THE WORKPLACE

Telecommuting, or working from home, was the popular mantra of the late twentieth century. However, this is rapidly being replaced by a new work concept: Work anywhere, anytime—in your car, your home, your office, even your client's office. It means a radical disaggregation of work, going beyond the walls and confines of the traditional office (O'Hamilton, Baker, & Vlasic, 1996). For example, Jarlath MacNamara, founder of the Dublin, Ireland–based Cabs-on-Line, fitted a Ford Galaxy taxi with a laptop with e-mail and a browser, a cell phone, and a wireless modem and fax (Lyons, 1998). The traditional corporation exemplified by private offices, elevators, and cubicled workspaces is giving way to informal gatherings and chatting among employees in community spaces, such as lunchrooms and lounges. Corporate America is changing and the walls of the corporation are falling down and being replaced by mobile office systems that conform to the needs of the team, not the other way around.

For example, at the Alcoa Aluminum Company of America, senior executives work in open cubicles and gather around "communications centers" replete with televisions, fax machines, newspapers, and tables that encourage impromptu meetings. CEO Paul H. O'Neill's favorite hangout is the kitchen, where he and his staff heat up take-out food and talk work (O'Hamilton, Baker, & Vlasic, 1996). This type of change is radical and it is at the heart of team redesign. By redesigning the environment that they work in, teams work more efficiently and effectively.

Indeed, technology that can boost employee efficiency and mobility is surpassing facilities and real estate as the second biggest corporate operating expense, after salaries and benefits (O'Hamilton et al., 1996). Increasingly, architects, interior designers, facilities managers, and furniture companies are assuming the new role of strategic design consultants not only with blueprints, but also with human behavior in the organization. This means that many of the old perks, such as large, private paneled offices and private lunchrooms, are disappearing. Instead, employees of every rank are out in the open. According to a 1995 survey by the International Facility Management Association, 83 percent of companies are embracing alternative office strategies. The following are some of the most promising options for maximizing team productivity in the new office space.

Virtual or Flexible Space

Virtual or flexible space is physical space that is used on a temporary and changing basis to meet different needs. Instead of physical space setting limits on managerial behavior, such as how many people can be in a meeting at any one time and what information technology is or is not available, virtual space means that people determine their needs first and design the space to fit those needs. It is an entirely different way of thinking about space. Most important, virtual or flexible space does not mean open, fixed cubicles. For example, Allan Alley, vice president of Focus Systems Inc., a Wilsonville, Oregon, maker of computer-projection systems, states that open cubicles are the "worst of both worlds. . . . No impromptu meetings and a lot of wasted space" (O'Hamilton et al., 1996, p. 113).

A prime example of virtual or flexible space is the "cave and commons" design: The idea is to balance individual work and teamwork, as well as privacy and community. At Minneapolis-based advertising agency Fallon-McElligott, when it is time to brainstorm, art directors, space buyers, account managers, and copywriters wheel special desks equipped with an employee's computer, files, and phone into flexible space. The room may hold 30 employees on Monday, none on Tuesday, and 10 or so on Wednesday, depending on what needs to be done. At any given time, team members may be working independently in their own cubicles or meeting at a center table.

At Procter & Gamble, project groups were the central design theme in their Cincinnati building. Members of teams work in open cubicles grouped together, and can all see each other, regardless of rank. File cases are on wheels, and offices are designed out of "bricks" that can be reconfigured in a jiffy. P&G personnel travel between floors by escalator, instead of elevators, which tend to halt conversation. "Huddle rooms" are strategically placed where teams can come together to brainstorm; and electronic whiteboards, which can convert scribble to e-mail, are present in lunchrooms and lounges. Corridors are deliberately wide so employees can stop for a chat. Furthermore, P&G designed features to help dual-career families: A dry cleaner, shoe repair shop, and take-out cafeteria are all on site.

Flexible Furniture

Furniture for the new space is key for productivity. Consider the "personal harbor," a small, cylindrical booth made by Steelcase Inc., with a door that can be closed; because it is curved, it has the effect of increasing interior space. There is enough room inside for a flat work surface, computer setup, phones, file drawer, and other standard desk items. There's even a whiteboard and built-in CD player. The important design feature is that the harbors are grouped around a large puzzle-like table that can be broken into several pieces. When harbor doors are open, people move in and out of the group space to talk to colleagues and participate in meetings. Whereas most norms state that people should never leave a traditional meeting room, with the personal harbor, people stay in a meeting long enough to contribute and then go back to work.

Some companies are even turning to custom designers and artists to get what they want. For example, when Fallon-McElligott wanted to create its flexible space, interior designer Gary E. Wheeler created the award-winning "free address lockers" that resemble armoires on wheels. They hold a computer, files, phone, and a desktop, as well as a special universal plug to simplify "docking" all the electronics (O'Hamilton et al., 1996).

Inhale Therapeutic Systems, a small Palo Alto start-up working on novel drug-delivery technology, uses "bullpens"—large cubicles containing four people of various ranks and functions—with no walls or barriers of any kind between people

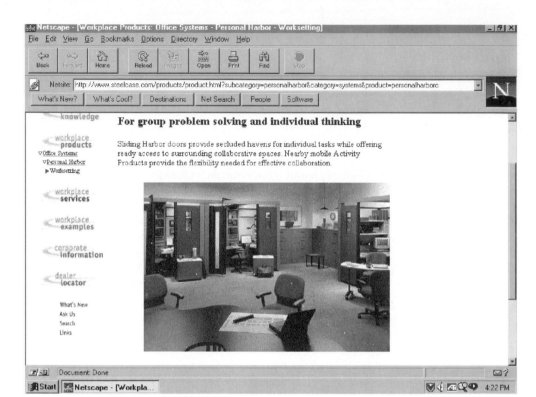

An office space using personal harbors designed by Steelcase, Inc.

Source: Steelcase, Inc.'s Web site at *www.steelcase.com.*

(O'Hamilton et al., 1996). These bullpens enable the employees to communicate more frequently and informally.

Hoteling

Employees are increasingly mobile, spending more of their work time on the road than in the office. However, the mobile employee still needs a place to meet with the rest of the sales team or client team. **Hoteling** is the provision of a building, office, or meeting rooms that can be reserved in advance, just like a hotel. For example, at Ernst & Young's Washington office, when employees call, they are asked for a personal ID and the dates they need "hotel" space. Within 30 seconds, the system confirms whether a workstation or a meeting room is available. Each hotel has a concierge to meet and help guests. When employees arrive, their name is on a door, and any files or supplies the employees have requested will be there too. Also, their phone numbers are forwarded. IBM has about 20,000 sales and service professionals nationwide using shared offices, which has cut about $1.4 billion from real-estate expenses (O'Hamilton et al., 1996). For hoteling to be effective, it must be hassle-free for the employee (Smith, 1997).

Hoteling can be extraordinarily cost-effective. It has allowed KPMG Peat Marwick LLP to hire new employees without leasing extra space. At Ernst & Young, staffers realize that the lack of individual offices shows up in the firm's profit margin, which, in turn, shows up in their bonuses (Smith, 1997).

Before Implementing Alternative Forms of Office Space . . .
(Becker, Quinn, Rappaport, & Sims, 1994)

1. The presence or absence of a strong champion is very important to the success/failure of the project.

2. Many issues that management may feel are barriers to implementing innovative ideas are perceived barriers.

3. A richer, more varied set of work settings that truly support the range of work activities must be provided.

4. A business approach to implementing innovations must be used instead of a cost approach.

5. User involvement is very critical to the success of the project.

6. Reinvesting a portion of the innovation cost savings is likely to result in a far higher level of employee satisfaction.

7. Using a pilot project to apply a standardized solution is ineffective.

8. The reassessment and data collection phase must not be eliminated.

9. Employees must be given time to adjust to the new work patterns.

However efficient, alternative forms of office space are not without problems. Implementing these types of alternative office space should be considered carefully. Consider the lessons in Box 12-2.

The new design of offices and furniture indicates that most managers and executives regard face-to-face communication to be the ideal—and the more of it the better. However, it is not always possible to bring team members together, especially those who are spread across the globe. The answer is the virtual team.

VIRTUAL TEAMS

A virtual team is a task-focused group that meets without all members necessarily being physically present or even working at the same time. Virtual teams work closely together even though they may be separated by many miles or even continents. Virtual teams may meet through conference calls, videoconferences, e-mail, or other communications tools, such as application sharing. Teams may include employees only, or they may include outsiders, such as a customer's employees. Virtual teams work well for global companies, but they can also benefit small companies operating from a single location, especially if decision makers are often at job sites or on the road. They can be short-lived, like the one that helped the VeriFone sales rep in Greece, or permanent, such as operational teams that run their companies virtually.

If a company has a need for virtual teams, the biggest challenge for productivity is *coordination of effort:* How to get people to work together compatibly and productively, even though face-to-face contact is limited and communication is confined to phone, fax, and e-mail. To deal with the coordination problem, the leaders of every virtual team at VeriFone must know and follow written procedures put together by the company's senior managers, whether the team is appointed (as in the case of the San Francisco staffer heading the team aiding the Greek sales rep), or self-selected (as in the case of a director of a long-term team monitoring day-to-day operations). Furthermore, before employees are permitted to form one of VeriFone's process-improvement teams, they must complete a 40-hour training program.

There are five crucial steps to creating (and maintaining) a successful virtual team (Pape, 1997). The first three steps are those that are required of any team.

1. *Have a clear, shared goal.* Teams must always be guided by a clear purpose, one that is shared by all team members. The purpose of the team will largely define issues such as who will be on the team, the process design, and the criteria that will be used to measure performance.
2. *Select members.* As with most teams, more is not better. The same is true for virtual teams: Most virtual teams should have three to seven members. More members mean greater process losses.
3. *Chart the course.* Team members tend to work to fill their time. Members of virtual teams will often be serving double or triple duty on other, local teams. It is important to set clear milestones for progress and give team members a clear sense of the likely duration of their work activity.
4. *Select technology tools.* Perhaps the most distinguishing aspect of virtual teams is the need to select a medium or media of communication. Any non-face-to-face communication medium will often entail considerable coordination loss if problems in using the technology are not adequately anticipated. Knowing what information technology to use when is key. For example, VeriFone teams use beepers, cellular phones, and voice mail for keeping in contact; and fax, e-mail, conference calls, and videoconferencing for disseminating information.
5. *Focus on the human factor.* Do not take it for granted that team members working virtually will develop cohesion on their own. However, it is neither practical nor realistic to create special face-to-face bonding opportunities for virtual teams before they work together. For example, Price-WaterhouseCoopers has 45,000 employees in 120 countries, and people work on projects with each other without having ever met in person. We discuss the human factor in more detail in the next section.

STRATEGIES FOR ENHANCING THE VIRTUAL TEAM

There are a variety of methods for creating rapport among team members. The trade-offs involve money and time. The following methods are used by various companies to address the rapport and trust problem that virtual teams encounter. Few of these methods have been tested in rigorous controlled research. We begin by discussing the most elaborate (and most expensive).

Collaboratory

A **collaboratory** is the combination of technology, tools, and infrastructure that allows scientists to work with remote facilities and each other as if they were co-located (Lederberg

& Uncaphor, 1989). It is a center without walls, in which scientists and technicians can perform research without regard to geographical location. Parallels in the business world include virtual corporations in the place of physical corporations (Davidow & Malone, 1992) and a global workplace instead of national or local workplaces (O'Hara-Devereaux & Johansen, 1994). Although the collaboratory requires no face-to-face contact, teams often need some degree of actual face-to-face contact to establish rapport. There are several types of interaction that will help develop rapport among team members and force them to work in a single geographic location. The length of the face-to-face interaction varies by method. Among them are initial face-to-face experience, temporary engagement, or the one-day videoconference.

Initial Face-to-Face Experience

Bringing together team members for a short, face-to-face experience is often used by companies who want to lay a groundwork of trust and communication for later teamwork that will be conducted strictly electronically. The idea here is that it is much easier for people to work together if they have actually met in a face-to-face encounter. Face-to-face contact humanizes people and creates expectations for team members to use in their subsequent long-distance work together.

Temporary Engagement

The idea here is to allow team members to work together in a sustained face-to-face fashion before separating them. For example, John Spencer, worldwide manager for the design and development of single-use cameras for Eastman Kodak Company in Rochester, New York, pulled together a project development team to design a new product that required the involvement of German design engineers. Spencer brought the German engineers to the United States for the initial 6 months of the project.

One-Day Videoconference

Chris Newell, executive director of the Lotus Institute, the research and education arm of Lotus Development Corp. in Cambridge, Massachusetts, believes that introductions via videoconference are crucial to develop trust and relationships before doing teamwork electronically. Thus, if an initial, face-to-face meeting is out of the question, an alternative may be to at least get everyone on-line so that people can attach a name to a face. Depending upon the size of the team and locations of different members, this alternative may be more feasible than a face-to-face meeting.

Touching Base

If teams do not have an opportunity to work together at the outset of a project, then providing an opportunity for them to touch base at some later point can be helpful. This method is most useful for teams in which one or two members are remotely located. For example, Barbara Recchia, communications program manager at Hewlett Packard in Palo Alto, California, lives and works in Santa Rosa. In the early months of her remote work arrangement, she felt hopelessly out of touch with her colleagues (Geber, 1995). Eventually, she decided to drop in once a week instead of once a month to maintain her connection to her team. There are often special problems when just one member of the team is remotely located from the rest of the local team. Because much teamwork is done informally at the water cooler or at lunch, the remote person often feels lonely and disconnected from the rest of the team, and the rest of the team may leave that person out of the loop—if not deliberately, then just because it is cumbersome to bring the outsider up to date on all team actions.

Schmoozing

Schmoozing (as described in chapter 4) is our name for superficial contact between people that has the psychological effect of having established a relationship with someone. There are a variety of non-face-to-face schmoozing strategies, such as exchanging pictures or biographical information or engaging in a simple get-acquainted e-mail exchange. The effectiveness of electronic schmoozing has been put to test and the results are dramatic: schmoozing increases liking and rapport and results in more profitable business deals than when people just get down to business (Moore, Kurtzberg, Thompson, & Morris, 1999). Perhaps the most attractive aspect of schmoozing is that it is relatively low-cost and efficient. Merely exchanging a few short e-mails describing yourself can lead to better business relations. However, you should not expect people to naturally schmooze—at least at the outset of a business relationship. Team members working remotely have a tendency to get down to business. As a start toward schmoozing, begin by telling the other person something about yourself that does not necessarily relate to the business at hand (e.g., "I really enjoy kayaking"); also, provide a context for your own work space (e.g., "It is very late in the day and there are 20 people at my door, so I don't have time to write a long message"). Furthermore, ask questions that show you are interested in the other party as a person; this is an excellent way to search for points of similarity. Finally, provide the link for the next e-mail or exchange (e.g., "I will look forward to hearing your reactions on the preliminary report and I will also send you the tapes you requested").

TRANSNATIONAL TEAMS[1]

Thus far, we have discussed teamwork via information technology as if it were strictly a burden or nuisance to be overcome. However, depending upon the goals of the company, it may be highly desirable to put together virtual teams, even when local teamwork is an alternative.

Many companies are international or multinational. A better goal might be to become a transnational company or team. A **transnational team** is a work group composed of multinational members whose activities span multiple countries; transnational teams have successfully transcended the cultural, geographic, and managerial barriers to team effectiveness (Snow, Snell, Davison, & Hambrick, 1996). Global teamwork may be the best ticket going to becoming truly transnational. As cases in point, consider the following companies (Snow et al., 1996):

- In 1985, Fuji-Xerox sent 15 of its most experienced Tokyo engineers to a Xerox Corporation facility in Webster, New York. For the next 5 years, the Japanese engineers worked with a group of American engineers to develop the "world copier"—a huge success in the global marketplace.

---

[1]This section draws heavily upon the work of Snow, Snell, Davison, and Hambrick (1996).

- In 1991, Eastman Kodak formed a team to launch its latest consumer product, the photo CD. That group of experts, based in London, developed a strategy for the simultaneous introduction of the photo CD in several European countries. The photo CD has been Kodak's most successful multicountry product introduction in the 1990s.
- At IBM–Latin America, in 1990, a group of managers and technical specialists formed their own team to market, sell, and distribute personal computers in 11 Latin American countries. It took the team leader about a year to convince his boss that the team should be formally recognized and allowed to operate as an autonomous business unit.

In each of these cases, a transnational team was key to the company's efforts to globalize and extend the firm's products and operations into international markets. Global competitive strategies are complex and expensive, and they are often administered by a transnational team of managers and specialists. For some examples of companies that missed the mark when attempting to cross cultural borders, see Sidebar 12-2.

Sidebar 12-2. Marketing "Cam-pains"

- Coors put its slogan, "Turn it loose," into Spanish, where it was read as "Suffer from diarrhea."
- Clairol introduced the Mist Stick, a curling iron, into Germany, only to find out that *mist* is slang for *manure*. Not too many people had use for the "manure stick."
- Scandinavian vacuum manufacturer Electrolux used the following in an American campaign: "Nothing sucks like an Electrolux."
- In Chinese, the Kentucky Fried Chicken slogan "Finger-lickin' good" came out as "Eat your fingers off."
- The American slogan for Salem cigarettes, "Salem—feeling free," was translated into the Japanese market as "When smoking Salem, you will feel so refreshed that your mind seems to be free and empty."
- When Gerber started selling baby food in Africa, they used the same packaging as in the United States, with the beautiful Caucasian baby on the label. Later, they learned that in Africa, companies routinely put pictures on the label of what's inside, since most people can't read English.
- Colgate introduced a toothpaste in France called Cue, the name of a notorious porno magazine.
- An American T-shirt maker in Miami printed shirts for the Spanish market which promoted the Pope's visit. Instead of "I saw the Pope" (el Papa), the shirts read "I saw the potato" (la papa).
- In Italy, a campaign for Schweppes Tonic Water translated the name into "Schweppes Toilet Water."
- Pepsi's "Come alive with the Pepsi Generation" translated into "Pepsi brings your ancestors back from the grave" in Chinese.
- We all know about GM's Chevy Nova meaning "won't go" in Spanish markets, but did you know that Ford had a similar problem in Brazil with the

Pinto? *Pinto* was Brazilian slang for "tiny male genitals." Ford renamed the automobile Corcel, meaning "horse."

- Hunt-Wesson introduced Big John products in French Canada as "Gros Jos." Later, they found out that in slang it means "big breasts."
- Frank Perdue's chicken slogan, "It takes a strong man to make a tender chicken," was translated into Spanish as "It takes an aroused man to make a chicken affectionate."
- When Parker Pen marketed a ball-point pen in Mexico, its ads were supposed to have read, "It won't leak in your pocket and embarrass you." Instead, the company thought that the word *embarazar* meant "to embarrass," when it actually meant "to impregnate," so the ad read: "It won't leak in your pocket and make you pregnant."
- The Coca-Cola name in China was first read as "Ke-kou-ke-la," meaning "Bite the wax tadpole" or "Female horse stuffed with wax," depending on the dialect. Coke then researched 40,000 characters to find a phonetic equivalent, "Ko-kou-ko-le," translating into "Happiness in the mouth."
- Some folks from England got a huge laugh from the name of an airline: The Trump Shuttle (Donald Trump's airline). They said that in England, *Trump* translated into "fart."
- And finally, not even Nike is exempt. Nike has a television commercial for hiking shoes that was shot in Kenya using Samburu tribesmen. The camera closes in on one tribesman who speaks in native Maa. As he speaks, the Nike slogan "Just do it" appears on the screen. Lee Cronk, an anthropologist at the University of Cincinnati, says the Kenyan is really saying, "I don't want these. Give me big shoes." Says Nike's Elizabeth Dolan, "We thought nobody in America would know what he said."

Like the other types of teams we have discussed, transnational teams come into existence in one of two primary ways: From the top down or from the bottom up. Most transnational teams are formed from the top down, as in the case of manager-led or self-managing teams. That is, senior managers see a competitive need, decide a transnational team should be formed, and put together a team with a particular mandate. For example, in 1991, Heineken formed the European Production task force, a 13-member team representing five countries. The task force wrestled with the issue of how many breweries the company should operate in Europe, what size and type they should be, and where they should be located. Eighteen months after it was formed, the task force presented its findings and recommendations to Heineken's board of directors, who enthusiastically accepted the recommendations.

In contrast, other transnational teams are emergent; like self-directing and self-governing teams, they evolve naturally from the existing network of individuals who depend on each other to accomplish their work objectives. These teams may cut across functions, business units, and countries and may even incorporate "outsiders" from other organizations, either temporarily or permanently. These teams may develop their own mandate and challenge higher managers to accept and support it. For example, the concept of one transnational team was instigated around a dinner table at an annual quality assurance convention held internally by Glaxo-Wellcome. They chose their own leader—a medical doctor—and she approached senior executives to obtain authorization and funding for the team.

Transnational teams are distinguished from other teams in terms of the complexity of their work and their multicultural membership. Transnational teams work on projects that are highly complex and have considerable impact on company objectives. It is imperative that transnational teams adeptly handle a variety of cross-cultural issues. In particular, transnational teams must take into account the degree of similarity among the cultural norms of the individuals on the team, language fluency, and leadership style (Snow et al., 1996). Here's where a clearly shared goal, well-articulated team member roles, shared values, and agreement upon performance criteria are critical. The more deliberate planning centered upon these factors that occurs on the front end of teamwork, the better.

Once formed, transnational teams can be used to accomplish a number of different objectives. Some firms use the teams primarily to help achieve global efficiency, to develop regional or worldwide cost advantages, and to standardize designs and operations (Ghoshal & Barlett, 1988). Other teams enable their companies to be locally responsive; they are expected to help their firms attend to the demands of different regions' market structures, consumer preferences, and political and legal systems. For example, local responsiveness was the main concern of Eastman Kodak's photo CD team as it sought to tailor the marketing strategy for the new product to each major country in the European market. A third use of transnational teams is for organizational learning, bringing together knowledge from various parts of the company, transferring technology, and spreading innovations throughout the firm. For example, IBM has a global network of experts, led by a core team of six people headquartered outside of London, that consults around the world for clients in the airline industry. That team, the International Airlines Solution Centre, is composed of permanent and temporary members who fuse technical, consulting, and industry expertise to provide information technology to airlines and airport authorities. The team identifies knowledge located in one part of the world and applies it to problems that arise in another.

CONCLUSIONS

Change is often disturbing for the corporate world, and technological change is often thought to be a "Frankenstein's monster." However, teams have been dealing with place and time issues for several decades. The older solution was to relocate employees; newer solutions are more varied, creative, (often) cheaper, and less permanent. There is a strong intuition in the business world that face-to-face communication is necessary for trust, understanding, and enjoyment. However, face-to-face communication in no way ensures higher team productivity—especially in the case of creative teams. Information technology can increase productivity of teams. The skilled manager knows when to use it, which obstacles are likely to crop up when using it, and how to address those obstacles.

Appendix 1

Managing Meetings: A Toolkit

The work of teams largely proceeds through meetings. Whether they are regularly scheduled or called out of need, effective meeting management is a key to success. Furthermore, people spend a lot of time in meetings. The average number of meetings jumped from 7 to 10 per week, based on surveys of business professionals between 1981 and 1995 by Mosvick and Nelson, authors of *We've Got to Start Meeting Like This!* (1995). Typical executives spend two-thirds of their time in scheduled meetings, and the amount of time managers spend in meetings increases with organizational level. Middle managers spend about 30 percent of their time in meetings; top management spends about 50 percent of their time in meetings. In addition to scheduled meetings, managers are involved in unscheduled and non-job-related meetings. In a study sponsored by the 3M Corporation, the number of meetings and conferences in industry nearly doubled during the previous decade and the cost of meetings nearly tripled. Most businesses spend 7 to 15 percent of their personnel budgets on meetings.

Perhaps meetings would not be a bad thing if they were economical and effective. Unfortunately, as much as 50 percent of meeting time is unproductive, and up to 25 percent of meeting time covers irrelevant issues. As one senior executive put it, "To waste your own time is unfortunate, but to waste the time of others is unforgivable." Companies are so overburdened with meetings that experts say it's a wonder any work gets done. Meetings also trigger stress. The 3M meeting network recently launched a World Wide Web site where workers describe their meeting horror stories. Not surprisingly, managers have resorted to using various tactics, which vary from the radical (removing all chairs to make people stand, locking the doors, requiring people to pay $0.25 before speaking, etc.) to the more tame (the example in Sidebar A1-1).

THE 4P MEETING MANAGEMENT MODEL

The 4P model is a method for designing and implementing effective meetings (Whetton & Cameron, 1991). It has four key steps (see Table A1-1): (1) specify the **purpose** of the meeting, (2) invite the right **people,** (3) carefully **plan** the meeting content and format, and (4) effectively manage the meeting's **process.**

Skilled meeting managers do not just sit at the head of the table and call upon people to speak in a round-robin fashion. Nor do they run a "talk show" by simply airing ideas, conflicts, and concerns. Skilled meeting managers do not write down everything that is said; rather, they call out and punctuate key themes. Skilled meeting

Sidebar A1-1. Meeting Tactics

The Test and Metrology Services Department of the Collins Commercial Avionics Division of Rockwell International in Cedar Rapids, Iowa, operates as a self-directed team. The key to their effective meeting management is amazingly cheap: cards. The card system came about because even with an agenda, lengthy weekly meetings among its 20 members exceeded the allotted time. In the card system, two 8×10 inch cards are passed out to each member at the beginning of the meeting. Each side is color-coded and inscribed with words: red and green on one card; white and yellow on the other. When an issue is brought before the team, all members display the red "needs discussion" card. If someone wasn't there to talk about the issue, she shows a white "need to talk" card to the facilitator, who recognizes the cardholder. As the discussion progresses, team members change their cards to green "ready to vote" cards. The facilitator terminates the discussion only when no more red "needs discussion" cards are displayed. When voting, team members can agree (green card), be neutral (white card), support but not like it (yellow card), or disagree (red card). The team members can hold up a yellow ("to task team") card that indicates more information is required. Lab manager George Fluharty states that the card system has had a dramatic impact on reducing the length of meeting time and providing team members with a voice. Another advantage to the card system is that everyone votes; no issue is dropped until the facilitator views each member's card. The cards have gone a long way to reduce side discussions and disruptive noise during meetings. However, like any system, there are disadvantages to the card system: Team members may form opinions quickly and show their votes before discussion is completed; the system also lends itself to subtle, nonverbal communication, such as when a member lays her cards on the table to signal her opinion. To stop that from happening, team members suggested that cards remain in laps until action is requested and side discussions can be conducted only with cards (Pettit, 1997).

managers do not verbally paraphrase members' ideas; rather, they record them visually. Skilled meeting managers do not try to induce dominant members to yield the floor by saying, "keep it short" or "we need to hear from everyone"; rather, they use brainwriting at select times. They do not organize the meeting by who is there; rather, by what is to be done (see Sidebar A1-2).

Sidebar A1-2. Announcements, Decisions, and Discussion

Most meetings are organized on the basis of who is there. Reports flow out person by person, department by department, often beginning with the most prestigious person and proceeding down. However, this type of round-robin format is inefficient. It is better to organize meetings by the content. Tropman, author of *Making Meetings Work* (1996), suggests that announcements should come first, then decisions, and finally discussion time, in that order.

TABLE A1-1   4P Meeting Management Model

Key Skill	*Questions to Ask*
Purpose • A complex problem needs to be resolved using the expertise of several people. • Team members' commitment to a decision or to each other needs to be enhanced. • Information needs to be shared simultaneously among several key people.	• What is the purpose of the meeting? • Is the purpose clear to participants? • Is a meeting the most appropriate means of accomplishing the goal? • Are key people available to attend the meeting? • Is the cost of the meeting in proportion to what will be accomplished?
Participants • The size of the team should be compatible with the task. • A balance between people with strong task orientations and those with strong interpersonal skills is desirable.	• Is the size of the meeting appropriate given the problem of coordination costs? • What diversity of skills and backgrounds is important to have in the meeting?
Plan • Provide for adequate physical space, etc. • Establish priorities by sequencing agenda items and allotting time limits to each item. • Prepare and distribute the agenda before or at the beginning of the meeting. • Organize the agenda by content, not by who is there. Use a three-step approach: announcements, decisions, discussion (Tropman, 1996). • Think about your visual aids: Visual aids are 43% more persuasive than no visuals (Armour, 1997). • Choose the most appropriate decision-making structure (e.g., brainstorming, normal group technique).	• Has an agenda been created? • Has the agenda for the meeting been distributed to members prior to the meeting? • Have members been forewarned if they will be asked to report? • Has the physical arrangement been considered (e.g., whiteboards, overheads, flipcharts)? • Has key information been put into proper information displays? • Has a note taker been assigned?
Process • At the beginning, restate the overall purpose of the meeting and review the agenda and time constraints. • Make note of the ground rules, such as how decisions will be made (e.g., raised hands, secret ballot). • Use techniques to ensure equal participation from members. • Conclude the meeting by summarizing key decisions, reviewing assignments, and determining objectives for the next meeting.	• If this is the first meeting of a team, has an icebreaker been included? • Does the icebreaker get people involved in a behavioral or emotional way (at a minimum, a handshake or high-five)? • Have the ground rules been determined and shared with members in advance of the meeting?

Sources: Adapted from Whetton, D.A., & Cameron, K.S. 1991. *Developing Management Skills* (2nd ed.). Harper-Collins; Armour, S. 1997, December 8. "Business' Black Hole." *USA Today,* p. 1A.

DEALING WITH PROBLEM PEOPLE IN MEETINGS

There is no surefire way to deal with "problem people." As a general principle, having structure helps. It can also be helpful to give group members a list of desirable and undesirable role descriptions prior to the meeting. Table A1-2 is a list of typical group members. Although stated in jest, each description has a ring of truth in it.

TABLE AI-2   Typical Group Members

Thelma Talk-a-Lot	("I just have to say this")
Sam Stall	("Let's not rush into this")
Don Domineering	(talks 75% of the time about his own ideas)
Nick Negative	(explains that someone has to be the devil's advocate)
Ted Theorizer	("It's really complex")
Nancy Nuts-'n'-Bolts	(always comes up with an impossible example to deal with)
Jim Just-a-Little-Bit-More-Information-on-This-Topic-Please	("I don't feel we should decide until we know more")
Herman Hypochondriacal	(is convinced that any path makes vulnerabilities increase)
Yolanda You're-Not-Going-to-Believe-What-Happened-to-Me	(uses immediate, personal events rather than overarching views to analyze problems)

Source: Tropman, J.E., & Morningstar, G. 1989. *Entrepreneurial Systems for the 1990s: Their Creation, Structure, and Management.* New York: Quorum Books. Reproduced with permission of Greenwood Publishing Group, Inc., Westport, CT.

ADVICE FOR MEETING ATTENDEES

The burden of effective meeting management does not rest solely on the shoulders of the leader. Group members need to engage in the following proactive strategies (Whetton & Cameron, 1991):

- **Determine if you need to attend the meeting.** Don't attend merely because you have been invited. If you have doubts about whether the meeting's agenda applies to you, discuss with the leader why he or she feels your presence is important.
- **Prepare.** Acquaint yourself with the agenda, and prepare any reports or information that will facilitate others' understanding of the issues. Come prepared with questions that will help you understand the issues.
- **Be on time.** Stragglers not only waste the time of other participants by delaying the meeting or by requiring summaries of what has happened, but they also hinder effective team building and hurt morale.
- **Ask for clarification on points that are unclear or ambiguous.** Most of the time, you will find that others in the room have the same question but are too timid to speak out.

- **When giving information, be precise and to the point.** Don't bore everyone with anecdotes and details that add little to your point.
- **Listen.** Keep eye contact with whoever is speaking, and try to ascertain the underlying ideas behind the comments. Be sensitive to the effect of your nonverbal behavior on speakers, such as slouching, doodling, or reading.
- **Be supportive of other group members.** Acknowledge and build on the comments of others (e.g., "As Jane was saying . . .").
- **Ensure equitable participation.** Take the lead in involving others so that everyone's talents are used. This is especially important if you know that some participants' points of view are not being included in the discussion. This can be accomplished by encouraging those who rarely participate (e.g., "Jim, your unit worked on something like this last year. What was your experience like?").
- **Make disagreements principle-based.** If it is necessary to disagree with, or challenge, the comments of others, follow the guidelines for collaborative conflict management (e.g., base your comments on commonly held princi-

ples or values; for example: "That's an interesting idea, Bill, but how does it square with the president's emphasis on cost-cutting?").

- **Act and react in a way that will enhance the group performance.** In other words, leave your personal agendas at the door and work toward the goals of the group.

COMMON MEETING DISEASES AND FALLACIES

It is almost impossible to predict where most meetings will go awry. The following is a description of the most common meeting diseases and some ideas on how to combat them.

The Overcommitment Phenomenon

Symptoms: Many people agree to perform tasks and accomplish goals that they cannot possibly do in the time allowed. In some cases, this problem is attributable to the pressures placed on managers to accomplish goals and say "yes." However, in many more instances, the overcommitment problem stems from a fundamental inability to estimate how long it will take to accomplish a task. In addition, people tend to make commitments in advance because their confidence in their ability to finish is higher when they are further away from the task (Gilovich, Kerr, & Medvec, 1993). Most people make subjective mental estimates of how long it will take to accomplish a task, such as writing a report, collecting information, or interviewing a recruit, by imagining the scenario and then estimating a time line based upon the running of the scenario. However, individuals' mental simulations fail to take into account the process losses that will inevitably thwart their efforts. For example, when they expect to spend 2 weeks writing a report, they fail to anticipate that their printer will break

down and that they will have to spend a day off-site. Consequently, most managers are consistently behind schedule.

In many cases, managers and executives are asked to commit themselves to perform tasks and events at some time in the distant future. For example, a team leader might be asked to enroll in a 3-day course next year, travel abroad to interview other team members, or attend a conference. Many people agree to these future invitations, but when the time approaches, regret that they have to do what they promised (Loewenstein & Prelic, 1991). People fail to adequately weigh the importance of their future opportunities and time constraints, so they commit to things in the future that they would most likely decline to do in the present.

Treatment: The easiest way to deal with the overcommitment problem is to simply double (or triple) the amount of time projected to accomplish a task. For example, publishers typically add 6 months to an author's projected completion time for a manuscript. Another way of combating the bias is to break the task down into its different elements and then estimate the time necessary to complete each part—people are more accurate at estimating the time necessary to accomplish smaller tasks. When someone asks you to do something, such as write a report, travel, or make a presentation, imagine that you are being asked to do this the next week, or even the next day. If you are disinclined, then it may not be a good idea to take it on.

Calls for More Information

Symptoms: Often, teams are uncomfortable making decisions. This is particularly true when the decision matter is complex and value-laden. Under such conditions, teams will do nearly anything to avoid making decisions. The manager faces an avoidance-avoidance conflict: Making a decision is difficult, but not making a decision makes one appear indecisive. Managers often respond to this avoidance-avoidance conflict by requesting more information. In theory, the amount of information relevant to any decision situation is boundless; however, at some point, decisions must be made. One way of avoiding decision making, but not appearing to be indecisive, is to request additional information. This makes people feel as though they are making progress, but actually, the additional information may not be diagnostic or useful. It is merely gathered so that the team members can better cognitively justify their decision. Decision avoidance is a particular concern when teams make negative decisions, such as downsizing.

Consider, for example, the following scenario (Savage, 1954):

> A businessman contemplates buying a certain piece of property. He considers the outcome of the next presidential election relevant to the attractiveness of the purchase. So, to clarify the matter for himself, he asks whether he would buy if he knew that the Republican candidate were going to win, and decides that he would do so. Similarly, he considers whether he would buy if he knew that the Democratic candidate were going to win, and again, finds that he would do so. Seeing that he would buy in either event, he decides that he should buy, even though he does not know which event obtains. (p. 21)

The preceding rationale is known as the **sure-thing principle** (Savage, 1954). It would seem irrational, or somewhat silly, if the businessperson in this case were to delay purchase until after the election, or to pay money to find out the election results ahead of time. Yet in organizations, decision makers often pursue noninstrumental information—information that appears relevant, but if available, would have no impact on choice. The problem does not end there: Once they pursue such information, people then use it to make their decision. Consequently, the pursuit of information that would have had no impact on choice leads people to make choices they otherwise would not have made (Bastardi & Shafir, 1998).

Treatment: The decision trap of calling for more information can best be dealt with by keeping a clear log that details the history of the decision. For example, a team member might say something like, "You know, this issue was first brought up two years ago, and it was agreed that a competitive analysis was necessary. This competitive analysis was performed and I brought you the results the following spring. Then, it was suggested that a task force be formed. We did this and came to some conclusions in a report circulated last fall. We agreed at that time that we would make a decision at this meeting. I realize that more information is always better, but I am beginning to wonder whether the costs of continuing to search for information are a way of avoiding a decision . . ." This strategy is especially important in teams where membership changes (and, hence, organizational memory is lost) and in teams that must make tough decisions (e.g., employment terminations).

Failed Memory and Reinventing the Wheel

Symptoms: Many teams face decisions that they make on a repeated basis. For example, merit review decisions, hiring decisions, admission decisions, funding decisions, and so on, are all decisions that must be made repeatedly. However, teams often exhibit a memory loss of sorts, in terms of how they made previous decisions. As a result, they spend precious time arguing with one another as to how they made the decision in the past, and memories prove to be fallible. The failed memory problem is most likely to afflict teams that have not created a sufficient organizational memory. The failed memory problem also haunts teams that experience turnover. Under these situations, team members who take notes, or have some kind of record, have an enormous advantage.

Treatment: The key here is to make the process explicit and then to have it recorded in some fashion so that it can be later retrieved. The problem is that most people trust their memories at the time they are discussing the issue or making the decision; consequently, they don't bother to write down what they believe will be burned into their memory.

Appendix 2

Special Tips for Consultants and Facilitators

One of the most challenging consulting tasks is to facilitate a meeting for a company. Many companies think this is easy work to do and, consequently, expect miracles to happen. When the meeting does not accomplish what was hoped for, it is easy to blame the consultant or facilitator. There is also an information asymmetry: The consultant/facilitator is not privy to key norms and personnel dynamics. Many companies expect consultants to be able to immediately dissect the motives of each member. Many mistakes are made prior to the beginning of the meeting. Often, teams that need outside facilitators are beseiged by thorny political and personnel issues. Even the issue of who hires the consultant can be a political one. Others may see the consultant as a hired gun.

What can an outside facilitator do to make the most out of meetings?

DO YOUR HOMEWORK

Find out as much as you can about the group, the company, and the individual members before the meeting. Ideally, interview the members of the group individually, either by phone, in person, or via a short questionnaire to determine their views of the issues to be addressed in the meeting and their major concerns about the ability of the meeting to accomplish these objectives. In

many cases, collecting this kind of information is not possible, is expensive to do, or takes too much time.

ORGANIZE THE PHYSICAL ENVIRONMENT

Your key materials for the meeting should include: A room large enough for people to sit comfortably, movable chairs, U-shaped seating, a pad of paper or notecards for each member and a pencil or pen, two or three flipcharts, and a whiteboard or a chalkboard. It is useful to also have an overhead projector. If you don't know the group ask for name badges or nameplates that are custom-printed. Usually, it is impossible to read handwriting on nametags unless you are standing only 2 feet away, and you will probably be about 15 to 20 feet away.

EXPLAIN WHO YOU ARE AND WHY YOU ARE THERE

You should begin the meeting by stating why you are there. You will be viewed as an outsider, or interloper, to the group. This creates tension. People will often feel defensive, paranoid, and suspicious of what is to come. You should immediately state that you are there to facilitate the process and to help the group make the best use of their time, and that you do not have a particular stake in the substantive issues. Above all, don't assume that the reasons for hiring a meeting facilitator have been accurately communicated to the group. Even if a memo was sent out, it may not have been read. Some people may feel strongly opposed to an outside facilitator. Tell the group who you are, but don't try to impress them. The objective is to give them confidence that you are qualified to do this job. Often, the group will feel somewhat defensive that they need to hire someone to manage themselves.

FIND OUT WHO THE GROUP IS

This is extremely tricky. The group members, in most cases, will know one another intimately, but you will not know them. Before the meeting, request information, such as biographies of the group members.

If the group members do not know one another well, it is useful for everyone to introduce themselves. If the group members do know one another well, having members talk about themselves is boring for other people. In this case, a useful technique is the **next-in-line strategy**, in which members introduce others in the group. For example, each person introduces the person to their left. This is more interesting for group members because they hear, perhaps for the first time, how they are viewed by others. This also serves as an icebreaker, because members are often touched at the admiration given to them by others. (Often, people sit by others whom they like, so having someone introduce the person sitting next to them ensures a favorable introduction.)

USE GROUND RULES

It is imperative to let the group know that you will be using and enforcing meeting ground rules. You may want to acknowledge that the ground rules may seem somewhat silly or reminiscent of their school days, but that companies that use these ground rules are more effective. It is usually a good idea to have a typed-up list of ground rules to pass around and briefly walk through with members. An example list of ground rules is presented in Table A2-1. You may not want to use all of these rules, but they give you a starting point. If there is time, it is good to ask members to add to this list.

The most difficult challenge facing the consultant is enforcing the ground rules. They will get broken and the temptation will be to excuse or ignore rule-breaking behavior. However, it is imperative to demonstrate that you will enforce these ground rules.

CREATE AN AGENDA

You should ideally have an agenda that is distributed to members in advance of the meeting. Expect to be challenged on the agenda either directly (e.g., "If you don't mind, I want to bring up x, y, and z") or indirectly (e.g., "Don't you think we should talk about x, y, and z before we do this?"). The best way of handling this is to create a postdiscussion

TABLE A2-1 Meeting Ground Rules

- Everyone stays for duration of meeting
- Form an agenda and stick to it
- Form a time line and stick to it
- No "new business"
- No semantic/philosophical discussions
- No "let's call for more information" (decision avoidance)
- No evaluation of ideas until evaluation period
- No more reports

agenda and explain that there may be time for these issues after the scheduled meeting.

CLOSING THE MEETING

It is important to bring the meeting to a close in a way that gives the members a sense of what has been accomplished and decided, what steps need to be taken before the next meeting, and what the goal of the next meeting will be (which should be scheduled with everyone present). Each one of the agenda items should be recapped, and homework or follow-up should be assigned to individual members. A summary of decision and action items should be distributed as soon as possible to the group.

SOLICIT FEEDBACK FOR YOURSELF AND THE GROUP

This step is important, especially if you have not worked with the group in the past. Distribute a short questionnaire to each participant that asks the following three questions: (1) What in this meeting went well and should be kept? (2) What in this meeting did not go so well and should be eliminated? (3) What in this meeting did not happen and should be included? (Tropman, 1996). If you will be working with the group again, you should aggregate the list of responses and circulate it among group members.

Appendix 3

A Guide for Creating Effective Study Groups

Most students enrolled in M.B.A. programs must work in groups to complete important projects and requirements en route to obtaining their degree. Some students work with the same group throughout their program; other students work with several different groups each semester. This is a guide for helping these groups to be as maximally effective as possible.

VERY EARLY ON

In the beginning, when the group is first forming, it is helpful to do some kind of structured exercise that moves beyond usual chit-chat. We suggest the "Team Management Skills Inventory" (exercise by Thompson, 1998)[1].

SOMETIME DURING THE FIRST WEEK OR TWO

There are a host of tensions and dilemmas that can threaten the effectiveness of any study group. We suggest the team meet and complete a "Team Contract" (exercise by Thompson, 1998).

---

[1]The exercises cited in this appendix are written for the Kellogg Teams and Groups Center (KTAG) and are available through the Dispute Resolution Research Center (DRRC), Kellogg Graduate School of Management, Northwestern University, 2001 Sheridan Road, Evanston, Illinois 60208-2011. Phone: (847) 491-8068; e-mail: drrc@kellogg.nwu.edu.

We also suggest that groups that will work together for long periods of time discuss the following issues in the first week or two:

Team Goals

- **Learning:** "Are we here to learn and to help others learn or are we here to get a good grade?" There is not a right answer to this question, but differing goals in the group can hurt later performance.
- **Standards:** "Is perfectionism more important than being on time, or vice versa?"
- **Performance:** "Are we a high-pass (dean's list) group or a pass (survival) group?"

Thought Questions

- What happens if the project leader has lower standards than some other members about writing a paper or report?
- What happens if one group member is not very skilled at some topic area (i.e., how do you utilize that member's input on group projects and incorporate ideas that do not appear to be adding value)?

Person-Task Mapping

- Is it best to capitalize on the existing strengths of team members or to play to people's weaknesses?
- Suppose your team has a quantitative guru in it. Do you want to assign the "quant jock" to do all the math and econometrics problems, or use this as an opportunity to let other team members learn?

Additional Questions

- **Member skills:** Do you want to use your study group meeting time to bring all group members up to speed or should those who need help get it on their own time?
- **Person-task focus:** Are people the group's first priority or is working the first priority?
- **Structure:** Should the team meeting be structured (e.g., agenda, timekeeper, assigned roles) or should it be free-form?
- **Interloper:** Are other people (outside the group) allowed to attend group meetings and have access to group notes, outlines, homework, and so on, or is group work considered confidential?
- **Communication standards:** Are group members expected to adapt to the most advanced methods of communication, or does group work happen at the lowest common denominator?
- **Project leader pacing:** There would seem to be an advantage for group members who volunteer early on for group projects because commitments and pressures build up later in the semester; how will the group meeting process adapt to increasing workloads?

AFTER THE GROUP IS WELL UNDER WAY

After the group is well under way, it is a good idea to take stock of how the group is working together. We suggest the "Group Assessment Inventory," ideally administered by a professor or another person acquainted with the study group (exercise by Thompson, Gruenfeld, Rothbard, & Naquin, 1999).

Another useful idea is to do some version of a peer-feedback performance review, wherein individuals receive confidential feedback and ratings about how they are viewed by other team members. This can often be completely computerized (see appendix 4).

ON A REGULAR BASIS

It is important that study groups revisit the team contract. Are the expectations being met? What issues and topics should be talked about that are not currently in the contract? What issues are in the contract that do not seem relevant?

SPECIAL TIPS FOR LONG-TERM STUDY GROUPS

Consider the actual advice from M.B.A. students who were enrolled in an intensive 2-year program. Their study groups were assigned to them and maintained throughout the 2-year program. During the time they worked together, members were asked for their input on what did and did not work in their study groups in regard to maximizing learning and using time effectively. Box A3-1 summarizes the students' responses.

Advice for Long-Term Study Groups

- An agenda should be distributed before each group meeting date so everyone can prepare properly. Decide upon the agenda for the next meeting before adjourning the current meeting.

- Define who is expected to do what for each project.

- A written outline or "straw man" is needed to focus the group discussion on any particular project. Several alternatives should be evaluated during the outline stage before selecting which alternative will be taken for any project.

- Each major group project has a project leader responsible for doing most of the writing (in some cases, all of the writing). Other group members provide input early in the project and after a draft has been written. Assignments can be done in parallel by using this method, which helps to meet deadlines.

- Some groups summarize class readings for the project leader during the weeks that they are busy completing the project.

- The workload is not divided equally on every project. Over a 2-year period everyone will get the chance to contribute.

- Rotate responsibilities with each module or semester. For example, one person in the group may be the agenda captain for an entire module. The agenda captain organizes the meeting agendas and runs the meetings for that entire module. Rotating responsibilities every week wastes time deciding who does what.

- Try to meet on the same day and time each week. This makes it easier to plan travel schedules in advance.

- At the end of each major assignment, review the effectiveness of the process used to fulfill requirements. Adjust the process to improve effectiveness.

- Improve communication within the group by using e-mail and standardized software.

- Focus on the goals of the meeting first, then socialize.

- Maintain a sense of humor!

Source: Taken from compiled lists from the Executive Masters Program, Kellogg School of Management, Northwestern University, Evanston, Illinois. Lists compiled by K. Murnighan (1998) and R. Weeks (1996).

Appendix 4

Example Items from Peer Evaluations and 360-Degree Performance Evaluations

Chapter 3 went into detail about the purpose and implementation of 360-degree evaluations. Some people, however, may be unfamiliar with what a typical 360-degree evaluation might look like. The fact is, there are no standards. In this appendix, we present examples of two 360-degree evaluation tools. The first one is a peer evaluation system; it is brief and is designed for students enrolled in a full-time M.B.A. program. The second one is much more extensive and designed to provide senior managers with confidential feedback about their leadership abilities and potential.

PETE: PERSONAL EFFECTIVENESS IN TEAM ENVIRONMENTS

Personal Effectiveness in Team Environments (PETE) is a Web-based peer evaluation system that enables students to give each other anonymous feedback on their team skills. The method is simple and completely automated. At the end of each academic quarter, students sign on to a Web page and provide anonymous feedback to their teammates by rating each other on 10 key criteria related to improving team-based outcomes (defined by Kellogg's Organization Behavior Department). The computer then compiles mean and standard deviation scores for each student. After all responses are compiled, students automatically receive a private e-mail with their personal scores from each of their teams. To enable them to track their progress in building their team skills over time, students also receive their scores from prior quarters.

The system allows students to get direct and timely feedback on their team skills. They can track their skill development in particular areas (e.g., leadership) over time and across different teams and projects to focus on skill development. What's more, students learn how to use peer-based reviews. The automated process means that the information is collected and disseminated efficiently.

Figure A4-1 illustrates how students using the PETE Web site can select the specific team and teammates they want to evaluate; Figure A4-2 illustrates a sample matrix for evaluating a teammate and lists all 10 items on the PETE questionnaire; and Figure A4-3 illustrates a sample of an output feedback that a student might receive from the PETE system.

Note: The values for this demonstration have been selected below and are reflected in subsequent figures.

Please select the course for the team you will be evaluating, and complete the related information:

Course/Section: | ACCT D30 Section 62 Tue–Fri 9:00–10:40 | ▼ |

Number of Teammates (**Do not count yourself**) | 4 | ▼ |

Hours/week of Team Meeting (avg.) | 3 | ▼ |

Team Selection Method | Assigned | ▼ |

Did you use a team consultant?   ○ Yes   ⊙ No

Please select the names of your teammates:

Have you been this person's teammate before?

		Yes	No
Teammate 1:	Joe Smith ▼	○	⊙
Teammate 2:	Jan Smith ▼	○	⊙
Teammate 3:	John Doe ▼	○	⊙
Teammate 4:	Jane Doe ▼	○	⊙

FIGURE A4-1   Selecting a Team to Evaluate Using PETE

Source: Adapted from PETE Web site at *http://faculty-web.at.nwu.edu/kellogg/pete/allenctr.html*

INDUSTRIAL EXAMPLE OF 360-DEGREE EVALUATIONS

The questionnaire in Table A4-1 from RHR Europe Company is designed to assess leadership behavior among senior employees. These behaviors encompass critical success factors in the company. The leaders choose at least nine people (one or two line managers; four or five peers; four or five subordinates) to complete the questionnaire, which is processed confidentially.

Each teammate receives feedback in the matrix below (one matrix per question; one question per Web site frame):

Teammate	Strongly Disagree 1	2	3	4	Neutral 5	6	7	8	9	Strongly Agree 10
Jane Doe	○	○	○	○	○	○	○	○	○	○
John Doe	○	○	○	○	○	○	○	○	○	○
Jan Smith	○	○	○	○	○	○	○	○	○	○
Joe Smith	○	○	○	○	○	○	○	○	○	○

Questions:

1. This teammate completed tasks on time and to specification.
2. This teammate encouraged innovation among teammates.
3. This teammate gave timely and honest feedback.
4. This teammate nondefensively accepted suggestions and critical comments.
5. This teammate shared essential information with teammates.
6. This teammate avoided destructive and divisive tactics, such as put-downs or playing games.
7. This teammate put self on the line to deal with difficult issues.
8. This teammate challenges the status quo when necessary.
9. This teammate communicates ideas efficiently.
10. This teammate balanced talking/telling with listening/hearing.

FIGURE A4-2   PETE Questionnaire Items and Rating System

Source: Adapted from PETE Web site at *http://faculty-web.at.nwu.edu/kellogg/pete/allenctr.html*

The **Mean** and *Standard Deviaiton* of the evaluations you received for each class are listed below.

The aggregate statistics combine all of the peer evaluations you reveived for all your classes last term, including classes that lacked sufficient respondents to report individually; however, stats for sections in which you did not complete a PETE evaluation are not included and are omitted in the aggretate stats.

John Doe

Scale: 1-strongly disagree 10-strongly agree *Fall 1998–1999*	Completed timely and accurate work	Encouraged innovation	Focused on goal	Took suggestions and criticism	Respectful of individuals	Created atmosphere of trust	Challenged majority opinion	Changed own opinion as needed	Communicated ideas efficiently	Balanced talking and listening
Accounting D30	9.3 *0.6*	7.7 *2.3*	9.3 *0.6*	9.7 *0.6*	9.7 *0.6*	9.7 *0.6*	9.3 *0.6*	9.3 *0.6*	9.7 *0.6*	10 *0*
Economics D30	*Sorry, Since you did not complete a PETE evaluation for this section, you are unable to receive scores for this section.*									
Management & Strategy D30	9 *1.7*	8.7 *2.3*	9 *1.7*	8.7 *2.3*	9 *1.7*	9.3 *1.2*	9 *1.7*	9.3 *1.2*	9 *1*	9.3 *1.2*
Marketing D30	*Fewer than three responses; insufficient number to report for this section.*									
Org. Behavior D30	9 *1.7*	8.3 *2.1*	8.7 *2.3*	8.7 *2.3*	9.3 *1.2*	9.3 *1.2*	9 *1.7*	9.3 *1.2*	9.3 *1.2*	9.3 *1.2*
Aggregate	9.1 *1.3*	8.2 *2*	9 *1.5*	9 *1.7*	9.3 *1.1*	9.4 *0.9*	9.1 *1.3*	9.3 *0.9*	9.3 *0.9*	9.6 *0.9*

FIGURE A4-3   Sample PETE Output Feedback Sheet

Note: The values for this demonstration do not reflect any student's actual scores.
Source: Adapted from PETE Web site at *http://faculty-web.at.nwu.edu/kellogg/pete/allenctr.html*

TABLE A4-1   360-Degree Leadership

Key Leadership Quality	Questions
Provide Vision: "Developing vision and demonstrating commitment to the company's strategies, and inspiring a sense of direction"	• Establishes initiatives that promote a global mindset in the organization • Creates a compelling scenario of the future involvement with the team and inspires buy-in • Identifies and applies models and processes that will stimulate behaviors in support of the company's vision • Puts the vision in practice by adopting desired behaviors and corresponding values • Actively gains information concerning markets and environment factors that can have an impact on strategies • Ensures that team and individual objectives support the company's vision • Creates a sense of team purpose according to vision and strategies • Shares insights and facilitates understanding and open communication around vision • Is able to imagine scenarios that are in discontinuity with the existing processes or products
Show Entrepreneurship: "Thinking ahead, seizing opportunities to develop new markets, products, or services and taking calculated risks to achieve growth"	• Demonstrates passion and energy to move forward • Invents strategies using various sources of data and individual experiences • Encourages proactive behaviors resulting in business growth • Takes calculated risks, then decides • Supports and rewards self-starting behaviors of collaborators • Seeks solutions beyond current practices • Demonstrates an action-oriented attitude • Explores and optimizes the use of resources and expertise available within the team • Communicates information and personal perceptions on new business opportunities for the company
Influence and Convince: "Persuading others to share a point of view, to adopt a specific position, or to take a course of action"	• Determines appropriate strategies to influence people • Builds networks and uses the authority or power of others to convince • Develops propositions tailored to the interest of the different parties involved • Builds a climate of trust • Expresses perspective with courage and integrity • Listens to others' viewpoints or objections and tests their ideas • Seeks to convince by underlining potential benefits of proposed solutions • Negotiates proposals to determine common course of action • Gains team adherence through effective communication

Note: All questions answered on 4-point scale: 1 = almost never; 2 = sometimes; 3 = usually; 4 = almost always; CS = can't say

Source: 360 Degree Leadership. RHR International Co., ©1998. Reprinted with permission from RHR International Co., Wood Dale, IL.

TABLE A4-1   360-Degree Leadership

Key Leadership Quality	Questions
Achieve Results: "Directing the activity of others by setting challenging goals for personal and team accomplishment and by controlling their achievements"	• Sets the example by showing high performance • Sets challenging goals that require a "step change" • Develops strategies and facilitates actions to overcome barriers • Initiates corrective actions to address performance problems • Supports and works alongside others to help improve performance and results • Introduces and applies new methods within the company • Communicates performance expectations to others • Creates a performance-oriented spirit within the team • Provides regular feedback on achieved performance • Puts in place performance measurement tools
Focus on Customer: "Managing proactively the various customer demands while maintaining a consistent level of effectiveness"	• Demonstrates a "customer first" attitude and meets with customers regularly • Is involved in the customer's decision-making process • Identifies customer needs and communicates relevant customer-related information • Acts as an advocate by influencing the company on the customer's behalf • Initiates actions that add value to the customer • Ensures team priorities and cooperation are in line with customer service requirements • Asks customers for feedback on service quality • Ensures that performance matches the customer's needs • Keeps close to customers' business evaluations • Is responsive to customer complaints and keeps word
Enhance Cooperation and Adaptation: "Managing people and teams across businesses and cultures"	• Creates an environment that fosters and rewards cooperation among diverse work teams • Identifies interdependencies and understands the dynamics of bringing different cultures together • Has gained credibility in managing outside home country • Challenges self and others to consider issues from a wider and more global perspective • Is sensitive and adaptable to other cultures • Understands the challenges and opportunities of doing business globally • Shares best practices, solutions, and a wide array of management processes across businesses • Explores diverse methods of learning and acting • Encourages relationships between people to enhance trust and communication across distances and differences

Key Leadership Quality	Questions
Empower: "Allocating decision-making authority and creating sense of ownership of the job, missions, or project assignments"	• Sets the example in creating a collaborative team spirit to stimulate initiative • Facilitates the free expression of ideas by showing tolerance such that others are willing to act • Approves and facilitates decision-making among collaborators and is supportive in times of crisis • Exposes staff to situations or challenges outside their area of responsibility • Gives credit to others for what they have accomplished • Builds trust and openness with others • Recognizes creativity in others and allows them to experiment • Shows the willingness to delegate authority to the lowest possible level • Communicates standards or criteria by which team members can measure their progress
Manage Change: "Fostering innovation and questioning the existing while maintaining constant effectiveness"	• Addresses the needs for change by anticipating and acting upon trends affecting markets and customers • Determines and explains implications of change on the various components of the organization • Creates an environment that encourages people through continuous improvement processes • Recognizes own mistakes and uses these as a learning opportunity • Thinks outside the box and does not hesitate to change habits • Creates a sense of urgency in others to achieve change • Questions self or solicits feedback to adapt to change requirements, and encourages others to do the same • Maintains operational effectiveness while implementing agreed changes • Ensures persistent follow-up of change strategies • Allows new ideas to emerge and ensures their purposeful development through team effort
Develop Talents: "Creating a learning and continuous improvement climate with an appropriate level of coaching and organizational support"	• Links business and individual development needs • Identifies potentials and develops them • Identifies areas of need and opportunities for self-development • Actively deploys feedback, guidance, and coaching to support people development • Creates opportunities for others to practice new behaviors and to develop skills for current and future role • Measures progress and evaluates benefits of talent development • Provides guidance, practical instructions, and directions in training activities • Recognizes the achievements and development progress of others • Takes charge of developing effective teams • Supports the development of collaborators even for responsibilities outside the entity

References

ABA Banking Journal 1985, July. "Hutton Aftermath: A Violation of Business Ethics or Downright Fraud?" Computers and Operations section, p. 30.

Abel, M. J. 1990. "Experiences in an Exploratory Distributed Organization." In J. Galegher, R. E. Kraut, & C. Egido (Eds.), *Intellectual Teamwork: Social and Technological Foundations of Cooperative Work* (pp. 489–510). Mahwah, NJ: Lawrence Erlbaum Associates.

Adams, S. 1965. "Inequity in Social Exchange." In L. Berkowitz (Ed.), *Advances in Experimental Social Psychology* (Vol. 2, pp. 267–299). New York: Academic Press.

Alderfer, C. P. 1976. "Boundary Relations and Organizational Diagnosis." In M. Meltzer & F. Wickert (Eds.), *Humanizing Organizational Behavior* (pp. 142–175). Springfield, IL: Charles C. Thomas.

Alderfer, C. P. 1977. "Group and Intergroup Relations." In J. R. Hackman & J. L. Suttle (Eds.), *Improving Life at Work* (pp. 227–296). Palisades, CA: Goodyear.

Allen, T. J. 1977. *Managing the Flow of Technology: Technology Transfer and the Dissemination of Technological Information within the R&D Organization.* Cambridge, MA: MIT Press.

Allen, V. L. 1965. "Situational Factors in Conformity." In L. Berkowitz (Ed.), *Advances in Experimental Social Psychology* (Vol. 2, pp. 267–299). New York: Academic Press.

Allison, S., & Messick, D. 1990. "Social Decision Heuristics and the Use of Shared Resources." *Journal of Behavioral Decision Making, 3,* 195–204.

Allmendinger, J. M., & Hackman, J. R. 1993. *The More, the Better? On the Inclusion of Women in Professional Organizations.* Report No. 5, Cross-National Study of Symphony Orchestras, Harvard University.

Allport, G. W., & Postman, L. 1947. *The Psychology of Rumor.* New York: H. Holt.

Altman, I., & Taylor, D. A. 1973. *Social Penetration: The Development of Interpersonal Relationships.* New York: Holt, Rinehart & Winston.

Amason, A. 1996. "Distinguishing the Effects of Functional and Dysfunctional Conflict on Strategic Decision Making: Resolving a Paradox for Top Management Teams." *Academy of Management Journal, 39*(1), 123–148.

Ancona, D. G. 1987. "Groups in Organizations: Extending Laboratory Models." In C. Hendrick (Ed.), *Annual Review of Personality and Social Psychology: Group and Intergroup Processes* (pp. 207–231). Beverly Hills, CA: Sage.

Ancona, D. G. 1990. "Outward Bound: Strategies for Team Survival in an Organization." *Academy of Management Journal, 33*(2), 334–365.

Ancona, D. G. 1993. "The Classics and the Contemporary: A New Blend of Small Group Theory." In J. K. Murnighan (Ed.), *Social Psychology in Organizations: Advances in Theory and Research.* Upper Saddle River, NJ: Prentice Hall.

Ancona, D. G., & Caldwell, D. F. 1987. "Management Issues Facing New-Product Teams in High Technology Companies." In D. Lewin, D. Lipsky, & D. Sokel (Eds.), *Advances in Industrial and Labor Relations* (Vol. 4, pp. 199–221). Greenwich, CT: JAI Press.

Ancona, D. G., & Caldwell, D. F. 1988. "Beyond Task and Maintenance: Defining External Functions in Groups." *Groups and Organizational Studies, 13,* 468–494.

Ancona, D. G., & Caldwell, D. F. 1991. *Bridging the Boundary: External Process and Performance in Organizational Teams.* Working paper 3305-91-BPS, Sloan School of Management, Cambridge, MA.

Ancona, D. G., & Caldwell, D. F. 1992. "Demography and Design: Predictors of New Product Team Performance." *Organization Science 3*(3), 321–341.

Ancona, D. G., & Nadler, D. A. 1989. "Top Hats and Executive Tales: Designing the Senior Team." *Senior Management Review, 31*(1), 19–28.

Anonymous 1996. "Microsoft Teamwork." *Executive Excellence, 13*(7): 6–7.

Argote, L. 1989. "Agreement about Norms and Work-Unit Effectiveness: Evidence from the Field." *Basic and Applied Social Psychology, 10*(2), 131–140.

Armstrong, D. J., & Cole, P. 1995. "Managing Distances and Differences in Geographically Distributed Work Groups." In S. E. Jackson & M. N. Ruderman (Eds.), *Diversity in Work Teams: Research Paradigms for a Changing Workplace* (pp. 187–215). Washington, DC: American Psychological Association.

Arnold, D. W., & Greenberg, C. I. 1980. "Deviate Rejection within Differentially Manned Groups." *Social Psychology Quarterly, 43*(4), 419–424.

Arrow, K. J. 1963. *Social Choice and Individual Values.* New York: John Wiley & Sons.

Asch, S. E. 1956. "Studies of Independence and Conformity: A Minority of One against a Unanimous Majority." *Psychological Monographs, 70*(9, Whole No. 416).

Asimov, I. 1982. *The Foundation Trilogy.* New York: Ballantine.

Associated Press. 1990, March 20. "Company: Miswiring Caused Satellite Deployment Failure."

Austin, J. T., Villanova, P., & Hindman, H. D. 1996. "Legal Requirements and Technical Guidelines Involved in Implementing Performance Appraisal Systems." In G. Ferris & R. M. Buckley (Eds.), *Human Resources Management: Perspectives, Context, Function, and Outcomes.* (3rd ed., p. 283). Upper Saddle River, NJ: Prentice Hall.

Babcock, L., Loewenstein, G., Issacharoff, S., & Camerer, C. 1995. "Biased Judgments of Fairness in Bargaining." *The American Economic Review, 85*(5), 1337–1343.

Babcock, L., & Olson, C. A. 1992. "The Causes of Impasses in Labor Disputes." *Industrial Relations, 31*(2), 348–360.

Back, K. W. 1951. "Influence through Social Communication." *Journal of Abnormal Social Psychology, 46,* 9–23.

Baldwin, T. T., & Ford, J. K. 1988. "Transfer of Training: A Review and Direction for Future Research." *Personnel Psychology, 41,* 63–105.

Bales, R. F. 1955. *How People Interact in Conferences.* New York: Scientific American.

Bales, T. 1958. "Task Roles and Social Roles in Problem-Solving Groups." In E. E. Maccoby, T. M. Newcomb, & E. I. Hartley (Eds.), *Readings in Social Psychology.* New York: Holt, Rinehart, & Winston.

Banaji, M. R., Hardin, C., & Rothman, A. J. 1993. "Implicit Stereotyping in Person Judgment." *Journal of Personality and Social Psychology, 65,* 272–281.

Barboza, D. 1998, September 20. "Loving a Stock, Not Wisely, but Too Well." *The New York Times,* Section 3, p. 1.

Barchas, P. R., & Fisek, M. H. 1984. "Hierarchical Differentiation in Newly Formed Groups of Rhesus and Humans." In P. R. Barchas (Ed.), *Essays toward a Sociophysiological Perspective* (pp. 23–33). Westport, CT: Greenwood Press.

Bargh, J. A., Chen, M., & Burrows, L. 1996. "Automaticity of Social Behavior: Direct Effects of Trait Construct and Stereotype Activation on Action." *Journal of Personality and Social Psychology, 71*(2), 230–244.

Barker, J. R. 1993. "Tightening the Iron Cage: Concertive Control in Self-Managing Teams." *Administrative Science Quarterly, 38,* 408–437.

Barley, S. R. 1996. "Technicians in the Workplace: Ethnographic Evidence for Bringing Work into Organization Studies." *Administrative Science Quarterly, 41*(3), 404–441.

Barron, R. S., Kerr, N. L., & Miller, N. 1992. *Group Process, Group Decision, Group Action.* Pacific Grove, CA: Brooks/Cole.

Basalla, G. 1988. *The Evolution of Technology.* New York: Cambridge University Press.

Bastardi, A., & Shafir, E. 1998. "On the Pursuit and Misuse of Useless Information." *Journal of Personality and Social Psychology, 75*(1), 19–32.

Baumeister, R. F. 1984. "Choking under Pressure: Self-Consciousness and Paradoxical Effects of Incentives on Skillful Performance." *Journal of Personality and Social Psychology, 46,* 610–620.

Baumeister, R. F., & Steinhilber, A. 1984. "Paradoxical Effects of Supportive Audiences on Performance under Pressure: The Home Field Disadvantage in Sports Championships." *Journal of Personality and Social Psychology, 47*(1), 85–93.

Bazerman, M., Mannix, E., & Thompson, L. 1988. "Groups as Mixed-Motive Negotiations." In E. J. Lawler & B. Markovsky (Eds.), *Advances in Group Processes: A Research Annal* (Vol. 5, pp. 195–216). Greenwich, CT: JAI Press.

Becker, F., Quinn, K. L., Rappaport, A. J., & Sims, W. R. 1994. *Implementing Innovative Workplaces.* NY State College of Human Ecology, Department of Design and Environmental Analysis Cornell University, Ithaca, NY.

Beer, M., Eisenstat, R. A., & Spector, B. 1990. *The Critical Path to Corporate Renewal.* Boston: Harvard Business School Press.

Bennis, W., & Nanus, B. 1985. *Leaders.* New York: Harper & Row.

Berger, J., Rosenholtz, S. J., & Zelditch, M. 1980. "Status Organizing Processes." *Annual Review of Sociology, 6,* 479–508.

Bergstrom, R. Y. 1997, February. "Be Prepared to Be Involved." *Automotive Manufacturing and Production, 109*(2), 66–69.

Bernardin, H. J. & Cascio, W. F. 1988. "Performance Appraisal and the Law." In R. S. Schuler, S.A. Youngblood, & V. L. Huber (Eds.), *Readings in Personnel and Human Resource Management* (3rd ed., p. 239). St. Paul, MN: West Publishing Company.

Bettencourt, B. A., Brewer, M. B., Croak, M. R., & Miller, N. 1992. "Cooperation and the Reduction of Intergroup Bias: The Role of Reward Structure and Social Orientation." *Journal of Experimental Social Psychology, 28*(4), 301–319.

Bettenhausen, K., & Murnighan, J. K. 1985. "The Emergence of Norms in Competitive Decision-Making Groups." *Administrative Science Quarterly, 30,* 350–372.

Blanchard, F. A., & Crosby, F. J. 1989. *Affirmative Action in Perspective.* New York: Springer.

Blinder, A. S. 1990. "Pay, Participation, and Productivity." *Brookings Review, 8*(1), 33–38.

Bloomfield, R., Libby, R., & Nelson, M. W. 1996. "Communication of Confidence as a Determinant of Group Judgment Accuracy." *Organization Behavior and Human Decision Processes, 68*(3), 287–300.

Bobo, L. 1983. "Whites' Opposition to Busing: Symbolic Racism or Realistic Group Conflict?" *Journal of Personality and Social Psychology, 45*(6), 1196–1210.

Bodenhausen, G. V. 1990. "Stereotypes as Judgmental Heuristics: Evidence of Circadian Variations in Discrimination." *Psychological Science, 1*(5), 319–322.

Bodenhausen, G. V., Macrae, C. N., & Milne, A. B. 1998. "Disregarding Social Stereotypes: Implications for Memory, Judgment, and Behavior." In J. M. Golding & C. M. MacLeod (Eds.), *Intentional Forgetting: Interdisciplinary Approaches* (pp. 349–368). Mahwah, NJ: Lawrence Erlbaum & Associates.

Bohrnstedt, G. W., & Fisher, G. A. 1986. "The Effects of Recalled Childhood and Adolescent Relationships Compared to Current Role Performances on Young Adults' Affective Functioning." *Social Psychology Quarterly, 49*(1), 19–32.

Boisjoly, R. M. 1987, December 13–18. *Ethical Decisions—Morton Thiokol and the Space Shuttle Challenger Disaster.* Speech presented at the American Society of Mechanical Engineers, Winter Annual Meeting, Boston, MA.

Bouma, G. D. 1980. "Keeping the Faithful: Patterns of Membership Retention in the Christian Reformed Church." *Sociological Analysis, 41,* 259–264.

Bradford, D. L., & Cohen, A. R. 1984. *Managing for Excellence.* New York: John Wiley & Sons.

Brawley, L. R., Carron, A. V., & Widmeyer, W. N. 1988. "Exploring the Relationship between Cohesion and Group Resistance to Disruption." *Journal of Sport and Exercise Psychology, 10*(2), 199–213.

Brewer, M. 1979. "Ingroup Bias in the Minimal Intergroup Situation: A Cognitive-Motivational Analysis." *Psychological Bulletin, 86,* 307–324.

Brewer, M. B., & Brown, R. J. 1998. "Intergroup Relations." In D. T. Gilbert, S. T. Fiske, & G. Lindzey (Eds.), *The Handbook of Social Psychology* (4th ed., Vol. 2, pp. 554–594). New York: McGraw-Hill.

Brickner, M. A., Harkins, S. G., & Ostrom, T. M. 1986. "Effects of Personal Involvement: Thought-Provoking Implications for Social Loafing." *Journal of Personality and Social Psychology, 51*(4), 763–770.

Brinkerhoff, M. B., & Burke, K. L. 1980. "Disaffiliation: Some Notes on 'Falling from the Faith.' " *Sociological Analysis, 41,* 41–54.

Brown, A. L. 1989. "Analogical Learning and Transfer: What Develops?" In S. Vosniadou & A. Ortony (Eds.), *Similarity and Analogical Reasoning* (pp. 369–412). New York: Cambridge University Press.

Brown, P., & Levinson, S. 1987. *"Politeness: Some Universals in Language Use."* Cambridge, England: Cambridge University Press.

Brown, R. J., Condor, F., Mathew, A., Wade, G., & Williams, J. A. 1986. "Explaining Intergroup Differentiation in an Industrial Organization." *Journal of Occupational Psychology, 59,* 273–286.

Burke, P. J. 1967. "The Development of Task and Social-Emotional Role Differentiation." *Sociometry, 30,* 379–392.

Burt, R. S. 1992. *The Social Structure of Competition.* Cambridge, MA: Harvard University Press.

Burt, R. S. 1999. "Entrepreneurs, Distrust, and Third Parties: A Strategic Look at the Dark Side of Dense Networks." In L. Thompson, J. Levine, & D. Messick (Eds.), *Shared Cognition in Organizations: The Management of Knowledge.* Mahwah, NJ: Lawrence Erlbaum & Associates.

Bushe, G. R. 1984. "Quality Circles in Quality of Work Life Projects: Problems and Prospects for Increasing Employee Participation." *Canadian Journal of Community Mental Health, 3*(2), 101–113.

Byrne, D. 1961. "Interpersonal Attraction and Attitude Similarity." *Journal of Abnormal and Social Psychology, 62,* 713–715.

Camacho, L. M., & Paulus, P. B. 1995. "The Role of Social Anxiousness in Group Brainstorming." *Journal of Personality and Social Psychology, 68,* 1071–1080.

Camerer, C. F., Loewenstein, G., & Weber, M. 1989. "The Curse of Knowledge in Economic Settings: An Experimental Analysis." *Journal of Political Economy, 97,* 1232–1254.

Caminiti, S. 1995. "What Team Leaders Need to Know." *Fortune, 131*(3), 93–100.

Campbell, D. T. 1965. "Ethnocentric and Other Altruistic Motives." In D. Levine (Ed.), *Nebraska Symposium on Motivation.* (pp. 283–311). Lincoln: University of Nebraska Press.

Cannon-Bowers, J. A., Salas, E., & Converse, S. A. 1993. "Shared Mental Models in Expert Team Decision Making." In N. J. Castellan (Ed.), *Individual and Group Decision Making* (pp. 221–246). Mahwah, NJ: Lawrence Erlbaum & Associates.

Cannon-Bowers, J. A., Tannenbaum, S. I., Salas, E., & Converse, S. A. 1991. "Toward an Integration of Training Theory and Technique." *Human Factors, 33*(3), 281–292.

Carnevale, P. J., Pruitt, D., & Seilheimmer, S. 1981. "Looking and Competing: Accountability and Visual Access in Integrative Bargaining." *Journal of Personality and Social Psychology, 40,* 111–120.

Carron, A. V., Widmeyer, W. N., & Brawley, L. R. 1988. "Group Cohesion and Individual Adherence to Physical Activity." *Journal of Sport and Exercise Psychology, 10*(2), 127–138.

Castore, C. H., & Murnighan, J. K. 1978. "Determinants of Support for Group Decisions." *Organizational Behavior and Human Performance, 22,* 75–92.

Caudron, S. 1996. "How Pay Launched Performance." *Personnel Journal* (now known as *Workforce), 75*(9), 70–76. Reprinted with permission.

Chechile, R. 1984. "Logical Foundations for a Fair and Rational Method of Voting." In W. Swapp (Ed.), *Group Decision Making* (pp. 97–114). Beverly Hills, CA: Sage.

Chen, X. P. 1996. "The Group-Based Binding Pledge as a Solution to Public Goods Problems." *Organization Behavior and Human Decision Processes, 66*(2), 192–202.

Chen, Z., & Daehler, M. W. 1989. "Positive and Negative Transfer in Analogical Problem Solving by Six-Year-Old Children." *Cognitive Development, 4*(4), 327–344.

Christensen, C., Larson, J. R., Abbott, A., Ardolino, A., Franz, T., & Pfeiffer, C. 1998. *Decision Making of Clinical Teams: Communication Patterns and Diagnostic Error.* Manuscript under review.

Cialdini, R. B. 1989. *Indirect Tactics of Image Management: Beyond Basking.* Mahwah, NJ: Lawrence Erlbaum & Associates.

Cini, M., Moreland, R. L., & Levine, J. M. 1993. "Group Staffing Levels and Responses to Prospective and New Members." *Journal of Personality and Social Psychology, 65,* 723–734.

Clark, K. B., & Fujimoto, T. 1987. *Overlapping Problem Solving in Product Development.* Working paper 87-048, Harvard University Graduate School of Business Administration, Cambridge, MA.

Clemmer, J. 1995. *Pathways to Performance: A Guide to Transforming Yourself, Your Team, and Your Organization.* Rocklin, CA: Macmillan Canada and Prima Publishing.

Cole, R. E. 1982. "Diffusion of Participating Work Structures in Japan, Sweden and the United States." In P.S. Goodman et al. (Eds.), *Change in Organizations* (pp. 166–225). San Francisco: Jossey-Bass.

Coleman, J. S. 1988. "Social Capital in the Creation of Human Capital." *American Journal of Sociology, 94,* S95–S120.

Collins, E. G., & Guetzkow, H. 1964. *A Social Psychology of Group Processes for Decision Making.* New York: Wiley.

Connolly, T., Routhieaux, R. L., & Schneider, S. K. 1993. "On the Effectiveness of Group Brainstorming: Test of One Underlying Cognitive Mechanism." *Small Group Research, 24,* 490–503.

Cota, A. L., & Dion, K. L. 1986. "Salience of Gender and Sex Composition of Ad Hoc Groups: An Experimental Test of Distinctiveness Theory." *Journal of Personality and Social Psychology, 50*(4), 770–776.

Craig, J. M., & Sherif, C. W. 1986. "The Effectiveness of Men and Women in Problem-Solving Groups as a Function of Group Gender Composition." *Sex Roles, 14*(7–8), 453–466.

Crisafi, M. A., & Brown, A. L. 1986. "Analogical Transfer of Very Young Children: Combining Two Separately Learned Solutions to Reach a Goal." *Child Development, 57*(4), 953–968.

Crocker, J., & McGraw, K. M. 1984. "What's Good for the Goose Is Not Good for the Gander: Solo Status as an Obstacle to Occupational Achievement for Males and Females." *American Behavioral Scientist, 27*(3), 357–369.

Crosby, F., Bromley, S., & Saxe, L. 1980. "Recent Unobtrusive Studies of Black and White Discrimination and Prejudice: A Literature Review." *Psychological Bulletin, 87,* 546–563.

Csikszentmihalyi, M. 1988. "Society, Culture and Person: A Systems View of Creativity." In R. Sternberg (Ed.), *The Nature of Productivity: Contemporary Psychological Perspectives.* New York: Cambridge University Press.

Cummings, T. G., & Mohrman, S. A. 1987. "Self-Designing Organizations: Towards Implementing Quality-of-Work-Life Innovations." In R. W. Woodman & W. A. Pasmore (Eds.), *Research in Organizational Change and Development* (Vol. 1, pp. 275–310). Greenwich, CT: JAI Press.

Cusumano, M. A. 1985. *The Japanese Automobile Industry: Technology and Management at Nissan and Toyota.* Cambridge, MA: Harvard University Press.

Cusumano, M. A. 1997. "How Microsoft Makes Large Teams Work Like Small Teams." *Sloan Management Review, 39*(1), 9–20.

Daft, R. L., & Lengel, R. H. 1984. "Information Richness: A New Approach to Managerial Behavior and Organization Design." *Research in Organization Behavior, 6,* 191–223.

Daft, R. L., Lengel, R. H., & Trevino, L. K. 1987. "Message Equivocality, Media Selection, and Manager Performance: Implications for Information Systems." *MIS Quarterly, 11*(3), 355–366.

Darley, J. M., & Batson, C. D. 1973. "From Jerusalem to Jericho: A Study of Situational and Dispositional Variables in Helping Behavior." *Journal of Personality and Social Psychology, 27,* 100–119.

Davidow, W. H., & Malone, M. S. 1992. *The Virtual Corporation: Structuring and Revitalizing the Corporation for the 21st Century.* New York: HarperCollins.

Davis, J. 1969. *Group Performance.* Reading, MA: Addison-Wesley.

Dawes, R., Orbell, J., & van de Kragt, A. 1988. "Not Me or Thee but We: The Importance of Group Identity in Eliciting Cooperation in Dilemma Situations." *Acta Psychologica, 68,* 83–97.

Dawes, R., van de Kragt, A., & Orbell, J. 1990. "Cooperation for the Benefit of Us—Not Me, or My Conscience." In J. Mansbridge (Ed.), *Beyond Self Interest* (pp. 97–110). Chicago: University of Chicago Press.

Deaux, K. 1985. "Sex and Gender." *Annual Review of Psychology, 36,* 49–81.

DeGroot, A. 1966. "Perception and Memory versus Thought. Some Old Ideas and Recent Findings." In B. Kleinmuntz (Ed.), *Problem Solving: Research, Method, and Theory* (pp. 19–50). New York: John Wiley & Sons.

DeMatteo, J. S., Eby, L. T., & Sundstrom, E. 1998. "Team-Based Rewards: Current Empirical Evidence and Directions for Future Research." *Research on Organization Behavior, 20,* 141–183.

DeMeyer, A. 1991. "Tech Talk: How Managers Are Stimulating Global R&D Communication." *Sloan Management Review, 32*(3), 49–58.

DeMeyer, A. 1993. "Internationalizing R&D Improves a Firm's Technical Learning." *Research-Technical Management, 36*(4), 42–49.

Dennis, A. R., Nunamaker, J. F., Jr., Paranka, D., & Vogel, D. R. A. 1990. "A New Role for Computers in Strategic Management." *Journal of Business Strategy, 11*(5), 38–42.

Deutsch, M. 1973. *The Resolution of Conflict.* New Haven, CT: Yale University Press.

Deutsch, M. 1975. "Equity, Equality, and Need: What Determines Which Value Will Be Used as the Basis of Distributive Justice?" *Journal of Social Issues, 31,* 137–149.

Deutsch, M., & Gerard, H. B. 1955. "A Study of Normative and Informational Social Influence upon Individual Judgment." *Journal of Abnormal and Social Psychology, 51,* 629–636.

Devadas, R., & Argote, L. 1995. *Organizational Learning Curves: The Effects of Turnover and Work Group Structure.* Invited paper presented at the annual meeting of the Midwestern Psychological Association, Chicago, IL.

Devine, P. G. 1989. "Stereotypes and Prejudice: Their Automatic and Controlled Components." *Journal of Personality and Social Psychology, 56,* 5–18.

Diehl, M., & Stroebe, W. 1987. "Productivity Loss in Brainstorming Groups: Toward a Solution of a Riddle." *Journal of Personality and Social Psychology, 53,* 497–509.

Dion, K. L. 1972. "Physical Attractiveness and Evaluations of Children's Transgressions." *Journal of Personality and Social Psychology, 24*(2), 207–213.

Dion, K. L., Berscheid, E., & Walster, E. 1972. "What Is Beautiful Is Good." *Journal of Personality and Social Psychology, 24,* 207–213.

Dion, K. L., & Evans, C. R. 1992. "On Cohesiveness: Reply to Keyton and Other Critics of the Construct." *Small Group Research, 23*(2), 242–250.

Dollard, J., Doob, L. W., Miller, N. E., Mowrer, O. H., & Sears, R. R. 1939. *Frustration and Aggression.* New Haven: Yale University Press.

Dow Jones News Service. 1998, April 14. *Japan's LTCB Asks Workers to Grade Executives.*

Drolet, A., Larrick, R., & Morris, M. W. 1998. "Thinking of Others: How Perspective-Taking Changes Negotiators' Aspirations and Fairness Perceptions as a Function of Negotiator Relationships." *Basic and Applied Social Psychology, 20*(1), 23–31.

Dubé, L., & Guimond, S. 1986. "Relative Deprivation and Social Protest: The Person-Group Issue." In J. Olson, C. P. Herman, & M. Zanna (Eds.), *Relative Deprivation and Social Comparison: The Ontario Symposium* (Vol. 4, pp. 201–216). Mahwah, NJ: Lawrence Erlbaum & Associates.

Dubrovsky, V. J., Keisler, S., & Sethna, B. N. 1991. "The Equalization Phenomenon: Status Effects in Computer-Mediated and Face-to-Face Decision-Making Groups." *Human-Computer Interaction, 6*(2), 119–146.

Dunbar, K. 1997. "How Scientists Think: On-Line Creativity and Conceptual Change in Science." In T. B. Ward, S. M. Smith, & J. Vaid (Eds.), *Creative Thought: An Investigation of Conceptual Structures and Processes.* Washington, DC: American Psychological Association.

Duncan, S. L. 1976. "Differential Social Perception and Attribution of Intergroup Violence: Testing the Lower Limits of Stereotyping Blacks." *Journal of Personality of Social Psychology, 34,* 590–598.

Durham, C., Knight, D., & Locke, E. A. 1997. "Effects of Leader Role, Team-Set Goal Difficulty, Efficacy, and Tactics on Team Effectiveness." *Organization Behavior and Human Decision Processes, 72*(2), 203–231.

Eisenberger, R., & Selbst, M. 1994. "Does Reward Increase or Decrease Creativity?" *Journal of Personality and Social Psychology, 49,* 520–528.

Eisenhardt, K. M., Kahwajy, J. L., & Bourgeois, L. J., III. 1997, July 1. "How Management Teams Can Have a Good Fight." *Harvard Business Review, 75*(4), 77–85.

Emery, F. E., & Trist, E. L. 1973. *Towards a Social Ecology: Contextual Appreciation of the Future in the Present.* New York: Plenum Press.

Erber, R., Wegner, D. M., & Bowman, R. (1996, May). *Ironic Effects of Trying Not to Be Sexist.* Paper presented at the 96th annual meeting of the Midwestern Psychological Association. Chicago, IL.

Etzkowitz, H., Kemelgor, C., & Uzzi, B. 1999. *Social Capital and Career Dynamics in Hard Science: Gender, Networks, and Advancement.* New York: Cambridge University Press.

Eveland, J. D., & Bikson, T. K. 1989. *Workgroup Structures and Computer Support: A Field Experiment.* Santa Monica, CA: Rand Corp.

Fairhurst, G. T., & Snavely, B. K. 1983. "Majority and Token Minority Group Relationships: Power Acquisition and Communication." *Academy of Management Review, 8*(2), 292–300.

Fan, E. T., & Gruenfeld, D. H. 1998. "When Needs Outweigh Desires: The Effects of Resource Interdependence and Reward Interdependence on Group Problem Solving." *Basic and Applied Social Psychology, 20*(1), 45–56.

Farwell, L., & Weiner, B. 1996. "Self-Perceptions of Fairness in Individual and Group Contexts." *Personality and Social Psychology Bulletin, 22*(9), 867–881.

Feld, S. L. 1982. "Social Structural Determinants of Similarity among Associates." *American Sociological Review, 47,* 797–801.

Feldman, D. C. 1977. "The Role of Initiation Activities in Socialization." *Human Relations, 30,* 977–990.

Ferdman, B. M. 1989. "Affirmative Action and the Challenge of the Color-Blind Perspective." In F. A. Blanchard & F. J. Crosby (Eds.), *Affirmative Action in Perspective* (pp. 169–176). New York: Springer.

Festinger, L., Riecken, H. W., & Schachter, S. 1956. *When Prophesy Fails.* Minneapolis: University of Minnesota Press.

Field, R. H. G., & House, R. J. 1990. "A Test of the Vroom-Yetton Model Using Manager and Subordinate Reports." *Journal of Applied Psychology, 75*(3), 362–366.

Fischhoff, B. 1975. "Hindsight Does Not Equal Foresight: The Effect of Outcome Knowledge on Judgment under Uncertainty." *Journal of Experimental Psychology: Human Perception and Performance, 1,* 288–299.

Fisher, R., & Ury, W. 1981. *Getting to Yes: Negotiating Agreement without Giving In.* Boston: Houghton Mifflin.

Fishman, C. 1996. "Whole Foods Is All Teams." *Fastcompany, 2,* 103.

Foa, U., & Foa, E. 1975. *Resource Theory of Social Exchange.* Morristown, NJ: General Learning Press.

Fontana, L. 1985. "Clique Formation in a Regional Health Planning Agency." *Human Relations, 38*(9), 895–910.

Forbus, K. D., Gentner, D., & Law, K. 1995. "MAC/FAC: A Model of Similarity-Based Retrieval." *Cognitive Science, 19*(2), 141–205.

Foushee, H. C., Lauber, J. K., Baetge, M. M., & Comb, D. B. 1986. *Crew Factors in Flight Operations: III. The Operational Significance of Exposure to Short-Haul Air Transport Operations* (NASA TM 88322). Moffett Field, CA: NASA Ames Research Center.

Frable, D. E., Blackstone, T., & Scherbaum, C. 1990. "Marginal and Mindful: Deviants in Social Interactions." *Journal of Personality and Social Psychology, 59*(1), 140–149.

Frank, M. G., & Gilovich, T. 1988. "The Dark Side of Self- and Social Perception: Black Uniforms and Aggression in Professional Sports." *Journal of Personality and Social Psychology, 54*(1), 74–85.

Frank, R. H., & Cook, P. J. 1995. *The Winner-Take-All Society.* New York: Penguin.

Freedman, J. L., Cunningham, J. A., & Krismer, K. 1992. "Inferred Values and the Reverse Incentive Effect in Induced Compliance." *Journal of Personality and Social Psychology, 62,* 357–368.

Friedlander, F. 1987. "The Design of Work Teams." In J. W. Lorsch (Ed.), *Handbook of Organizational Behavior.* Upper Saddle River, NJ: Prentice Hall.

Fry, W. R., Firestone, I., & Williams, D. L. 1983. "Negotiation Process and Outcome of Stranger Dyads and Dating Couples: Do Lovers Lose?" *Basic and Applied Social Psychology, 4,* 1–16.

Gabrenya, W. K., Latané, B., & Wang, Y. 1983. "Social Loafing in Cross-Cultural Perspective: Chinese on Taiwan." *Journal of Cross-Cultural Psychology, 14*(3), 368–384.

Gaertner, S. L., & Dovidio, J. F. 1986. "The Aversive Form of Racism." In S. L. Gaertner & J. F. Dovidio, (Eds.), *Prejudice, Discrimination, and Racism* (pp. 61–89). New York: Academic Press.

Galagan, P. 1986. "Work Teams That Work." *Training & Development Journal, 40*(11), 33–35.

Galegher, J., Kraut, R. E., & Egido, C. (Eds.). 1990. *Intellectual Teamwork: Social and Technological Foundations of Cooperative Work.* Hillsdale, NJ: Erlbaum.

Gallupe, R. B. 1992. "Electronic Brainstorming and Group Size." *Academy of Management Journal, 35,* 351–353.

Gardner, W. L. 1992. "Lessons in Organizational Dramaturgy: The Art of Impression Management." *Organizational Dynamics, 21*(1), 33–46.

Garfield, C. 1992. *Second to None* (p. 252). New York: Avon.

Gauron, E. F., & Rawlings, E. I. 1975. "A Procedure for Orienting New Members to Group Psychotherapy." *Small Group Behavior, 6,* 293–307.

Geber, B. 1995, April. "Virtual Teams." *Training Magazine, 32*(4), 36–40.

Gendron, G. 1998, May. "FYI: Growing by Design." *Inc., 20*(6), 9.

Gentner, D., Brem, S., Ferguson, R., & Wolff, P. 1997. "Analogy and Creativity in the Works of Johannes Kepler." In T. B. Ward, S. M. Smith, et al. (Eds.), *Creative Thought: An Investigation of Conceptual Structures and Processes* (pp. 403–459). Washington, DC: American Psychological Association.

Gentner, D., & Gentner, D. R. 1983. "Flowing Waters or Teeming Crowds: Mental Models of Electricity." In D. Gentner & A. Stevens (Eds.), *Mental Models.* Mahwah, NJ: Lawrence Erlbaum & Associates.

Gentner, D., & Landers, R. 1985. "Analogical Reminding: A Good Match Is Hard to Find." *Proceedings of the International Conference on Cybernetics and Society* (pp. 607–613), Tucson, AZ. New York: Institute of Electrical and Electronics Engineers.

Gentner, D., & Markman, A. B. 1997. "Structure Mapping in Analogy and Similarity." *American Psychologist, 52*(1), 45–56.

Gentner, D., Rattermann, M. J., & Forbus, K. D. 1993. "The Roles of Similarity in Transfer: Separating Retrievability from Inferential Soundness." *Cognitive Psychology, 25*(4), 524–575.

Gerard, H. 1983. "School Desegregation: The Social Science Role." *American Psychologist, 38,* 869–878.

Gersick, C. J. C. 1988. "Time and Transition in Work Teams: Toward a New Model of Group Development." *Academy of Management Journal, 31,* 9–41.

Ghoshal, S., & Barlett, C. A. 1988. "Innovation Processes in Multinational Corporations." In M. L. Tushman & W. L. Moore (Eds.), *Readings in the Management of Innovation* (2nd ed.). Cambridge, MA: Harper & Row.

Gibb, J. R. 1951. *Dynamics of Participative Groups.* Boulder: University of Colorado.

Gick, M. L., & Holyoak, K. J. 1980. "Analogical Problem-Solving." *Cognitive Psychology, 12,* 306–355. Adapted from Duncker, K. 1945. *On Problem Solving.* Psychological Monographs 58, no. 270.

Gick, M. L., & Holyoak, K. J. 1983. "Schema Induction and Analogical Transfer." *Cognitive Psychology, 15,* 1–38. Reprinted in Holyoak, K.J., & Thagard, P. 1995. *Mental Leaps: Analogy in Creative Thought.* Cambridge, MA: MIT Press.

Gigone, D., & Hastie, R. 1993. "The Common Knowledge Effect: Information Sharing and Group Judgment." *Journal of Personality and Social Psychology, 65*(5), 959–974.

Gigone, D., & Hastie, R. 1997. "The Impact of Information on Small Group Choice." *Journal of Personality and Social Psychology, 72*(1), 132–140.

Gilovich, T. 1987. "Secondhand Information and Social Judgment." *Journal of Experimental Social Psychology, 23*(1), 59–74.

Gilovich, T., Kerr, M., & Medvec, V. H. 1993. "The Effect of Temporal Perspective on Subjective Confidence." *Journal of Personality and Social Psychology, 64*(4), 552–560.

Gilovich, T., Savitsky, K., & Medvec, V. H. 1998. "The Illusion of Transparency: Biased Assessments of Others' Ability to Read One's Emotional States." *Journal of Personality and Social Psychology, 75*(2), 332–346.

Glasser, I. 1988. "Affirmative Action and the Legacy of Racial Injustice." In P. A. Katz & D. A. Taylor (Eds.), *Eliminating Racism.* New York: Plenum.

Glickman, A. S., Zimmer, S., Montero, R. C., Guerette, P. J., et al. 1987. "The Evolution of Teamwork Skills: An Empirical Assessment with Implications for Training." *US Naval Training Systems Center Technical Reports,* No. 87-016.

Gold, M., & Yanof, D. S. 1985. "Mothers, Daughters, and Girlfriends." *Journal of Personality and Social Psychology, 49*(3), 654–659.

Goldberg, P. 1968. "Are Women Prejudiced against Women?" *Transaction, 5,* 28–30.

Goldstein, I. L. 1989. "Critical Training Issues: Past, Present, and Future." In I. L. Goldstein et al., *Training and Development in Organizations.* San Francisco: Jossey-Bass.

Goleman, D. 1988, June. "Recent Studies Explain Why Some Meetings Fail." *The New York Times,* p. C1.

Goleman, D. 1991, October 15. "Happy or Sad, a Mood Can Prove Contagious." *The New York Times,* pp. C1, C8.

Goodman, P. S., & Garber, S. 1988. "Absenteeism and Accidents in a Dangerous Environment: Empirical Analysis of Underground Coal Mines." *Journal of Applied Psychology, 73*(1), 81–86.

Goodman, P. S., & Leyden, D. P. 1991. "Familiarity and Group Productivity." *Journal of Applied Psychology, 76*(4), 578–586.

Granovetter, M. 1973. "The Strength of Weak Ties." *American Journal of Sociology, 78,* 1360–1379.

Greek, D. 1997. "Steel Rewrites the Rules." *Professional Engineering, 10*(13), 19–20.

Greenberg, J. 1988. "Equity and Workplace Status: A Field Experiment." *Journal of Applied Psychology, 75,* 561–568.

Greenberg, J. 1996. *Managing Behavior in Organizations.* Upper Saddle River, NJ: Prentice Hall. (p. 189).

Greenwald, A. G., & Banaji, M. 1995. "Implicit Social Cognition: Attitudes, Self-Esteem, and Stereotypes." *Psychological Review, 102*(1), 4–27.

Griffin, D. W., & Ross, L. 1991. "Subjective Construal, Social Inference, and Human Misunderstanding." In M. P. Zanna (Ed.), *Advances in Experimental Social Psychology* (Vol. 24, pp. 319–359). San Diego, CA: Academic Press.

Griffith, J. 1989. "The Army's New Unit Personnel Replacement System and Its Relationship to Unit Cohesion and Social Support." *Military Psychology, 1,* 17–34.

Griffith, V. 1997, July 18. "Teamwork's Own Goals." *Financial Times,* p. 12.

Grimsley, K. D. 1997, May 26. "Racial Bias Suit Stirs Debate at Bell Atlantic; Firm Says Its Workforce Is a 'Reflection of Society'." *Washington Post,* Final Edition, p. A01.

Gross, S. E. 1995. *Compensation for Teams: How to Design and Implement Team-Based Reward Programs.* New York: AMACOM.

Grossman, J. 1998, April. "We've Got to Start Meeting Like This." *Inc. Magazine.*

Grossman, S. R., Rodgers, B. E., & Moore, B. R. 1989, December. "Turn Group Input into Stellar Output." *Working Woman,* 36–38.

Gruenfeld, D. H. 1994. "Status and Integrative Complexity in Decision-Making Groups: Evidence from the United States Supreme Court and a Laboratory Experiment." *Dissertation Abstracts International, Section B: The Sciences & Engineering, 55*(2-B), 630.

Gruenfeld, D. H. 1995. "Status, Ideology and Integrative Complexity on the U.S. Supreme Court: Rethinking the Politics of Political Decision Making." *Journal of Personality and Social Psychology, 68*(1), 5–20.

Gruenfeld, D.H. 1997. Integrating across teams: Formal structural solutions. Presentation at J.L. Kellogg School, May 1997, Evanston, IL; also based on Mohrman S.A., Cohen, S.G., & Mohrman, A.M. 1995. *Designing Team-Based Organizations.* San Francisco: Jessey-Bass

Gruenfeld, D. H. (Ed.). 1998. *Composition.* Stamford, CT: JAI Press.

Gruenfeld, D. H., & Fan, E. T. 1999. "What Newcomers See and What Oldtimers Say: Discontinuities in Knowledge Exchange." In L. Thompson, J. Levine, & D. Messick (Eds.), *Shared Cognition in Organizations: The Management of Knowledge.* Mahwah, NJ: Lawrence Erlbaum & Associates.

Gruenfeld, D. H., Keltner, D. J., & Anderson, C. 1998. *The Effects of Power on Those Who Possess It.* Working paper, J. L. Kellogg Graduate School of Management, Northwestern University.

Gruenfeld, D. H., Mannix, E. A., Williams, K. Y., & Neale, M. A. 1996. "Group Composition and Decision Making: How Member Familiarity and Information Distribution Affect Process and Performance." *Organization Behavior and Human Decision Processes, 67*(1), 1–15.

Gruenfeld, D. H., Martorana, P., & Fan, E. T. 1999. *What Do Groups Learn from Their Worldiest Members?: Direct and Indirect Influence in Dynamic Teams.* Working paper, J. L. Kellogg Graduate School of Management, Northwestern University.

Gruenfeld, D. H., Thomas-Hunt, M. C., & Kim, P. 1998. "Cognitive Flexibility, Communication Strategy, and Integrative Complexity in Groups: Public Versus Private Reactions to Majority and Minority Status." *Journal of Experimental Social Psychology, 34,* 202–226.

Guetzkow, H., & Gyr, J. 1954. "An Analysis of Conflict in Decision-Making Groups." *Human Relations, 7,* 367–381.

Guilford, J. P. 1959. *Personality.* New York: McGraw-Hill.

Guilford, J. P. 1967. "The Nature of Human Intelligence." *Intelligence, 1,* 274–280.

Guzzo, R. A., Salas, E., & Associates. 1995. *Team Effectiveness and Decision Making in Organizations.* San Francisco: Jossey-Bass.

Hackman, J. R. 1987. "The Design of Work Teams." In J. W. Lorsch (Ed.), *Handbook of Organizational Behavior.* Upper Saddle River, NJ: Prentice Hall.

Hackman, J. R. 1990. "Introduction: Work Teams in Organizations: An Oriented Framework." In J. Hackman (Ed.), *Groups That Work and Those That Don't.* San Francisco: Jossey-Bass.

Hackman, J. R., Brousseau, K. R., & Weiss, J. A. 1976. "The Interaction of Task Design and Group Performance Strategies in Determining Group Effectiveness." *Organization Behavior and Human Performance, 16,* 350–365.

Hackman, J. R., & Morris, C. G. 1975. "Group Tasks, Group Interaction Process and Group Performance Effectiveness. A Review and Proposed Integration." In L. Berkowitz (Ed.), *Advances in Experimental Social Psychology* (Vol. 8, pp. 45–99). New York: Academic Press.

Hackman, R. April, 1996. Presentation on group behavior, J. L. Kellogg Graduate School of Management, Evanston, Illinois.

Hains, S. C., Hogg, M. A., & Duck, J. M. 1997. "Self-Categorization and Leadership: Effects of Group Prototypicality and Leader Stereotypicality." *Personality and Social Psychology Bulletin, 23*(10), 1087–1099.

Hall, F. 1997. "Effective Delegation." In D. D. Brown, R. J. Lewicki, D. T. Hall, & F. S. Hall (Eds.), *Experiences in Management and Organizational Behavior* (4th ed.). New York: John Wiley & Sons. Reprinted with permission.

Hambrick, D. C. 1995. "Fragmentation and the Other Problems CEOs Have with Their TMT's." *California Management Review, 37*(3), 110–127.

Hambrick, D. C. 1997. "Corporate Coherence and the TMT." *Planning Review, 25*(5), 24–29.

Hanks, M., & Eckland, B. K. 1978. "Adult Voluntary Association and Adolescent Socialization." *Sociological Quarterly, 19*(3), 481–490.

Harber, K. D. 1998. "Feedback to Minorities: Evidence of a Positive Bias." *Journal of Personality and Social Psychology, 74*(3), 622–628.

Harkins, S. G., & Jackson, J. M. 1985. "The Role of Evaluation in Eliminating Social Loafing." *Personality and Social Psychology Bulletin, 11,* 457–465.

Harkins, S. G., & Szymanski, K. 1987. *Social Loafing and Social Facilitation: New Wine in Old Bottles.* Beverly Hills, CA: Sage.

Harvey, J. 1974. "The Abilene Paradox: The Management of Agreement." *Organizational Dynamics, 3*(1), 63–80. © American Management Association International. Reprinted with permission.

Harvey, O. J., & Consalvi, C. 1960. "Status and Conformity to Pressure in Informal Groups." *Journal of Abnormal and Social Psychology, 60,* 182–187.

Haslam, S. A., McGarty, C., Brown, P. M., Eggins, R. A., Morrison, B. E., & Reynolds, K. J. 1998. "Inspecting the Emperor's Clothes: Evidence That Random Selection of Leaders Can Enhance Group Performance." *Group Dynamics: Theory, Research, and Practice, 2*(3), 168–184.

Hastie, R., Penrod, S., & Pennington, N. 1983. *Inside the Jury.* Cambridge, MA: Harvard University Press.

Hatfield, E., & Sprecher, S. 1986. "Measuring Passionate Love in Intimate Relationships." *Journal of Adolescence, 9*(4), 383–410.

Heath, C. 1998. *On the Social Psychology of Agency Relationships: Lay Theories of Motiva-tion Overemphasize Extrinsic Rewards.* Unpublished manuscript, Duke University, Durham, NC.

Heilman, M. E., Hornstein, H. A., Cage, J. H., & Herschlag, J. K. 1984. "Reactions to Prescribed Leader Behavior as a Function of Role Perspective: The Case of the Vroom-Yetton Model." *Journal of Applied Psychology, 69*(1), 50–60.

Hequet, M. 1994, April. "Teams at the Top." *Training,* 7–9.

Higgins, E. T. 1999. " 'Saying Is Believing' Effects: When Sharing Reality about Something Biases Knowledge and Evaluations." In L. Thompson, J. M. Levine, & D. M. Messick (Eds.), *Shared Cognition in Organizations: The Management of Knowledge.* Mahwah, NJ: Lawrence Erlbaum & Associates.

Hill, M. 1982. "Group versus Individual Performance: Are N+1 Heads Better Than One?" *Psychological Bulletin, 91,* 517–539.

Hill, S. 1995. "The Social Organization of Boards of Directors." *British Journal of Sociology, 46*(2), 245–278.

Hillkirk, J. 1993, July 26. "Tearing Down Walls Builds GE." *USA Today,* p. 5B.

Hiltz, S. R., Johnson, K., & Turoff, M. 1986. "Experiments in Group Decision Making: Communication Process and Outcome in Face-to-Face versus Computerized Conferences." *Human Communication Research, 13*(2), 225–252.

Hinde, R. A. 1979. *Non-Verbal Communication.* Cambridge, England: Cambridge University Press.

Hof, R. D., Browder, S., & Elstrom, P. 1997, May 5. "Internet Communities." *Business Week,* no. 3525, pp. 64–80.

Hoffman, L. R., & Maier, N. R. F. 1966. "An Experimental Reexamination of the Similarity-Attraction Hypothesis." *Journal of Personality and Social Psychology, 3,* 145–152.

Hoffman, R. 1995, April. "Ten Reasons You Should Be Using 360-Degree Feedback." *HR Magazine, 40*(4), 82–85.

Hogg, M. A. 1987. "Social Identity and Group Cohesiveness." In J. C. Turner, M. A. Hogg, P. J. Oakes, S. D. Reicher, & M. Wetherell (Eds.), *Rediscovering the Social Group: A Self-Categorization Theory* (pp. 89–116). Oxford, England: Basil Blackwell.

Hogg, M., & Turner, J. C. 1987. "Intergroup Behaviour, Self-Stereotyping and the Salience of Social Categories." *British Journal of Social Psychology, 26,* 325–340.

Holland, K. 1996. "Sexual Healing at Mitsubishi?" *Business Week,* no. 3477, p. 48.

Hollingshead, A. B. 1996. "The Rank-Order Effect in Group Decision Making." *Organizational Behavior and Human Decision Processes, 68*(3), 181–193.

Holyoak, K. J., & Koh, K. 1987. "Surface and Structural Similarity in Analogical Transfer." *Memory and Cognition, 15*(4), 332–340.

Hopkins, K. R., Nestleroth, S. L., & Bolick, C. 1991. *Help Wanted: How Companies Can Survive and Thrive in the Coming Worker Shortage.* New York: McGraw-Hill.

Horn, E. M. 1993. *The Influence of Modality Order and Break Period on a Brainstorming Task.* Unpublished honors thesis, University of Texas at Arlington.

Howells, L. T., & Becker, S. W. 1962. "Seating Arrangements and Leadership Emergence." *Journal of Abnormal and Social Psychology, 64,* 148–150.

Huber, V. L., Neale, M. A., & Northcraft, G. B. 1987. "Judgment by Heuristics: Effects of Ratee and Rater Characteristics and Performance Standards on Performance-Related Judgments." *Organization Behavior and Human Decision Processes, 40,* 149–169.

Huey, J. 1994, February 21. "The New Post Heroic Leadership." *Fortune,* pp. 42–50.

Huseman, R. C., & Driver, R. W. 1979. "Groupthink: Implications for Small Group Decision Making in Business." In R. Huseman & A. Carroll (Eds.), *Readings in Organizational Behavior* (pp. 100–110). Boston: Allyn & Bacon.

Ibarra, H. 1995. "Race, Opportunity, and Diversity of Social Circles in Managerial Networks." *Academy of Management Journal, 38*(3), 673–703.

Ickes, W. 1983. "A Basic Paradigm for the Study of Unstructured Dyadic Interaction." *New Directions for Methodology of Social and Behavioral Science, 15,* 5–21.

Ickes, W., & Turner, M. 1983. "On the Social Advantages of Having an Older, Opposite-Sex Sibling: Birth Order Influences in Mixed-Sex Dyads." *Journal of Personality and Social Psychology, 45*(1), 210–222.

Imperato, G. 1997. "Harley Shifts Gears." *Fastcompany, 9,* 104.

Insko, C., Pinkley, R., Hoyle, R., Dalton, B., Hong, G., Slim, R., Landry, P., Holton, B., Ruffin, P., & Thibaut, J. 1987. "Individual Versus Group Discontinuity: The Role of a Consensus Rule." *Journal of Experimental Social Psychology, 23,* 250–267.

Izraeli, D. N. 1983. "Sex Effects or Structural Effects? An Empirical Test of Kanter's Theory of Proportions." *Social Forces, 62*(1), 153–165.

Jackson, J. M., & Harkins, S. G. 1985. "Equity in Effort: An Explanation of the Social Loafing Effect." *Journal of Personality and Social Psychology, 49,* 1199–1206.

Jackson, L. A., Gardner, P. D., & Sullivan, L. A. 1992. "Explaining Gender Differences in Self-Pay Expectations: Social Comparison Standards and Perceptions of Fair Pay." *Journal of Applied Psychology, 77*(5), 651–663.

Jackson, L. A., & Grabski, S. V. 1988. "Perceptions of Fair Pay and the Gender Wage Gap." *Journal of Applied Social Psychology, 18*(7, Part I), 606–625.

Jackson, S. E. 1992. "Team Composition in Organizational Settings: Issues in Managing an Increasingly Diverse Work Force." In S. Worchel, W. Wood, & J. A. Simpson (Eds.), *Group Process and Productivity* (pp. 138–173). Newbury Park: Sage.

Jackson, S. E., Brett, J. F., Sessa, V. I., Cooper, D. M., Julin, J. A., & Peyronnin, K. 1991. "Some Differences Make a Difference: Individual Dissimilarities and Group Heterogeneity as Correlates of Recruitment, Promotions, and Turnover." *Journal of Applied Psychology, 76*(5), 675–689.

Jacobs, R. C., & Campbell, D. T. 1961. "The Perpetuation of an Arbitrary Tradition through Several Generations of a Laboratory Microculture." *Journal of Abnormal and Social Psychology, 62,* 649–658.

Janis, I. L. 1972. *Victims of Groupthink.* Boston: Houghton Mifflin.

Janis, I. L. 1982. *Victims of Groupthink* (2nd ed.). Boston: Houghton Mifflin.

Janis, I. L., & Mann, L. 1977. *Decision Making: A Psychological Analysis of Conflict, Choice, and Commitment* (p. 130). New York: The Free Press, a Division of Simon & Schuster. Reprinted with permission.

Jarman, M. 1998, April 19. "Complete Turnaround: 360-degree Evaluations Gaining Favor with Workers, Management." *The Arizona Republic,* p. D1.

Jehn, K. A. 1997. "A Qualitative Analysis of Conflict Types and Dimensions in Organizational Groups." *Administrative Science Quarterly, 42,* 530–557.

Jessup, L. M., & Valacich, J. S., (Eds.). 1993. *Group Support Systems.* New York: Macmillan.

Johnson-Laird, P. N. 1980. "Mental Models in Cognitive Science." *Cognitive Science, 4*(1), 71–115.

Johnston, W. B., & Packer, A. E. 1987. *Workforce 2000: Work and Workers for the Twenty-First Century.* Indianapolis, IN: Hudson Institute.

Jones, E. E., Stires, L. K., Shaver, K. G., & Harris, V. A. 1968. "Evaluation of an Ingratiator by Target Persons and Bystanders." *Journal of Personality, 36*(3), 349–385.

Jones, J. M. 1983. "The Concept of Race in Social Psychology: From Color to Culture." In L. Wheeler & P. Shaver (Eds.), *Review of Personality and Social Psychology* (Vol. 4). Newbury Park, CA: Sage.

Jourard, S. M. 1971. *Self-Disclosure: An Experimental Analysis of the Transparent Self.* New York: John Wiley & Sons.

Judd, C. M., & Park, B. 1988. "Out-Group Homogeneity: Judgments of Variability at the Individual and Group Levels." *Journal of Personality and Social Psychology, 54*(5), 778–788.

Kahneman, D., & Tversky, A. 1979. "Prospect Theory: An Analysis of Decision under Risk." *Econometrica, 47,* 263–291.

Kameda, T., Ohtsubo, Y., & Takezawa, M. 1997. "Centrality in Sociocognitive Networks and Social Influence: An Illustration in a Group Decision-Making Context." *Journal of Personality and Social Psychology, 73*(2), 296–309.

Kanter, R. M. 1977. "Some Effects of Proportions on Group Life: Skewed Sex Ratios and Responses to Token Women." *American Journal of Sociology, 82,* 465–490.

Karau, S. J., & Williams, K. D. 1993. "Social Loafing: A Meta-Analytic Review and Theoretical Integration." *Journal of Personality and Social Psychology, 65,* 681–706.

Katz, D., & Braly, K. 1933. "Racial Stereotypes of 100 College Students." *Journal of Abnormal and Social Psychology, 28,* 280–290.

Katz, D., & Kahn, R. L. 1978. *The Social Psychology of Organizations* (2nd ed.). New York: John Wiley & Sons.

Katz, R. 1982. "The Effects of Group Longevity on Project Communication and Performance." *Administrative Science Quarterly, 27,* 81–104.

Katzenbach, J. R., & Smith, D. K. 1993, March–April. "The Discipline of Teams." *Harvard Business Review, 71*(2), 111–120.

Keisler, S., & Sproull, L. 1992. "Group Decision Making and Communication Technology." *Organization Behavior and Human Decision Processes, 52,* 96–123.

Keisler, S., Zubrow, D., Moses, A., & Gellar, V. 1985. "Affect in Computer-Mediated Communication: An Experiment in Synchronous Terminal-to-Terminal Discussion." *Human Computer Interaction, 1*(1), 77–104.

Keller, G., & McGahan, A. 1994. "Saturn: A Different Kind of Car Company." Harvard Business School Case No. 9-795-010. Prepared by G. Keller, under the supervision of A. M. McGahan and in consultation with A. Hax. Boston: Harvard Business School Publishing.

Kelley, H. H., & Thibaut, J. 1978. *Interpersonal Relations: A Theory of Interdependence.* New York: Wiley.

Kelley, H. H. 1962. *The Development of Cooperation in the "Minimal Social Situation."* Washington, DC: American Psychological Association.

Kelley, H. H. 1983. "The Situational Origins of Human Tendencies: A Further Reason for the Formal Analysis of Structures." *Personality and Social Psychology Bulletin, 9*(1), 8–36.

Kelly, J. R., Futoran, G. C., & McGrath, J. E. 1990. "Capacity and Capability: Seven Studies of Entrainment of Task Performance Rates." *Small Group Research, 21*(3), 283–314.

Kelly, J. R., & McGrath, J. E. 1985. "Effects of Time Limits and Task Types on Task Performance and Interaction of Four-Person Groups." *Journal of Personality and Social Psychology, 49*(2), 395–407.

Kempton, W. 1986. "Two Theories of Home Heat Control." *Cognitive Science, 10,* 75–90.

Kempton, W. 1987. *Two Theories of Home Heat Control.* New York: Cambridge University Press.

Kerr, N. L. 1989. "Illusions of Efficacy: The Effects of Group Size on Perceived Efficacy in Social Dilemmas." *Journal of Experimental Social Psychology, 25,* 287–313.

Kerr, N. L. 1983. "Motivation Losses in Small Groups: A Social Dilemma Analysis." *Journal of Personality and Social Psychology, 45,* 819–828.

Kerr, N. L., & Bruun, S. 1981. "Ringelmann Revisited: Alternative Explanations for the Social Loafing Effect." *Journal of Personality and Social Psychology, 37,* 224–231.

Keysar, B. 1994. "The Illusory Transparency of Intention: Linguistic Perspective-Taking in Text." *Cognitive Psychology, 26*(2), 165–208.

Keysar, B. 1998. "Language Users as Problem Solvers: Just What Ambiguity Problem Do They Solve?" In S. R. Fussell & R. J. Kreuz (Eds.), *Social and Cognitive Approaches to Interpersonal Communication* (pp. 175–200). Mahwah, NJ: Lawrence Erlbaum & Associates.

Kidder, T. 1981. *Soul of a New Machine.* New York: Avon.

King, R. T., Jr. 1998, May 20. "Levi's Factory Workers Are Assigned to Teams, and Morale Takes a Hit." *Wall Street Journal,* p. 1.

Kipnis, D. 1957. *The Effects of Style of Leadership and Incentives upon the Inducement of an Attitude Change.* Thesis, New York University.

Kirsner, S. 1998. "Total Teamwork: SEI Investments." *Fastcompany, 14,* 130.

Klein, J. A. 1984, September–October. "Why Supervisors Resist Employee Involvement." *Harvard Business Review,* 87–95.

Klimoski, R., & Inks, L. 1990, April. "Accountability Forces in Performance Appraisal." *Organization Behavior and Human Decision Processes, 45*(2), 194–208.

Klimoski, R., & Mohammed, S. 1997. "Team Mental Model: Construct or Metaphor?"

[Special issue]. *Journal of Management, 20*(2), 403–437.

Knight-Ridder Newspapers. 1991, October 13. "Whites' IDs of Blacks in Crime Cases Often Wrong, Studies Show." *Columbus Dispatch.*

Kohn, A. 1993, September–October. "Why Incentive Plans Cannot Work." *Harvard Business Review, 71,* 54–63.

Komorita, S., & Chertkoff, J. 1973. "A Bargaining Theory of Coalition Formation." *Psychological Review, 80,* 149–162.

Komorita, S., & Parks, C. 1994. *Social Dilemmas.* Madison, WI: Brown & Benchmark.

Kotovsky, L., & Gentner, D. 1996. "Comparison and Categorization in the Development of Relational Similarity." *Child Development, 67*(6), 2797–2822.

Kraiger, K., & Ford, J. K. 1985, February. "A Meta-Analysis of Ratee Race Effects in Performance Ratings." *Journal of Applied Psychology, 70*(1), 56–65.

Kramer, M. W., Kuo, C. L., & Dailey, J. C. 1997. "The Impact of Brainstorming Techniques on Subsequent Group Processes: Beyond Generating Ideas." *Small Group Research, 28*(2), 218–242.

Kramer, R. M. 1999. "Social Uncertainty and Collective Paranoia in Knowledge Communities: Thinking and Acting in the Shadow of Doubt." In L. Thompson, J. Levine, & D. Messick (Eds.), *Social Cognition in Organizations: The Management of Knowledge.* Mahwah, NJ: Lawrence Erlbaum Associates.

Krauss, R. M., & Fussell, S. R. 1991. "Perspective-Taking in Communication: Representations of Others' Knowledge in Reference." *Social Cognition, 9,* 2–24.

Krauss, R. M., & Fussell, S. R. 1996. "Social Psychological Models of Interpersonal Communication." In E. T. Higgins & A. W. Kruglanski, (Eds.), *Social Psychology: Handbook of Basic Principles* (pp. 655–701). New York: Guilford.

Kravitz, D. A., & Martin, B. 1986. "Ringelmann Rediscovered: The Original Article." *Journal of Personality and Social Psychology, 50*(5), 936–941.

Kresa, K. 1991. "Aerospace Leadership in a Vortex of Change." *Financier, 15*(1), 25–28.

"Labor Letter: Training Holds." 1992, July 14. *Wall Street Journal,* p. A-1.

"Labor Letter: Training the Workforce— Corporate Commitment." 1991, October 22. *Wall Street Journal,* p. A-1.

Landy, D., & Sigall, H. 1974. "Beauty Is Talent: Task Evaluation as a Function of the Performer's Physical Attractiveness." *Journal of Personality and Social Psychology, 29,* 299–304.

Larson, C. E., Foster-Fishman, P. G., & Keys, C. B. 1994. "Discussion of Shared and Unshared Information in Decision-Making Groups." *Journal of Personality and Social Psychology, 67*(3), 446–461.

Larson, C. E., & LaFasto, F. M. 1989. *Teamwork: What Must Go Right/What Can Go Wrong.* Newbury Park, CA: Sage.

Larson, J. R., & Christensen, C. 1993. "Groups as Problem-Solving Units: Toward a New Meaning of Social Cognition" [Special Issue: Social Processes in Small Groups I: Theoretical Perspectives]. *British Journal of Social Psychology, 32*(1), 5–30.

Larson, J. R., Christensen, C., Franz, T. M., & Abbott, A. S. 1998. "Diagnosing Groups: The Pooling, Management, and Impact of Shared and Unshared Case Information in Team-Based Medical Decision Making." *Journal of Personality and Social Psychology, 75*(1), 93–108.

Larson, J. R., Foster-Fishman, P. G., & Franz, T. M. 1998. "Leadership Style and the Discussion of Shared and Unshared Information in Decision-Making Groups." *Personality and Social Psychology Bulletin, 24*(5), 482–495.

Latané, B. 1981. "The Psychology of Social Impact." *American Psychologist, 36,* 343–356.

Latané, B., & Darley, J. M. 1968. "Group Inhibition of Bystander Intervention in Emergencies." *Journal of Personality and Social Psychology, 10,* 215–221.

Latané, B., & Darley, J. M. 1970. *The Unresponsive Bystander: Why Doesn't He Help?* New York: Appleton-Century-Crofts.

Laughlin, P. R. 1980. "Social Combination Processes of Cooperative Problem-Solving Groups on Verbal Interactive Tasks." In M. Fishbein (Ed.), *Progress in Social Psychology*

(Vol. 1). Mahwah, NJ: Lawrence Erlbaum & Associates.

Lawler, E. E. 1988. "Choosing an Involvement Strategy." *Academy of Management Executive, 11*(3), 197–204.

Lawler, E. E. 1990. *Strategic Pay: Aligning Organizational Strategies and Pay Systems.* San Francisco, CA: Jossey-Bass.

Lawler, E. E. 1992. *The Ultimate Advantage: Creating the High-Involvement Organization.* San Francisco: Jossey-Bass.

Lawler, E. E., Mohrman, S. A., & Ledford, G. E. Jr. 1995. *Creating High Performance Organizations: Practices and Results of Employee Involvement and Total Quality Management in Fortune 1000 Companies.* San Francisco: Jossey-Bass.

Leary, M. 1995. *Self-Presentation: Impression Management and Behavior.* Dubuque, IA: Brown & Benchmark.

Lederberg, J., & Uncaphor, K. 1989. *Towards a National Collaboratory.* Report of an invitational workshop at the Rockefeller University, Washington, DC: NSF, Directorate for Computer and Information Science and Engineering.

LeJeune, M. 1997, December. "Beat, Meter Latest Team Building Ideas." *Colder County Business Report.*

Levine, J. M. 1989. "Reaction to Opinion Deviance in Small Groups." In P. Paulus (Ed.), *Psychology of Group Influence* (2nd ed., pp. 187–231). Mahwah, NJ: Lawrence Erlbaum & Associates.

Levine, J. M., & Moreland, R. L. 1985. "Innovation and Socialization in Small Groups." In S. Moscovici, G. Mugny, & E. van Avermaet (Eds.), *Perspectives on Minority Influence* (pp. 143–169). Cambridge, England: Cambridge University Press.

Levine, J. M., & Moreland, R. L. 1991. "Culture and Socialization in Work Groups." In L. B. Resnick, J. M. Levine, & S. D. Teasley (Eds.), *Perspectives on Socially Shared Cognition* (pp. 585–634). Washington, DC: American Psychological Association.

Levine, J. M., & Moreland, R. L. 1994. "Group Socialization: Theory and Research." In W. Stroebe & M. Hewstone (Eds.), *The European*

Review of Social Psychology (Vol. 5, pp. 305–336). Chichester, England: Wiley.

Levine, J. M., Resnick, L. B., & Higgins, E. T. 1993. "Social Foundations of Cognition." *Annual Review of Psychology, 44,* 585–612.

LeVine, R. A., & Campbell, D. T. 1972. *Ethnocentrism: Theories of Conflict, Ethnic Attitudes and Group Behavior.* New York: John Wiley & Sons.

Levinger, G. K., & Rausch, H. L. 1977. *Close Relationships: Perspectives on the Meaning of Intimacy.* Amherst, MA: University of Massachusetts Press.

Levinger, G. K., & Snoek, J. D. 1972. *Attraction in Relationship: A New Look at Interpersonal Attraction.* Morristown, NJ: General Learning Press.

Levinson, S. C. 1983. *Pragmatics* (p. 264). Cambridge, England: Cambridge University Press.

Lewin, K. 1943. "Forces behind Food Habits and Methods of Change." *Bulletin of the National Research Council, 108,* 35–65.

Lewin, K. 1947. "Frontiers in Group Dynamics: Concept, Method, and Reality in Social Science." *Human Relations, 1,* 5–42.

Lewis, B. P., & Linder, D. E. 1997. "Thinking about Choking? Attentional Processes and Paradoxical Performance." *Personality and Social Psychology Bulletin, 23*(9), 937–944.

Lewis, S. A., Langan, C. J., & Hollander, E. P. 1972. "Expectation of Future Interaction and the Choice of Less Desirable Alternatives in Conformity." *Sociometry, 35,* 440–447.

Liang, D. W., Moreland, R. L., & Argote, L. 1995. "Group versus Individual Training and Group Performance: The Mediating Role of Transactive Memory." *Personality and Social Psychology Bulletin, 21*(4), 384–393.

Libby, R., Trotman, K. T., & Zimmer, I. 1987. "Member Variation, Recognition of Expertise, and Group Performance." *Journal of Applied Psychology, 72*(1), 81–87.

Liberman, N., & Trope, Y. 1998. "The Role of Feasibility and Desirability Considerations in Near and Distant Future Decisions: A Test of Temporal Construal Theory." *Journal of Personality and Social Psychology, 75*(1), 5–18.

Liden, R. C., & Graen, G. 1980. "Generalizability of the Vertical Dyad Linkage Model of Leadership." *Academy of Management Journal, 23*(3), 451–465.

Lind, A., Kray, L., & Thompson, L. 1998. "The Social Construction of Injustice: Fairness Judgments in Response to Own and Others' Unfair Treatment by Authorities." *Organization Behavior and Human Decision Processes, 75*(1), 1–22.

Lind, E. A., & Tyler, T. R. 1988. *The Social Psychology of Procedural Justice.* New York: Plenum.

Linville, P. W., Fischer, G. W., & Salovey, P. 1989. "Perceived Distributions of the Characteristics of In-Group and Out-Group Members: Empirical Evidence and a Computer Simulation." *Journal of Personality and Social Psychology, 57,* 165–188.

Littlepage, G., Robison, W., & Reddington, K. 1997. "Effects of Task Experience and Group Experience on Group Performance, Member Ability, and Recognition of Expertise." *Organization Behavior and Human Decision Processes, 69*(2), 133–147.

Loewenstein, J. 1997. *Using Comparison to Improve Preschoolers' Spatial Mapping Ability."* Poster presented at the Biennial meeting of the Society for Research in Child Development, Washington, DC.

Loewenstein, J., & Gentner, D. In preparation. *Comparison and Mapping in Preschoolers.*

Loewenstein, J., & Prelic, D. 1991. "Negative Time Preference." *AEA Papers and Proceedings, 81*(2), 347–352.

Loewenstein, J., Thompson, L., & Gentner, D. In press. "Analogical Encoding Facilitates Knowledge Transfer in Negotiation." *Psychonomic Bulletin and Review.*

Lord, C., & Saenz, D. 1985. "Memory Deficits and Memory Surfeits: Differential Cognitive Consequences of Tokenism for Tokens and Observers." *Journal of Personality and Social Psychology, 49,* 918–926.

Los Angeles Times 1992, May 18. "Coming Renaissance of the LAPD; the Importance of Police Reform—and Willie L. Williams." p. B4.

Louis, M. R. 1980. "Surprise and Sense Making: What Newcomers Experience in Entering Unfamiliar Organizational Settings." *Administrative Science Quarterly, 25,* 226–251.

Lublin, J. S. 1995, April 12. "My Colleague, My Boss." *Wall Street Journal,* p. R4.

Lynn, M. 1997. "Board Games: Those Who Make It to the Top Are Not Usually Shy, Retiring Types, and Cadbury Only Increases the Likelihood of Conflict." *Management Today,* 30–34.

Lyons, M. 1998, April 8. "Taxi a High-Tech Office on Wheels." *The Irish Times,* p. 16.

MacKenzie, M., Cambrosio, A., & Keating, P. 1988. "The Commercial Application of a Scientific Discovery: The Case of the Hybridoma Technique." *Research and Policy, 17*(3), 155–170.

Macrae, C. N., Bodenhausen, G. V., Milne, A. B., & Jetten, J. 1994. "Out of Mind but Back in Sight: Stereotypes on the Rebound." *Journal of Personality and Social Psychology, 67*(5), 808–817.

Magaro, P. A., & Ashbrook, R. M. 1985. "The Personality of Societal Groups." *Journal of Personality and Social Psychology, 48*(6), 1479–1489.

Maier, N. R. F. 1952. *Principles of Human Relations, Applications to Management.* New York: John Wiley & Sons.

Maio, G. R., & Esses, V. M. 1998. "The Social Consequences of Affirmative Action: Deleterious Effects on Perceptions of Groups." *Personality and Social Psychology Bulletin, 24*(1), 65–74.

Maisonneuve, J., Palmade, G., & Fourment, C. 1952. "Selective Choices and Propinquity." *Sociometry, 15,* 135–140.

Manning, J. F., & Fullerton, T. D. 1988. "Health and Well-Being in Highly Cohesive Units of the U.S. Army." *Journal of Applied Social Psychology, 18,* 503–519.

Mannix, E. 1993. "Organizations as Resource Dilemmas: The Effects of Power Balance on Coalition Formation in Small Groups." *Organization Behavior and Human Decision Processes, 55,* 1–22.

Mannix, E., & Loewenstein, G. 1993. "Managerial Time Horizons and Inter-Firm Mobility: An Experimental Investigation." *Organization Behavior and Human Decision Processes, 56,* 266–284.

Mannix, E., Thompson, L., & Bazerman, M. H. 1989. "Negotiation in Small Groups." *Journal of Applied Psychology, 74,* 508–517.

Marchetti, M. 1997. "Why Teams Fail." *Sales and Marketing Management, 149*(6), 91.

Markham, S. E., Dansereau, F., & Alutto, J. A. 1982. "Group Size and Absenteeism Rates: A Longitudinal Analysis." *Academy of Management Journal, 25*(4), 921–927.

May, K. 1982. "A Set of Independent, Necessary and Sufficient Conditions for Simple Majority Decisions." In B. Barry & R. Hardin (Eds.), *Rational Man and Irrational Society* (pp. 299–303). Beverly Hills, CA: Sage.

Mazur, A. 1985. "A Biosocial Model of Status in Face-to-Face Groups." *Social Forces, 64,* 377–402.

McAlister, L., Bazerman, M. H. & Fader, R. 1986. "Power and Goal Setting in Channel Negotiations." *Journal of Marketing Research, 23,* 238–263.

McCallum, D., Harring, K., Gilmore, R., Drenan, S., Chase, J., Insko, C., & Thibaut, J. 1985. "Competition and Cooperation between Groups and between Individuals." *Journal of Experimental Social Psychology, 21,* 301–320.

McCaskey, M. B. 1995. "Framework for Analyzing Work Groups." Harvard Business School Case No. 480-009. Boston, MA: Harvard Business School Publishing.

McCauley, C. 1998. "Groupthink Dynamics in Janis's Theory of Groupthink: Backward and Forward." *Organizational Behavior & Human Decision Processes, 73*(2–3), 142–162.

McCauley, C., Stitt, C. L., & Segal, M. 1980. "Stereotyping: From Prejudice to Prediction." *Psychological Bulletin, 87*(1), 195–215.

McClintock, C., Messick, D., Kuhlman, D., & Campos, F. 1973. "Motivational Bases of Choice in Three-Choice Decomposed Games." *Journal of Experimental Social Psychology, 57,* 250–260.

McGrath, J. E. 1984. *Groups: Interaction and Performance.* Upper Saddle River, NJ: Prentice Hall.

McGrath, J. E. 1990. "Time Matters in Groups." In J. Galegher, R. E. Kraut, & C. Egido (Eds.), *Intellectual Teamwork: Social and Technological Foundations of Cooperative Work.* Mahwah, NJ: Lawrence Erlbaum & Associates.

McGrath, J. E., Kelly, J. R., & Machatka, D. E. 1984. "The Social Psychology of Time: Entrainment of Behavior in Social and Organizational Settings." *Applied Social Psychology Annual, 5,* 21–44.

McGregor, D. 1960. *"The Human Side of Enterprise."* New York: McGraw-Hill.

McGuire, T., Keisler, S., & Siegel, J. 1987. "Group and Computer-Mediated Discussion Effect in Risk Decision-Making." *Journal of Personality and Social Psychology, 52*(5), 917–930.

McGuire, W. J., & Padawer-Singer, A. 1976. "Trait Salience in the Spontaneous Self-Concept." *Journal of Personality and Social Psychology, 33,* 743–754.

McPherson, J. M., & Smith-Lovin, L. 1986. "Sex Segregation in Voluntary Associations." *American Sociology Review, 5*(1), 61–79.

Meherabian, A. 1971. *Silent Messages.* Belmont, CA: Wadsworth.

Meindl, J. R., & Lerner, M. O. 1984. "Exacerbation of Extreme Responses to an Out-Group." *Journal of Personality and Social Psychology, 47*(1), 71–84.

Messick, D. 1993. "Equality as a Decision Heuristic." In B. A. Mellers & J. Baron (Eds.), *Psychological Perspectives on Justice* (pp. 11–31). New York: Cambridge University Press.

Michaels, S. W., Brommel, J. M., Brocato, R. M., Linkous, R. A., & Rowe, J. S. 1982. "Social Facilitation in a Natural Setting." *Replication in Social Psychology, 4*(2), 21–24.

Michel, J. G., & Hambrick, D. C. 1992. "Diversification Posture and Top Management Team Characteristics." *Academy of Management Journal, 35*(1), 9–37.

Milgram, S. 1963. "Behavioral Study of Obedience." *Journal of Abnormal and Social Psychology, 67,* 371–378.

Miller, C. E., Jackson, P., Mueller, J., & Schersching, C. 1987. "Some Social Psychological Effects of Group Decision Rules." *Journal of Personality and Social Psychology, 52,* 325–332.

Miller, C. T. 1982. "The Role of Performance-Related Similarity in Social Comparison of Abilities: A Test of the Related Attributes Hypothesis." *Journal of Experimental Social Psychology, 18,* 513–523.

Miller, D. T., & Ratner, R. 1998. "The Disparity between the Actual and Assumed Power of Self-Interest." *Journal of Personality and Social Psychology, 74*(1), 53–62.

Milliken, W. F. 1996. "The Eastman Way." *Quality Progress, 29*(10), 57–62.

Milliman, J. F., Zawacki, R. F., Norman, C., Powell, L., & Kirksey, J. 1994, November. "Companies Evaluate Employees from All Perspectives." *Personnel Journal, 73*(11), 99–103.

Mintzberg, H. 1973. *The Nature of Managerial Work.* New York: Harper & Row.

Mohrman, S. A., Lawler, E. E., & Mohrman, A. M. 1992. "Applying Employee Involvement in Schools." *Educational Evaluation and Policy Analysis, 14*(4), 347–360.

Moore, D., Kurtzberg, T., Thompson, L., & Morris, M. 1999. "Long and Short Routes to Success in Electronically-Mediated Negotiations: Group Affiliations and Good Vibrations." *Organization Behavior and Human Decision Processes, 77*(1), 22–43.

Moreland, R. L. 1985. "Social Categorization and the Assimilation of "New" Group Members." *Journal of Personality and Social Psychology, 48*(5), 1173–1190.

Moreland, R. L., Argote, L., & Krishnan, R. 1996. "Socially Shared Cognition at Work." In J. L. Nye & A. M. Brower (Eds.), *What's Social about Social Cognition?* Thousand Oaks, CA: Sage.

Moreland, R. L., Argote, L., & Krishnan, R. 1998. "Training People to Work in Groups." In R. S. Tindale et al. (Eds.), *Theory and Research on Small Groups.* New York: Plenum Press.

Moreland, R. L., & Levine, J. M. 1982. "Socialization in Small Groups: Temporal Changes in Individual-Group Relation." In L. Berkowitz (Ed.), *Advances in Experimental Social Psychology* (Vol. 15, pp. 137–192). New York: Academic Press.

Moreland, R. L., & Levine, J. M. 1984. "Role Transitions in Small Groups." In V. L. Allen & E. van de Vliert (Eds.), *Role Transitions: Explorations and Explanations* (pp. 181–195). New York: Plenum Press.

Moreland, R. L., & Levine, J. M. 1988. "Group Dynamics over Time: Development and Socialization in Small Groups." In J. E. McGrath (Ed.), *The Social Psychology of Time: New Perspectives* (pp. 151–181). Newbury Park, CA: Sage.

Moreland, R. L., & Levine, J. M. 1989. "Newcomers and Oldtimers in Small Groups." In P. Paulus (Ed.), *Psychology or Group Influence* (2nd ed., pp. 143–186). Mahwah, NJ: Lawrence Erlbaum & Associates.

Moreland, R. L., & Levine, J. M. 1992. "The Composition of Small Groups." In E. J. Lawler, B. Markovsky, C. Ridgeway, & H. A. Walker (Eds.), *Advances in Group Processes* (Vol. 9, pp. 237–280). Greenwich, CT: JAI Press.

Mosvick, R., & Nelson, R. B. 1996. *We've Got to Start Meeting Like This!: A Guide to Successful Meeting Management* (rev. ed.). Indianapolis, IN: Park Avenue.

Mullen, B. 1983. "Operationalizing the Effect of the Group on the Individual: A Self-Attention Perspective." *Journal of Experimental Social Psychology, 19,* 295–322.

Mullen, B., Johnson, C., & Salas, E. 1991. "Productivity Loss in Brainstorming Groups: A Meta-Analytic Integration." *Basic and Applied Social Psychology, 12,* 3–23.

Mulvey, P. W., Veiga, J. F., & Elsass, P. M. 1996. "When Teammates Raise a White Flag." *Academy of Management Executive, 10*(1), 40–49.

Murnighan, J. K. 1992. *Bargaining Games.* New York: William Morrow and Co., Inc. Reprinted with permission.

Nadler, J., Thompson, L., & Morris, M. 1999. "Schmooze or Lose: The Efforts of Rapport and Gender in E-mail Negotiations." Paper presented at the Academy of Management Annual conference, August 1999, Chicago IL.

Nagasundaram, M., & Dennis, A. R. 1993. "When a Group Is Not a Group: The Cognitive Foundation of Group Idea Generation." *Small Group Research, 24,* 463–489.

Nahavandi, A., & Aranda, E. 1994. "Restructuring Teams for the Re-engineered Organization." *Academy of Management Review, 8*(4), 58–68.

Nelson, B. 1994. *1001 Ways to Reward Employees.* New York: Workman Publishing Co., Inc. Reprinted with permission.

Nemeth, C. 1994. "The Value of Minority Dissent." In S. Moscovici, A. Mucchi-Faina, et al. (Eds.), *Minority Influence: Nelson-Hall Series in Psychology* (pp. 3–15). Chicago: Nelson-Hall Publishers.

Nemeth, C., & Wachtler, J. 1974. "Creating the Perceptions of Consistency and Confidence: A Necessary Condition for Minority Influence." *Sociometry, 37*(4), 529–540.

Nemeth, C. J. 1995. "Dissent as Driving Cognition, Attitudes, and Judgments." *Social Cognition, 13,* 273–291.

Nemeth, C. J., & Kwan, J. L. 1987. "Minority Influence, Divergent Thinking and Detection of Correct Solutions." *Journal of Applied Social Psychology, 17*(9), 788–799.

Nemeth, C. J., & Wachtler, J. 1983. "Creative Problem Solving as a Result of Majority vs. Minority Influence." *European Journal of Social Psychology, 13*(1), 45–55.

Nieva, V. F., & Gutek, B. A. 1981. *Women and Work: A Psychological Perspective.* New York: Praeger.

Nieva, V. F., Myers, D., & Glickman, A. S. 1979, July. "An Exploratory Investigation of the Skill Qualification Testing System." *U.S. Army Research Institute for the Behavioral and Social Sciences,* TR 390.

Novak, C. J. 1997, April. "Proceed with Caution When Paying Teams." *HR Magazine, 42*(4), 73–78.

Novick, L. R. 1988. "Analogical Transfer, Problem Similarity, and Expertise." *Journal of Experimental Social Psychology: Learning, Memory and Cognition, 14*(3), 510–520.

Novick, L. R., & Holyoak, K. J. 1991. "Mathematical Problem Solving by Analogy." *Journal of Experimental Social Psychology: Learning, Memory and Cognition, 17*(3), 398–415.

Nunamaker, J. F., Jr., Briggs, R. O., & Mittleman, D. D. 1995. "Electronic Meeting Systems: Ten Years of Lessons Learned." In D. Coleman & R. Khanna (Eds.), *Groupware: Technology and Applications* (pp. 149–193). Upper Saddle River, NJ: Prentice Hall.

O'Connor, K. M. 1994. *Negotiation Teams: The Impact of Accountability and Representation Structure on Negotiator Cognition and Performance.* Eugene, OR: International Association of Conflict Management.

O'Hamilton, J., Baker, S., & Vlasic, B. 1996, April. "The New Workplace." *Business Week, 3473,* 106–117.

O'Hara-Devereaux, M., & Johansen, R. 1994. *Global Work: Bridging Distance, Culture and Time.* San Francisco: Jossey-Bass.

O'Reilly, C. A., & Caldwell, D. F. 1985. "The Impact of Normative Social Influence and Cohesiveness on Task Perceptions and Attitudes: A Social-Information Processing Approach." *Journal of Occupational Psychology, 58,* 193–206.

O'Reilly, C. A., Chatman, J. F., & Caldwell, D. F. 1991. "People and Organizational Culture: A Profile Comparison Approach to Assessing Person-Organization Fit." *Academy of Management Journal, 34,* 487–516.

Oaksford, M., & Chater, N. 1994. "A Rational Analysis of the Selection Task as Optimal Data Selection." *Psychological Review, 101,* 608–631.

Oberle, J. 1990. "Teamwork in the Cockpit." *Training, 27*(2), 34–38.

Oddou, G. 1987. "Rock Climbing, Rappelling, and Sailing: Effective Management and Organization Development Tools?" *Consultation: An International Journal, 6*(3), 145–157.

Offner, A. K., Kramer, T. J., & Winter, J. P. 1996. "The Effects of Facilitation, Recording, and Pauses on Group Brainstorming." *Small Group Research, 27,* 283–298.

Oldham, J. 1998, May 18. "Conflict and Cookies: Companies Coax Problems Out into the Open and Use Them to Make Working Groups More Effective." *Los Angeles Times,* p. 22.

Olson, M. 1965. *The Logic of Collective Action.* Cambridge, MA: Harvard University Press.

Ordeshook, P. 1986. *Game Theory and Political Theory: An Introduction.* Cambridge, England: Cambridge University Press.

Orsburn, J. D., Moran, L., Musselwhite, E., & Zenger, J. H. 1990. *Self-Directed Work Teams: The New American Challenge.* Chicago: Irwin.

Osborn, A. F. 1957. *Applied Imagination* (rev. ed.). New York: Scribner.

Osborn, A. F. 1963. *Applied Imagination* (3rd ed.). New York: Scribner.

Osgood, C. E. 1979. *GRIT 1.* Dundas, Ontario: Peace Research Reviews (vol. 8, no. 1, 0553-4283).

Oxley, N. L., Dzindolet, M. T., & Paulus, P. B. 1996. "The Effects of Facilitators on the Performance of Brainstorming Groups." *Journal of Social Behavior and Personality, 11*(4), 633–646.

Pape, W. R. 1997, July 15. "Group Insurance." *Inc.* (Technology Supplement), *19*(9), 29–31.

Park, B., & Rothbart, M. 1982. "Perception of Outgroup Homogeneity and Levels of Social Categorization: Memory for Subordinate Attitudes of Ingroup and Outgroup Members." *Journal of Personality and Social Psychology, 42,* 1050–1068.

Parks, C. D., & Cowlin, R. A. 1996. "Acceptance of Uncommon Information into Group Discussion When That Information Is or Is Not Demonstrable." *Organization Behavior and Human Decision Processes, 66*(3), 307–315.

Parnell, C. 1998. "Teamwork: Not a New Idea, but It's Transforming the Workplace." *Executive Speeches, 12*(3), 35–40.

Parnes, S. J., & Meadow, A. 1959. "Effect of 'Brainstorming' Instructions on Creative Problem-Solving by Trained and Untrained Subjects." *Journal of Educational Psychology, 50,* 171–176.

Parsons, T., Bales, R. F., & Shils, E. 1953. *Working Paper in the Theory of Action.* Glencoe, IL: Free Press.

Pascale, R. 1998. "Grassroots Leadership—Royal Dutch/Shell." *Fastcompany, 14,* 110.

Pascarella, P. 1997. "Compensating Teams." *Across the Board, 34*(2), 16–22.

Paulus, P. B. 1998. "Developing Consensus about Groupthink after All These Years." *Organization Behavior and Human Decision Processes, 73*(2–3), 362–374.

Paulus, P. B., & Dzindolet, M. T. 1993. "Social Influence Processes in Group Brainstorming." *Journal of Personality and Social Psychology, 64,* 575–586.

Paulus, P. B., Larey, T. S., Brown, V., Dzindolet, M. T., Roland, E. J., Leggett, K. L., Putman, V. L., & Coskun, H. 1998, June. *Group and Elec-*

tronic Brainstorming: Understanding Production Losses and Gains in Idea Generating Groups. Paper presented at Learning in Organizations Conference, Carnegie-Mellon University, Pittsburgh, PA.

Paulus, P. B., Larey, T. S., & Ortega, A. H. 1995. "Performance and Perceptions of Brainstormers in an Organizational Setting." *Basic and Applied Social Psychology, 17,* 249–265.

Paulus, P. B., Larey, T. S., Putman, V. L., Leggett, K. L., & Roland, E. J. 1996. "Social Influence Process in Computer Brainstorming." *Basic and Applied Social Psychology, 18,* 3–14.

Paulus, P. B., Putman, V. L., Coskun, H., Leggett, K. L., & Roland, E. J. 1996. *Training Groups for Effective Brainstorming.* Presented at the Fourth Annual Advanced Concepts Conference on Work Teams–Team Implementation Issues, Dallas, TX.

Perkins, D. V. 1982. "Individual Differences and Task Structure in the Performance of a Behavior Setting: An Experimental Evaluation of Barker's Manning Theory." *American Journal of Community Psychology, 10*(6), 617–634.

Perrow, C. 1984. *Normal Accidents: Living with High-Risk Technologies.* New York: Basic Books.

Peterson, R. S., & Nemeth, C. J. 1996. "Focus versus Flexibility: Majority and Minority Influence Can Both Improve Performance." *Personality and Social Psychology Bulletin, 22*(1), 14–23.

Peterson, R. S., Owens, P. D., Tetlock, P. E., Fan, E. T., & Martorana, P. 1998. "Group Dynamics in Top Management Teams: Groupthink, Vigilance, and Alternative Models of Organizational Failure and Success." *Organization Behavior and Human Decision Processes, 73,* 272–305.

Pettit, J. 1997, January. "Team Communication: It's in the Cards." *Training and Development, 15*(1), 12–14.

Petty, R. E., Cacioppo, J. T., & Kasmer, J. 1985. *Effects of Need for Cognition on Social Loafing.* Paper presented at the Midwestern Psychology Association Meeting, Chicago, IL.

Petty, R. M., & Wicker, A. W. 1974. "Degree of Manning and Degree of Success of a Group as Determinants of Members' Subjective Experiences and Their Acceptance of a New Group Member." *Catalog of Selected Documents in Psychology, 4,* 43.

Pfeffer, J. 1983. "Organizational Demography." In B. M. Staw & L. L. Cummings (Eds.), *Research in Organizational Behavior* (Vol. 5, pp. 299–359). Greenwich, CT: JAI Press.

Phelps, R. 1996, September. "Cadbury Trusts in Teamwork." *Management Today,* 110.

Philip, G., & Young, E. S. 1987. "Man-Machine Interaction by Voice: Developments in Speech Technology. Part I: The State-of-the-Art." *Journal of Information Science Principles and Practice, 13*(1), 3–14.

Plott, C. 1976. "Axiomatic Social Choice Theory: An Overview and Interpretation." *American Journal of Political Science, 20,* 511–596.

Plott, C., & Levine, M. 1978. "A Model of Agenda Influence on Committee Decisions." *American Economic Review, 68,* 146–160.

Podolny, J. M., & Baron, J. N. 1997. "Resources and Relationships: Social Networks and Mobility in the Workplace." *American Sociological Review, 62*(5), 673–693.

Pope, S. 1996. "The Power of Guidelines, Structure, and Clear Goals." *Journal for Quality and Participation, 19*(7), 56–60.

Poza, E. J., & Marcus, M. 1980, Winter. "Success Story: The Team Approach to Work Restructuring." *Organizational Dynamics, 8*(3), 3–25.

Prentice, D. A., Miller, D. T., & Lightdale, J. R. 1994. "Asymmetries in Attachments to Groups and to Their Members: Distinguishing between Common-Identity and Common-Bond Groups." *Personality and Social Psychology Bulletin, 20,* 484–493.

Prentice-Dunn, S., & Rogers, R. W. 1989. "Deindividuation and the Self-Regulation of Behavior." In P. B. Paulus (Ed.), *Psychology of Group Influence* (2nd ed.), Mahwah, NJ: Lawrence Erlbaum & Associates.

PR Newswire 1998, February 26. "RSA's Secret-Key Challenge Solved by Distributed Team in Record Time; Team of Computer Enthusiasts Cracks Government-Endorsed DES Algorithm in Less Than Half the Time of Previous Challenge."

Pruitt, D. G., & Lewis, S. A. 1975. "Development of Integrative Solutions in Bilateral Negotiation." *Journal of Personality and Social Psychology, 31,* 621–630.

Raiffa, H. 1982. *The Art and Science of Negotiation.* Cambridge, MA: Belknap.

Rand, K. A., & Carnevale, P. J. 1994. *The Benefits of Team Support in Bilateral Negotiations.* Unpublished manuscript, University of Illinois, Urbana, IL.

Raven, B. H., & Rubin, J. Z. 1976. *Social Psychology: People in Groups.* New York: John Wiley & Sons.

Reeves, L., & Weisberg, R. W. 1994. "The Role of Content and Abstract Information in Analogical Transfer." *Psychological Bulletin, 115*(3), 381–400.

Rhoades, J. A., & O'Connor, K. M. 1996. "Affect in Computer-Mediated and Face-to-Face Work Groups: The Construction and Testing of a General Model." *Computer Supported Cooperative Work, 4,* 203–228.

Rickards, T. 1993. "Creative Leadership: Messages from the Front Line and the Back Room." *Journal of Creative Behavior, 27,* 46–56.

Ridgeway, C. L. 1982. "Status in Groups: The Importance of Motivation." *American Sociological Review, 47,* 76–88.

Riess, M. 1982. "Seating Preferences as Impression Management: A Literature Review and Theoretical Integration." *Communication, 11,* 85–113.

Riess, M., & Rosenfeld, P. 1980. "Seating Preferences as Nonverbal Communication: A Self-Presentational Analysis." *Journal of Applied Communications Research, 8,* 22–30.

Ringelmann, M. 1913. *Aménagement des fumiers et des purins.* Paris: Librarie agricole de la Maison rustique.

Robinson, R. J., & Keltner, D. 1996. "Much Ado about Nothing? Revisionists and Traditionalists Choose an Introductory English Syllabus." *Psychological Science, 7*(1), 18–24.

Rogelberg, S. G., Barnes-Farrell, J. L., & Lowe, C. A. 1992. "The Stepladder Technique: An Alternative Group Structure Facilitating Effective Group Decision Making." *Journal of Applied Psychology, 77*(5), 730–737.

Rogelberg, S. G., & O'Connor, M. S. 1998. "Extending the Stepladder Technique: An Examination of Self-Paced Stepladder Groups." *Group Dynamics: Theory, Research, and Practice, 2*(2), 82–91.

Rogers, R. W., & Prentice-Dunn, S. 1981. "Deindividuation and Anger-Mediated Interracial Aggression: Unmasking Regressive Racism." *Journal of Personality and Social Psychology, 4*(1), 63–73.

Rosenthal, E. A. 1996. *Social Networks and Team Performance.* Unpublished Ph.D. dissertation, University of Chicago.

Rosenthal, R., & Jacobson, L. 1968. *Pygmalion in the Classroom: Teacher Expectation and Pupils' Intellectual Development.* New York: Holt.

Ross, B. H. 1987. "This Is Like That: The Use of Earlier Problems and the Separation of Similarity Effects." *Journal of Experimental Psychology: Learning, Memory and Cognition, 13*(4), 629–639.

Ross, J., & Staw, B. M. 1993, August. "Organizational Escalation and Exit: Lessons from the Shoreham Nuclear Power Plant." *Academy of Management Journal, 36*(4), 701–732.

Ross, L. 1977. "The Intuitive Psychologist and His Shortcomings: Distortions in the Attribution Process." In L. Berkowitz (Ed.), *Advances in Experimental Social Psychology* (Vol. 10, pp. 173–220). Orlando, FL: Academic Press.

Ross, L., & Samuels, S. M. 1993. *The Predictive Power of Personal Reputation vs. Labels and Construal in the Prisoner's Dilemma Game.* Stanford University, Stanford, CA.

Rothbart, M., & Hallmark, W. 1988. "In-Group and Out-Group Differences in the Perceived Efficacy of Coercion and Conciliation in Resolving Social Conflict." *Journal of Personality and Social Psychology, 55,* 248–257.

Rouse, W., & Morris, N. 1986. "On Looking into the Black Box: Prospects and Limits in the Search for Mental Models." *Psychological Bulletin, 100,* 359–363.

Roy, M. C., Gauvin, S., & Limayem, M. 1996. "Electronic Group Brainstorming: The Role of Feedback on Productivity." *Small Group Research, 27,* 215–247.

Royal, E. G., & Golden, S. B. 1981. "Attitude Similarity and Attraction to an Employee Group." *Psychology Reports, 48*(1), 251–254.

Ruder, M. K., & Gill, D. L. 1982. "Immediate Effects of Win-Loss on Perceptions of Cohesion in Intramural and Intercollegiate Volleyball

Teams." *Journal of Sport Psychology, 4*(3), 227–234.

Rutkowski, G. K., Gruder, C. L., & Romer, D. 1983. "Group Cohesiveness, Social Norms, and Bystander Intervention." *Journal of Personality and Social Psychology, 44*(3), 545–552.

Sanfey, A., & Hastie, R. 1998. "Does Evidence Presentation Format Affect Judgment? An Experimental Evaluation of Displays of Data for Judgments." *Psychological Science, 9*(2), 99–103.

Savage, L. J. 1954. *The Foundations of Statistics.* New York: John Wiley & Sons.

Schein, E. H. 1988. *Process Consultation: Its Role in Organization Development* (Vol. 1). Reading, MA: Addison-Wesley.

Schofield, J. W. 1986. "Black and White Contact in Desegregated Schools." In M. Hewstone & R. J. Brown (Eds.), *Contact and Conflict in Intergroup Encounters* (pp. 79–92). Oxford, England: Blackwell.

Schrage, M. 1995. *No More Teams!: Mastering the Dynamics of Creative Collaboration.* New York: Currency Doubleday.

Schrage, M. 1998, October 5. "Why Your Department Needs to Implement 360s." *Computerworld,* p. 33.

Schuman, H., Steeh, C., & Bobo, L. 1985. *Racial Attitudes in America: Trends and Interpretations.* Cambridge, MA: Harvard University Press.

Schutte, J. G. 1996. *Virtual Teaching in Higher Education: The New Intellectual Superhighway or Just Another Traffic Jam?* Working paper, California State University, Northridge, CA.

Schwartz, B. 1986. *The Battle for Human Nature: Science, Morality, and Modern Life.* New York: Norton.

Sears, D. O., & Allen, H. M. Jr. 1984. "The Trajectory of Local Desegregation Controversies and Whites' Opposition to Busing." In N. Miller & M. Brewer (Eds.), *Groups in Contact: The Psychology of Desegregation* (pp. 123–151). New York: Academic Press.

Sears, D. O., & Funk, C. L. 1990. "The Limited Effect of Economic Self-Interest on the Political Attitudes of the Mass Public." *Journal of Behavioral Economics, 19*(3), 247–271.

Sears, D. O., & Funk, C. L. 1991. "Graduate Education in Political Psychology. Annual Meeting of International Society of Political Psychology, Washington, DC." *Political Psychology, 12*(2), 345–362.

Secord, P. F., & Backman, C. W. 1964. *Social Psychology.* New York: McGraw-Hill.

Sedekides, C., Campbell, W. K., Reeder, G. D., & Elliot, A. J. 1998. "The Self-Serving Bias in Relational Context." *Journal of Personality and Social Psychology, 74*(2), 378–386.

Segal, M. W. 1974. "Alphabet and Attraction: An Unobtrusive Measure of the Effect of Propinquity in a Field Setting." *Journal of Personality and Social Psychology, 30*(5), 654–657.

Selbert, R. 1987, November. "Women at Work." *Future Scan, 554,* 1–3.

Senge, P. M. 1996. "Leading Learning Organizations: The Bold, the Powerful, and the Invisible." In F. Hesselbein, M. Goldsmith, & R. Beckhard (Eds.), *The Leader of the Future: New Visions, Strategies, and Practices for the Next Era* (pp. 41–57). San Francisco: Jossey-Bass.

Seta, J. J. 1982. "The Impact of Comparison Processes on Coactors' Task Performance." *Journal of Personality and Social Psychology, 42,* 281–291.

Shah, P. P., & Jehn, K. A. 1993. "Do Friends Perform Better Than Acquaintances? The Interaction of Friendship, Conflict, and Task." *Group Decision and Negotiation, 2*(2), 149–165.

Shaw, M. E. 1981. *Group Dynamics: The Psychology of Small Group Behavior,* (3rd Ed.). New York: McGraw-Hill.

Shea, G. P., & Guzzo, R. A. 1987, Spring." Group Effectiveness: What Really Matters?" *Sloan Management Review, 28*(3), 25–31.

Sheehan, N., et al. 1971. *The Pentagon Papers: As Published by The New York Times, Based on the Investigative Reporting by Neil Sheehan, Written by Neil Sheehan [and others].* Articles and documents edited by G. Gold, A. M. Siegal, & S. Abt. New York, Toronto: Bantam.

Shepherd, M. M., Briggs, R. O., Reinig, B. A., Yen, J., & Nunamaker, J. F., Jr. 1995–1996. "Invoking Social Comparison to Improve Electronic Brainstorming: Beyond Anonymity." *Journal of Management Information Systems, 12,* 155–170.

Shepperd, J. A. 1993. "Productivity Loss in Performance Groups: A Motivation Analysis." *Psychological Bulletin, 113,* 67–81.

Sherif, M. 1966. *In Common Predicament: Social Psychology of Intergroup Conflict and Cooperation.* Boston: Addison-Wesley.

Short, J., Williams, E., & Christie, B. 1976. *The Social Psychology of Telecommunications.* London, New York: John Wiley & Sons.

Shure, G. H., Rogers, M. S., Larsen, I. M., & Tasson, J. 1962. "Group Planning and Task Effectiveness." *Sociometry, 25,* 263–282.

Siegel, J., Dubrovsky, V., Keisler, S., & McGuire, T. 1986. "Group Processes in Computer-Mediated Communication." *Organizational Behavior, 37,* 157–187.

Silberman, M. 1990. *Active Training: A Handbook of Techniques, Designs, Case Examples, and Tips.* San Diego, CA, Lexington, MA: University Associates, Inc., Lexington Books/D. C. Heath and Company.

Simonton, D. K. 1987. *Why Presidents Succeed: A Political Psychology of Leadership.* New Haven, CT: Yale University Press.

Sims, R. R. 1992. "Linking Groupthink to Unethical Behavior in Organizations." *Journal of Business Ethics, 11*(9), 651–662.

Smith, C. M., Tindale, R. S., & Dugoni, B. L. 1996. "Minority and Majority Influence in Freely Interacting Groups: Qualitative vs. Quantitative Differences." *British Journal of Social Psychology, 35,* 137–149.

Smith, S. 1997, February 24. "Accountants Adopt Hoteling Idea Without Reservations." *San Francisco Business Times.*

Smith-Lovin, L., & Robinson, D. T. 1992. "Gender and Conversational Dynamics." In C. Ridgeway (Ed.), *Gender, Interaction and Inequality.* New York: Springer-Verlag.

Snow, C. C., Snell, S. A., Davison, S. C., & Hambrick, D. C. 1996. "Use Transnational Teams to Globalize Your Company." *Organizational Dynamics, 24*(4), 50–67.

Snyder, M. 1984. "When Belief Creates Reality." In L. Berkowitz (Ed.), *Advances in Experimental Social Psychology* (Vol. 18, pp. 248–306). New York: Academic Press.

Snyder, M., Tanke, E. D., & Berscheid, E. 1977. "Social Perception and Interpersonal Behavior: On the Self-Fulfilling Nature of Social Stereotypes." *Journal of Personality and Social Psychology, 35,* 656–666.

Sommer, R. 1969. *Personal Space: The Behavioral Basis of Design.* Upper Saddle River, NJ: Prentice Hall.

South, S. J., Bonjean, C. M., Markham, W. T., & Corder, J. 1982. "Social Structure and Intergroup Interaction: Men and Women of the Federal Bureaucracy." *American Sociological Review, 47,* 587–599.

Sparrowe, R. T., & Popielarz, P. A. 1995. *Weak Ties and Structural Holes: The Effects of Network Structure on Careers.* Paper presented at the annual meetings of the Academy of Management, Vancouver, B.C.

Sproull, L., & Keisler, S. 1991. *Connections: New Ways of Working in the Networked Organization.* Cambridge, MA: MIT Press.

Stark, R., & Bainbridge, W. S. 1980. "Toward a Theory of Religion: Religious Commitment." *Journal for Scientific Study of Religion, 19,* 114–128.

Stasser, G. 1988. "Computer Simulation as a Research Tool: The DISCUSS Model of Group Decision Making." *Journal of Experimental Social Psychology, 24*(5), 393–422.

Stasser, G. 1992. "Information Salience and the Discovery of Hidden Profiles by Decision-Making Groups: A 'Thought' Experiment." *Organization Behavior and Human Decision Processes, 52,* 156–181.

Stasser, G., & Stewart, D. D. 1992. "Discovery of Hidden Profiles by Decision-Making Groups: Solving a Problem versus Making a Judgment." *Journal of Personality and Social Psychology, 63,* 426–434.

Stasser, G., Stewart, D. D., & Wittenbaum, G. M. 1995. "Expert Roles and Information Exchange during Discussion: The Importance of Knowing Who Knows What." *Journal of Experimental Social Psychology, 31,* 244–265.

Stasser, G., Taylor, L. A., & Hanna, C. 1989. "Information Sampling in Structured and Unstructured Discussions of Three- and Six-Person Groups." *Journal of Personality and Social Psychology, 57,* 67–78.

Stasser, G., & Titus, W. 1985. "Pooling of Unshared Information in Group Decision Making: Biased Information Sampling During Discussion." *Journal of Personality and Social Psychology, 48,* 1467–1478.

Stasser, G., & Titus, W. 1987. "Effects of Information Load and Percentage of Shared Information on the Dissemination of Unshared Information in Group Discussion." *Journal of Personality and Social Psychology, 53,* 81–93.

Staw, B. H. 1976. "Knee-Deep in the Big Muddy: A Study of Escalating Commitment to a Chosen Course of Action." *Organization Behavior and Human Decision Processes, 16*(1), 27–44.

Steele, C. M. 1997. "A Threat in the Air: How Stereotypes Shape the Intellectual Identities and Performance of Women and African Americans." *American Psychologist, 52,* 613–629.

Steiner, I. 1972. *Group Process and Productivity.* New York: Academic Press.

Stewart, D. D., Billings, R. S., & Stasser, G. 1998. "Accountability and the Discussion of Unshared, Critical Information in Decision Making Groups." *Group Dynamics: Theory, Research, and Practice, 2*(1), 18–23.

Stewart, D. D., & Stasser, G. 1995. "Expert Role Assignment and Information Sampling during Collective Recall and Decision-Making." *Journal of Personality and Social Psychology, 69,* 619–628.

Stogdill, R. M. 1972. "Group Productivity, Drive, and Cohesiveness." *Organizational Behavior and Human Performance, 8*(1), 26–43.

Stokes, J. P. 1983. "Components of Group Cohesion: Inter-Member Attraction, Instrumental Value, and Risk Taking." *Small Group Behavior, 14,* 163–173.

Stoner, J. A. F. 1961. *A Comparison of Individual and Group Decisions Involving Risk.* Thesis, Massachusetts Institute of Technology.

Strodtbeck, F. L., & Hook, L. H. 1961. "The Social Dimensions of a 12-Man Jury Table." *Sociometry, 24*(4), 397–415.

Stroebe, W., Diehl, M., & Abakoumkin, G. 1992. "The Illusion of Group Effectivity." *Personality and Social Psychology Bulletin, 18*(5), 643–650.

Stroebe, W., Lenkert, A., & Jonas, K. 1988. "Familiarity May Breed Contempt: The Impact of Student Exchange on National Stereotypes and Attitudes." In W. Stroebe, A. W. Kruglanski, D. Bar-Tal, & M. Hewstone (Eds.), *The Social Psychology of Intergroup Conflict* (167–187). New York: Springer-Verlag.

Sumner, W. 1906. *Folkways.* New York: Ginn.

Sundstrom, E. D., & Sundstrom, M. G. 1986. *Work Places: The Psychology of the Physical Environment in Offices and Factories.* Cambridge, England: Cambridge University Press.

Sutton, R. I., & Hargadon, A. 1996. "Brainstorming Groups in Context: Effectiveness in a Product Design Firm." *Administrative Science Quarterly, 41,* 685–718.

Swensen, C. H. 1973. *Introduction to Interpersonal Relations.* Glenview, IL: Scott Foreman.

Tajfel, H. 1982. "Social Psychology of Intergroup Relations." *Annual Review of Psychology, 33,* 1–39.

Tajfel, H., (Ed.). 1978. *Differentiation between Social Groups: Studies in the Social Psychology of Intergroup Relations.* New York: Academic Press.

Tajfel, H., & Turner, J. C. 1986. "The Social Identity Theory of Intergroup Behavior." In S. Worchel & W. G. Austin (Eds.), *Psychology of Intergroup Relations* (pp. 7–24). Chicago: Nelson-Hall.

Taylor, D. M., Moghaddam, F. M., Gamble, I., & Zellerer, F. 1987. "Disadvantaged Group Responses to Perceived Inequality: From Passive Acceptance to Collective Action." *Journal of Social Psychology, 127,* 259–272.

Taylor, D. M., Wright, S. C., Moghaddam, F. M., & Lalonde, R. N. 1990. "The Personal/Group Discrimination Discrepancy: Perceiving My Group, but Not Myself, to Be the Target of Discrimination." *Personality and Social Psychology Bulletin, 16,* 254–262.

Taylor, D. W., & Faust, W. L. 1952. "Twenty Questions: Efficiency of Problem-Solving as a Function of the Size of the Group." *Journal of Experimental Social Psychology, 44,* 360–363.

Taylor, F. W. 1911. *Shop Management.* New York: Harper & Brothers.

Taylor, S. E., Fiske, S. T., Etcoff, N. L., & Ruderman, A. J. 1978. "Categorical and Contextual Bases of Person Memory and Stereotyping." *Journal of Personality and Social Psychology, 36,* 778–793.

Terry, D.J., & Callan, V. J. 1998. "In-Group Bias in Response to an Organizational Merger." *Group Dynamics: Theory, Research, and Practice, 2*(2), 67-81.

Tetrault, L. A., Schriescheim, C. A., & Neider, L. L. 1988. "Leadership Training Interventions: A Review." *Organizational Development Journal, 6*(3), 77–83.

"The Trouble With Teams: Management Focus." *Economist*, 1995, January 14, 61.

Thibaut, J., & Kelley, H. 1959. *The Social Psychology of Groups.* New York: John Wiley & Sons.

Thompson, J. 1967. *Organizations in Action.* New York: McGraw-Hill.

Thompson, L. 1991. "Information Exchange in Negotiation." *Journal of Experimental Social Psychology, 27,* 161–179.

Thompson, L. 1998. *The Mind and Heart of the Negotiator.* Upper Saddle River, NJ: Prentice Hall.

Thompson, L., & DeHarpport, T. 1994. "Social Judgment, Feedback, and Interpersonal Learning in Negotiation." *Organization Behavior and Human Decision Processes, 58,* 327–345.

Thompson, L., & DeHarpport, T. 1998. "Relationships, Good Incompatibility, and Communal Orientation in Negotiations." *Basic and Applied Social Psychology, 20*(1), 33–43.

Thompson, L., Gentner, D., & Lowenstein, J. (in press) "Avoiding Missed Opportunities in Managerial Life: Analogical Training More Powerful than Individual Case Training." In press, *Organizational Behavior and Human Decision Processes.*

Thompson, L., & Hastie, R. 1990. "Social Perception in Negotiation." *Organization Behavior and Human Decision Processes, 47,* 98–123.

Thompson, L., & Hrebec, D. 1996. "Lose-Lose Agreements in Interdependent Decision Making." *Psychological Bulletin, 120*(3), 396–409.

Thompson, L., Kray, L., & Lind, A. 1998. "Cohesion and Respect: An Examination of Group Decision Making in Social and Escalation Dilemmas." *Journal of Experimental Social Psychology, 34,* 289–311.

Thompson, L., & Loewenstein, J. 1992. "Egocentric Interpretations of Fairness and Negotiation." *Organization Behavior and Human Decision Processes, 51,* 176–197.

Thompson, L., Mannix, E., & Bazerman, M. 1988. "Group Negotiation: Effects of Decision Rule, Agenda, and Aspiration." *Journal of Personality and Social Psychology, 54,* 86–95.

Thompson, L., Peterson, E., & Brodt, S. 1996. "Team Negotiation: An Examination of Integrative and Distributive Bargaining." *Journal of Personality and Social Psychology, 54,* 86–95.

Thompson, L., Valley, K. L., & Kramer, R. M. 1995. "The Bittersweet Feeling of Success: An Examination of Social Perception in Negotiation." *Journal of Experimental Social Psychology, 31*(6), 467–492.

Tickle-Degnen, L., & Rosenthal, R. 1987. "Group Rapport and Nonverbal Behavior." In *Review of Personality and Social Psychology* (Vol. 9, pp. 113–136). Beverly Hills, CA: Sage.

Tippett, D. D., & Peters, J. F. 1995. "Team Building and Project Management: How Are We Doing?" *Project Management Journal, 26*(4), 29–37.

Totterdell, P., Kellett, S., Teuchmann, K., & Briner, R. 1998. "Evidence of Mood Linkage in Work Groups." *Journal of Personality and Social Psychology, 74*(6), 1504–1515.

Train, J. 1995, June 24. "Learning from Financial Disaster." *Financial Times* (Weekend Money Markets), p. II.

Triandis, H. C. 1977. "Cross-Cultural Social and Personality Psychology." *Personality & Social Psychology Bulletin, 3*(2), 143–158.

Tropman, J.E. & Morningstar, G. 1989. *Entrepreneurial Systems of the 1990s: Their Creation, Structure, and Management.* New York: Quorum Books. Reproduced with permission of Greenwood Publishing Group, Inc., Westport, CT

Tropman, J. E. 1996. *Making Meetings Work: Achieving High Quality Group Decisions.* Thousand Oaks, CA: Sage.

Tuch, S. A., & Martin, J. K. 1991. "Race in the Workplace: Black and White Differences in the Sources of Job Satisfaction." *Sociological Quarterly, 32*(1), 103–116.

Turkle, S. 1995. *Life on the Screen: Identity in the Age of the Internet.* New York: Simon & Schuster.

Turner, M. E., & Pratkanis, A. R. 1998. "A Social Identity Maintenance Model of Groupthink."

Organizational Behavior and Human Decision Processes, 73(2–3), 210–235.

Turner, M. E., Probasco, P., Pratkanis, A. R., & Leve, C. 1992. "Threat, Cohesion, and Group Effectiveness: Testing a Social Identity Maintenance Perspective on Groupthink." *Journal of Personality and Social Psychology, 63,* 781–796.

Tversky, A., & Kahneman, D. 1973. "Availability: A Heuristic for Judging Frequency and Probability." *Cognitive Psychology, 5,* 207–232.

Tversky, A., & Kahneman, D. 1974. "Judgment under Uncertainty: Heuristics and Biases." *Science, 185,* 1124–1131.

Tyler, T. R. 1990. *Why People Obey the Law.* New Haven, CT: Yale University Press.

Tyler, T. R. 1997. "The Psychology of Legitimacy: A Relational Perspective on Voluntary Deference to Authorities." *Personality and Social Psychology Review, 1*(4), 323–345.

Tyler, T. R., & Smith, H. J. 1998. "Social Justice and Social Movements." In D. Gilbert, S. T. Fiske, & G. Lindzey (Eds.), *Handbook of Social Psychology* (4th ed.). New York: McGraw-Hill.

U. S. Bureau of the Census. 1995. *Labor Force Statistics from the Current Population Survey. A Joint Project between the Bureau of Labor Statistics and the Bureau of Census.* Washington, DC.

U. S. Bureau of Labor Statistics. 1993. *Average Wages Earned by Women Compared to Men.* Washington, DC.

Uzzi, B. 1997. "Social Structure and Competition in Interfirm Networks: The Paradox of Embeddedness." *Administrative Science Quarterly, 42,* 35–67.

Uzzi, B., & Gillespie, J. J. 1999. "Access and Governance Benefits of Social Relationships and Networks: The Case of Collateral, Availability, and Bank Spreads." In H. Rosenblum (Ed.), *Business Access to Capital and Credit.* Washington, DC: Federal Reserve Bank.

van Avermaet, E. 1974. *Equity: A Theoretical and Experimental Analysis.* Unpublished doctoral dissertation, University of California, Santa Barbara.

Van Maanen, J. 1977. "Experiencing Organization: Notes on the Meaning of Careers and Socialization." In J. Van Maanen (Ed.), *Organizational Careers: Some New Perspectives* (pp. 15–45). New York: John Wiley & Sons.

van Oostrum, J., & Rabbie, J. M. 1995. "Intergroup Competition and Cooperation within Autocratic and Democratic Management Regimes." *Small Group Research, 26*(2), 269–295.

Vanneman, S., & Pettigrew, T.F. 1972. "Race and Relative Deprivation in Urban United States." *Race, 13,* 461–486.

Van Vianen, A. E., & Willemsen, T. M. 1992. "The Employment Interview: The Role of Sex Stereotypes in the Evaluation of Male and Female Job Applicants in the Netherlands." *Journal of Applied Social Psychology, 22*(6), 471–491.

von Hippel, E. A. 1988. *Task Partitioning: An Innovation Process Variable* (Working Paper No. 2030-88). Sloan School of Management, Cambridge, MA.

Vroom, V. H., & Jago, A. G. 1978. "The Validity of the Vroom-Yetton Model." *Journal of Applied Psychology, 63*(2), 151–162.

Vroom, V. H., & Jago, A. G. 1988. *The New Leadership: Managing Participation in Organizations.* Upper Saddle River, NJ: Prentice Hall.

Vroom, V.H., & Yetton, P.W. 1973. *Leadership and Decision-Making.* Pittsburgh, PA: University of Pittsburgh Press.

Wageman, R. 1995. "Interdependence and Group Effectiveness." *Administrative Science Quarterly, 40*(1), 145–180.

Wageman, R. 1997. "Case Study: Critical Success Factors for Creating Superb Self-Managing Teams at Xerox." *Compensation & Benefits Review, 29*(5), 31–41.

Wagner, G., Pfeffer, J., & O'Reilly, C. 1984. "Organizational Demography and Turnover in Top Management Groups." *Administrative Science Quarterly, 29,* 74–92.

Walton, R. E. 1977. "Work Innovations at Topeka: After Six Years." *Journal of Applied Psychology, 63,* 81–88.

Walton, R. E., & Hackman, J. R. 1986. "Groups under Contrasting Management Strategies." In P. S. Goodman et al. (Eds.), *Designing Effective Workgroups.* San Francisco: Jossey-Bass.

Wanous, J. P. 1980. *Organizational Entry: Recruitment, Selection, and Socialization of Newcomers.* Reading, MA: Addison-Wesley.

Wason, P. C., & Johnson-Laird, P. N. 1972. *Psychology of Reasoning: Structure and Content.* Cambridge, MA: Harvard University Press.

Watson, W. E., Keimar, K., & Michaelsen, L. K. 1993. "Cultural Diversity's Impact on Interaction Process and Performance: Comparing Homogeneous and Diverse Task Groups." *Academy of Management Journal, 36*(3), 590–602.

Webb, S., & Smith, A. 1991. "IS Training Survey: Manufacturing Training Holds up as Recession Continues." *Industrial Society,* 13–15.

Weber, M. 1958. *The Protestant Ethic and the Spirit of Capitalism.* Translated by T. Parsons. New York: Scribner's.

Weber, M. 1978. *Economy and Society: An Outline of Interpretive Sociology* (G. Roth & C. Wittich, Trans.). Berkeley: University of California Press.

Wegner, D. M. 1986. "Transactive Memory: A Contemporary Analysis of the Group Mind." In B. Mullen & G. Goethals (Eds.), *Theories of Group Behavior* (pp.185–208). New York: Springer-Verlag.

Wegner, D. M. 1994. "Ironic Processes of Mental Control." *Psychological Review, 101,* 34–52.

Wegner, D. M., & Bargh, J. A. 1998. "Control and Automaticity in Everyday Life." In D. Gilbert, S. T. Fiske, & G. Lindzey (Eds.), *Handbook of Social Psychology* (4th ed., pp. 446–496). Boston: McGraw-Hill.

Wegner, D. M., Giuliano, T., & Hertel, P. 1995. "Cognitive Interdependence in Close Relationships." In W. J. Ickes (Ed.), *Compatible and Incompatible Relationships* (pp. 253–276). New York: Springer-Verlag.

Weick, K. E., & Gilfillan, D. P. 1971. "Fate of Arbitrary Traditions in a Laboratory Microculture." *Journal of Personality and Social Psychology, 17,* 179–191.

Weingart, L. R. 1992. "Impact of Group Goals, Task Component Complexity, Effort, and Planning on Group Performance." *Journal of Applied Psychology, 77,* 682–693.

Weingart, L. R., Bennett, R., & Brett, J. F. 1993. "The Impact of Consideration of Issues and Motivational Orientation on Group Negotiation Process and Outcome." *Journal of Applied Psychology, 78,* 504–517.

Weisberg, R. W. 1986. *Creativity, Genius and Other Myths.* New York: Freeman.

Weisberg, R. W. 1993. *Creativity: Beyond the Myth of Genius.* San Francisco: Freeman.

Weisberg, R. W. 1997. "Case Studies of Creative Thinking." In S. M. Smith, T. B. Ward, & R. A. Finke (Eds.), *The Creative Cognition Approach.* Cambridge, MA: MIT Press.

Weitzman, M. 1984. *The Share Economy.* Cambridge, MA: Harvard University Press.

Wellens, A. R. 1989, September. "Effects of Telecommunication Media upon Information Sharing and Team Performance: Some Theoretical and Empirical Findings." *IEEE AES Magazine, 4,* 14.

Wellins, R. S. 1992. "Building a Self-Directed Work Team." *Training and Development, 46*(12), 24–28.

Wellins, R.S., Byham, W.C., & Wilson, J.M. 1991. *Empowered Teams* (p. 26). San Francisco: Jessey-Bass, Inc., Publishers.

Werner, D., Ember, C. R., & Ember, M. 1981. *Anthropology: Study Guide and Workbook.* Upper Saddle River, NJ: Prentice Hall.

Whetton, D. A., & Cameron, K. S. 1991. *Developing Management Skills* (2nd ed.). New York: HarperCollins.

Wicker, A. W., Kermeyer, S. L., Hanson, L., & Alexander, D. 1976. "Effects of Manning Levels on Subjective Experiences, Performance, and Verbal Interaction in Groups." *Organization Behavior and Human Performance, 17,* 251–274.

Wicker, A. W., & Mehler, A. 1971. "Assimilation of New Members in a Large and a Small Church." *Journal of Applied Psychology, 55,* 151–156.

Wild, T. C., Enzle, M. E., Nix, G., & Deci, E. L. 1997. "Perceiving Others as Intrinsically or Extrinsically Motivated: Effects on Expectancy Formation and Task Engagement." *Personality and Social Psychology Bulletin, 23*(8), 837–848.

Wilder, D. A. 1986a. "Social Categorization: Implications for Creation and Reduction of Intergroup Bias." In L. Berkowitz (Ed.), *Advances in Experimental Social Psychology* (Vol. 19, pp. 291–355). Orlando, FL: Academic Press.

Wilder, D. A. 1986b. "Cognitive Factors Affecting the Success of Intergroup Contact." In S. Worchel & W. Austin (Eds.), *Psychology of Intergroup Relations* (pp. 49–66). Chicago: Nelson-Hall.

Wilder, D. A., & Allen, V. L. 1977. "Veridical Social Support, Extreme Social Support, and Conformity." *Representative Research in Social Psychology, 8,* 33–41.

Wilder, D. A., & Shapiro, P. N. 1989. "Role of Competition-Induced Anxiety in Limiting the Beneficial Impact of Positive Behavior by an Out-Group Member." *Journal of Personality & Social Psychology, 56,* 60–69.

Williams, K. D., Harkins, S. G., & Latané, B. 1981. "Identifiability as a Deterrant to Social Loafing: Two Cheering Experiments." *Journal of Personality & Social Psychology, 40*(2), 303–311.

Williams, K. D. In press. "Social Ostracism." In R. Kowalski (Ed.), *Aversive Interpersonal Behaviors.* New York: Plenum.

Williams, K. D. 1981. "The Effects of Group Cohesiveness on Social Loafing in Simulated Word-Processing Pools." *Dissertation Abstracts International, 42*(2-B), 838.

Williams, K. D., & Williams, K. B. 1984. *Social Loafing in Japan: A Cross-Cultural Development Study.* Paper presented at the Midwestern Psychological Association Meeting, Chicago.

Wittenbaum, G. M. In press. "Information Sampling in Decision-Making Groups: The Impact of Members' Task-Relevant Status." *Small Group Research.*

Word, C. O., Zanna, M. P., & Cooper, J. 1974. "The Nonverbal Mediation of Self-Fulfilling Prophecies in Interracial Interaction." *Journal of Experimental Social Psychology, 10,* 109–120.

Worringham, C. J., & Messick, D. M. 1983. "Social Facilitation of Running: An Unobtrusive Study." *Journal of Social Psychology, 121,* 23–29.

Wright, S. C., Aron, A., McLaughlin-Volpe, T., & Ropp, S. A. 1997. "The Extended Contact Effect: Knowledge of Cross-Group Friendships and Prejudice." *Journal of Personality and Social Psychology, 73*(1), 73–90.

Wright, S. C., Taylor, D. M., & Moghaddam, F. M. 1990. "Responding to Membership in a Disadvantaged Group: From Acceptance to Collective Protest." *Journal of Personality and Social Psychology, 58,* 994–1003.

Yukl, G. A. 1981. *Leadership in Organizations.* London: Prentice-Hall International.

Zaccaro, S. J. 1984. "Social Loafing: The Role of Task Attractiveness." *Personality and Social Psychology Bulletin, 10,* 99–106.

Zachary, G. P. 1996. "Beyond the Minimum Wage." *In These Times, 20*(19), 27.

Zajonc, R. 1968. "Attitudinal Effects of Mere Exposure." *Journal of Personality and Social Psychology, 9*(monograph supplement, No. 2, Part 2).

Ziller, R. C. 1957. "Four Techniques of Group Decision-Making under Uncertainty." *Journal of Applied Psychology, 41,* 384–388.

Zimbardo, P. G., Weisenberg, M., Firestone, I., & Levy, M. 1965. "Communicator Effectiveness in Producing Public Conformity and Private Attitude Change." *Journal of Personality, 33,* 233–255.

Zurcher, L. A. 1965. "The Sailor Aboard Ship: A Study of Role Behavior in a Total Institution." *Social Forces, 43,* 389–400.

Zurcher, L. A. 1970. "The 'Friendly' Poker Game: A Study of an Ephemeral Role." *Social Forces, 49,* 173–186.

Author Index

A

ABA Banking Journal, 113
Abakoumkin, G., 167
Abbott, A. S., 93, 94
Abel, M. J., 235
Adams, S., 145
Alderfer, C. P., 2, 6, 170
Alexander, D., 66
Allen, H. M. Jr., 215
Allen, T. J., 234
Allen, V. L., 111, 112
Allison, S., 147
Allmendinger, J. M., 230
Allport, G. W., 221
Altman, I., 21
Alutto, J. A., 65
Amason, A., 133
Ancona, D. G., 5, 59, 170, 171, 172, 173, 174, 187
Anderson, C., 223
Anonymous, 6, 32
Aranda, E., 6
Ardolino, A., 93
Argote, L., 78, 100, 101, 103, 104, 105
Armour, S., 257
Armstrong, D. J., 232, 236
Arnold, D. W., 66
Aron, A., 228
Arrow, K. J., 138
Asch, S. E., 110, 111
Ashbrook, R. M., 71
Associated Press, 85
Austin, J. T., 50

B

Babcock, L., 146, 148
Back, K. W., 112
Backman, C. W., 21
Baetge, M. M., 98
Bainbridge, W. S., 71
Baker, S., 244, 245, 246
Baldwin, T. T., 100
Bales, R. F., 76
Banaji, M. R., 83, 223, 224, 225
Barboza, D., 119
Barchas, P. R., 77
Bargh, J. A., 225, 226
Barker, J. R., 207
Barlett, C. A., 253
Barley, S. R., 238
Barnes-Farrell, J. L., 162
Baron, J. N., 179
Barron, R. S., 228, 229
Basalla, G., 153
Bastardi, A., 260
Batson, C. D., 193
Baumeister, R. F., 20, 22
Bazerman, M., 138, 139, 142, 144, 145
Becker, F., 247
Becker, S. W., 196
Beer, M., 209
Benne, K. D., 68
Bennett, R., 142
Bennis, W., 51
Berger, J., 77
Bergstrom, R. Y., 128
Bernardin, H. J., 49
Berscheid, E., 195, 223
Bettencourt, B. A., 218
Bettenhausen, K., 76, 77, 145
Bikson, T. K., 241
Billings, R. S., 94
Blackstone, T., 72
Blanchard, F. A., 226
Blinder, A. S., 43
Bloomfield, R., 96
Bobo, L., 214, 223
Bodenhausen, G. V., 226, 229
Bohrnstedt, G. W., 74
Boisjoly, R. M., 109
Bolick, C., 70
Bonjean, C. M., 72
Bouma, G. D., 71
Bourgeois, L. J. III, 134
Bowman, R., 226
Bradford, D. L., 227
Braly, K., 220
Brawley, L. R., 79, 80
Brem, S., 154, 156
Brett, J. F., 70, 142
Brewer, M. B., 218, 227
Brickner, M. A., 26, 27
Briggs, R. O., 161, 164
Briner, R., 200
Brinkerhoff, M. B., 71
Brocato, R. M., 22
Brodt, S., 144
Bromley, S., 223
Brommel, J. M., 22
Brousseau, K. R., 61
Browder, S., 240
Brown, A. L., 157
Brown, P. M., 196
Brown, P., 88
Brown, R. J., 227
Brown, V., 167
Bruun, S., 26
Burke, K. L., 71
Burke, P. J., 76
Burrows, L., 225
Burt, R. S., 173, 175, 176, 179, 180, 181
Bushe, G. R., 19
Byham, W. C., 209
Byrne, D., 185

C

Cacioppo, J. T., 26
Cage, J. H., 204
Caldwell, D. F., 79, 173, 187, 221
Callan, V. J., 219

Camacho, L. M., 160, 161
Cambrioso, A., 234
Camerer, C. F., 87, 148
Cameron, K. S., 255, 257, 258
Caminiti, S., 188
Campbell, D. T., 75, 77, 214
Campbell, W. K., 79
Campos, F., 145
Cannon-Bowers, J. A., 98
Carnevale, P. J., 144, 215
Carron, A. V., 79, 80
Cascio, W. F., 49
Castore, C. H., 144
Caudron, S., 56
Chase, J., 215
Chater, N., 122
Chatman, J. F., 221
Chechile, R., 139
Chen, M., 225
Chen, X. P., 136
Chen, Z., 157
Chertkoff, J., 147
Christensen, C., 93, 94, 96
Christie, B., 240
Cialdini, R. B., 100
Cini, M., 67
Clark, K. B., 169
Clemmer, J., 201, 206
Cohen, A. R., 227
Cohen, S. G., 183
Cole, P., 232, 236
Cole, R. E., 6
Coleman, J. S., 175
Collins, E. G., 33
Comb, D. B., 98
Condor, F., 227
Conger, J. A., 211
Connolly, T., 161
Consalvi, C., 112
Converse, S. A., 98
Cook, P. J., 6
Cooper, D. M., 70
Cooper, J., 194
Corder, J., 72
Coskun, H., 161, 167
Cota, A. L., 72
Cowlin, R. A., 94
Craig, J. M., 72
Crisafi, M. A., 157
Croak, M. R., 218
Crocker, J., 72
Crosby, F. J., 223, 226
Csikszentmihalyi, M., 152
Cummings, T. G., 19
Cunningham, J. A., 53
Cusumano, M. A., 7, 182

D

Daehler, M. W., 157
Daft, R. L., 233
Dailey, J. C., 168
Dalton, B., 215

Dansereau, F., 65
Darley, J. M., 25, 123, 193
Davidow, W. H., 249
Davis, J., 33
Davison, S. C., 250, 253
Dawes, R., 51, 136
Deaux, K., 220
Deci, E. L., 199
DeGroot, A., 153
DeHarpport, T., 140, 141
DeMatteo, J. S., 39
DeMeyer, A., 233, 234
Dennis, A. R., 165, 166, 167
Deutsch, M., 112, 135, 145
Devadas, R., 105
Devine, P. G., 225
Diehl, M., 159, 160, 167
Dion, K. L., 72, 79, 195, 223
Dollard, J., 224
Doob, L. W., 224
Dovidio, J. F., 223, 224
Dow Jones News Service, 46
Drenan, S., 215
Driver, R. W., 113
Drolet, A., 83
Dubé, L., 216
Dubrovsky, V. J., 243, 244
Duck, J. M., 199
Dugoni, B. L., 152, 157
Dunbar, K., 150
Duncan, S. L., 221
Durham, C., 200
Dzindolet, M. T., 161, 167

E

Eby, L. T., 39
Eckland, B. K., 74
Economist, 6
Eggins, R. A., 196
Egido, C., 21, 234
Eisenberger, R., 53
Eisenhardt, K. M., 134
Eisenstat, R. A., 209
Elliot, A. J., 79
Elsass, P. M., 126
Elstrom, P., 240
Ember, C. R., 23
Ember, M., 23
Emery, F. E., 237
Enzle, M. E., 199
Erber, R., 226
Esses, V. M., 230
Etcoff, N. L., 71
Etzkowitz, H., 181, 182
Evans, C. R., 79
Eveland, J. D., 241

F

Fader, R., 145
Fairhurst, G. T., 72
Fan, E. T., 64, 65, 114, 174, 182, 184

Farwell, L., 147
Faust, W. L., 23
Feld, S. L., 71
Feldman, D. C., 75
Ferdman, B. M., 226
Ferguson, R., 154, 156
Festinger, L., 192, 193
Field, R. H. G., 204
Firestone, I., 141, 192
Fischer, G. W., 220
Fischhoff, B., 15
Fisek, M. H., 77
Fisher, G. A., 74
Fisher, R., 140
Fishman, C., 3, 26, 31
Fiske, S. T., 71
Foa, E., 136
Foa, U., 136
Fontana, L., 71
Forbus, K. D., 156
Ford, J. K., 51, 100
Foster-Fishman, P. G., 95
Fourment, C., 185
Foushee, H. C., 98
Frable, D. E., 72
Frank, M. G., 224
Frank, R. H., 6
Franz, T. M., 93, 94, 95
Freedman, J. L., 53
Friedlander, F., 6
Fry, W. R., 141
Fujimoto, T., 169
Fullerton, T. D., 80
Funk, C. L., 51
Fussell, S. R., 86, 88
Futoran, G. C., 186

G

Gabrenya, W. K., 23
Gaertner, S. L., 223, 224
Galagan, P., 19
Galegher, J., 21, 234
Gallupe, R. B., 166
Gamble, I., 216
Garber, S., 105
Gardner, P. D., 220
Gardner, W. L., 100
Garfield, C., 36, 57
Gauron, E. F., 75
Gauvin, S., 161
Geber, B., 236, 249
Gellar, V., 240
Gendron, G., 158
Gentner, D. R., 96
Gentner, D., 96, 154, 156, 157
Gerard, H. B., 112, 227
Gersick, C. J. C., 77
Ghoshal, S., 253
Gibb, J. R., 23
Gick, M. L., 154, 155, 156, 157
Gigone, D., 88, 95, 96
Gilfillan, D. P., 78

Gill, D. L., 80
Gillespie, J. J., 181
Gilmore, R., 215
Gilovich, T., 87, 100, 224, 259
Giuliano, T., 99
Glasser, I., 226
Glickman, A. S., 65, 80
Gold, M., 74
Goldberg, P., 224
Golden, S. B., 71
Goldstein, I. L., 100
Goleman, D., 113, 200
Goodman, P. S., 105
Grabski, S. V., 220
Graen, G., 20
Granovetter, M., 177
Greek, D., 5
Greenberg, C. I., 66
Greenberg, J., 24, 26
Greenwald, A. G., 83, 223, 224
Griffin, D. W., 87
Griffith, J., 105
Griffith, V., 8
Grimsley, K. D., 213
Gross, S. E., 36, 38, 39, 40, 41, 54, 57
Grossman, S. R., 168
Grossmann, J., 164
Gruder, C. L., 79
Gruenfeld, D. H., 29, 64, 65, 96, 100,
        152, 174, 182, 183, 184, 223,
        268
Guerette, P. J., 80
Guetzkow, H., 33, 132
Guilford, J. P., 151, 157
Guimond, S., 216
Gutek, B. A., 220
Guzzo, R. A., 19, 39, 80, 109
Gyr, J., 132

H

Hackman, J. R., 2, 3, 4, 18, 20, 29, 30,
        61, 65, 100, 201, 230
Hackman, R., 10
Hains, S. C., 199
Hall, F., 205
Hallmark, W., 146, 147
Hambrick, D. C., 79, 209, 210, 250, 253
Hanks, M., 74
Hanna, C., 92, 94
Hanson, L., 66
Harber, K. D., 224
Hardin, C., 225
Hargadon, A., 168
Harkins, S. G., 26, 27, 161
Harring, K., 215
Harris, V. A., 84, 198
Harvey, J., 124, 125, 126
Harvey, O. J., 112
Haslam, S. A., 196
Hastie, R., 88, 95, 96, 140, 144, 197
Hatfield, E., 195
Heath, C., 50, 51

Heilman, M. E., 204
Hequet, M., 189
Herschlag, J. K., 204
Hertel, P., 99
Higgins, E. T., 86, 152
Hill, M., 8
Hill, S., 18
Hillkirk, J., 46
Hiltz, S. R., 241
Hinde, R. A., 21
Hindman, H. D., 50
Hof, R. D., 240
Hoffman, L. R., 118
Hoffman, R., 48
Hogg, M. A., 80, 112, 199
Holland, K., 5
Hollander, E. P., 112
Hollingshead, A. B., 95
Holton, B., 215
Holyoak, K. J., 154, 155, 156, 157
Hong, G., 215
Hook, L. H., 195
Hopkins, K. R., 70
Horn, E. M., 162
Hornstein, H. A., 204
House, R. J., 204
Howells, L. T., 196
Hoyle, R., 215
Hrebec, D., 140
Huber, V. L., 50
Huey, J., 206
Huseman, R. C., 113

I

Ibarra, H., 179
Ickes, W., 74
Imperato, G., 5
Inks, L., 52
Insko, C., 215
Issacharoff, S., 148
Izraeli, D. N., 72

J

Jackson, J. M., 26, 161
Jackson, L. A., 220
Jackson, P., 112
Jackson, S. E., 70, 152
Jacobs, R. C., 75, 78
Jacobson, L., 193
Jago, A. G., 202
Janis, I. L., 112, 113, 117, 129
Jarman, M., 46
Jehn, K. A., 133, 134
Jessup, L. M., 164
Jetten, J., 226
Johansen, R., 249
Johnson, C., 159, 160, 162
Johnson, K., 241
Johnson-Laird, P. N., 96, 122
Johnston, W. B., 70
Jonas, K., 227

Jones, E. E., 84, 198
Jones, J. M., 216
Jourard, S. M., 21
Judd, C. M., 220
Julin, J. A., 70

K

Kahn, R. L., 33
Kahneman, D., 197, 243
Kahwajy, J. L., 134
Kameda, T., 179
Kanter, R. M., 72
Karau, S. J., 160
Kasmer, J., 26
Katz, D., 33, 220
Katz, R., 106, 107
Katzenbach, J. R., 11, 27
Keating, P., 234
Keimar, K., 70
Keisler, S., 234, 240, 241, 242, 243,
        244
Keller, G., 201
Kellett, S., 200
Kelley, H. H., 28, 74
Kelly, J. R., 186
Keltner, D. J., 222, 223
Kemelgor, C., 181, 182
Kempton, W., 97
Kermeyer, S. L., 66
Kerr, M., 259
Kerr, N. L., 25, 26, 27, 65, 228, 229
Keys, C. B., 95
Keysar, B., 87, 239
Kidder, T., 174
Kim, P., 152
King, R. T. Jr., 36
Kipnis, D., 185
Kirksey, J., 48
Kirsner, S., 59
Klein, J. A., 188
Klimoski, R., 52, 97
Knight, D., 200
Knight-Ridder Newspapers, 220
Koh, K., 156
Kohn, A., 53
Komorita, S., 144, 147
Kotovsky, L., 157
Kraiger, K., 51
Kramer, M. W., 168
Kramer, R. M., 114, 143, 218
Kramer, T. J., 161
Krauss, R. M., 86, 88
Kraut, R. E., 21, 234
Kravitz, D. A., 23
Kray, L., 79, 116, 122
Kresa, K., 6
Krishnan, R., 100, 101, 104
Krismer, K., 53
Kuhlman, D., 145
Kuo, C. L., 168
Kurtzberg, T., 140, 250
Kwan, J. L., 152, 157

L

Labor Letter, 100
LaFasto, F. M., 62, 63, 89, 150
Lalonde, R. N., 216
Landers, R., 156
Landry, P., 215
Landy, D., 195, 224
Langan, C. J., 112
Larey, T. S., 161, 167
Larrick, R., 83
Larsen, I. M., 61
Larson, C. E., 62, 63, 89, 150
Larson, J. R., 93, 94, 95, 96
Latané, B., 23, 25, 26, 65, 123
Lauber, J. K., 98
Laughlin, P. R., 33, 95
Law, K., 156
Lawler, E. E., 35, 38, 39, 42, 43, 44,
    50, 204, 207
Leary, M., 160
Lederberg, J., 248
Ledford, G. E. Jr., 35, 50
Leggett, K. L., 161, 167
LeJeune, M., 79
Lengel, R. H., 233
Lenkert, A., 227
Lerner, M. O., 215
Leve, C., 116, 117
Levine, J. M., 67, 74, 75, 78, 102, 112,
    133, 145, 152
Levine, M., 139
LeVine, R. A., 214
Levinger, G. K., 21
Levinson, S. C., 88
Levy, M., 192
Lewin, K., 17
Lewis, B. P., 22
Lewis, S. A., 112, 141
Leyden, D. P., 105
Liang, D. W., 103
Libby, R., 96, 102
Liberman, N., 118
Liden, R. C., 20
Lightdale, J. R., 80
Limayem, M., 161
Lind, A., 79, 116, 122
Lind, E. A., 53
Linder, D. E., 22
Linkous, R. A., 22
Linville, P. W., 220
Littlepage, G., 105
Locke, E. A., 200
Loewenstein, G. F., 87, 136, 146, 147,
    148
Loewenstein, J., 156, 157, 259
Lord, C., 71, 72
Los Angeles Times, 8
Louis, M. R., 75, 79
Lowe, C. A., 162
Lublin, J. S., 35
Lynn, M., 131, 134
Lyons, M., 244

M

Machatka, D. E., 186
MacKenzie, M., 234
Macrae, C. N., 226
Magaro, P. A., 71
Maier, N. R. F., 117, 118
Maio, G. R., 230
Maisonneuve, J., 185
Malone, M. S., 249
Mann, L., 113
Manning, J. F., 80
Mannix, E. A., 96, 100, 136, 138,
    139, 142, 144, 145
Marchetti, M., 1
Marcus, M., 19
Markham, S. E., 65
Markham, W. T., 72
Markman, A. B., 157
Martin, B., 23
Martin, J. K., 70
Martorana, P., 114, 184
Mathew, A., 227
May, K., 139
Mazur, A., 77
McAlister, L., 145
McCallum, D., 215
McCaskey, M. B., 185
McCauley, C., 116, 214
McClintock, C., 145
McGahan, A., 201
McGarty, C., 196
McGrath, J. E., 65, 186, 241
McGraw, K. M., 72
McGregor, D., 50, 207
McGuire, T., 241, 243, 244
McGuire, W. J., 72
McLaughlin-Volpe, T., 228
McPherson, J. M., 71
Meadow, A., 159
Medvec, V. H., 87, 259
Meherabian, A., 234
Mehler, A., 66
Meindl, J. R., 215
Messick, D., 22, 145, 147
Michaels, S. W., 22
Michaelsen, L. K., 70
Michel, J. G., 79
Milgram, S., 191
Miller, C. E., 112
Miller, C. T., 214
Miller, D. T., 51, 80
Miller, N. E., 224
Miller, N., 218, 228, 229
Milliken, W. F., 169
Milliman, J. F., 48
Milne, A. B., 226
Mintzberg, H., 20
Mittleman, D. D., 164
Moghaddam, F. M., 216
Mohammed, S., 97
Mohrman, A. M., 39, 183
Mohrman, S. A., 19, 35, 39, 50, 183

Montero, R., 80
Moore, B. R., 168
Moore, D., 140, 250
Moran, L., 4
Moreland, R. L., 67, 74, 75, 78, 100,
    101, 102, 103, 104, 133, 145
Morningstar, G., 258
Morris, C. G., 100
Morris, M. W., 83
Morris, M., 140, 250
Morris, N., 96
Morrison, B. E., 196
Moses, A., 240
Mosvick, R., 255
Mowrer, O. H., 224
Mueller, J., 112
Mullen, B., 72, 159, 160, 162
Mulvey, P. W., 126
Murnighan, J. K., 23, 76, 77, 144,
    145, 268, 269
Musselwhite, E., 4
Myers, D., 65

N

Nadler, D. A., 5
Nadler, J., 140
Nagasundaram, M., 167
Nahavandi, A., 6
Nanus, B., 51
Naquin, C., 268
Neale, M. A., 50, 96, 100
Neider, L. L., 105
Nelson, B., 42
Nelson, M. W., 96
Nelson, R. B., 255
Nemeth, C. J., 133, 152, 157, 196
Nestleroth, S. L., 70
Nieva, V. F., 65, 220
Nix, G., 199
Norman, C., 48
Northcraft, G. B., 50
Novak, C. J., 45
Novick, L. R., 156
Nunamaker, J. F. Jr., 161, 164, 165, 166

O

O'Connor, K. M., 144, 240
O'Connor, M. S., 163
O'Hamilton, J., 244, 245, 246
O'Hara-Devereaux, M., 249
O'Reilly, C. A., 70, 79, 221
Oaksford, M., 122
Oberle, J., 105
Oddou, G., 105
Offner, A. K., 161
Ohtsubo, Y., 179
Oldham, J., 135
Olson, C. A., 146
Olson, M., 27
Orbell, J., 51, 136
Ordeshook, P., 139, 144

Orsburn, J. D., 4
Ortega, A. H., 167
Osborn, A. F., 158, 159, 162
Osgood, C. E., 228
Ostrom, T. M., 26, 27
Owens, P. D., 114
Oxley, N. L., 161

P

Packer, A. E., 70
Padawer-Singer, A., 72
Palmade, G., 185
Pape, W. R., 231, 248
Paranka, D., 165, 166
Park, B., 220
Parks, C. D., 94, 144
Parnell, C., 1, 64
Parnes, S. J., 159
Parsons, T., 76
Pascale, R., 9
Pascarella, P., 38, 41
Paulus, P. B., 160, 161, 162, 167
Pennington, N., 144
Penrod, S., 144
Perkins, D. V., 66
Perrow, C., 98
Peters, J. F., 60
Peterson, E., 144
Peterson, R. S., 114, 152
Pettigrew, T. F., 216
Pettit, J., 256
Petty, R. E., 26
Petty, R. M., 66
Peyronnin, K., 70
Pfeffer, J., 70
Pfeiffer, C., 93
Phelps, R., 28
Philip, G., 235
Pinkley, R., 215
Plott, C., 139
Podolny, J. M., 179
Pope, S., 60
Popielarz, P. A., 179
Postman, L., 221
Powell, L., 48
Poza, E. J., 19
PR Newswire, 27-28
Pratkanis, A. R., 116, 117
Prelic, D., 259
Prentice, D. A., 80
Prentice-Dunn, S., 65, 224
Probasco, P., 116, 117
Pruitt, D. G., 141, 215
Putman, V. L., 161, 167

Q

Quinn, K. L., 247

R

Rabbie, J. M., 215
Raiffa, H., 143

Rand, K. A., 144
Rappaport, A. J., 247
Ratner, R., 51
Rattermann, M. J., 156
Rausch, H. L., 21
Raven, B. H., 113
Rawlings, E. I., 75
Reddington, K., 105
Reeder, G. D., 79
Reeves, L., 156
Reinig, B. A., 161
Resnick, L. B., 152
Reynolds, K. J., 196
Rhoades, J. A., 240
Rickards, T., 168
Ridgeway, C. L., 72
Riecken, H. W., 192, 193
Riess, M., 196
Ringelmann, M., 23
Robinson, D. T., 72
Robinson, R. J., 222
Robison, W., 105
Rodgers, B. E., 168
Rogelberg, S. G., 162, 163
Rogers, M. S., 61
Rogers, R. W., 65, 224
Roland, E. J., 161, 167
Romer, D., 79
Ropp, S. A., 228
Rosenfeld, P., 196
Rosenholtz, S. J., 77
Rosenthal, E. A., 179
Rosenthal, R., 193, 235
Ross, B. H., 156
Ross, J., 120, 122
Ross, L., 87, 190, 195
Rothbard, N., 268
Rothbart, M., 146, 147, 220
Rothman, A. J., 225
Rouse, W., 96
Routhieaux, R. L., 161
Rowe, J. S., 22
Roy, M. C., 161
Royal, E. G., 71
Rubin, J. Z., 113
Ruder, M. K., 80
Ruderman, A. J., 71
Ruffin, P., 215
Rutkowski, G. K., 79

S

Saenz, D., 71, 72
Salas, E., 98, 109, 159, 160, 162
Salovey, P., 220
Samuels, S. M., 195
Sanfey, A., 197
Savage, L. J., 260
Savitsky, K., 87
Saxe, L., 223
Schachter, S., 192, 193
Schein, E. H., 77
Scherbaum, C., 72

Schersching, C., 112
Schneider, S. K., 161
Schofield, J. W., 226, 227
Schrage, M., 47, 232, 242
Schriescheim, C. A., 105
Schuman, H., 223
Schutte, J. G., 238
Schwartz, B., 51
Sears, D. O., 51, 215
Sears, R. R., 224
Secord, P. F., 21
Sedekides, C., 79
Segal, M. W., 185, 214
Seilheimmer, S., 215
Selbert, R., 70
Selbst, M., 53
Senge, P. M., 205
Sessa, V. I., 70
Seta, J. J., 161
Sethna, B. N., 243, 244
Shafir, E., 260
Shah, P. P., 134
Shapiro, P. N., 229
Shaver, K. G., 84, 198
Shaw, M., 66, 69, 147
Shea, G. P., 19, 39, 80
Sheats, P., 68
Sheehan, N., 119
Shepherd, M. M., 161
Shepperd, J. A., 160
Sherif, C. W., 72
Sherif, M., 170
Shils, E., 76
Short, J., 240
Shure, G. H., 61
Siegel, J., 241, 243, 244
Sigall, H., 195, 224
Silberman, M., 105
Simonton, D. K., 189
Sims, R. R., 113
Sims, W. R., 247
Slim, R., 215
Smith, A., 100
Smith, C. M., 152, 157
Smith, D. K., 11, 27
Smith, H. J., 137
Smith, S., 246
Smith-Lovin, L., 71, 72
Snavely, B. K., 72
Snell, S. A., 250, 253
Snoek, J. D., 21
Snow, C. C., 250, 253
Snyder, M., 195, 216
Sommer, R., 195
South, S. J., 72
Sparrowe, R. T., 179
Spector, B., 209
Sprecher, S., 195
Sproull, L., 234, 240, 241, 242
Stark, R., 71
Stasser, G., 91, 92, 94, 95, 96, 102
Staw, B. M., 120, 121, 122
Steeh, C., 223

Steele, C. M., 221
Steiner, I., 20, 33, 65
Steinhilber, A., 22
Stewart, D. D., 94, 95, 96, 102
Stires, L. K., 84, 198
Stitt, C. L., 214
Stogdill, R. M., 79
Stokes, J. P., 80
Stoner, J. A. F., 128
Strodtbeck, F. L., 195
Stroebe, W., 159, 160, 167, 227
Sullivan, L. A., 220
Sumner, W., 218
Sundstrom, E. D., 39, 80
Sundstrom, M. G., 80
Sutton, R. I., 168
Swensen, C. H., 21
Szymanski, K., 26

T

Tajfel, H., 112, 215, 218
Takezawa, M., 179
Tanke, E. D., 195
Tannenbaum, S. I., 98
Tasson, J., 61
Taylor, D. A., 21
Taylor, D. M., 216
Taylor, D. W., 23
Taylor, F. W., 50
Taylor, L. A., 92, 94
Taylor, S. E., 71
Terry, D. J., 219
Tetlock, P. E., 114
Tetrault, L. A., 105
Teuchmann, K., 200
Thibaut, J., 74, 215
Thomas-Hunt, M. C., 152
Thompson, J., 63
Thompson, L., 79, 116, 122, 138, 139,
    140, 141, 142, 143, 144, 146,
    147, 148, 156, 157, 218, 233,
    239, 250, 267, 268
Tickle-Degnen, L., 235
Tindale, R. S., 152, 157
Tippett, D. D., 60
Titus, W., 91, 92
Totterdell, P., 200
Train, J., 119
Trevino, L. K., 233
Triandis, H. C., 21
Trist, E. L., 237
Trope, Y., 118

Tropman, J. E., 256, 257, 258, 265
Trotman, K. T., 102
Tuch, S. A., 70
Turkle, S., 240
Turner, J. C., 112, 215, 218
Turner, M. E., 116, 117
Turner, M., 74
Turoff, M., 241
Tversky, A., 197, 243
Tyler, T. R., 51, 53, 137, 198

U

U.S. Bureau of Labor Statistics, 37
U.S. Bureau of Census, 37
Uncaphor, K., 249
Ury, W., 140
Uzzi, B., 83, 181, 182

V

Valacich, J. S., 164
Valley, K. L., 143, 218
van Avermaet, E., 147
van de Kragt, A., 51, 136
Van Maanen, J., 75, 79
van Oostrum, J., 215
Van Vianen, A. E., 221
Vanneman, S., 216
Veiga, J. F., 126
Villanova, P., 50
Vlasic, B., 244, 245, 246
Vogel, D. R. A., 165, 166
von Hippel, E. A., 169
Vroom, V. H., 202, 203

W

Wachtler, J., 152, 196
Wade, G., 227
Wageman, R., 39, 60
Wagner, G., 70
Walster, E., 223
Walton, R. E., 19, 201
Wang, Y., 23
Wanous, J. P., 75
Wason, P. C., 122
Watson, W. E., 70
Webb, S., 100
Weber, M., 87, 207
Weeks, R., 268, 269
Wegner, D. M., 99, 226
Weick, K. E., 78

Weiner, B., 147
Weingart, L. R., 61, 142
Weisberg, R. W., 153, 156
Weisenberg, M., 192
Weiss, J. A., 61
Weitzman, M., 42
Wellens, A. R., 234
Wellins, R. S., 209
Werner, D., 23
Whetton, D. A., 255, 257, 258
Wicker, A. W., 66
Widmeyer, W. N., 79, 80
Wild, T. C., 199
Wilder, D. A., 111, 216, 229
Willemsen, T. M., 221
Williams, D. L., 141
Williams, E., 240
Williams, J. A., 227
Williams, K. B., 23
Williams, K. D., 23, 26, 27, 78, 160
Williams, K. Y., 96, 100
Wilson, J. M., 209
Winter, J. P., 161
Wittenbaum, G. M., 96, 102
Wolff, P., 154, 157
Word, C. O., 194
Worringham, C. J., 22
Wright, S. C., 216, 228

Y

Yanof, D. S., 74
Yen, J., 161
Yetton, P. W., 202, 203
Young, E. S., 235
Yukl, G. A., 189

Z

Zaccaro, S. J., 26
Zachary, G. P., 7
Zajonc, R., 83, 199
Zanna, M. P., 194
Zawacki, R. F., 48
Zelditch, M., 77
Zellerer, F., 216
Zenger, J. H., 4
Ziller, R. C., 23
Zimbardo, P. G., 192
Zimmer, I., 102
Zimmer, S., 80
Zubrow, D., 240
Zurcher, L. A., 75

Subject Index

A

Abilene paradox, 124–28
abstraction. *See* comparison and
    abstraction
accountability, 27, 94
advisor, 174
affective conflict, 132, 133, 134
affirmative action, 229–30
agenda, 28, 264–65
agentic activities, 72
analogical reasoning, 154–57
announcements, in meetings, 256
anticipation, 102
Arrow paradox, 138
attitudes, instant, 83
A-type conflict, 132, 133, 134
autocratic decision method, 202
autonomy, 12
avoidance-avoidance conflict, in
    meetings, 259–60
awareness, 199

B

bandwagon bias, 52
base pay, 38
BATNA principle, 140–46
behavioral stability, 106
behavioral synchrony, 199
benchmarks, for brainstorming, 161
best alternative to a negotiated
    agreement. *See* BATNA
    principle
bias, 213
    in communication, 86–88
    about conflict, 132
    hindsight, 15
    homogeneity, 51, 71
    in-group, 218, 219
    physical attractiveness, 194–95

ratee, 52–54
rater, 50–52
biased interpretation, 87
biased interview process, 194
blind faith, 191–93
blinding, 225–26
blind justice, 145
bonding, 79–80
bonus pay, 39
boundaries, 170
boundary spanner, 174, 176–77
boundedness, 2
brainstorming
    electronic, 164–68
    group, 158–63
    individual, 159
brainwriting, 162
broadcasting teams, 171
bufferer, 174
bureaucratic organizations, 201
bystander effect, 123

C

calculated trust, 81
capability problems, 186
capacity problems, 186
card test, 122
cash awards, 40–42
categorization
    and behavior, 216–17
    creativity through, 151–52
    need for, 216
cautious shift, 128
clique networks, 175–76, 178, 181
close-mindedness, 114
coaching function, 10
coalitions, 144–45
cognitive conflict, 132–34
cognitive flexibility, creativity
    through, 152

cohesion, 79–80
collaboratory, 248–49
collective intelligence, 85–86
    team mental models, 96–99
    transactive memory systems,
        99–105
    See also information dependence
        problem
commitment, 74. *See also* escalation
    of commitment
commitment organizations, 201
common knowledge effect, 88–91
communal activities, 72
communication, 85–86
    biases in, 86–88
    and compensation, 57
    links in, 29
    place-time model of, 233–40
    and rater bias, 52
    See also discussion; information
        dependence problem
comparison and abstraction, 156–57
compensation, 35–38, 58
    gainsharing, 42–43
    guiding principles, 54–57
    incentive pay, 38–39
    profit sharing, 42
    recognition, 39–42
competencies, 38–39
competency-based pay, 44–45
competition, 6, 136–37
conflict, 10, 131, 148
    biases about, 132
    in democracy, 137–46
    escalation, 146–48
    in meetings, 259–60
    realistic group, 214
    symbolic, 214
    team dilemma, 135–37
    types of, 132–35
conformity, 110–12, 160

consciousness-raising, 226–27
consensus building, 202
consultants, special tips for, 263–65
consultative decision method, 202
contact
    face-to-face, 84, 242, 249
    mere, 227–28
    and prejudice, 227–28
context, team, 18–20
context dependence, creativity
        through, 152
contingency contracts, 142–43
contracts, team, 27
contribution-based distribution, 145
convergent thinking, 157–58
cooperation, enhancing, 136–37
coordination problems, 160
coordination strategies, 27–29
coordinator, 174
correspondence, between team
        mental models, 98–99
covert racism, 223–24
creative teams, 63
creativity, 150, 168
    analogical reasoning, 154–57
    defining, 151–52
    divergent versus convergent
        thinking, 157–58
    electronic brainstorming,
        164–68
    group brainstorming, 158–63
    individual and team, 152–54
C-type conflict, 132–34
culture, team, 19–20
curse of knowledge, 87

D

decision analysis model, 202–4
decision making, 109–10, 129–30
    and conformity, 110–12
    and information dependence
        problem, 94
    in meetings, 256, 259–60
    pitfalls
        Abilene paradox, 124–28
        escalation of commitment,
            118–24
        group polarization, 128–29
        groupthink, 112–18
        unanimous, 138
decision tree model, 204
deindividuation, 25
delegation, 202, 204–5
Delphi technique, 163
democracy, perils and pitfalls of
    BATNA principle, 140–46
    group negotiation, 139–40
    voting, 137–39
demonstrable tasks, 65
description, 17
design, team, 19

design function, 10
diagnosis, accuracy of, 14–15
differences, leveraging, 142–43
different place, different time com-
        munication, 238–40
different time, same place commu-
        nication, 237–38
discrimination, 214, 224–25
discussion
    and information dependence
        problem, 93–94
    in meetings, 256
    sequential, 142
    See also communication
disembedded exchange networks,
        182
distance, 184–86
divergent thinking, 157–58
diversity, 68–69
    creating, 72–73
    and creativity, 151–52
    of networks, 181–82
    SWOT analysis of, 69–72

E

effort, 23–27
egocentric bias, 52–53
electronic brainstorming (EBS),
        164–68
e-mail, 238–40, 242
embedded networks, 181
emotional conflict. *See* A-type con-
        flict
empowerment
    effects of, 207–8
    encouraging, 204–7
    and fragmentation, 210
    red flags, 210–11
    top management teams, 208–10
entrepreneurial opportunities,
        177
entrepreneur network, 178
"envelopes and money" game, 23
equality, 145, 166
equifinality, 32–33
equity, 145
equity method, determination
        of, 55
escalation of commitment, 118–24
ethnocentrism, 181, 218
experience effect, 52
expertise, 22, 156
external environment, 169–70,
        186–87
    boundaries, 170
    distance, 184–86
    identity, 173
    interteam relations, 170–73
    member roles, 173, 174
    networking, 173, 175–84
    time, 186

extremism, 222–23
extrinsic incentives bias, 50–52

F

face-saving mechanisms, 116
face-to-face contact, 233–35
    and technology, 242
    and trust, 84
    and virtual teams, 249
facilitators
    for brainstorming, 161
    special tips for, 263–65
failed memory, 260–61
failures
    circumstantial, 10–11
    experimenting with, 8, 10
    misattribution error, 8
    perspective-taking, 87
fairness, 53–54, 145–46
faith
    blind, 191–93
    and trust, 80–81
familiarity, 199
fatigue reduction, 229
feedback, 27, 236, 265
financial measures, 55
fixed-pie fallacy, 140
flaming, 239
flattery, 83–84
flexibility, 151
flexible furniture, 245–46
flexible space, 244–45
fluency, 151
4P meeting management model,
        255–56, 257
framing effect, 243
free riders, 24–25
functional distance, 185
functional ethnocentrism, 181
functional expertise, 67
fundamental attribution error, 51,
        190
furniture, flexible, 245–46

G

gains, 197–98
gainsharing, 42–43
gatekeeper, 174
gender, and social capital, 182
global teams, 250–53
Good Samaritans, 193
Graduated and Reciprocal
        Initiative in Tension
        Reduction (GRIT),
        228, 229
Great Opportunity theory,
        189–96
Great Person theory, 189–90
ground rules, for facilitators, 264
group brainstorming, 158–63

group interests, versus individual interests, 135–37
group membership, 215–25
    categorization, 216–17
    discrimination, 224–25
    extremism, 222–23
    in-groups, 217–19
    minority groups, 220–22
    out-groups, 217–18, 219–20
    performance evaluation, 222
    racism, 223–24
    See also interteam relations; relationships; team members
group negotiation, 139–40
group polarization, 128–29
group socialization, 74–75
groupthink, 112–18

H

halo bias, 51
head of the table effect, 195–96
heterogeneity aversion, 71–72
hidden profile, 91–93
hierarchical networks, 182
hindsight bias, 15
homogeneity, 106–7, 219–20
homogeneity bias, 51, 71
hoteling, 246–47
human capital, 175–76
humanitarian leadership, 193
human resources, optimizing, 102

I

ideas
    categorization of, 151–52
    parallel entry of, 165
    refinement and evaluation of, 166
identity, 136, 173, 198–99. *See also* group membership
imperfect markets, 175
implementation power, 207
implicit trust, 83–84
impossibility theorem, 138
incentive pay, 38–39, 137
indirect speech acts, 87–88
individual brainstorming, 159
individual growth, 31, 32
individual interests, versus group interests, 135–37
inert knowledge problem, 156
informal communication, loss of, 236
informal modeling, loss of, 236
information
    providing, 141
    sharing, 140–41
    vivid, 197–200
information age, and teams, 7
informational clones, 89
information broker, 178

information dependence problem, 88
    common knowledge effect, 88–91
    hidden profile, 91–93
    inadequate solutions, 93–94
    interventions, 94–96
information dependent individuals, 110–11
information exchange, and technology, 242
information managers, 94–96
information redundancy, 90
information systems (IS), and 360-degree program, 47
information technology, 231–32
    and local teamwork, 244–47
    place-time model, 233–40
    and social behavior, 240–44
    transnational teams, 250–53
    virtual teams, 247–450
in-group bias, 218, 219
in-groups, 217–19
innovation, versus routinization, 105–8
instant attitudes, 83
insulating teams, 171
integration, 31, 182–84
interdependence, 2, 63–64
interpersonal skills, 67–68
interpreter, 174
interteam relations, 170–73
    group membership, 215–25
    overview, 213–15
    and prejudice, 225–30
    See also group membership; relationships; team members
intervention, theory-based, 15
intrinsic interest, and ratee bias, 53
intuition, 143
iron cage, 207

J

job-based pay, 44
job interviewing, 194
job involvement, 206
journey, 97
justice, norms of, 145–46

K

knowledge
    curse of, 87
    and performance, 20–22

L

labels, power of, 195
latent stereotype, 221–22
leaders
    information managers, 94–96
    random selection of, 196

leadership, 10, 211–12
    decision analysis model, 202–4
    and empowerment, 207–8
    and Great Opportunity theory, 189–96
    and Great Person theory, 189–90
    and participative management, 204–11
    and senior team fragmentation, 210
    and team empowerment, 208–9
    team paradox, 188–89
    and teamwork, 200–201
    360-degree, 274–76
leadership behavior, 197–200
leveraging differences, 142–43
lightning bolts, 40–42
light of day test, 239
lobbyist, 174
local teamwork, enhancing, 244–47
lose-lose outcome, 140
losses, 197–98

M

majority rules, 138, 144
manager-led teams, 3
managers
    information managers, 94–96
    minority, 179
    and misattribution error, 8
    and networking, 179–80
    team-building responsibilities, 8, 9
    team survey, 11–15
manufactured product model, 97
marketing teams, 172
markets, perfect and imperfect, 175
marriage model, 97
mediator, 174
medical diagnosis, hidden profiles in, 93
meetings, 255
    advice for attendees, 258–59
    diseases and fallacies, 259–61
    facilitator/consultant tips, 263–65
    4P management model, 255–56
    problem people in, 257
memory, failed, 260–61
mental models, team, 96–97
mere contact, 227–28
mere exposure, 83, 199
message distortion, 86
message tuning, 86
metacommunication, 239
mimicking, 83
minority groups, 220–22
minority managers, 179
misattribution error, 8
motivation, 23–27
multiple offers, 141–42

multirater feedback program. *See* 360-degree program

N

negotiation
   group, 139–40
   role, 75–77
   team-on-team, 144
negotiator, 174
networking, 173
   boundary spanning and structural holes, 176–77
   human capital and social capital, 175–76
   and managers, 179–80
   perfect and imperfect markets, 175
   structural positioning, 180–84
   types of, 177–79
   See also social networks
next-in-line strategy, 264
nominal group technique, 162, 163
noncash awards, 40–42
nondemonstrable tasks, 65
norms, 19–20
   development and enforcement, 77–79
   of justice, 145–46
   social, and technology, 243

O

obedience to authority principle, 190–91
observational learning, loss of, 236
office space, redesigning, 244–47
on-line planning, 61
operational measures, 55
organizational context, 19
organizational involvement, 206–7
organizational productivity, 31–32
organizations, teams in. *See* teams
originality, 151
ostracism, 78
out-groups, 217–18, 219–20
out-of-the-loop employees, 236–37
overbounded teams, 170
overcommitment phenomenon, 259
overt racism, 223–24

P

parallel entry of ideas, 165
parallel suggestion involvement, 206
participative management. *See* empowerment
pay. *See* compensation
peer evaluations. *See also* performance appraisal; Personal Effectiveness in Team Environments; 360-degree programs

people. *See* team members
perfect markets, 175
performance, 33–34
   coordination strategies, 27–29
   criteria, 29–33
   effort and motivation, 23–27
   equation for, 33
   integrated model, 18
   knowledge and skill, 20–22
   standards, 29
   and team context, 18–20
   and technology, 243–44
   and transactive memory systems, 100
performance appraisal, 35–36, 43–44, 58
   competency-based, 44–45
   job-based, 44
   PETE. *See* Personal Effectiveness in Team Environments
   ratee bias, 52–54
   rater bias, 50–52
   skill-based, 44
   360-degree program, 45–50, 68, 274–76
   and group membership, 222
performance threats, 33
Personal Effectiveness in Team Environments (PETE), 271, 272, 273
perspective-taking failures, 87
physical attractiveness bias, 194–95
physical environment, and facilitators, 263
place-time model, 233–40
pledges, 136–37
pluralistic ignorance, 124
polarization, group, 128–29
pooled interdependence, 63–64
postsettlement settlements, 143
potential productivity, 33
power, and information technology, 240–41
powerlessness, 210–11
practice, 22, 29
praise, 42
prejudice, 214, 225–30
preplanning, 61
prescription, 17
prescriptive norm, 19
primacy, 198
primacy bias, 52
private votes, 127
problem identification, 202, 204
problem people, in meetings, 257
problem-solving teams, 62–63
process, 33
process loss, 33
productivity, 29–30, 31–33
profit sharing, 42
project determinants, 120
propinquity effect, 185

proscriptive norm, 19
pseudostatus characteristics, 76–77
psychological determinants, 120–22
public posting, 26

R

racism, overt and covert, 223–24
raising the bar, 57
ratee bias, 52–54
rater bias, 50–52
realistic group conflict, 214
real status characteristics, 76
recency bias, 52
reciprocal interdependence, 64
reciprocity bias, 52
recognition awards, 39–40, 41–42
reference point, 198
rehearsal, 22, 29
reinventing the wheel, 260–61
relational similarity, 157
relationships, 60, 73–74
   cohesion, 79–80
   group norms, 77–79
   group socialization, 74–75
   role negotiation, 75–77
   trust, 80–84
   See also group membership; interteam relations; team members
resources, 33
responsibility
   and Abilene paradox, 127–28
   diffusion of, 25
   team building, 8, 9
   and team performance, 27
   See also team building, managers' responsibilities
results, 38–39
retaliation effect, 224
retreats, 11
rewards. *See* compensation; performance appraisals
richness, 233
risk averse, 197–98
risk seeking, 197–98
risk taking, and technology, 243
risk technique, 117
risky shift, 128
role differentiation, 107
role negotiation, 75–77
role transition, 74–75
rolling average method, 57
rotating nominal group technique, 163
routinization, versus innovation, 105–8

S

same time, different place communication, 235–36
satisfaction, 30–31, 32

schmoozing, 83, 250
screen loading, 239
scripts, 181
selective exposure, 106
self-affirmation, 198–99
self-directing teams, 4–5
self-efficacy, reduced sense of, 25
self-fulfilling prophecy, 72, 193–95
self-governing teams, 5
self-identity, 198–99
self-limiting behavior, 124, 126
self-managing teams, 3–4
self-rationalization, 191
self-reporting, 68
self-stereotyping, 222
sequential interdependence, 64
shared aspects, 157
similarity-attraction effect, 71
similarity-based trust, 82
skill, and performance, 20–22
skill assessment, 13
skill-based pay, 44, 45
skill development, 13–15
social behavior, and information
        technology, 240–44
social capital, 175–76, 182
social comparison, and ratee
        bias, 53
social contagion, 83
social determinants, 122
social embeddedness, 82
social facilitation, 22
social impairment, 22
social interaction. *See*
        communication
socialization, group, 74–75
social loafing, 23, 160
social networks
    and technology, 241–42
    and trust, 82–83
    See also networking
social norms, and technology, 243
socioemotional master, 76
solitary writing, 162
specialization, 6
spokesperson, 174
sports model, 97
spot awards, 40–42
stability, 2
status
    and information technology,
        240–41
    minimizing differences, 127
status competition, 76
stepladder technique, 162–63
stereotyping, 214, 221–22
strategic manipulation, 139
strategist, 174
stress reduction, 229
strike behavior, 146
structural determinants, 123
structural holes, 176–77

structural positioning, 180–84
structured discussion principles, 117
study groups, 267–69
sucker effects, 25
sunk costs, 123–24
sure-thing principle, 260
surveying teams, 172–73
SWOT analysis, of diversity, 69–72
symbolic conflict, 214
synergy, 33

T

tacit coordination, 100
tactical teams, 62
task analysis, 60, 61–67
task performance, and technology,
        243–44
task-management skills, 67, 68
tasks
    and Abilene paradox, 127
    delegation, 204–5
    involving, attractive, and interest-
        ing, 26
team bonding, 79–80
team building, 59–60, 84
    managers' responsibilities, 8, 9
    people, 67–73
    relationships, 73–84
    task analysis, 61–67
team context, 18–20
team dilemma, 135 37
team members, 60
    appraisal of, 68
    conflict among, 10, 11
    diversity, 68–73
    external roles of, 173, 174
    skills, 67–68
    See also group membership; in-
        terteam relations; rela-
        tionships
team mental models, 96–97
team-on-team negotiation, 144
team paradox, 188–89, 200–201
teams, 1–2, 15–16
    autonomy versus manager con-
        trol, 12
    contracts, 27
    culture, 19–20
    defined, 2–3
    design, 19
    identity, 136
    importance of, 5–7
    longevity, 12, 105–8
    most common, 11
    observations about, 7–11
    size, 11
        and Abilene paradox, 127
        and brainstorming, 165
        and groupthink, 116
        and information dependence
            problem, 94

    and performance, 27, 28
    and task analysis, 65–67
    skill assessment, 13
    skill development, 13–15
    transnational, 250–53
    types of, 3–5
    virtual, 247–50
    See also collective intelligence;
        communication; compen-
        sation; conflict; creativity;
        decision making; empow-
        erment; external environ-
        ment; information tech-
        nology; interteam
        relationships; leadership;
        performance; perfor-
        mance appraisals
team therapy, 148
teamwork
    frustrating aspects of, 12
    local, 244–47
    observations about, 7–11
technical expertise, 67
temporary engagement, 249
theory-based intervention, 15
therapy, team, 148
360-degree programs, 45–50
    industrial example of, 272,
        274–76
    and skill assessment, 68
time, 118, 186
top management teams (TMT),
        208–10
touching base, 249–50
training, 29
    and groupthink, 117
    and transactive memory systems,
        100–105
transactive memory systems
        (TMS), 99–105
transnational teams, 250–53
transparency illusion, 87
trust, 27
    and BATNA principle, 140–41
    calculated, 81
    developing, 81–82
    and faith, 80–81
    implicit, 83–84
    similarity-based, 82
    and social networks, 82–83
tunnel vision, 123
turnover, 105

U

underbounded teams, 170
uniformity, pressures toward, 114

V

variable pay, 38
videoconference, one-day, 249

virtual space, 244–47
virtual teams, 247–50
vivid information, 197–200
voting, 137–39

W

"weak get strong" effect, 240–41
welfare-based justice, 145
well-being, 30–31, 32
women

compensation of, 37
and social capital, 182
and technology, 241
working group, 2
workplace, redesigning, 244–47
work planning, 102